The Best Test Preparation for the

AP
Calculus
AB & BC Exams

With CD-ROM for Windows®

Norman Levy, Ph.
Certified Mathematics Teacher
New York State

Research & Education Association
Visit our website at
www.rea.com

Research & Education Association
61 Ethel Road West
Piscataway, New Jersey 08854
E-mail: info@rea.com

The Best Test Preparation for the
AP CALCULUS AB & BC EXAMS
With TEST*ware*® on CD-ROM

Printed in the United States of America

Library of Congress Control Number 2006933675

International Standard Book Number 0-7386-0286-8

Windows® is a registered trademark of Microsoft Corporation.

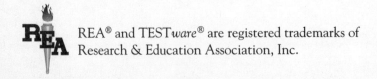

CONTENTS

ABOUT OUR AUTHOR

Dr. Norman Levy is the Director of Mathematics and Testing for NJL College Preparation and Learning Center, as well as Math Coordinator of Hebrew Academy of Nassau County, N.Y., where he supervises the mathematics staff, selects textbooks, implements programs, holds teacher-training workshops, and teaches SAT math skills to students. He is a certified mathematics teacher for grades 7-12 in New York State and the respected author and coauthor of more than a dozen academic study and test preparation guides for college-bound students and teacher candidates. Dr. Levy and his wife, Dr. Joan Levy, are directors of NJL College Preparation in Albertson, N.Y., which offers test preparation classes and counseling for college-bound students.

AUTHOR ACKNOWLEDGMENTS

The author gratefully acknowledges NJL College Preparation for its resources and technical support; Joshua Levy for his technical support and computer competence; J. Dawn Levy for her technical support and computer competence; Julia Brown for her technical competence and unrelenting attention to detail in the math, and the REA Editorial staff for all manner of help.

ABOUT RESEARCH & EDUCATION ASSOCIATION

Founded in 1959, Research & Education Association (REA) is dedicated to publishing the finest and most effective educational materials—including software, study guides, and test preps—for students in middle school, high school, college, graduate school, and beyond.

REA's test preparation series includes books and software for all academic levels in almost all disciplines. REA publishes test preps for students who have not yet entered high school, as well as high school students preparing to enter college. Students from countries around the world seeking to attend college in the United States will find the assistance they need in REA's publications. For college students seeking advanced degrees, REA publishes test preps for many major graduate school admission examinations in a wide variety of disciplines, including engineering, law, and medicine. Students at every level, in every field, with every ambition can find what they are looking for among REA's publications.

REA's series presents tests that accurately depict the official exams in both degree of difficulty and types of questions. REA's practice exams are always based upon the most recently administered exams, and include every type of question that can be expected on the actual exams.

REA's publications and educational materials are highly regarded and continually receive an unprecedented amount of praise from professionals, instructors, librarians, parents, and students. Our authors are as diverse as the subject matter represented in the books we publish. They are well known in their respective disciplines and serve on the faculties of prestigious colleges and universities throughout the United States and Canada.

Today, REA's wide-ranging catalog is a leading resource for teachers, students, and professionals.

We invite you to visit us at *www.rea.com* to find out how "REA is making the world smarter."

ACKNOWLEDGMENTS

In addition to our author, we would like to thank Larry B. Kling, Vice President, Editorial, for supervising development; Pam Weston, Vice President, Publishing, for production integrity and managing the publication to completion; John Cording, Vice President, Technology, for coordinating the design and development of REA's TEST*ware*®; Diane Goldschmidt, Senior Editor, for coordinating revisions and quality assurance; Sandra Rush for her expert copyediting; Heena Patel and Michelle Boykins, Technology Project Managers, for their design contributions and software testing efforts; Jeff LoBalbo, Senior Graphic Artist, for his graphic arts contributions and post-production file mapping; Christine Saul, Senior Graphic Artist, for designing our cover; and Aquent Publishing Services for typesetting this edition.

STUDY SCHEDULE
AP Calculus AB

The following study schedule allows for thorough preparation for the AP Calculus AB examination. Although it is designed for six weeks, it can be reduced to a three-week course by collapsing each two-week period into one. Be sure to set aside enough time (at least two hours each day) to study. But no matter which study schedule works best for you, the more time you spend studying, the more prepared and relaxed you will feel on the day of the exam.

Week	Activity
1	Take Practice Exam 1 on CD-ROM to determine your strengths and weaknesses. You can then determine the areas in which you need to strengthen your skills.
2	Carefully read and study the AP Calculus Course Review included in this book, paying particular attention to the content that will be on the Calculus AB exam.
3	Take Practice Exam 2 on CD-ROM, and after scoring your exam, carefully review all incorrect answer explanations. If there are any types of questions or particular subjects that seem difficult to you, review those subjects by going over the appropriate section of the AP Calculus review.
4	Take Practice Exam 3 in this book, and after scoring your exam, carefully review all incorrect answer explanations. If there are any types of questions or particular subjects that seem difficult to you, review those subjects by going over the appropriate section of the AP Calculus review.
5	Take Practice Exam 4 in this book, and after scoring your exam, carefully review all incorrect answer explanations. If there are any types of questions or particular subjects that seem difficult to you, review those subjects by going over the appropriate section of the AP Calculus review.
6	Take Practice Exam 5 in this book, and after scoring your exam, carefully review all incorrect answer explanations. If there are any types of questions or particular subjects that seem difficult to you, review those subjects by going over the appropriate section of the AP Calculus review. If time allows, study any areas you consider to be your weaknesses by using the Course Review in this book and any other study resources you have. Review the practice exams one more time to be sure you understand the problems that you originally answered incorrectly.

STUDY SCHEDULE
AP Calculus BC

The following study schedule allows thorough preparation for the AP Calculus BC examination. Although it is designed for four weeks, it can be reduced to a two-week course by collapsing each two-week period into one. Be sure to set aside enough time (at least two hours each day) to study. But no matter which study schedule works best for you, the more time you spend studying, the more prepared and relaxed you will feel on the day of the exam.

Week	Activity
1	Take Practice Exam 1 on CD-ROM for the AP Calculus BC exam to determine your strengths and weaknesses. You can then determine the areas in which you need to strengthen your skills.
2	Carefully read and study the AP Calculus Course Review included in this book, paying particular attention to the content that will be on the Calculus BC exam.
3	Take Practice Exam 2 for AP Calculus BC in this book, and after scoring your exam, carefully review all incorrect answer explanations. If there are any types of questions or particular subjects that seem difficult to you, review those subjects by going over the appropriate section of the AP Calculus review.
4	Take Practice Exam 3 for AP Calculus BC in this book, and after scoring your exam, carefully review all incorrect answer explanations. If time allows, study any areas you consider to be your weaknesses by using the course review in this book and any other study resources you have. Review the practice exams one more time to be sure you understand the problems that you originally answered incorrectly.

INSTALLING REA's TEST*ware*®

SYSTEM REQUIREMENTS

Pentium 75 MHz (300 MHz recommended) or a higher or compatible processor; Microsoft Windows 98 or later; 64 MB available RAM; Internet Explorer 5.5 or higher

INSTALLATION

1. Insert the AP Calculus AB & BC TEST*ware*® CD-ROM into the CD-ROM drive.
2. If the installation doesn't begin automatically, from the Start Menu choose the RUN command. When the RUN dialog box appears, type *d*:\setup (where *d* is the letter of your CD-ROM drive) at the prompt and click OK.
3. The installation process will begin. A dialog box proposing the directory "Program Files\REA\APCalculus" will appear. If the name and location are suitable, click OK. If you wish to specify a different name or location, type it in and click OK.
4. Start the AP Calculus AB & BC TEST*ware*® application by double-clicking on the icon.

REA's AP Calculus AB & BC TEST*ware*® is **EASY** to **LEARN AND USE**. To achieve maximum benefits, we recommend that you take a few minutes to go through the on-screen tutorial on your computer. The "screen buttons" are also explained here to familiarize you with the program.

SSD ACCOMMODATIONS FOR STUDENTS WITH DISABILITIES

Many students qualify for extra time to take the AP exams, and our TEST*ware*® can be adapted to accommodate your time extension. This allows you to practice under the same extended-time accommodations that you will receive on the actual test day. To customize your TEST*ware*® to suit the most common extensions, visit our website at *www.rea.com/ssd*.

TECHNICAL SUPPORT

REA's TEST*ware*® is backed by customer and technical support. For questions about **installation or operation of your software**, contact us at:

Research & Education Association
Phone: (732) 819-8880 (9 a.m. to 5 p.m. ET, Monday–Friday)
Fax: (732) 819-8808
Website: http://www.rea.com
E-mail: info@rea.com

Note to Windows XP Users: In order for the TEST*ware*® to function properly, please install and run the application under the same computer administrator-level user account. Installing the TEST*ware*® as one user and running it as another could cause file-access path conflicts.

INTRODUCTION

AP Calculus AB & BC

Chapter 1

EXCELLING ON THE AP CALCULUS AB & BC EXAMS

ABOUT THIS BOOK AND TEST*ware*®

This book, along with the accompanying CD, provides an accurate and complete representation of the Advanced Placement examinations in Calculus AB and BC. Our practice exams are based on the format of the most recently administered Advanced Placement Calculus AB and BC exam. Each practice exam in this book includes every type of question that you can expect to encounter on the real exam. Following each of our practice exams is an answer key complete with detailed explanations designed to clarify the material for you. By using the subject reviews, completing all the appropriate practice exams for Calculus AB & BC, as necessary, and studying the explanations that follow, you will pinpoint your strengths and weaknesses and, above all, put yourself in the best possible position to score well.

Three practice exams are also included on the enclosed TEST*ware*® CD-ROM—two for the AP Calculus AB exam and one for the AP Calculus BC exam. The software provides timed conditions for instantaneous, accurate scoring, which makes it all the easier to pinpoint your strengths and weaknesses.

ABOUT THE EXAM

The Advanced Placement Calculus AB & BC examinations are offered each May at participating schools and multi-school centers throughout the world.

The Advanced Placement Program is designed to allow high school students to pursue college-level studies while attending high school. In turn, participating colleges and universities in the United States and more than 30 countries around the world, grant credit and/or advanced placement to students who do well on the examinations.

FORMAT OF THE AP CALCULUS AB & BC EXAMS

The AP Calculus AB & BC exams are each approximately three hours and fifteen minutes long. The exams are divided into two sections. Each section of both exams is timed and completed separately, and each counts for half of the student's score.

Section	Part	Number of Questions	Question Numbers*	Type	Calculator**	Time
I	A	28	1–28	Multiple-choice	No	55 min
	B	17	76–92	Multiple-choice	Required	50 min
II	A	3	1–3	Free response	Required	45 min
	B	3	4–6	Free response	No	45 min
Total		45 + 6				3 hr 15 min

Note: *Oddly enough,   Q1–28 are question numbers 1–28

Q29–45 are question numbers 76–92

**If you finish Section II Part B early, you may return to Section II Part A. However, you do NOT get to use your calculator.

CONTENT OF THE AP CALCULUS AB & BC EXAMS

Although the content of the Calculus AB & BC exams changes slightly from year to year, the following outline shows the topics usually found on the exams. Items marked with an asterisk (*) are found only on the BC exam. All other topics are common to both exams.

  I. Functions and Relations
        Graphical Analysis
        Limits
        Continuity
        Discontinuity
        Parametric and Polar*
        Vector valued functions*

  II. Derivatives
        Definition
        Derivatives of elementary functions
        Chain rule
        Implicit differentiation
        Mean value theorem
        Inverse functions

III. Applications of Derivatives
    Curve Analysis
    Related Rates
    Optimization
    L'Hospital's Rule*
    Motion

IV. Integrals
    Fundamental Theorem of Calculus
    Riemann Sums (right, left, midpoint)/Trapezoidal Rule
    Antidifferentiation including u-substitution
    Antidifferentiation including partial fractions and by parts*
    Improper integrals*

V. Applications of Integrals
    Area
    Volume
    Average value
    Arc length*
    Motion

VI. Differential Equations
    Slope fields
    Euler's method*
    Separation of variables

VII. Series*
    Convergence testing
    Radius/interval of convergence
    Taylor and Maclaurin series
    Lagrange form of the Taylor error bound

VIII. Parametric and Polar*
    Curve Analysis
    Arc length
    Area
    Motion

USE OF CALCULATORS

1.	Allowed:	The College Board publishes a continually changing list of sanctioned calculators.
	Not allowed:	• QWERTY keyboard • computers • pen-input driven devices • electronic pads • non-graphing calculators
2.	Memory:	Memories will NOT be cleared.
3.	Capabilities Required:	• Plot a function in a viewing window • Find the roots of functions (solve equations numerically) • Numerically calculate the derivative of a function • Numerically calculate the value of a definite integral
4.	What work do I show?	• The set-up of the problem i.e.: Area $= \int_{2}^{4}\left[(\sin x)^2 - (\cos 3x)^2\right] dx =$ • Do <u>NOT</u> write the math in calculator syntax. • All capabilities above can only be used to check your answer. You must show your handwritten work.

HOW TO USE THIS BOOK AND TEST*ware*®

Developing a plan of attack

This book, along with our TEST*ware*® software package of computerized practice exams, affords you the most relevant, targeted prep available for the AP Calculus AB & BC Exams. Our book features a no-nonsense subject review that covers exactly the material you need to master to do well on the AP exam. If it's in our review, you need to know it! And it's formatted in a way to perfectly complement your calculus textbook.

Here are the working assumptions that informed how our book and software were tailored:

- You've taken—or are taking—a course in calculus or otherwise have some familiarity with the subject.

- You already possess one of those 800-plus page calculus textbooks that cover the subject matter exhaustively.

- You need a quick and concise review of the subject matter modeled on the actual AP exams.

- If you're getting ready to sit for the AP Calculus AB or BC Exams, you already have a knowledge of basic algebra, geometry, algebra 2, trigonometry, pre-calculus, and calculus.

- Furthermore, bear in mind that this is a math test; thus, it is math rules and illustrations that are needed for review. And that's precisely what we give you.

How, then, to put it all together? Read over our course review and our suggestions for test taking. Next, take the first practice exam on CD-ROM under the appropriate heading (AB or BC) to audit your strengths and weaknesses; this book combines coverage of Calculus AB and BC, and the tests on CD correspond to our book's printed exams for AB Practice Exams 1 and 2 and BC Practice Exam 1. We provide distinct practice and review for both exams, with the step-by-step problem-solving attacks you need to ace the exam included in our detailed explanations with each exam answer. Those explanations will equip you with a systematic way of pinpointing your weakest areas so that you can bolster your total performance—and reinforce what you've learned in the classroom!

Be sure to take all the applicable practice tests.

To make the best use of your study time, follow our test-specific study schedules, which you will find in the front of the book.

SSD accommodations for students with disabilities

Many students qualify for extra time to take the AP exams, and our TEST*ware*® can be adapted to accommodate your time extension. This allows you to practice under the same extended-time accommodations that you will receive on the actual test day. To customize your TEST*ware*® to suit the most common extensions, visit our website at *www.rea.com/ssd*.

When should I start studying?

It is never too early to start studying for the AP Calculus AB & BC examinations. The earlier you begin, the more time you will have to sharpen your skills. Do not procrastinate!

ABOUT OUR REVIEW SECTION

This book contains an AP Calculus AB & BC course review, which you can use both as a primer and as a quick reference while taking the practice exams. Our course review is meant to complement your AP Calculus AB & BC textbook and is by no means exhaustive. By studying our review along with your text, you will be well prepared for the exam.

SCORING REA's PRACTICE EXAMS

Scoring the Multiple-Choice Section

$$\frac{}{\text{Number Correct}} \times 1 = \frac{}{a}$$

$$\frac{}{\text{Number Wrong}} \times \tfrac{1}{4} = \frac{}{b}$$

Multiple-Choice Raw Score: $(a - b) \times 1.2 = \underline{}$
$$\text{Multiple-Choice Raw Score}$$

Scoring the Free-Response Section

The score for each problem should reflect how completely the question was answered—that is, the solution that was produced and the steps taken. You should gauge at what point a mistake was made, and determine whether any use of calculus or mathematics was incorrect. Each problem is given a score of 0 to 9 points. More points should be given for correct answers that include all work in the answer explanation, and fewer points should be given for incorrect answers and for the failure to write down necessary work.

For the free-response section, use this formula to calculate your raw score.

$$\frac{}{Q1} + \frac{}{Q2} + \frac{}{Q3} + \frac{}{Q4} + \frac{}{Q5} + \frac{}{Q6} = \frac{}{\text{Free-Response Raw Score}}$$

Converting Raw Score to Scaled Score

Final Score out of 108:

Multiple Choice: $(a - b)\,(1.2) =$ Raw Score (MC)
Free Response: 0 to 54   = Raw Score (FR)

Raw Score (MC) + Raw Score (FR)			
AB	**BC**	**Scaled Score**	**Description**
72–108	66–108	5	Extremely well qualified
56–71	54–65	4	Well qualified

39–55	36–53	3	Qualified
25–38	29–35	2	Possibly qualified
0–24	0–28	1	No recommendation

Most colleges will grant either college credit or advanced placement to students who earn a 3 or above.

SCORING THE OFFICIAL EXAMS

The College Board creates a formula (which changes slightly every year) to convert raw scores into composite scores grouped into broad AP grade categories.

The AP free-response problems are graded by teacher volunteers. Past grading illustrations are available to teachers from the College Board and may be ordered using the contact information given on page 11. These actual examples of student responses and a grade analysis can be of great assistance to both the student and the teacher as a learning or review tool.

Calculus AB Subscore Grade for the Calculus BC Exam

The College Board provides AP Calculus BC test takers with two scores: the score you received for the Calculus BC exam and the grade you would have received if you had taken the Calculus AB exam. This is called the AB subscore and is based on your performance on the portion of the exam devoted to Calculus AB topics. If you are familiar with the more complex BC topics, you have nothing to lose by taking the BC exams because of the AB subscore.

When will I know my score?

In July, a grade report will be sent to you, your high school, and the college you chose to notify. The report will include scores for all the AP exams you have taken up to that point.

Your grade will be used by your college of choice to determine placement in its Calculus AB & BC program. This grade will vary in significance from college to college and is used with other academic information to determine placement. Normally, colleges participating in the Advanced Placement Program will recognize grades of 3 or better. Contact your college admissions office for more information regarding its use of AP grades.

STUDYING FOR YOUR EXAM

It is very important for you to choose the time and place for studying that works best for you. Work out a study routine and stick to it.

When you take the practice tests, create an environment as much like the actual testing environment as possible. Turn your television and radio off, and sit down at a quiet table free from distraction. Make sure to time yourself, breaking the test down by section.

As you complete each practice test, score your test and thoroughly review the explanations to the questions you answered incorrectly. Concentrate on one problem area at a time by reviewing the question and explanation and by studying our review until you are confident that you completely understand the material.

Keep track of your scores. You should carefully study the reviews that cover areas with which you have difficulty.

TEST-TAKING TIPS

If you are not be familiar with standardized tests such as the AP Calculus AB & BC exams, there are many ways to become accustomed to the AP exams.

Become comfortable with the format of the exam. Stay calm and pace yourself. After simulating the test a couple of times, you will boost your chances of doing well, and you will be able to sit for the actual exam with more confidence.

Read all of the possible answers. Just because you think you have found the correct response, do not automatically assume that it is the best answer. Read through each choice to be sure that you are not making a mistake by jumping to conclusions.

Use the process of elimination. Go through each answer to a question and eliminate as many of the answer choices as possible. By eliminating just two answer choices, you give yourself a better chance of choosing the correct answer.

Work quickly and steadily. Work quickly and steadily and avoid focusing on any one question too long. Taking the practice tests in this book will help you learn to budget your time.

Beware of test vocabulary. Words such as *always*, *every*, *none*, *only*, and *never* indicate there should be no exceptions to the answer you choose. Words like *generally*, *usually*, *sometimes*, *seldom*, *rarely*, and *often* indicate there may be exceptions to your answer.

Learn the directions and format for each section of the test. Familiarizing yourself with the directions and format of the exam will save you valuable time on the day of the actual test.

TEST SMARTS FOR AP CALCULUS

- When you write a decimal answer, be accurate to 3 decimal places.
- Each part of a free response question is scored separately. A mistake in one part counts for point loss only in that part. If a future part of the question requires use of previous answer and you work out the new part with the proper procedure utilizing the previous wrong answer, it will be counted as CORRECT.
- Do not show your work in the free response section in calculator "language." For example:

  $6 * 3$ is not math

  $6 \wedge 3$ is not math

  NINT $(x^2, x, 3)$ is not math

  Solve $(2x - y = 6, x)/y = 7$ is not math

THE DAY OF THE EXAM

Before the Exam

- Get a good night's sleep
- Prepare all your "bring to the exam" items
- Relax! You've prepared for the test

The Day of the Exam

- Wake up early
- Eat breakfast
- Dress comfortably
- Plan to arrive early
- Make sure to have your social security number, a picture identification (i.e., a driver's license or student identification card), school code and admissions ticket
- Bring several No. 2 pencils with erasers and several black or blue pens
- Bring a watch
- Bring an approved calculator and batteries

During the Exam

Once you enter the test center, follow all of the rules and instructions given by the test supervisor. If you do not, you risk being dismissed from the test and having your scores canceled.

You may wear a watch, but only one without a beeper or an alarm. No dictionaries, textbooks, notebooks, compasses, correction fluid, highlighters, rulers, computers, cell phones, beepers, PDAs, scratch paper, listening and recording devices, briefcases, or packages will be permitted, and drinking, smoking, and eating are prohibited while taking the test.

After the Exam

You may immediately register when taking the exam to have your score sent to the college of your choice; you may also wait and later request to have your AP score reported to the college of your choice.

CONTACTING THE AP PROGRAM

For registration bulletins or more information about the AP Calculus AB & BC exams, contact:

AP Services
Educational Testing Service
P.O. Box 6671
Princeton, NJ 08541-6671
Phone: (609) 771-7300 or (888) 225-5427
E-mail: apexams@ets.org
Website: *www.collegeboard.com*

COURSE REVIEW

AP Calculus AB & BC

Chapter 2

PRECALCULUS FACTS

GUIDE TO BASIC FUNCTION GRAPHS

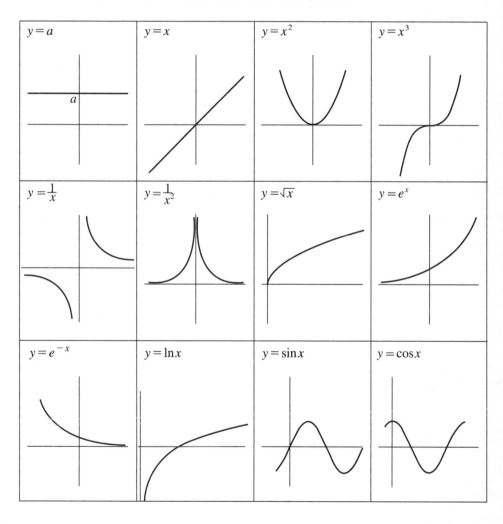

BASIC FUNCTION TRANSFORMATIONS

Notation	How $f(x)$ changes	
$f(x) + a$	moves up a units	
$f(x) - a$	moves down a units	
$f(x + a)$	moves left a units	
$f(x - a)$	moves right a units	
$af(x)$	$(a > 1)$ vertical stretch	
$af(x)$	$(0 < a < 1)$ vertical shrink	
$f(ax)$	$(a > 1)$ horizontal shrink	
$f(ax)$	$(0 < a < 1)$ horizontal stretch	
$-f(x)$	reflection x-axis	
$f(-x)$	reflection y-axis	

BASIC TRIGONOMETRIC IDENTITIES

Tangent and Cotangent Identities

$$\tan\theta = \frac{\sin\theta}{\cos\theta} \qquad \cot\theta = \frac{\cos\theta}{\sin\theta}$$

Reciprocal Identities

$$\sec\theta = \frac{1}{\cos\theta} \qquad \csc\theta = \frac{1}{\sin\theta}$$

Pythagorean Identities

$$\sin^2\theta + \cos^2\theta = 1$$
$$\tan^2\theta + 1 = \sec^2\theta$$
$$\cot^2\theta + 1 = \csc^2\theta$$

Double-Angle Formulas

$$\sin 2\theta = 2\sin\theta\,\cos\theta$$
$$\cos 2\theta = \cos^2\theta - \sin^2\theta$$
$$= 1 - 2\sin^2\theta$$
$$= 2\cos^2\theta - 1$$
$$\tan 2\theta = \frac{2\tan\theta}{1 - \tan^2\theta}$$

Power-Reduction Formulas

$$\sin^2\theta = \frac{1 - \cos 2\theta}{2}$$
$$\cos^2\theta = \frac{1 + \cos 2\theta}{2}$$
$$\tan^2\theta = \frac{1 - \cos 2\theta}{1 + \cos 2\theta}$$

Half Angle Formulas

$$\sin\frac{1}{2}\theta = \pm\sqrt{\frac{1 - \cos\theta}{2}}$$
$$\cos\frac{1}{2}\theta = \pm\sqrt{\frac{1 + \cos\theta}{2}}$$
$$\tan\frac{1}{2}\theta = \frac{1 - \cos\theta}{\sin\theta} = \frac{\sin\theta}{1 + \cos\theta}$$

Sum and Difference Formulas

$$\sin(u \pm v) = \sin u\cos v \pm \cos u\sin v$$
$$\cos(u \pm v) = \cos u\cos v \mp \sin u\sin v$$
$$\tan(u \pm v) = \frac{\tan u \pm \tan v}{1 \mp \tan u\tan v}$$

BASIC LOGARITHM RULES

$$\ln(ab) = \ln a + \ln b$$

$$\ln\left(\frac{a}{b}\right) = \ln a - \ln b$$

$$\ln(a^b) = b \ln a$$

$$\ln e^x = x$$

$$e^{\ln x} = x$$

$$\log_a b = \frac{\ln b}{\ln a}$$

Chapter 3

LIMITS AND CONTINUITY

EVALUATING LIMITS

Basic Limits

$\lim_{x \to a} c = c$ where c is a constant	$\lim_{x \to a} x = a$

To find $\lim_{x \to a} h(x)$

If $h(a) =$	Action to find $\lim_{x \to a} h(x)$	
N^*	$\lim_{x \to a} h(x) = N$	
$\dfrac{N}{\infty}$	$\lim_{x \to a} h(x) = 0$	
$\dfrac{N}{0}$	**If**	**Then**
	• $\lim_{x \to a^-} h(x) = \lim_{x \to a^+} h(x) = \infty$	$\lim_{x \to a} h(x) = \infty$
	• $\lim_{x \to a^-} h(x) = \lim_{x \to a^+} h(x) = -\infty$	$\lim_{x \to a} h(x) = -\infty$
	• $\lim_{x \to a^-} h(x) \neq \lim_{x \to a^+} h(x)$	$\lim_{x \to a} h(x) = \text{DNE}$
$\dfrac{0}{0}, \dfrac{\infty}{\infty}$ (Indeterminate)	Try one of the following: • Factor, and then take the limit • Rationalize, and then take the limit • Use **L'Hospital's Rule** If $h(x) = \dfrac{f(x)}{g(x)}$ and $h(a) = \dfrac{0}{0}$ or $\dfrac{\infty}{\infty}$ assuming $f'(x)$ and $g'(x)$ exist, and $g'(x) \neq 0$, then $$\lim_{x \to a} \frac{f(x)}{g(x)} = \lim_{x \to a} \frac{f'(x)}{g'(x)}$$	

*N is a real number.

(*Continued*)

If $h(a) =$	Action to find $\lim\limits_{x \to a} h(x)$
Other Indeterminate Forms: $0 \cdot \infty, \infty - \infty, 0^{\circ}, \infty^{\circ}, 1^{\infty}$	Create a $\dfrac{0}{0}$ or $\dfrac{\infty}{\infty}$ such that L'Hospital's Rule can apply

*N is a real number.
DNE = does not exist

Polynomial Division as $x \to \infty$

Let ax^n be the highest powered term of $P_1(x)$
$\quad bx^m$ be the highest powered term of $P_2(x)$

If $h(x) = \dfrac{P_1(x)}{P_2(x)} = \dfrac{\text{Polynomial 1}}{\text{Polynomial 2}}$,

then $\lim\limits_{x \to \infty} h(x) = \lim\limits_{x \to \infty} \dfrac{ax^n}{bx^m}$

If $n = m$ $\qquad\qquad$ then $\lim\limits_{x \to \infty} h(x) = \dfrac{a}{b}$

$\quad m > n$ $\qquad\qquad\qquad \lim\limits_{x \to \infty} h(x) = 0$

$\quad n > m$ $\qquad\qquad\qquad \begin{cases} \lim\limits_{x \to \infty} h(x) = +\infty \text{ for } ab > 0 \\[2mm] \lim\limits_{x \to \infty} h(x) = -\infty, \text{ for } ab < 0 \end{cases}$

LIMIT PROPERTIES

If $\lim\limits_{x \to a} f(x) = P$ and $\lim\limits_{x \to a} g(x) = Q$, then:

Type	Property
Multiplicative constant c	$\lim\limits_{x \to a} c f(x) = cP$
Addition	$\lim\limits_{x \to a} [f(x) + g(x)] = P + Q$
Subtraction	$\lim\limits_{x \to a} [f(x) - g(x)] = P - Q$

(Continued)

Type	Property
Multiplication	$\lim\limits_{x \to a} [f(x) \cdot g(x)] = P \cdot Q$
Division	$\lim\limits_{x \to a} \dfrac{f(x)}{g(x)} = \dfrac{P}{Q}$, provided $Q \neq 0$
nth power (n is a positive integer)	$\lim\limits_{x \to a} [f(x)]^n = P^n$
nth root (n is an even integer)	$\lim\limits_{x \to a} \sqrt[n]{f(x)} = \sqrt[n]{P}$, $P > 0$
nth root (n is an odd integer)	$\lim\limits_{x \to a} \sqrt[n]{f(x)} = \sqrt[n]{P}$
Composite	If $\lim\limits_{x \to a} g(x) = Q$ and $\lim\limits_{x \to Q} f(x) = f(Q)$. $\lim\limits_{x \to a} f(g(x)) = f\left(\lim\limits_{x \to a} g(x)\right) = f(Q)$

Special Limits

$\lim\limits_{x \to 0} \dfrac{\sin x}{x} = 1$	$\lim\limits_{x \to 0} \dfrac{\cos x - 1}{x} = 0$
$\lim\limits_{x \to \infty} \dfrac{x^n}{e^x} = 0$, for all n	$\lim\limits_{x \to \infty} \left(1 + \dfrac{1}{x}\right)^x = e$
$\lim\limits_{x \to 0} \dfrac{\tan x}{x} = 1$	$\lim\limits_{x \to \infty} x^n = 0$, $|x| < 1$
$\lim\limits_{x \to \infty} \dfrac{x^n}{n!} = 0$	$\lim\limits_{n \to \infty} \dfrac{\ln n}{n} = 0$
$\lim\limits_{n \to \infty} \sqrt[n]{n} = 1$	$\lim\limits_{n \to \infty} \sqrt[n]{x} = 1$, $x > 0$
$\lim\limits_{x \to 0} \dfrac{e^x - 1}{x} = 1$	$\lim\limits_{x \to 0} (1 + x)^{\frac{1}{x}} = e$

Example 1

Evaluate	$\lim\limits_{x\to3}\dfrac{x+3}{x-5}$
Solution: Substitute:	$\dfrac{x+3}{x-5} \Rightarrow \dfrac{3+3}{3-5} = \dfrac{6}{-2} = \boxed{-3}$

Example 2

Evaluate	$\lim\limits_{x\to3}\dfrac{x^2-9}{x-3}$
Solution: Substitute:	$\dfrac{x^2-9}{x-3} \Rightarrow \dfrac{0}{0}$ (Indeterminate)
Method 1:	Factor $$\lim_{x\to3}\frac{x^2-9}{x-3} = \lim_{x\to3}\frac{(x+3)(x-3)}{(x-3)} = \lim_{x\to3}(x+3) = \boxed{6}$$
Method 2:	L'Hospital's Rule $$\lim_{x\to3}\frac{x^2-9}{x-3} = \lim_{x\to3}\frac{2x}{1} = \boxed{6}$$

Example 3

Evaluate	$\lim\limits_{x\to\infty}\dfrac{7x^2-3x+2}{9x^2-2x+1}$
Solution: Substitute:	$\dfrac{7x^2-3x+2}{9x^2-2x+1} \Rightarrow \dfrac{\infty}{\infty}$ (Indeterminate)
Method 1:	Polynomial Division $$\lim_{x\to\infty}\frac{7x^2-3x+2}{9x^2-2x+1} = \lim_{x\to\infty}\frac{7x^2}{9x^2} = \boxed{\frac{7}{9}}$$
Method 2:	L'Hospital's Rule $$\lim_{x\to\infty}\frac{7x^2-3x+2}{9x^2-2x+1} = \lim_{x\to\infty}\frac{14x-3}{18x-2} = \lim_{x\to\infty}\frac{14}{18} = \boxed{\frac{7}{9}}$$

Example 4

Evaluate $\qquad \lim\limits_{x \to 0}(1+x)^{\frac{1}{x}}$

Solution:

Substitute: $\quad (1+0)^{\frac{1}{0}} \Rightarrow 1^{\infty}$ (Indeterminate Form)

$$\text{Let } y = (1+x)^{\frac{1}{x}} \quad \Rightarrow \quad \ln y = \ln(1+x)^{\frac{1}{x}}$$

$$\lim_{x \to 0}[\ln y] = \lim_{x \to 0}\left[\frac{1}{x}\ln(1+x)\right]$$

$$= \lim_{x \to 0}\frac{\ln(1+x)}{x} \qquad \leftarrow \begin{array}{l} \text{L'Hospital's Rule} \\ \text{Applies } \left(\frac{0}{0}\right) \end{array}$$

$$= \lim_{x \to 0}\frac{1}{1+x} = 1$$

$$\therefore \lim_{x \to 0}[\ln y] = 1$$

$$\lim_{x \to 0} y = e^{1} = \boxed{e}$$

$$\lim_{x \to 0}(1+x)^{\frac{1}{x}} = \boxed{e}$$

CONTINUITY

Continuity at a Point

A function f is continuous at point c if:
1. $f(c)$ is defined
2. $\lim\limits_{x \to c} f(x)$ exists
3. $f(c) = \lim\limits_{x \to c} f(x)$

Continuity on an Open Interval

A function f is continuous on an open interval (a, b) if it is continuous at each point in the interval.

Continuity on a Closed Interval

A function f is continuous on the closed interval $[a, b]$ if:
- it is continuous on the open interval (a, b) and

- $\lim\limits_{x \to a^+} f(x) = f(a)$

- $\lim\limits_{x \to b^-} f(x) = f(b)$

Intermediate Value Theorem — General

If $f(x)$ is continuous on the closed interval $[a, b]$ and if k is any number between $f(a)$ and $f(b)$, then there is at least one number c in $[a, b]$ such that $f(c) = k$.

Intermediate Value Theorem — Root Related

If $f(x)$ is continuous on the closed interval $[a, b]$ and if $f(a)$ and $f(b)$ have opposite signs, then there is at least one number c in $[a, b]$ such that $f(c) = 0$.

Squeeze Theorem

If $g(x) \le f(x) \le h(x)$
for all x in an open interval containing c, except possibly at c itself, and if

$$\lim\limits_{x \to a} g(x) = \lim\limits_{x \to a} h(x) = L$$

then

$$\lim\limits_{x \to a} f(x) = L.$$

Chapter 4

DERIVATIVES

NOTATION/SYMBOLS

function	$f(x), y$
1st derivative	$f'(x), y', \dfrac{dy}{dx}, D_x$
2nd derivative	$f''(x), y'', \dfrac{d^2y}{dx^2}, D_x^2$

DEFINITION OF DERIVATIVE

$$f'(x) = \lim_{h \to 0} \frac{f(x+h) - f(x)}{h}$$

or

$$f'(a) = \lim_{x \to a} \frac{f(x) - f(a)}{x - a} = \lim_{x \to a} \frac{f(a+h) - f(a)}{h}$$

CHAIN RULE

$$\frac{dy}{dx} = \frac{dy}{du} \cdot \frac{du}{dx}$$

or

$$\frac{d}{dx}[f(g(x))] = f'(g(x)) \cdot g'(x)$$

GENERAL RULES

$$\frac{d}{dx}(c) = 0$$

$$\frac{d}{dx}(x) = 1$$

$$\frac{d}{dx}(cu) = c\frac{du}{dx}$$

$$\frac{d}{dx}(u \pm v) = \frac{du}{dx} \pm \frac{dv}{dx}$$

$$\frac{d}{dx}(u \cdot v) = u\frac{dv}{dx} + v\frac{du}{dx}$$

$$\frac{d}{dx}\left(\frac{u}{v}\right) = \frac{v\dfrac{du}{dx} - u\dfrac{dv}{dx}}{v^2} \qquad (v \neq 0)$$

where u and v are functions of x, and c is a constant

BASIC DERIVATIVES

Basic Rules	Basic Rules for Composite Functions
$\dfrac{d}{dx}(x^n) = nx^{n-1}$	$\dfrac{d}{dx}(u^n) = nu^{n-1}\dfrac{du}{dx}$
$\dfrac{d}{dx}(\sin x) = \cos x$	$\dfrac{d}{dx}(\sin u) = \cos u\dfrac{du}{dx}$
$\dfrac{d}{dx}(\cos x) = -\sin x$	$\dfrac{d}{dx}(\cos u) = -\sin u\dfrac{du}{dx}$
$\dfrac{d}{dx}(\tan x) = \sec^2 x$	$\dfrac{d}{dx}(\tan u) = \sec^2 u\dfrac{du}{dx}$
$\dfrac{d}{dx}(\cot x) = -\csc^2 x$	$\dfrac{d}{dx}(\cot u) = -\csc^2 u\dfrac{du}{dx}$

$\dfrac{d}{dx}(\sec x) = \sec x \tan x$	$\dfrac{d}{dx}(\sec u) = \sec u \tan u \dfrac{du}{dx}$
$\dfrac{d}{dx}(\csc x) = -\csc x \cot x$	$\dfrac{d}{dx}(\csc u) = -\csc u \cot u \dfrac{du}{dx}$
$\dfrac{d}{dx}(e^x) = e^x$	$\dfrac{d}{dx}(e^u) = e^u \dfrac{du}{dx}$
$\dfrac{d}{dx}(a^x) = a^x \ln a$	$\dfrac{d}{dx}(a^u) = a^u \ln a \dfrac{du}{dx}$
$\dfrac{d}{dx}(\ln x) = \dfrac{1}{x}$	$\dfrac{d}{dx}(\ln u) = \dfrac{1}{u}\dfrac{du}{dx}$
$\dfrac{d}{dx}(\log_a x) = \dfrac{1}{x}\cdot\dfrac{1}{\ln a}$	$\dfrac{d}{dx}(\log_a u) = \dfrac{1}{u}\cdot\dfrac{1}{\ln a}\dfrac{du}{dx}$
$\dfrac{d}{dx}(\sin^{-1} x) = \dfrac{1}{\sqrt{1-x^2}}$	$\dfrac{d}{dx}(\sin^{-1} u) = \dfrac{1}{\sqrt{1-u^2}}\dfrac{du}{dx}$
$\dfrac{d}{dx}(\tan^{-1} x) = \dfrac{1}{1+x^2}$	$\dfrac{d}{dx}(\tan^{-1} u) = \dfrac{1}{1+u^2}\dfrac{du}{dx}$
$\dfrac{d}{dx}(\sec^{-1} x) = \dfrac{1}{|x|\sqrt{x^2-1}}$	$\dfrac{d}{dx}(\sec^{-1} u) = \dfrac{1}{|u|\sqrt{u^2-1}}\dfrac{du}{dx}$

Example 1

$$y = \sin 3x, \quad \dfrac{dy}{dx} =$$

Solution:

$$\text{Use } \dfrac{d}{dx}(\sin u) = \cos u \dfrac{du}{dx}, \text{ where } u = 3x$$

$$\therefore \dfrac{d}{dx}(\sin 3x) = \cos(3x)\dfrac{d(3x)}{dx} = \cos(3x)\cdot 3 = \boxed{3\cos(3x)}$$

Example 2

$$y = e^{2x} \cdot (x+1)^2, \frac{dy}{dx} =$$

Solution:

Use the product rule first

$$y = e^{2x} \cdot (x+1)^2$$

$$\frac{dy}{dx} = e^{2x} \frac{d(x+1)^2}{dx} + (x+1)^2 \frac{d(e^{2x})}{dx}$$

Use rules for $\frac{d}{dx}(u^n)$ and $\frac{d}{dx}(e^u)$,

$$= e^{2x}\left[2(x+1)^1(1)\right] + (x+1)^2\left[e^{2x} \cdot 2\right]$$

$$= 2(x+1)\,e^{2x}[1+(x+1)]$$

$$= \boxed{2(x+1)(x+2)e^{2x}}$$

Example 3

Find the equation of the line tangent to $f(x) = x^2 - 3x + 1$ at $x = 1$

Solution:

when $x = 1$, $y = (1)^2 - 3(1) + 1 = -1$

$m = f'(x) = 2x - 3$, at $x = 1$, $m = -1$

$\therefore$ Using $(y - y_1) = m(x - x_1)$

$$\boxed{(y + 1) = -1(x - 1)}$$

or

$$\boxed{y = -x}$$

IMPLICIT DIFFERENTIATION

Finding $\dfrac{dy}{dx}$ Implicitly

To find $\dfrac{dy}{dx}$ implicitly:

- Take the derivative with respect to x of both sides of the equation.
- Use the chain rule at each occurrence of y:

  For example, $\dfrac{d}{dx}(3y^2) = 6y\dfrac{dy}{dx}$
- Solve the resulting equation for $\dfrac{dy}{dx}$

Example

If $y^2 + \sin(xy) = 2$, find $\dfrac{dy}{dx}$

Solution:

$$\frac{d}{dx}[y^2 + \sin(xy)] = \frac{d}{dx}(2)$$

$$= 2y\frac{dy}{dx} + \left[\cos(xy)\frac{d(xy)}{dx}\right] = 0$$

Note: xy is a product

$$= 2y\frac{dy}{dx} + \left[\cos(xy)\left(x\frac{dy}{dx} + y\right)\right] = 0$$

$$\frac{dy}{dx} = \boxed{\frac{-y\cos(xy)}{2y + x\cos(xy)}}$$

FINDING THE DERIVATIVE OF $f^{-1}(x)$

Let $g(x) = f^{-1}(x)$

$$\boxed{g'(x) = \frac{1}{f'(g(x))}}, \quad f'(g(x)) \neq 0$$

Example

If $g(x) = f^{-1}(x)$ and $f(x) = x^5 + x + 7$, find $g'(9)$ Note: $(1, 9)$ is a point on $f(x)$
Solution: If the point $(1, 9)$ is on $f(x)$, then $(9, 1)$ is on $g(x)$ $\qquad \therefore g(9) = 1$ $\qquad\qquad f(x) = x^5 + x + 7$ $\qquad\qquad f'(x) = 5x^4 + 1$ $\qquad\qquad f'(1) = 6$ $\qquad\qquad g'(x) \qquad = \dfrac{1}{f'(g(x))}$ $\qquad\qquad g'(9) \qquad = \dfrac{1}{f'(g(9))} = \dfrac{1}{f'(1)} = \boxed{\dfrac{1}{6}}$

RATE OF CHANGE

Average Rate of Change

1. The average rate of change is always calculated over an interval.
2. It is the slope of the secant line joining the end points of the interval.

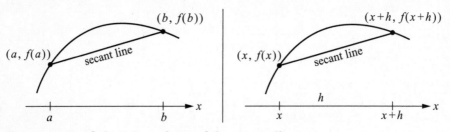

Average rate of change = slope of the secant line $\Rightarrow m_{\text{sec}}$

$$= \frac{\Delta y}{\Delta x}$$

$$= \frac{f(b) - f(a)}{b - a}$$

$$= \frac{f(x + h) - f(x)}{h}$$

3. Average velocity $= \dfrac{\Delta s}{\Delta t}$, where s = position and t = time

4. Average acceleration $= \dfrac{\Delta v}{\Delta t}$, where v = velocity and t = time

Instantaneous Rate of Change

1. The instantaneous rate of change is always calculated at a single point
2. It is the slope of the tangent line at the point

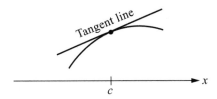

Instantaneous rate of change = slope of the tangent line $\Rightarrow m_{tan}$

$$= \frac{dy}{dx}$$

$$= \lim_{h \to 0} \frac{f(x+h) - f(x)}{h}$$

Instantaneous velocity = $\dfrac{ds}{dt}$, where s = position and t = time

Instantaneous acceleration = $\dfrac{dv}{dt}$, where v = velocity and t = time

A FUNCTION DOES *NOT* HAVE A DERIVATIVE AT $x = c$ IF:

The function is discontinuous at $x = c$	The function has a vertical tangent at $x = c$
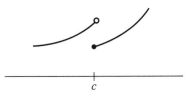	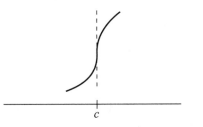

(Continued)

The function has a cusp at $x = c$	The function has a corner at $x = c$
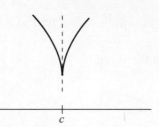	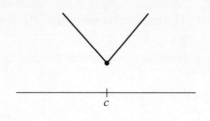

The function has a vertical asymptote at $x = c$

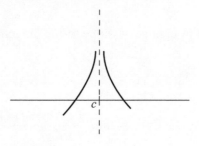

Note: The function is undefined at $x = c$.

ROLLE'S THEOREM

Let $f(x)$ be continuous on $[a, b]$ and differentiable on (a, b). If $f(a) = f(b)$, then there is at least one number c in (a, b) such that
$$f'(c) = 0$$

MEAN VALUE THEOREM (MVT)

Let $f(x)$ be continuous on $[a, b]$ and differentiable on (a, b). Then there is at least one number c in (a, b) such that
$$f'(c) = \frac{f(b) - f(a)}{b - a}$$

Example

Find the value of c that satisfies the Mean Value Theorem for the function $f(x) = \sqrt{x}$ on the interval $[1, 9]$

Solution:

$$f'(x) = \frac{1}{2\sqrt{x}}, f(1) = 1, f(9) = 3$$

$$\text{MVT:} \quad f'(c) = \frac{f(b) - f(a)}{b - a}$$

$$\frac{1}{2\sqrt{c}} = \frac{3 - 1}{9 - 1} = \frac{2}{8} = \frac{1}{4}$$

$$\therefore c = 4$$

This satisfies the MVT because 4 is in the interval $(1, 9)$

Chapter 5

APPLICATIONS OF DERIVATIVES

APPROXIMATIONS

Use this figure to define the notation for the approximations that follow:

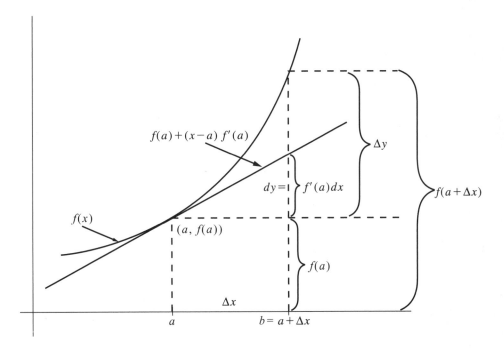

Linear/Tangent Line Approximation

To estimate the value of the function f at a point $x = b$ near $x = a$:

$$f(b) \approx f(a) + (b - a) f'(a)$$

Approximation Using Differentials

To estimate the change in the function f (referred to as ΔY) at a point $x = b$ near $x = a$:

$$\boxed{\Delta Y \approx dy = f'(a)\,dx}, \quad \text{where } dx = \Delta x = (b - a)$$

To estimate the value of the function f at $x = b$ near $x = a$:

$$\boxed{f(b) = f(a + \Delta x) \approx f(a) + f'(a)dx},$$

where $dx = \Delta x = (b - a)$

Example 1

Use a tangent line approximation to estimate the value of $\sqrt{26}$.

Solution:
$$f(x) = \sqrt{x} = x^{\frac{1}{2}}, \quad f'(x) = \frac{1}{2\sqrt{x}}$$

Use $x = 25$ to estimate $x = 26$ $\therefore a = 25$ and $b = 26$

$$f(b) \approx f(a) + (b - a)f'(a)$$

$$f(26) \approx f(25) + (26 - 25)f'(25)$$

$$\approx 5 + 1\left(\frac{1}{2\sqrt{25}}\right) = 5 + (1)\left(\frac{1}{10}\right) = \boxed{5.1}$$

Example 2

Use differentials to estimate the value of $\sqrt{26}$.

Solution:
$$f(x) = \sqrt{x} = x^{\frac{1}{2}}, \quad f'(x) = \frac{1}{2\sqrt{x}}$$

Use $x = 25$ to estimate $x = 26$ $\therefore a = 25, \quad b = 26,$ $\Delta x = 1$

$$f(b) = f(a + \Delta x) \approx f(a) + f'(a)\,dx$$

$$f(26) = f(25 + 1) \approx f(25) + f'(25) \cdot (1)$$

$$\approx 5 + \frac{1}{10}(1) = \boxed{5.1}$$

Propagated Error Approximation

Let $y = f(x)$.

To estimate the error in y (referred to as Δy) based on the measurement error in x (referred to as Δx) near a measurement of $x = a$:

propagation error $= \Delta y \approx dy = f'(a)\, dx$, where $dx = \Delta x$

$$\therefore \boxed{\text{Propagation Error} \approx f'(a)\, dx}$$

Relative Error/Percentage Error Approximation

$$\text{Relative Error in } y \approx \frac{dy}{y}$$

$$\text{\% Error in } y \approx \frac{dy}{y}(100)$$

If y is a measured value, then dy is a measurement error

If y is a computed value, then dy is the propagated error

Example 1

The side of a square is measured as $10 \pm .05$ inches. What is the propagated measurement error for the area of the square?

Solution: $A = s^2 \Rightarrow dA = 2s\,ds$, where $s = 10$ and $\Delta s = ds = \pm .05$

$$\Delta A \approx dA = 2s\,ds$$
$$= 2(10)(\pm .05) = \pm 1$$

the propagated measurement error for the area is $\boxed{\pm 1}$

Example 2

Based on Example 1 above, what are the relative error and percent error in the area?

Solution: $A = s^2 = 10^2 = 100, \quad dA = \pm 1$

$$\text{Relative Error} = \boxed{\frac{1}{100} = .01}$$

$$\text{\% Error} = \boxed{1\%}$$

GRAPHING

Holes

Let $f(x) = \dfrac{g(x)}{h(x)}$, $h(x) \neq 0$

1. Factor $g(x)$ and $h(x)$ completely.

2. Cancel all common factors. Typical factors appear as $(x - c)$.

3. There is a hole in the graph of $f(x)$ at the point where $x = c$.

Note that canceling the common factors removes the hole.

Vertical Asymptote

Let $f(x) = \dfrac{g(x)}{h(x)}$, $h(x) \neq 0$

1. Remove any holes from $f(x)$ by canceling common factors.

2. Set the resulting $h(x) = 0$ and solve for x.

3. Assuming solutions of the form $x = a$ or $x = b$, then $x = a$ and $x = b$ are both vertical asymptotes.

Horizontal Asymptote

Let $f(x) = \dfrac{g(x)}{h(x)}$, $h(x) \neq 0$

1. Remove any holes from $f(x)$ by canceling common factors.

2. For the new $f(x)$, if $\lim\limits_{x \to \infty} f(x) = a$,   where a is a real number, then $y = a$ is horizontal asymptote on the right.

3. For the new $f(x)$, if $\lim\limits_{x \to -\infty} f(x) = b$, where b is a real number, then $y = b$ is a horizontal asymptote on the left.

4. Usually $a = b$, but not always.

Critical Numbers

If the function f is defined at $x = a$, then a is a critical number if either

- $f'(a) = 0$

or

- $f'(a)$ is not defined

Relative Minimum/Maximum Points

If $f'(c) = 0$, we can determine whether $f(c)$ is a relative minimum or a relative maximum in either of two ways:

- The first derivative test

- The second derivative test

The first derivative test

1. Plot all critical values and values of x that are not in the domain of $f(x)$ on a number line.

2. Between these values determine whether $f'(x)$ is positive or negative, and mark the number line with $+$ or $-$ signs as applicable.

3. If $f'(x)$ changes from $-$ to $+$ over a critical value c, then $f(c)$ is a relative minimum, provided $f(c)$ exists

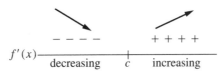

4. If $f'(x)$ changes from $+$ to $-$ over a critical value c, then $f(c)$ is a relative maximum, provided $f(c)$ exists

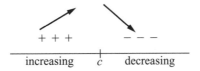

The second derivative test

> Assuming $f(x)$ is twice differentiable
>
> If $f''(c) > 0$, $f(c)$ is a relative minimum
>
> $f''(c) < 0$, $f(c)$ is a relative maximum
>
> $f''(c) = 0$,   inconclusive

Relative Min/Max points vs critical numbers

> If the function f has a relative minimum or relative maximum at $x = a$, then a is a critical number of f.

Absolute minimum/maximum on a closed interval [*a*, *b*]

> 1. Find all the critical numbers on (a, b).
> 2. Evaluate the function at each critical number.
> 3. Evaluate the function at each end point.
> 4. The least of these function values is the absolute minimum on the interval, and the greatest of these function values is the absolute maximum on the interval.

Extreme Value Theorem

> If the function f is continuous on $[a, b]$, then f has both a minimum and maximum in the interval.

Finding Inflection Points

> 1. On a number line, plot all values of x for which $f''(x) = 0$ or f'' is undefined and the values of x that are not in the domain of $f(x)$.
> 2. Between these values, determine whether $f''(x)$ is positive or negative, and mark the number line with $+$ or $-$ signs as applicable.

3. If $f''(x)$ changes from $-$ to $+$ over the value $x = c$, then $(c, f(c))$ is an inflection point, provided $f(c)$ exists

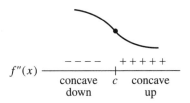

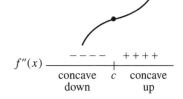

4. If $f''(x)$ changes from $+$ to $-$ over the values $x = c$, then $(c, f(c))$ is an inflection point, provided $f(c)$ exists

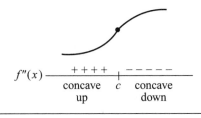

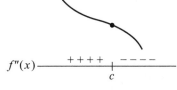

Graphical Meanings of f(x), f'(x), f''(x)

$f(x)$

$f(x)$ is the function of x

Values of x for which $f(x) = 0$ are called roots, zeroes, or x-intercepts.	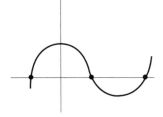

If $f(x) > 0$ on (a, b), the graph is *above* the x-axis 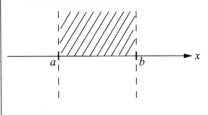	If $f(x) < 0$ on (a, b), the graph is *below* the x-axis 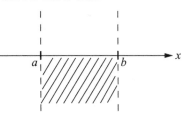

$f'(x)$

$f'(x)$ is the first derivative of $f(x)$	
Values of x for which $f'(x)=0$ indicate critical values. These are possible min/max points.	
If $f'(x)>0$ on (a, b), the graph is *increasing* 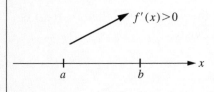	If $f'(x)<0$ on (a, b), the graph is *decreasing* 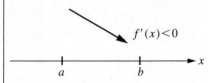
$f'(x)$ changes sign from $+$ to $-$. There is a relative maximum at $x = a$ provided $f(a)$ exists 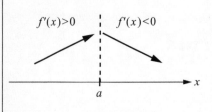	$f'(x)$ changes sign from $-$ to $+$. There is a relative minimum at $x = a$ provided $f(a)$ exists 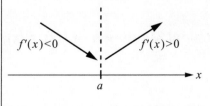

$f''(x)$

$f''(x)$ is the second derivative of $f(x)$	
Values of x for which $f''(x)=0$ indicate points of inflection.	
If $f''(x) > 0$ on (a, b), the graph is *concave up* 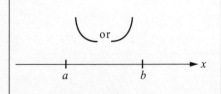	If $f''(x) < 0$ on (a, b), the graph is *concave down* 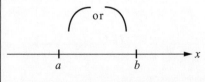

If $f''(x)$ changes sign at $x = a$, a is a point of inflection provided $f(a)$ exists

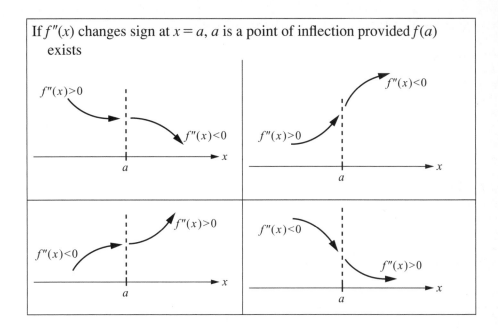

Things to Consider when Sketching a Graph

As appropriate and practical, the following properties of a graph should be considered for sketching purposes.

Based on:	Property of $F(x)$ that can be determined:
$f(x)$	• Domain • Range • x-intercept(s), root(s), zero(s) • y-intercept • Symmetry • Vertical Asymptote(s) • Horizontal Asymptote(s) • Oblique Asymptote
$f'(x)$	• increasing • decreasing • relative minimum/maximum points
$f''(x)$	• concave up • concave down • point(s) of inflection
—	• Test points

Graphical Analysis of a Rational Function

Example

	Analyze and sketch the graph of $f(x) = \frac{(x+1)(x-2)(x-3)}{(x+2)(x-3)}$
	Solution:
Hole	• Cancel the common factor $(x-3)$. This indicates a hole at $x=3$
Revised $f(x)$	• Continue the analysis with the new $\boxed{f(x) = \frac{(x+1)(x-2)}{(x+2)}}$, which is identical to the original $f(x)$ except it does *not* have a hole Note: the hole is at $x=3$, $y = \frac{(3+1)(3-2)}{(3+2)} = \frac{4}{5}$ $\boxed{\text{hole: } (3, \frac{4}{5})}$
x-intercept(s)	• To find the x-intercepts, solve $f(x)=0$ $\boxed{x\text{-intercepts are } x=-1 \text{ and } x=2}$
y-intercept	• To find the y-intercept, let $x=0$ $$f(x) = y = \frac{(0+1)(0-2)}{(0+2)} = -1$$ $\boxed{y\text{-intercept is } (0, -1)}$
Vertical Asymptote	• To find the vertical asymptote(s), set the denominator equal to 0. $(x+2)=0 \quad \therefore \boxed{x=-2 \text{ is a vertical asymptote}}$
Horizontal Asymptote	• To find horizontal asymptote, take the limit as $x \to \infty$. $$\lim_{x\to\infty} \frac{(x+1)(x-2)}{(x+2)} = \lim_{x\to\infty} \frac{x^2-x-2}{(x+2)} = \infty$$ $\therefore \boxed{\text{No Horizontal Asymptote}}$ Note: $y = x-3$ is an oblique asymptote.

Derivatives	$f(x) = \dfrac{x^2 - x - 2}{x + 2}$, $\quad f'(x) = \dfrac{x^2 + 4x}{(x+2)^2}$, $\quad f''(x) = \dfrac{8}{(x+2)^3}$
First Derivative Analysis	Critical values: Solve $\dfrac{x^2 + 4x}{(x+2)^2} = 0$ $\boxed{x = 0 \text{ or } x = -4}$ Also use $\boxed{x = -2}$, because the function is undefined at $x = -2$ Determine how the first derivative behaves between each critical value. $f'(x)$: increases $(-\infty, -4)$ has a relative maximum at $x = -4$, $y = -9$ decreases $(-4, -2)$ decreases $(-2, 0)$ has a relative minimum at $x = 0$, $y = -1$ increases $(0, \infty)$
Second Derivative Analysis	Solve $\dfrac{8}{(x+2)^3} = 0$. There are no solutions. Also use $\boxed{x = -2}$, because the function is undefined at $x = -2$. Note: $x = -2$ is not an inflection point because the function is not defined at $x = -2$.

Putting it all
together

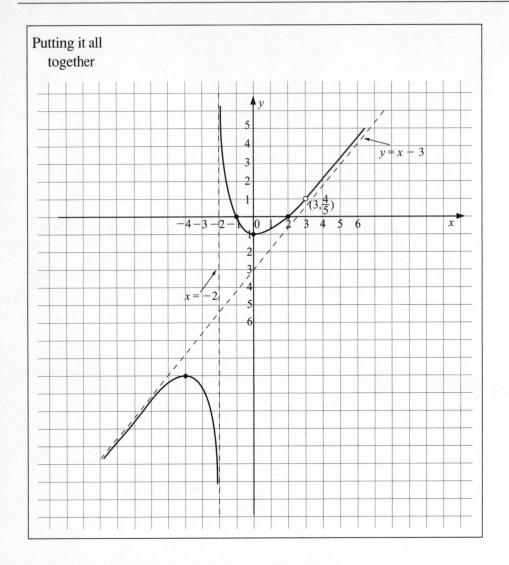

APPLIED OPTIMIZATION PROBLEMS

1. Draw and label a good sketch, if applicable.
2. Based on the text, assign meaningful variables to relevant un-
   knowns.
3. Write an objective equation relating the item to be optimized as a
   function of other variables.
4. Write supporting equations expressing interrelationships of the
   variables and the given data.
5. Use the geometry of the problem to develop equations, if applicable.

6. Algebraically manipulate the equations to express the variable to be optimized as a function of a single secondary variable.

7. Determine domain constraints, if applicable, for the secondary variable.

8. Take the derivative of the objective equation with respect to the secondary variable, set it equal to 0, and solve for the critical values of the secondary variable. These are *potential*, minimum/maximum values.

9. Test these critical values to determine whether they are relative minimums, relative maximums, or neither. Use the first derivative or second derivative test.

10. If the secondary variable is constrained, find the values of the objective variable at each endpoint of the constraint and at each applicable critical value within the constraint, and choose the value that optimizes the problem.

Example

Find the dimensions of the rectangle with greatest area that can be inscribed in the semicircle $y = \sqrt{9 - x^2}$

Solution: • Sketch a diagram

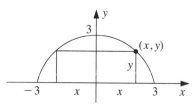

• The area of the rectangle $A = 2xy$, where $y = \sqrt{9 - x^2}$

$$\therefore A = 2x\sqrt{9 - x^2}$$

• Note that the value of x is limited to the interval $(0, 3)$

• Set $\dfrac{dA}{dx} = 0$ and solve for x

(Continued)

$$\frac{dA}{dx} = 2x\frac{d}{dx}(9-x^2)^{\frac{1}{2}} + (9-x^2)^{\frac{1}{2}}\frac{d}{dx}(2x)$$

$$= 2x\left[\frac{1}{2}(9-x^2)^{-\frac{1}{2}}(-2x)\right] + (9-x^2)^{\frac{1}{2}}(2)$$

$$= 2(9-x^2)^{-\frac{1}{2}}[-2x^2+9]$$

$$= \frac{18-4x^2}{\sqrt{9-x^2}} = 0$$

$$\therefore x = \frac{3\sqrt{2}}{2} \approx 2.12$$

- Use the first derivative test to show that $x = \frac{3\sqrt{2}}{2}$ gives a relative maximum

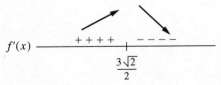

$$f'(x)$$

- To determine the absolute maximum over the interval (0, 3), test the endpoints of the interval and the relative maximum point to determine which area is greatest.

x	Area
0	0
$\frac{3\sqrt{2}}{2}$	9
3	0

Choose $x = \frac{3\sqrt{2}}{2}$

$$\therefore y = \sqrt{9-x^2} = \frac{3\sqrt{2}}{2}$$

the dimensions ($2x$ by y) are: $3\sqrt{2}$ by $\frac{3\sqrt{2}}{2}$

RELATED RATES

1. Draw and label a good sketch, if applicable.
2. Develop an equation that relates the relevant variables.
3. Differentiate each side of the equation with respect to time t to create a rate equation. Use implicit differentiation.
4. Substitute the given data into the rate equation and calculate the required unknown.

Example

A 17-foot ladder is leaning against a brick wall at a height greater than 8 ft. The bottom of the ladder is slipping away from the wall at a constant rate of 1 ft/sec. At what speed is the top of the ladder sliding down the wall when the top is 8 ft above the ground?

Solution:
- Draw a diagram

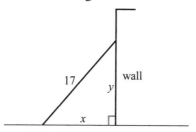

- Establish an equation
$$x^2 + y^2 = 17^2$$
- Create a rate equation by differentiating with respect to t
$$2x\frac{dx}{dt} + 2y\frac{dy}{dt} = 0$$
- Given $\dfrac{dx}{dt} = 1$, $y = 8 \therefore x = 15$

The problem is asking to determine $\dfrac{dy}{dt}$:
$$2(15)(1) + 2(8)\frac{dy}{dt} = 0$$
$$\frac{dy}{dt} = \frac{-15}{8}\ \text{ft/sec} = -1.875\ \text{ft/sec}$$

Answer: $\boxed{\dfrac{15}{8}}$ or 1.875 ft/sec

Note: the minus sign indicates the downward motion.

Chapter 6

INTEGRATION

DISCRETE AREA UNDER A CURVE

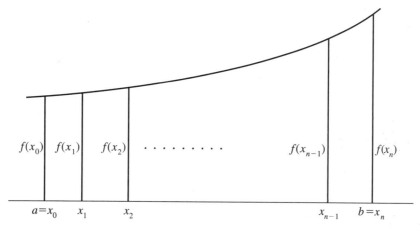

- In the given figure, the interval $[a, b]$ is divided into n equal subintervals of length $\frac{b-a}{n}$.
- $x_0 = a$ is the left endpoint of the first interval.
- $x_n = b$ is the right endpoint of the last interval.

The area under the curve $f(x)$ can be estimated via several approximation techniques.

Technique	Area approximation
Left-Endpoint Rule	$\frac{b-a}{n}\left[f(x_0)+f(x_1)\cdots+f(x_{n-1})\right]$
Right-Endpoint Rule	$\frac{b-a}{n}\left[f(x_1)+f(x_2)\cdots+f(x_n)\right]$
Midpoint Rule	$\frac{b-a}{n}\left[f\left(\frac{x_0+x_1}{2}\right)+f\left(\frac{x_1+x_2}{2}\right)\cdots+f\left(\frac{x_{n-1}+x_n}{2}\right)\right]$

Trapezoidal Rule	$\dfrac{b-a}{2n}\left[f(x_0)+2f(x_1)+2f(x_2)\cdots+2f(x_{n-1})+f(x_n)\right]$ Note that the Trapezoidal Rule is the average of the Left-Endpoint and Right-Endpoint Rules.
Simpson's Rule	$\dfrac{b-a}{3n}[f(x_0)+4f(x_1)+2f(x_2)+4f(x_3)\cdots$ $+2f(x_{n-2})+4f(x_{n-1})+f(x_n)]$ (n must be even)

Example

Estimate the area under the graph $y=x^2$ (and above the x-axis) from $x=1$ to $x=7$. Use 6 equal subintervals

Solution: Draw a sketch.

Calculate $\dfrac{b-a}{n}=\dfrac{7-1}{6}=1$

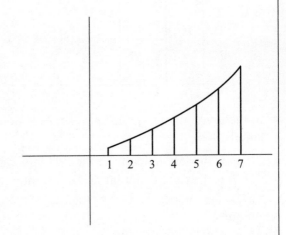

Left-hand Sum $= 1[1^2+2^2+3^2+4^2+5^2+6^2]=91$

Right-hand Sum $= 1[2^2+3^2+4^2+5^2+6^2+7^2]=139$

Midpoint Rule $= 1\left[(1.5)^2+(2.5)^2+(3.5)^2+(4.5)^2+(5.5)^2+(6.5)^2\right]=113.5$

Trapezoidal Rule $= \dfrac{1}{2}[1^2+2(2^2)+2(3^2)+2(4^2)+2(5^2)$

$+2(6^2)+7^2]=115$

Simpson's Rule $= \dfrac{1}{3}[1^2 + 4(2^2) + 2(3^2) + 4(4^2) + 2(5^2)$

$$+ 4(6^2) + 7^2] = 114$$

Note: Actual area $= \displaystyle\int_1^7 x^2 dx = 114$

BASIC INTEGRALS

$\displaystyle\int kf(u)\,du = k\int f(u)\,du$ k is a constant	$\displaystyle\int du = u + C$
$\displaystyle\int [f(u) \pm g(u)]\,du = \int f(u)\,du \pm \int g(u)\,du$	$\displaystyle\int \sin u\,du = -\cos u + C$
$\displaystyle\int u^n\,du = \dfrac{u^{n+1}}{n+1} + C \quad n \neq -1$	$\displaystyle\int \cos u\,du = \sin u + C$
$\displaystyle\int \dfrac{1}{u}\,du = \ln |u| + C$	$\displaystyle\int \tan u\,du = -\ln |\cos u| + C$
$\displaystyle\int e^u\,du = e^u + C$	$\displaystyle\int \sec u\,du = \ln |\sec u + \tan u| + C$
$\displaystyle\int a^u\,du = \dfrac{a^u}{\ln a} + C$	$\displaystyle\int \sec^2 u\,du = \tan u + C$
$\displaystyle\int \dfrac{du}{a^2 + u^2} = \dfrac{1}{a}\tan^{-1}\left(\dfrac{u}{a}\right) + C$	$\displaystyle\int \sec u \tan u\,du = \sec u + C$
$\displaystyle\int \dfrac{du}{\sqrt{a^2 - u^2}} = \sin^{-1}\left(\dfrac{u}{a}\right) + C$	$\displaystyle\int \dfrac{du}{u\sqrt{u^2 - a^2}} = \dfrac{1}{a}\sec^{-1}\left(\dfrac{u}{a}\right) + C$

FUNDAMENTAL THEOREM OF CALCULUS

If $f(x)$ is continuous on $[a, b]$ and $F(x)$ is the antiderivative of $f(x)$, then

$$\int_a^b f(x)\,dx = F(x)\Big|_a^b = F(b) - F(a)$$

Note: The antiderivative F is a function whose derivative equals f.

FUNDAMENTAL THEOREM OF CALCULUS —PART 2

If $f(x)$ is continuous on $[a, b]$, then for every x in the interval $[a, b]$

$$\frac{d}{dx}\left[\int_a^x f(t)\,dt\right] = f(x)$$

and $\dfrac{d}{dx}\left[\displaystyle\int_a^{g(x)} f(t)\,dt\right] = f(g(x)) \cdot g'(x)$

MEAN VALUE THEOREM FOR INTEGRALS

If $f(x)$ is continuous on $[a, b]$, there is a number c between a and b such that

$$\int_a^b f(t)\,dt = f(c)[b - a]$$

AVERAGE VALUE OF *f(x)* OVER THE INTERVAL [*a, b*]

If $f(x)$ is continuous on $[a, b]$, the average value over the interval $[a, b]$ *is*

$$\frac{1}{b-a}\int_a^b f(x)\,dx$$

PROPERTIES OF DEFINITE INTEGRALS

$\displaystyle\int_a^b f(x)\,dx =$ the *net signed area** between the curve $f(x)$ and the x-axis

*Area above the x-axis is considered positive; area below the x-axis is considered negative

$\displaystyle\int_a^a f(x) = 0$	$\displaystyle\int_a^b kf(x)\,dx = k\int_a^b f(x)\,dx,$ k is a constant

(Continued)

$$\int_a^b [f(x) + g(x)] dx =$$
$$\int_a^b f(x) dx + \int_a^b g(x) dx$$

$$\int_a^b f(x) dx = -\int_b^a f(x) dx$$

a, *b*, and *c* are in any order

$$\int_a^b f(x) dx = \int_a^c f(x) dx + \int_c^b f(x) dx$$

Example 1

If $y = \int_3^{x^5} \sin t \, dt$, find $\dfrac{dy}{dx}$.

Solution:
$$\frac{d}{dx} \left[\int_3^{x^5} \sin t \, dt \right] = \sin(x^5) \cdot 5x^4 = \boxed{5x^4 \sin(x^5)}$$

Example 2

Find the average value of $f(x) = x^2$ over the interval $[1, 4]$

Solution:
$$\text{Average value} = \frac{1}{4-1} \int_1^4 x^2 dx = \frac{1}{3} \left[\frac{x^3}{3} \right]_1^4 = \boxed{7}$$

Example 3

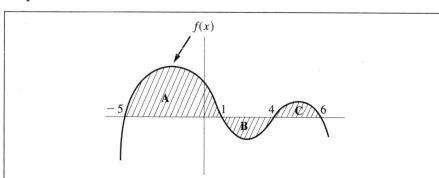

If the areas of the regions **A**, **B**, and **C** are 8, 3, and 2, respectively, then
$$\int_{-5}^{6} f(x) dx =$$

Solution:

The integral is the sum of the signed area from $x = -5$ to $x = 6$. Note the signed area of region B is -3

$$\int_{-5}^{6} f(x)\,dx = 8 - 3 + 2 = \boxed{7}$$

INTEGRATION TECHNIQUES

Substitutions

Assign a dummy variable equal to $g(x)$ to simplify the given integral into a basic form. Two common types are:

- u-substitution
- trigonometric substitution

Integration by Parts

$$\int u\,dv = uv - \int v\,du$$

Partial Fractions

Used to decompose rational functions when the denominator is factorable.

Example 1

$$\int xe^{3x^2}\,dx =$$

Solution: Use u-substitution

let $u = 3x^2 \Rightarrow du = 6x\,dx$

$$\int xe^{3x^2}\,dx = \int e^{3x^2} \cdot x\,dx = \frac{1}{6}\int e^{3x^2} \cdot 6x\,dx = \frac{1}{6}\int e^u\,du$$

$$= \frac{1}{6}e^u + C \Rightarrow \boxed{\frac{1}{6}e^{3x^2} + C}$$

Example 2

$$\int \frac{dx}{\sqrt{9+x^2}} =$$

Solution: Use trigonometric substitution

Let $x = 3\tan\theta \Rightarrow dx = 3\sec^2\theta\,d\theta$

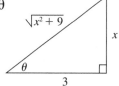

$$\int \frac{dx}{\sqrt{9+x^2}} = \int \frac{3\sec^2\theta}{\sqrt{9+(3\tan\theta)^2}}\,d\theta = \int \frac{3\sec^2\theta}{\sqrt{9(1+\tan^2\theta)}}\,d\theta = \int \frac{3\sec^2\theta}{3\sec\theta}\,d\theta$$

$$= \int \sec\theta\,d\theta = \ln|\sec\theta + \tan\theta| + C$$

$$= \ln\left|\frac{\sqrt{x^2+9}}{3} + \frac{x}{3}\right| + C = \boxed{\ln\left|\frac{\sqrt{x^2+9}+x}{3}\right| + C}$$

Example 3

$$\int x\sin x\,dx =$$

Solution: Use integration by parts

let $u = x \Rightarrow du = dx$; let $dv = \sin x\,dx \Rightarrow v = -\cos x$

$$\therefore \int \underset{u}{x}\,\underset{dv}{\sin x\,dx} = \underset{u}{x}\,\underset{v}{(-\cos x)} - \int \underset{v}{(-\cos x)}\,\underset{du}{dx}$$

$$= -x\cos x + \int \cos x\,dx$$

$$= -x\cos x + \sin x + C$$

Example 4

$$\int \frac{1}{x^2 - 3x - 4}\,dx =$$

Solution: Use partial fractions

$$\frac{1}{x^2-3x-4} = \frac{1}{(x-4)(x+1)} = \frac{A}{x-4} + \frac{B}{x+1} \Rightarrow A = \frac{1}{5}$$

$$B = -\frac{1}{5}$$

$$\int \frac{1}{x^2-3x-4}\,dx = \int \left(\frac{\frac{1}{5}}{x-4} + \frac{-\frac{1}{5}}{x+1}\right)dx = \frac{1}{5}\int \left(\frac{1}{x-4} - \frac{1}{x+1}\right)dx$$

$$= \frac{1}{5}\Big[\ln|x-4| - \ln|x+1|\Big] + C$$

$$= \frac{1}{5}\left[\ln\left|\frac{x-4}{x+1}\right|\right] + C$$

IMPROPER INTEGRALS

If $f(x)$ is continuous on $(-\infty, b]$

$\displaystyle\int_{-\infty}^{b} f(x)\,dx = \lim_{a\to-\infty}\int_{a}^{b} f(x)\,dx$, if the limit exists

$\qquad$ = diverges, $\qquad$ if the limit does *not* exist

If $f(x)$ is continuous on $[a, \infty)$

$\displaystyle\int_{a}^{\infty} f(x)\,dx = \lim_{b\to\infty}\int_{a}^{b} f(x)\,dx$, if the limit exists

$\qquad$ = diverges, $\qquad$ if the limit does *not* exist

If $f(x)$ is continuous on $(-\infty, \infty)$

$\displaystyle\int_{-\infty}^{\infty} f(x)\,dx = \int_{-\infty}^{c} f(x)\,dx + \int_{c}^{\infty} f(x)$, if the limits exist

$\qquad$ = diverges, $\qquad$ if *either* limit does *not* exist

Example

$$\int_{1}^{\infty} \frac{3}{x^3}\,dx =$$

Solution:

$$\int_{1}^{\infty} \frac{3}{x^3}\,dx = \lim_{b\to\infty}\int_{1}^{b} 3x^{-3}\,dx = \lim_{b\to\infty}\left.\frac{-3}{2x^2}\right|_{1}^{b}$$

$$= \lim_{b\to\infty}\left[\frac{-3}{2b^2} + \frac{3}{2}\right] = \boxed{\frac{3}{2}}$$

Chapter 7

APPLICATIONS OF INTEGRALS

AREAS

Area Between Two Curves

If the area between two curves over the interval $[a, b]$ can be viewed as a sum of vertical rectangles, then

$$\text{Area} = \int_a^b (\text{top curve} - \text{bottom curve}) \, dx$$

$$= \int_a^b [f(x) - g(x)] \, dx$$

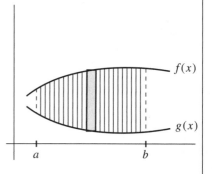

If the area between two curves over the interval $y = a$ to $y = b$ can be viewed as a sum of horizontal rectangles, then

$$\text{Area} = \int_a^b (\text{right curve} - \text{left curve}) \, dy$$

$$= \int_a^b [f(y) - g(y)] \, dy$$

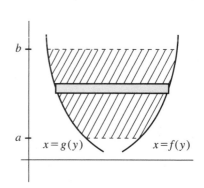

VOLUME DISKS AND WASHERS

When the region to be rotated can be viewed as the sum of rectangles *perpendicular* to the axis of rotation, use this method:

$$\text{Volume} = \pi \int_a^b \left[(r_{\text{outer}})^2 - (r_{\text{inner}})^2 \right] dx$$

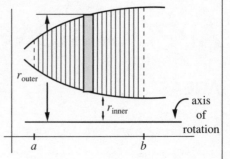

or

$$= \pi \int_a^b \left[(r_{\text{outer}})^2 + (r_{\text{inner}})^2 \right] dy$$

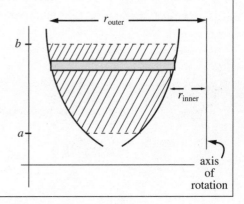

Shells

When the region to be rotated can be viewed as the sum of rectangles *parallel* to the axis of rotation, use this method:

$$\text{Volume} = 2\pi \int_a^b (\text{Area of region} \times \text{mean distance}) \, dx$$

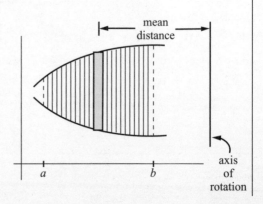

or

$$= 2\pi \int_a^b (\text{Area of region} \times \text{mean distance})\, dy$$

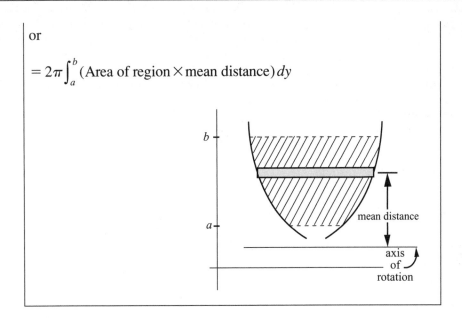

Cross-Section (Slicing)

If the cross-sectional area of a three-dimensional solid can be expressed in terms of a single variable x, then

$$\text{Volume} = \int_a^b (\text{Cross-sectional area}) (\text{thickness})$$

$$= \int_a^b A(x)\, dx$$

Example 1

Find the area between $y = x^2$ and $y = \sqrt{x}$ from $x = 2$ to $x = 5$.

Solution: A sketch is helpful.

$$A = \int_2^5 (x^2 - x^{\frac{1}{2}})\, dx \approx 33.43$$

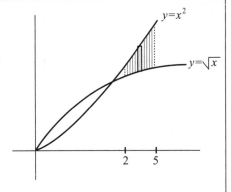

Example 2

Let the region R be the area between $y = x$ and $y = x^2$ bounded between $x = 0$ and $x = 1$. Find the volume of region R when rotated about the x-axis.

Solution:
A sketch is helpful. Note that in the interval $(0,1)$, $x > x^2$ and $\sqrt{y} > y$.

1. Using disks/washers

$$V = \pi \int_{x=0}^{1} [(x)^2 - (x^2)^2]dx = \frac{2\pi}{15}$$

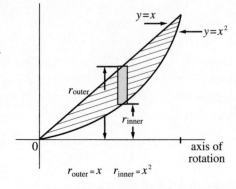

2. Using shells

$$V = 2\pi \int_{y=0}^{1} (\sqrt{y} - y) \cdot y \, dy = \frac{2\pi}{15}$$

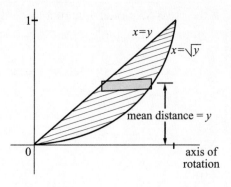

Example 3

The base of a solid is in the first quadrant and can be represented by the circle $x^2 + y^2 = 1$. If each cross-sectional area is a square with its side perpendicular to the x-axis, what is the volume of the resulting solid?

Solution: A sketch is helpful.

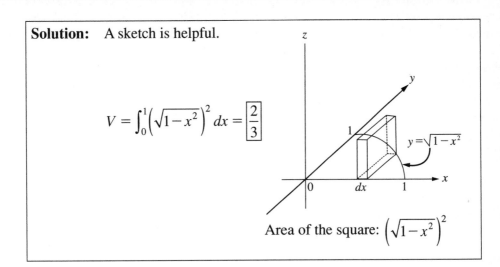

$$V = \int_0^1 \left(\sqrt{1-x^2}\right)^2 dx = \boxed{\dfrac{2}{3}}$$

Area of the square: $\left(\sqrt{1-x^2}\right)^2$

ARC LENGTH

If $y = f(x)$, the arc length S on the interval $[a, b]$ is

$$S = \int_a^b \sqrt{1+[f'(x)]^2}\ dx$$

If $x = g(x)$, the arc length S from $y = a$ to $y = b$ is

$$S = \int_a^b \sqrt{1+[g'(y)]^2}\ dy$$

Example 1

Find the length of the graph $y = x^2$ from $x = 1$ to $x = 2$.

Solution:
$$S = \int_a^b \sqrt{1+[f'(x)]^2}\ dx \qquad \begin{aligned} f(x) &= x^2 \\ f'(x) &= 2x \end{aligned}$$

$$= \int_1^2 \sqrt{1+(2x)^2}\ dx \approx \boxed{3.168}$$

Chapter 8

DIFFERENTIAL EQUATIONS

DEFINITIONS

Term	Definition
Differential Equation	An equation involving an unknown function and one or more of its derivatives
General Solution	A function that satisfies the differential equation. It represents a family of curves because it contains unspecified constants
Particular Solution	A function that satisfies the differential equation in which the value of the constants are known because of initial condition data
Separation of Variables	A differential equation that can be written as: $f(x)\,dx = g(y)\,dy$
Slope field or Direction field	<ul><li>The slope field displays graphically a small line segment at each (x, y) coordinate pair that reflects the value of $\frac{dy}{dx}$.</li><li>The line segments represent tangent lines to the general solution.</li><li>The slope field provides a pictorial outline of the family of curves represented by the general solution.</li></ul>
Euler's Method	An iterative process that approximates the particular solution to a differential equation of the form: $\frac{dy}{dx} = f(x, y)$

Euler's Method

Given: (x_0, y_0) and $\dfrac{dy}{dx} = f(x, y)$

use: incremental changes $= \Delta x$

step			(x, y)
0	Given: (x_0, y_0)		(x_0, y_0)
1	$x_1 = x_0 + \Delta x$	$y_1 = y_0 + \Delta x \cdot f(x_0, y_0)$	(x_1, y_1)
. . .			
n	$x_n = x_{n-1} + \Delta x$	$y_n = y_{n-1} + \Delta x \cdot f(x_{n-1}, y_{n-1})$	(x_n, y_n)

Example

For the differential equation $\dfrac{dy}{dx} + 1 = x$,

    a) Find the general solution.
    b) Find the particular solution if $(0,1)$ is in the solution.
    c) Sketch a slope field by using integer values of x, $-1 \le x \le 2$, and integer values of y, $-2 \le y \le 2$

Solution: (a) Separate the variables and integrate

$$\frac{dy}{dx} + 1 = x \Rightarrow \frac{dy}{dx} = x - 1 \Rightarrow dy = (x-1)\,dx$$

$$\int dy = \int (x-1)\,dx$$

$$\boxed{y = \frac{x^2}{2} - x + c}$$

(b) If $y = 1$ when $x = 0$,

$$1 = \frac{0^2}{2} - 0 + C \Rightarrow C = 1$$

$$\therefore \boxed{y = \frac{x^2}{2} - x + 1}$$

(c)

x	y	$\dfrac{dy}{dx}$
-1	-2	-2
	-1	-2
	0	-2
	1	-2
	2	-2
0	-2	-1
	-1	-1
	0	-1
	1	-1
	2	-1
1	-2	0
	-1	0
	0	0
	1	0
	2	0
2	-2	1
	-1	1
	0	1
	1	1
	0	1

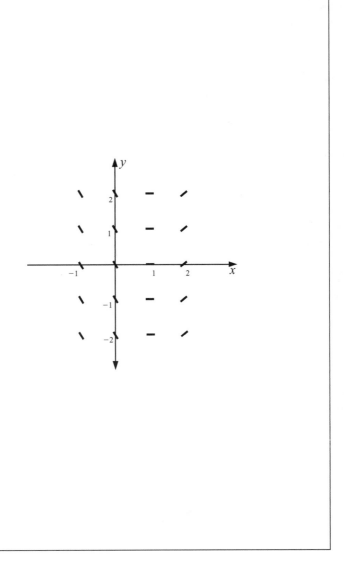

SPECIAL DIFFERENTIAL EQUATIONS

Population Grows at a Rate Proportional to the Population

Equation	Solution	Graph
$\dfrac{dP}{dt} = kP$ $P(t_0) = P_0$	$P(t) = P_0 e^{k(t-t_0)}$	

Newton's Law of Cooling

Rate of change of temperature T of an object placed in a medium at constant temperature C is negatively proportional to the difference between T and C

Equation	Solution	Graph
For: $T > C$ $\dfrac{dT}{dt} = -k(T - C)$	$T(t) = C + (T_0 - C)e^{-kt}$	
For: $T < C$ $\dfrac{dT}{dt} = -k(C - T)$	$T(t) = C - (C - T_0)e^{-kt}$	
$T(0) = T_0$	$\lim_{t \to \infty} T(t) = C$	

Logistic Growth:

Equation	Solution	Graph
$\dfrac{dP}{dt} = kP\left(1 - \dfrac{P}{N}\right)$ or $\dfrac{dP}{dt} = \dfrac{k}{N}P(N - P)$ $P(0) = P_0$ $N = \max$ value of $P(t)$	$P(t) = \dfrac{N}{1 + \left(\dfrac{N}{P_0} - 1\right)e^{-kt}}$ $\lim\limits_{t \to \infty} P(t) = N$	

Chapter 9

PARAMETRIC EQUATIONS AND POLAR COORDINATES

ORGANIZED FACTS

Parametric Equations	Polar Coordinates
$x = f(t), y = g(t)$	Parametric form $x = r\cos\theta \qquad x = f(\theta)\cos\theta$ $y = r\sin\theta \qquad y = f(\theta)\sin\theta$ where $r = f(\theta)$
$\dfrac{dy}{dx} = \dfrac{\left(\dfrac{dy}{dt}\right)}{\left(\dfrac{dx}{dt}\right)} = \dfrac{dy}{dt}\cdot\dfrac{dt}{dx}, \quad \dfrac{dx}{dt} \neq 0$	$\dfrac{dy}{dx} = \dfrac{\left(\dfrac{dy}{d\theta}\right)}{\left(\dfrac{dx}{d\theta}\right)} = \dfrac{\dfrac{dr}{d\theta}\sin\theta + r\cos\theta}{\dfrac{dr}{d\theta}\cos\theta - r\sin\theta}, \quad \dfrac{dx}{d\theta} \neq 0$
$\dfrac{d^2y}{dx^2} = \dfrac{\dfrac{d}{dt}\left(\dfrac{dy}{dx}\right)}{\left(\dfrac{dx}{dt}\right)}, \quad \dfrac{dx}{dt} \neq 0$	$\dfrac{d^2y}{dx^2} = \dfrac{\dfrac{d}{d\theta}\left(\dfrac{dy}{dx}\right)}{\left(\dfrac{dx}{d\theta}\right)}, \quad \dfrac{dx}{d\theta} \neq 0$
Arc length $S = \displaystyle\int_a^b \sqrt{\left(\dfrac{dx}{dt}\right)^2 + \left(\dfrac{dy}{dt}\right)^2}\, dt$	Arc length $S = \displaystyle\int_a^b \sqrt{r^2 + \left(\dfrac{dr}{d\theta}\right)^2}\, d\theta$
	Area $A = \dfrac{1}{2}\displaystyle\int_a^b r^2 d\theta$
	Area between two polar graphs $A = \dfrac{1}{2}\displaystyle\int_a^b (r_2^2 - r_1^2)\, d\theta$

Example 1

Find the perimeter of the cardioid $r = 1 + \cos\theta$.

Solution: perimeter = arc length from $\theta = 0$ to $\theta = 2\pi$

$$S = \int_a^b \sqrt{r^2 + \left(\frac{dr}{d\theta}\right)^2}\, d\theta$$

$$r = 1 + \cos\theta \Rightarrow \frac{dr}{d\theta} = -\sin\theta$$

$$S = \int_0^{2\pi} \sqrt{(1+\cos\theta)^2 + (-\sin\theta)^2}\, d\theta$$

$$= \int_0^{2\pi} \sqrt{1 + 2\cos\theta + \cos^2\theta + \sin^2\theta}\, d\theta$$

$$= \int_0^{2\pi} \sqrt{2 + 2\cos\theta}\, d\theta = \boxed{8}$$

Example 2

If $x = t + 1$ and $y = 2t^2 + 3$, find the equation of the tangent line when $t = 1$.

Solution:

$$\frac{dy}{dx} = \frac{\left(\dfrac{dy}{dt}\right)}{\left(\dfrac{dx}{dt}\right)} = \frac{4t}{1}\bigg|_{t=1} = 4 = \text{slope}$$

$$\therefore m = \frac{dy}{dx} = 4, \quad x = t+1\big|_{t=1} = 2, \quad y = 2t^2 + 3\big|_{t=1} = 5$$

tangent line equation: $\boxed{(y-5) = 4(x-2)}$

Chapter 10

SEQUENCES AND SERIES

TESTS FOR CONVERGENCE

Geometric

$\sum\limits_{n=1}^{\infty} ar^{n-1}$	converges if:	converges to:	diverges if:
	$\lvert r \rvert < 1$	$\dfrac{a}{1-r}$	$\lvert r \rvert \geq 1$

p-Series

$\sum\limits_{n=1}^{\infty} \dfrac{1}{n^p}, \quad p>0$	converges if:	diverges if:
	$p>1$	$0<p\leq 1$

Harmonic (*p*-series, with *p*=1)

$\sum\limits_{n=1}^{\infty} \dfrac{1}{n}$	—	diverges:
		Always

*n*th term

$\sum\limits_{n=1}^{\infty} a_n$	—	diverges if:
		$\lim\limits_{n\to\infty} a_n \neq 0$

Integral

$$\sum_{n=1}^{\infty} a_n = \sum_{n=1}^{\infty} f(n)$$ Note: $f(x)$ is a continuous, positive, decreasing function	converges if:	diverges if:
	$\int_1^{\infty} f(x)\,dx$ converges	$\int_1^{\infty} f(x)\,dx$ diverges

Comparison

$$\sum_{n=1}^{\infty} a_n$$ $(a_n > 0)$	converges if:	diverges if:
	$b_n \ge a_n > 0$ and $\sum_{n=1}^{\infty} b_n$ converges	$a_n \ge b_n > 0$ and $\sum_{n=1}^{\infty} b_n$ diverges

Limit Comparison

$$\sum_{n=1}^{\infty} a_n$$ $(a_n > 0)$	converges if:	diverges if:
	$\lim_{n \to \infty} \dfrac{a_n}{b_n} > 0$ and finite and $\sum_{n=1}^{\infty} b_n$ converges $(b_n > 0)$	$\lim_{n \to \infty} \dfrac{a_n}{b_n} > 0$ and finite and $\sum_{n=1}^{\infty} b_n$ diverges $(b_n > 0)$

Ratio

$$\sum_{n=1}^{\infty} a_n$$ $(a_n > 0)$	converges if:	diverges if:	No conclusion if:
	$\lim_{n \to \infty} \left\| \dfrac{a_{n+1}}{a_n} \right\| < 1$	$\lim_{n \to \infty} \left\| \dfrac{a_{n+1}}{a_n} \right\| > 1$	$\lim_{n \to \infty} \left\| \dfrac{a_{n+1}}{a_n} \right\| = 1$

Root

$$\sum_{n=1}^{\infty} a_n$$ $(a_n > 0)$	converges if:	diverges if:	No conclusion if
	$\lim_{n \to \infty} \sqrt[n]{\|a_n\|} < 1$	$\lim_{n \to \infty} \sqrt[n]{\|a_n\|} > 1$	$\lim_{n \to \infty} \sqrt[n]{\|a_n\|} = 1$

Alternating Series

	converges if:	
$\displaystyle\sum_{n=1}^{\infty}(-1)^{n-1}a_n$	$a_n \geq a_{n+1} > 0$ and $$\lim_{n\to\infty} a_n = 0$$	—

Note:

$\displaystyle\sum_{n=1}^{\infty} a_n$ is *absolutely convergent* if $\displaystyle\sum_{n=1}^{\infty}|a_n|$ converges

$\displaystyle\sum_{n=1}^{\infty} a_n$ is *conditionally convergent* if $\displaystyle\sum_{n=1}^{\infty} a_n$ converges

but $\displaystyle\sum_{n=1}^{\infty}|a_n|$ diverges

Example 1

Test $\displaystyle\sum_{n=1}^{\infty} \frac{1}{n^2+1}$ for convergence or divergence

Solution: Since $\dfrac{1}{n^2+1}$ is positive, continuous, and decreasing, use the integral test.

$$\int_1^{\infty} \frac{1}{x^2+1}\,dx = \lim_{b\to\infty} \int_1^b \frac{1}{x^2+1}\,dx = \lim_{b\to\infty}\left[\tan^{-1}x\right]_1^b$$

$$= \lim_{b\to\infty}\left[\tan^{-1}b - \tan^{-1}1\right] = \frac{\pi}{2} - \frac{\pi}{4} = \frac{\pi}{4}$$

$$\therefore \sum_{n=1}^{\infty} \frac{1}{n^2+1} \boxed{\text{converges}}$$

Example 2

Test $\displaystyle\sum_{n=1}^{\infty} \frac{2^n}{n!}$ for convergence or divergence

Solution: Use the ratio test.

$$\lim_{n\to\infty} \frac{\left(\frac{2^{n+1}}{(n+1)!}\right)}{\left(\frac{2^n}{n!}\right)} = \lim_{n\to\infty} \frac{2}{n+1} = 0$$

$$\therefore \sum_{n=1}^{\infty} \frac{2^n}{n!} \boxed{\text{converges}}$$

Example 3

Does $\displaystyle\sum_{n=1}^{\infty}\frac{n}{n+5}$ converge or diverge?

Solution: Use the nth term test

$$\lim_{n\to\infty}\frac{n}{n+5}=1$$

$$\therefore \sum_{n=1}^{\infty}\frac{n}{n+5}\ \boxed{\text{diverges}}$$

Example 4

Does $\displaystyle\sum_{n=1}^{\infty}\frac{7}{3^n+2}$ converge or diverge?

Solution: Since $\frac{7}{3^n+2}<\frac{7}{3^n}$ and $\frac{7}{3^n}$ is a convergent geometric series, the comparison test concludes that

$$\sum_{n=1}^{\infty}\frac{7}{3^n+2}\ \boxed{\text{converges}}$$

Example 5

Does $\displaystyle\sum_{n=1}^{\infty}\frac{1}{\sqrt{n}}$ converge or diverge?

Solution: this is a p-series with $p=\frac{1}{2}$ $\therefore$ $\boxed{\text{diverges}}$

TYPES OF SERIES

Taylor Polynomial

$$f(x)\approx P_n(x)=f(a)+f'(a)(x-a)+\frac{f''(a)(x-a)^2}{2!}+\cdots+\frac{f^n(a)(x-a)^n}{n!}$$

for the function f, expanded about $x=a$

MacLaurin Polynomial

$$f(x) \approx P_n(x) = f(0) + f'(0)x + \frac{f''(0)x^2}{2!} + \frac{f'''(0)x^3}{3!} + \cdots + \frac{f^n(0)x^n}{n!}$$

Note: This is the Taylor Polynomial with $a = 0$.

Power Series

$$\sum_{n=0}^{\infty} a_n(x-a)^n = a_0 + a_1(x-a) + a_2(x-a)^2 + \cdots + a_n(x-a)^n$$

Radius and Interval of Convergence

Given: $\displaystyle\sum_{0}^{\infty} a_n(x-a)^n$, a power series centered at a. Then one of the following MUST be true:

1. It converges only for $x = a$ $\Rightarrow r = 0$

or

2. It converges for all x $\qquad \Rightarrow r = \infty$

or

3. It converges for some x $\qquad \Rightarrow |x - a| < r \Rightarrow a - r < x < a + r$

and it diverges for some x $\qquad \Rightarrow |x - a| > r$

where $r =$ radius of convergence and $(a - r, a + r)$ is the interval of convergence

Remember to check the endpoints regarding inclusion in the interval.

REMAINDER (ERROR)

Taylor Remainder

$$f(x) = P_n(x) + R_n(x)$$

$$R_n(x) = \text{Remainder} = \frac{f^{(n+1)}(c)}{(n+1)!}(x-a)^{n+1}, \quad \text{where } c \text{ is between } a \text{ and } x.$$

Lagrange Form of the Taylor Polynomial Remainder

$$f(x) = \sum_{n=0}^{n} \frac{f^n(a)}{n!}(x-a)^n + R_n(x) = \text{Taylor Polynomial} + \text{Remainder (Error)}$$

$$\text{where } |R_n(x)| = \left| \frac{f^{(n+1)}(c)}{(n+1)!}(x-a)^{n+1} \right| \quad a \le c \le x$$

1. If $\lim_{n\to\infty} R_n(x) = 0$, then $f(x) = \sum_{n=0}^{\infty} \frac{f^n(a)}{n!}(x-a)^n.$

2. If $\left| f^{(n+1)}(c) \right|$ is maximized, it creates an upper bound on the error, $|R_n(x)|$.

Error Bound for Alternating Series

For converging alternating series with decreasing terms, the error is always less than or equal to the absolute value of the first omitted term.

Example 1

Develop a MacLaurin 5th degree polynomial to approximate $\ln(x+1)$		
Solution:	$f(x) = \ln(x+1)$	$f(0) = \ln(1) = 0$
	$f'(x) = \dfrac{1}{x+1}$	$f'(0) = 1$
	$f''(x) = \dfrac{-1}{(x+1)^2}$	$f''(0) = -1$
	$f'''(x) = \dfrac{2}{(x+1)^3}$	$f'''(0) = 2 = 2!$
	$f^{iv}(x) = \dfrac{-6}{(x+1)^4}$	$f^{iv}(0) = -6 = -(3!)$

$$f^n(x) = \frac{(-1)^{n-1}(n-1)!}{(x+1)^n} \qquad f^n(0) = (-1)^{n-1}(n-1)!$$

$$\therefore P_n(x) = f(0) + f'(0)x + \frac{f''(0)x^2}{2!} + \frac{f'''(0)x^3}{3!} + \cdots + \frac{f^n(0)x^n}{n!}$$

$$= 0 + 1x - \frac{x^2}{2!} + \frac{2!x^3}{3!} - \frac{3!x^4}{4!} + \cdots + \frac{(-1)^{n-1}(n-1)!x^n}{n!}$$

$$f(x) \approx P(x) = \boxed{x - \frac{x^2}{2} + \frac{x^3}{3} - \frac{x^4}{4} + \frac{x^5}{5}}$$

Note: If the series

$$\ln w = (w-1) - \frac{(w-1)^2}{2} + \frac{(w-1)^3}{3} + \cdots + \frac{(-1)^{n-1}(w-1)^n}{n}$$

is known, let $w = x + 1$, to get:

$$\ln(x+1) = x - \frac{x^2}{2} + \frac{x^3}{3} - \frac{x^4}{4} + \frac{x^5}{5}$$

Example 2

Find the radius of convergence and the interval of convergence for $\sum\limits_{n=1}^{\infty} (\frac{x}{7})^n$

Solution: Apply the ratio test

$$\lim_{x \to \infty} \left| \frac{(\frac{x}{7})^{n+1}}{(\frac{x}{7})^n} \right| = \lim_{n \to \infty} \left| \frac{x}{7} \right|$$

this converges when $\left| \frac{x}{7} \right| < 1 \Rightarrow |x| < 7$ centered at zero

$\therefore$ | the radius of converges is 7

To fully determine the interval of convergence, test the end points -7 and 7:

$$\sum_{n=1}^{\infty} \left(\frac{7}{7} \right)^n = \sum_{n=1}^{\infty} 1^n \quad \text{diverges, as does } \sum_{n=1}^{\infty} (-1)^n$$

$\therefore$ the interval of convergence is $(-7, 7)$

SOME BASIC POWER SERIES

Power Series	Interval of convergence
$(1+x)^n = 1 + nx + \dfrac{n(n-1)x^2}{2!} + \dfrac{n(n-1)(n-2)x^3}{3!} + \cdots$	$-1 < x < 1$
$e^x = 1 + x + \dfrac{x^2}{2!} + \dfrac{x^3}{3!} + \cdots + \dfrac{x^n}{n!}$	$-\infty < x < \infty$
$\ln x = (x-1) - \dfrac{(x-1)^2}{2} + \dfrac{(x-1)^3}{3} + \cdots + \dfrac{(-1)^{n-1}(x-1)^n}{n}$	$0 < x \leq 2$
$\ln(x+1) = x - \dfrac{x^2}{2} + \dfrac{x^3}{3} - \dfrac{x^4}{4} + \cdots + \dfrac{(-1)^{n+1}(x)^n}{n}$	$-1 < x \leq 1$
$\ln\left(\dfrac{1+x}{1-x}\right) = 2\left(x + \dfrac{x^3}{3} + \dfrac{x^5}{5} + \dfrac{x^7}{7} + \cdots + \dfrac{x^{2n+1}}{2n+1}\right)$	$-1 < x < 1$
$\sin x = x - \dfrac{x^3}{3!} + \dfrac{x^5}{5!} + \cdots + \dfrac{(-1)^n x^{2n+1}}{(2n+1)!}$	$-\infty < x < \infty$
$\cos x = 1 - \dfrac{x^2}{2!} + \dfrac{x^4}{4!} + \cdots + \dfrac{(-1)^n x^{2n}}{(2n)!}$	$-\infty < x < \infty$
$\tan^{-1} x = x - \dfrac{x^3}{3} + \dfrac{x^5}{5} + \cdots + \dfrac{(-1)^n x^{2n+1}}{2n+1}$	$-1 \leq x \leq 1$
$\dfrac{1}{1-x} = 1 + x + x^2 + x^3 + \cdots + x^n$	$-1 < x < 1$
$\dfrac{1}{1+x^2} = 1 - x^2 + x^4 - x^6 + \cdots + (-1)^n x^{2n}$	$-1 < x < 1$

POWER SERIES OPERATIONS

For $f(x) = \sum\limits_{n=0}^{\infty} a_n x^n$, $g(x) = \sum\limits_{n=0}^{\infty} b_n x^n$, $c = $ constant

ALGEBRA	1.	$cx^r f(x) = \sum\limits_{n=0}^{\infty} ca_n x^{n+r}$
	2.	$f(cx) = \sum\limits_{n=0}^{\infty} a_n (cx)^n$
	3.	$f(x^r) = \sum\limits_{n=0}^{\infty} a_n (x^r)^n$
	4.	$f(x) \pm g(x) = \sum\limits_{n=0}^{\infty} (a_n \pm b_n) x^n$
	5.	$f(x) \cdot g(x)$ $\dfrac{f(x)}{g(x)}$ $=$ multiply (divide) in a manner similar to polynomial products and quotients
CALCULUS	6.	$f'(x) = \sum\limits_{n=1}^{\infty} na_n x^{n-1}$
	7.	$\int f(x)\,dx = \sum\limits_{n=0}^{\infty} \dfrac{a_n x^{n+1}}{n+1} + c$
Note:		The radius of convergence as a result of differentiating or integrating is the same as that of the original series. The interval of convergence may differ at the endpoints.

Example

If $f(x) = \cos x = \sum\limits_{n=0}^{\infty} \dfrac{(-1)^n x^{2n}}{(2n)!}$,   find   (a) $\cos 3x$
                                                          (b) $-\sin x$

Solution:

    (a) Use $f(cx) = \sum\limits_{n=0}^{\infty} a_n (cx)^n$

        $\therefore$ replace x with $3x$

(Continued)

$$\cos(3x) = \boxed{\sum_{n=0}^{\infty} \frac{(-1)^n (3x)^{2n}}{(2n)!}}$$

(b) $-\sin x$ is the derivative of $\cos x$

$$\frac{d}{dx}\left[\sum_{n=0}^{\infty} \frac{(-1)^n x^{2n}}{(2n)!}\right] = \sum_{n=1}^{\infty} \frac{(-1)^n (2n) x^{2n-1}}{(2n)!}$$

$$\therefore -\sin x = \boxed{\sum_{n=1}^{\infty} \frac{(-1)^n x^{2n-1}}{(2n-1)!}}$$

Chapter 11

VECTOR VALUED FUNCTIONS AND MOTION

MOTION

$s = s(t) =$ position,	$v = v(t) =$ velocity,
$a = a(t) =$ acceleration,	speed $= |$velocity$|$

Average	Instantaneous
$v_{avg} = \dfrac{\Delta s}{\Delta t}$	$v(t) = \dfrac{ds}{dt}$
$a_{avg} = \dfrac{\Delta v}{\Delta t}$	$a(t) = \dfrac{dv}{dt}$
	$s(t) = \displaystyle\int v(t)\,dt$
	$v(t) = \displaystyle\int a(t)\,dt$

VECTOR FUNCTIONS

position vector: $\langle x(t), y(t) \rangle = \vec{s}(t) = x(t)\boldsymbol{i} + y(t)\boldsymbol{j}$

velocity vector: $\langle x'(t), y'(t) \rangle = \vec{v}(t) = x'(t)\boldsymbol{i} + y'(t)\boldsymbol{j}$

speed: magnitude of the velocity vector $= |\vec{v}(t)| = \sqrt{[x'(t)]^2 + [y'(t)]^2}$

acceleration vector: $\langle x''(t), y''(t) \rangle = \vec{a}(t) = x''(t)\boldsymbol{i} + y''(t)\boldsymbol{j}$

MOTION—PART 2

velocity $= v(t)$	magnitude and direction
speed $\quad= |v(t)|$	magnitude only

(Continued)

Velocity $v(t)$	Acceleration $a(t)$	Result
0	0	standing still
0	+	standing still
0	−	standing still
+	0	constant speed to the right
+	+	speeding up, moving to the right
+	−	slowing down, moving to the right
−	0	constant speed to the left
−	+	slowing down, moving to the left
−	−	speeding up, moving to the left

Example 1

If the position vector of a particle is $\left\langle t, \frac{1}{t} \right\rangle = \vec{s}(t)$, find its speed at $t = 1$

Solution: $\vec{s}(t) = \left\langle t, \frac{1}{t} \right\rangle \Rightarrow \vec{v}(t) = \left\langle 1, -\frac{1}{t^2} \right\rangle$

$$\vec{v}(1) = \langle 1, -1 \rangle$$

$$\text{speed} = |\vec{v}(1)| = \sqrt{(1)^2 + (-1)^2} = \boxed{\sqrt{2}}$$

Example 2

A particle moves in such a way that its velocity vector is $\left\langle 2t, 3t^2 + 2 \right\rangle$. Find the coordinates of the particle at $t = 2$ if at $t = 1$ it is located at $(4, -1)$

Solution: $\vec{v}(t) = \left\langle 2t, 3t^2 + 2 \right\rangle$

$$\vec{s}(t) = \left\langle \frac{2t^2}{2} + c_1, \frac{3t^3}{3} + 2t + c_2 \right\rangle$$

$$\vec{s}(1) = \langle 1 + c_1, 1 + 2 + c_2 \rangle = (4, -1)$$

$$\therefore c_1 = 3 \text{ and } c_2 = -4$$

$$\vec{s}(t) = \left\langle t^2 + 3, t^3 + 2t - 4 \right\rangle$$

$$\vec{s}(2) = \langle 7, 8 \rangle \Rightarrow \boxed{(7, 8)}$$

PRACTICE EXAMS

AP Calculus AB

PRACTICE EXAM 1

This exam is also on CD-ROM in our
special interactive AP Calculus TESTware®

AP Calculus AB

Section I

PART A

Time: 55 minutes
28 questions

(Answer sheets appear in the back of this book.)

DIRECTIONS: Solve each of the following problems, select the best answer choice, and fill in the corresponding oval on the answer sheet.

Calculators may NOT be used for this section of the exam.

NOTES:

(1) Unless otherwise specified, the domain of a function f is assumed to be the set of all real numbers x for which $f(x)$ is a real number.

(2) The inverse of a trigonometric function f may be indicated by using the inverse function notation f^{-1} or with the prefix "arc" (e.g., $\sin^{-1} x = \arcsin x$).

1. $\displaystyle\int_{-2}^{-1} \sqrt{2}x^{-2}dx =$

(A) $-\sqrt{2}$

(B) $-\dfrac{\sqrt{2}}{2}$

(C) $\dfrac{\sqrt{2}}{2}$

(D) 1

(E) $\sqrt{2}$

(handwritten work):

$-2 \quad \sqrt{2} \quad x^{-3}$

$\left[-\sqrt{2}\, x^{-1} \right]_{-2}$

$\sqrt{2} - \left(\tfrac{1}{2}\sqrt{2} \right)$

2. If $f(x) = \pi^3$, then $f'(1) =$

   (A) $\dfrac{\pi^4}{4}$

   (B) π^3

   (C) $3\pi^2$

   (D) 2π

   (E) 0

3. If $y = \dfrac{1}{\sqrt[3]{e^x}}$, then $y'(1) =$

   (A) $3e^{-\frac{1}{3}}$

   (B) $\dfrac{1}{3}e^{-\frac{1}{3}}$

   (C) $3e^{\frac{1}{3}}$

   (D) $-\dfrac{1}{3}e^{-\frac{1}{3}}$

   (E) $-\dfrac{1}{3}e^{\frac{1}{3}}$

$$\left(e^x\right)^{-\frac{1}{3}}$$

$$-\frac{1}{3}\left(e^x\right)^{-\frac{4}{3}}$$

4. $\displaystyle\lim_{h \to 0} \dfrac{\sin(\pi + h) - \sin\pi}{h} =$

   (A) $-\infty$

   (B) -1

   (C) 0

   (D) 1

   (E) ∞

$\cos\theta$

5. What is the slope of the line tangent to the curve $y^3 + x^2y^2 - 3x^3 = 9$ at the point $(1, 2)$?

   (A) $\dfrac{1}{16}$

   (B) $\dfrac{1}{8}$

   (C) $\dfrac{1}{4}$

   (D) $-\dfrac{1}{4}$

   (E) $-\dfrac{1}{8}$

$$3y^2\frac{dy}{dx} + 2xy^2 + 2x^2y\frac{dy}{dx} - 4x^2 = 0$$

$$3y^2\frac{dy}{dx} + 2x^2y\frac{dy}{dx} = 9x^2 - 2xy^2$$

$$\frac{dy}{dx} = \frac{9x^2 - 2xy^2}{3y^2 + 2x^2y} = \frac{9 - 2(4)}{12 + 4}$$

6. If $f'(x) = \sin x$ and $f(\pi) = 3$, then $f(x) =$

    (A) $4 + \cos x$

    (B) $3 + \cos x$

    (C) $2 - \cos x$

    (D) $4 - \cos x$

    (E) $-2 - \cos x$

    Handwritten: $-\cos x + C$
    $-\cos \pi + C = 3$
    $1 + C = 3$

7. The position of a particle moving along a straight line at any time t is given by $s(t) = 2t^3 - 4t^2 + 2t - 1$. What is the acceleration of the particle when $t = 2$?

    (A)   32

    (B)   16

    (C)   8

    (D)   4

    (E)   0

    Handwritten: $6t^2 - 8t + 2$
    $12t - 8$

8. If $f(x) = 3^{2x}$, then $f'(x) =$

    (A) $2 \cdot 3^{2x}$

    (B) 6^{2x}

    (C) $9^x (\ln 6)$

    (D) $9^x (\ln 9)$

    (E) $\dfrac{9^x}{\ln 9}$

    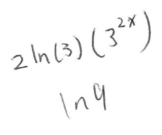

    Handwritten: $2 \ln(3)(3^{2x})$
    $\ln 9$

9. Find the horizontal asymptote(s) of $f(x) = \dfrac{1 - |x|}{x}$

    (A) $y = 1$ only

    (B) $y = -1$ only

    (C) $x = 0, x = 1, x = -1$

    (D) $y = 0$ only

    (E) $y = 1, y = -1$

    Handwritten: $y \to -\infty \quad \dfrac{-\infty}{+\infty} = 1$
    $y \to \infty : \dfrac{-\infty}{\infty} = y$
    $1.$

10. The graph of the function f is shown in the figure below. Which of the following statements is (are) true?

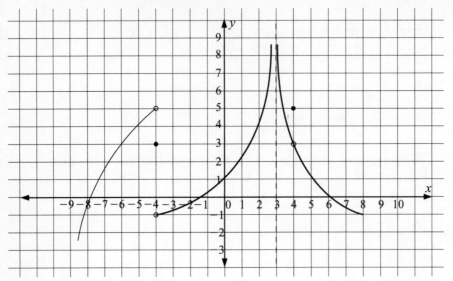

    I. $\lim\limits_{x \to -4} f(x) = 3$

    II. $f(-4) = 3$

    III. $\lim\limits_{x \to 4} f(x) = 5$

    (A) I only

    (B) II only

    (C) III only

    (D) I and II only

    (E) I, II, and III

11. $\displaystyle\int_{1}^{e^2} \frac{\ln x^2}{x}\,dx =$

    (A) 2

    (B) 4

    (C) 6

    (D) 8

    (E) 10

12.

x	1	3	5	7	9
$h(x)$	2	3	3	4	5

Using the table of value shown above for the continuous function $h(x)$, which of the following is the approximation of $\int_1^9 h(x)\,dx$ using trapezoids with equal subintervals?

(A) 27

(B) 26

(C) 24

(D) 22

(E) 20

13. If $y = \arccos(\cos^4 x - \sin^4 x)$, then $\dfrac{d^2 y}{dx^2} =$

(A) 0

(B) 1

$\cos^2 x - \cos \sin^2 \theta$

(C) $-2(\cos x - \sin x)$

(D) $-2(\cos x + \sin x)$

(E) $\sin x + \cos x$

14. Which of the following best states a property of the function $f(x) = x^3 - x$?

(A) There is a relative maximum at $x = \dfrac{\sqrt{3}}{3}$.

(B) There is a relative minimum at $x = \dfrac{\sqrt{3}}{3}$.

$3x^2 - 1 = 0$

(C) There is a relative maximum at $x = \sqrt{3}$.

(D) There is a relative minimum at $x = \sqrt{3}$.

$\pm \dfrac{\sqrt{3}}{3}$

(E) There is a relative minimum at $x = \dfrac{-\sqrt{3}}{2}$.

15. $\lim\limits_{\theta \to 0} \dfrac{\sin^2 2\theta}{2\theta} =$

(A) $-\infty$

$6 \times 4 \wedge 1$

$\sin 2\theta \, (1)$

(B) -1

(C) 0

(D) 1

(E) ∞

16. If $y = (3x)^x$, then $y' =$

(A) $x(3x)^{x-1}$

(B) $3x(3x)^{x-1}$

(C) $(3x)^{x-1} \ln (3x)$

(D) $(3x)^x \ln (3x)$

(E) $(3x)^x (1 + \ln (3x))$

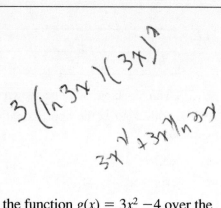

17. What is the average rate of change for the function $g(x) = 3x^2 - 4$ over the interval $[-1, 3]$?

(A) 0

(B) 2

(C) 5

(D) 6

(E) 8

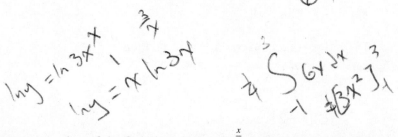

18. What is the average value of the function $f(x) = 2e^{\frac{x}{4}}$ on the interval $[0, 4]$?

(A) $2(e - 1)$

(B) $2e$

(C) $2 \ln 4$

(D) $e^2 - 1$

(E) $e + 2$

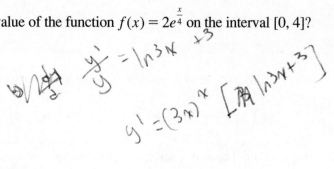

19. Using the graph of $f(x)$ shown below, what is the value of $\int_{-7}^{6} f(x) \, dx$?

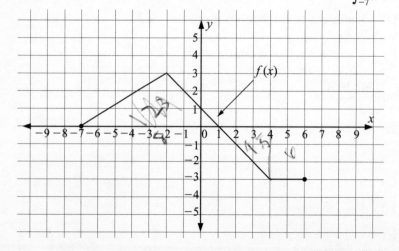

(A) $\dfrac{45}{2}$

(B) $\dfrac{27}{2}$

(C) $\dfrac{17}{2}$

(D) $\dfrac{9}{2}$

(E) $\dfrac{3}{2}$

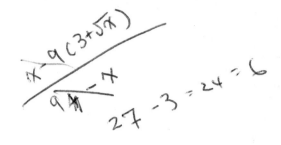

20. $\displaystyle\lim_{x\to 9}\frac{x-9}{3-\sqrt{x}} =$

(A) -12

(B) -6

(C) 0

(D) 6

(E) ∞

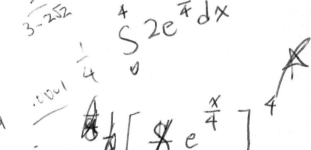

21. Let $f(x) = x^3$. Find the value of c that satisfies the Mean Value Theorem on the closed interval $[1, 3]$.

(A) $-\sqrt{\dfrac{13}{3}}$

(B) $-\sqrt{\dfrac{13}{2}}$

(C) $\sqrt{\dfrac{5}{2}}$

(D) $\sqrt{\dfrac{11}{3}}$

(E) $\sqrt{\dfrac{13}{3}}$

22. A particle moves along the x-axis such that its position s at any time t is given by $s(t) = \dfrac{2t^3}{3} - \dfrac{5t^2}{2} + 2t - 54$. For what value(s) of t is the particle at rest?

(A) $t = 1$ only

(B) $t = 2$ only

(C) $t = \dfrac{1}{2}$ or $t = 2$

(D) $t = \dfrac{1}{2}$ or $t = 3$

(E) $t = 3$ only

23. $\dfrac{d}{dx}\left[\displaystyle\int_{153}^{x^2} t^3\, dt \right] =$

(A) $x^6 - (153)^3$

(B) $3x^6 - 153$

(C) $2x^7 - 3x^6$

(D) x^6

(E) $2x^7$

24. Over which interval(s) is the function $f(x) = 8x^3 + 18x^2 - 24x + 11$ decreasing?

(A) $(-\infty, -2)$ and $\left(\dfrac{1}{2}, \infty\right)$

(B) $\left(-\infty, -\dfrac{1}{2}\right)$ and $(2, \infty)$

(C) $\left(-2, \dfrac{1}{2}\right)$

(D) $\left(-\dfrac{1}{2}, 2\right)$

(E) $(2, \infty)$

25. Which of the following are properties of definite integrals?

I. $\displaystyle\int_a^b c\, f(x)\, dx = c \int_a^b f(x)\, dx$

II. $\displaystyle\int_a^b f(x)\, dx = -\int_b^a f(x)\, dx$

III. $\displaystyle\int_a^b [f(x) \cdot g(x)]\, dx = \int_a^b f(x)\, dx \cdot \int_a^b g(x)\, dx$

(A) I only

(B) II only

(C) III only

(D) I and II only

(E) I, II, and III

26. Let R represent the region enclosed by the graphs $y = x$ and $y = x^2$ over the interval $[0, 1]$. What is the volume of the solid that results when R is revolved about the line $y = 2$?

(A) $\pi \int_0^1 [(2 - x^2)^2 - (2 - x)^2] dx$

(B) $\pi \int_0^1 [(2 - x)^2 - (2 - x^2)^2] dx$

(C) $\pi \int_0^1 [(\sqrt{y})^2 - (y)^2] dy$

(D) $\pi \int_0^1 [(y)^2 - (\sqrt{y})^2] dy$

(E) $\pi \int_0^2 [(2 - y)^2 - (2 - \sqrt{y})^2] dy$

27.

x	$f(x)$	$g(x)$	$f'(x)$	$g'(x)$
1	2	5	1	2
2	3	3	3	4
3	4	1	5	6

Using the table of values shown above, what is the value of $\dfrac{d}{dx}[f(g(2))]$?

(A) 5

(B) 10

(C) 15

(D) 20

(E) 25

28. If $f(x) = \begin{cases} x + 1, & x \le 1 \\ 3 + ax^2, & x > 1 \end{cases}$, what is the value of a for which $f(x)$ is continuous for all values of x?

(A) -2

(B) -1

(C) 0

(D) $\dfrac{1}{2}$

(E) 1

STOP

This is the end of Section I, Part A.
If time still remains, you may check your work only in this section.
Do not begin Section I, Part B until instructed to do so.

Section I

PART B

Time: 50 minutes
      17 questions

(Answer sheets appear in the back of this book.)

DIRECTIONS: Solve each of the following problems, select the best answer choice, and fill in the corresponding oval on the answer sheet.

Calculators MAY be used for this section of the exam.

NOTES:

(1) The exact numerical value of the correct answer does not always appear among the choices given. When this happens, select the number from among the choices that best approximates the exact numerical value.

(2) Unless otherwise specified, the domain of a function f is assumed to be the set of all real numbers x for which $f(x)$ is a real number.

(3) The inverse of a trigonometric function f may be indicated by using the inverse function notation f^{-1} or with the prefix "arc" (e.g., $\sin^{-1} x = \arcsin x$).

76. The figure below shows the graphs of $y = x + 1$ and $y = 2x^2$. What is the area of the shaded region?

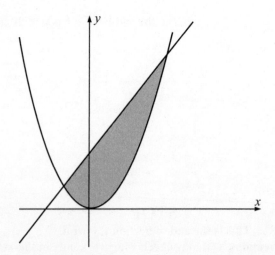

(A) $\dfrac{3}{4}$

(B) $\dfrac{7}{8}$

(C) $\dfrac{9}{8}$

(D) $\dfrac{5}{4}$

(E) $\dfrac{11}{8}$

77. Find the slope of the line tangent to $3y^2 - 2x^2 = 5xy$ at the point $(1, 2)$.

(A) -1

(B) -2

(C) 0

(D) 1

(E) 2

78. Let the piecewise function f be defined as follows:

$$f(x) = \begin{cases} \dfrac{x^2 - 4}{x - 2}, & \text{for } x \ne 2 \\ 2, & \text{for } x = 2 \end{cases}$$

Which of the following are true about the function f?

   I. $f(2) = 2$

   II. $\lim\limits_{x \to 2} f(x) = 2$

   III. $f(x)$ is continuous at $x = 2$

(A) I only

(B) III only

(C) I and II only

(D) I and III only

(E) I, II, and III

79. For which point on the graph of $f(x)$ shown below is $f(x)$, $f'(x)$, and $f''(x)$ negative?

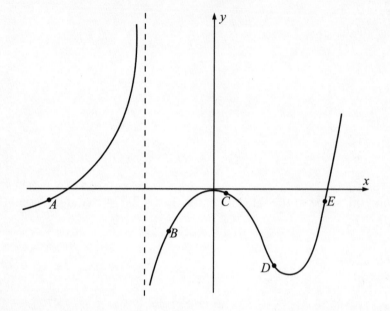

(A) A

(B) B

(C) C

(D) D

(E) E

80. Let $h(x)$ be the antiderivative of $g(x)$. If $g(x) = e^x \sqrt{1 - e^x}$ and $h\left(\ln \dfrac{3}{4}\right) = \dfrac{11}{12}$, find $h(-2)$.

(A) .464

(B) .487

(C) .535

(D) .541

(E) .739

81. The acceleration of a particle moving on a line is given by:

$$a(t) = \frac{1}{\sqrt{t}} + 3\sqrt{t}$$

If the particle starts from rest, what is the distance traveled from $t = 0$ to $t = 3.61$?

(A) 20.21

(B) 28.95

(C) 65.78

(D) 300.1

(E) 632.15

82. At each point (x, y) on a curve, the slope of the curve is $3x^2(y - 6)$. If the curve contains the point $(0, 7)$, then which of the following is the equation of the curve?

(A) $y = 6e^{x^3} + 1$

(B) $y = x^3 + 7$

(C) $y = e^{x^3} + 7$

(D) $y^2 = x^3 + 49$

(E) $y = e^{x^3} + 6$

83. If $g(x) = \dfrac{-x - f(x)}{f(x)}$, $f(1) = 4$ and $f'(1) = 2$, then $g'(1) =$

(A) $-\dfrac{1}{2}$

(B) $-\dfrac{1}{8}$

(C) $\dfrac{1}{8}$

(D) $\dfrac{3}{16}$

(E) $\dfrac{11}{8}$

84. The volume V (in^3) of unmelted ice remaining from a melting ice cube after t seconds is given by $V(t) = 2000 - 40t + 0.2t^2$. How fast is the volume changing when $t = 40$ seconds?

(A) -26 in^3/sec

(B) -24 in^3/sec

(C) -20 in^3/sec

(D) -8 in^3/sec

(E) 20 in^3/sec

85. Which of the following is (are) antiderivatives of $f(x) = \dfrac{3\ln^2 x}{2x}$?

I. $\dfrac{\ln^3 x}{2}$

II. $\dfrac{1}{x}\ln x^2 - \ln^2 x$

III. $\dfrac{\ln^3 x + 11}{2}$

(A) I only

(B) II only

(C) I and II only

(D) I and III only

(E) II and III only

86.

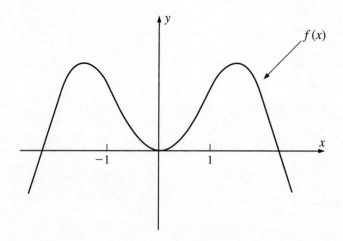

The graph of $f(x)$ is shown in the figure above. Which of the following could be the graph of $f''(x)$?

(A)

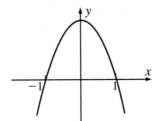

(B)

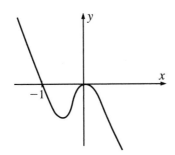

(C)

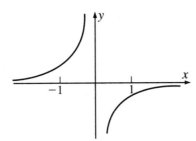

(D)

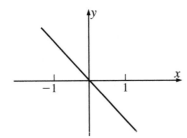

(E)

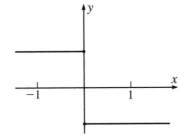

87. If $f(x) = \frac{1}{2}x^3 - x + 5$ and $g(x) = f^{-1}(x)$, find $g'(7)$.

    Note: $f(2) = 7$.

    (A) $\frac{1}{7}$

    (B) $\frac{1}{6}$

    (C) $\frac{1}{5}$

    (D) $\frac{1}{4}$

    (E) $\frac{1}{3}$

88. $\int_{-2}^{1} |x+1|\, dx =$

    (A) $\frac{3}{2}$

    (B) 2

    (C) $\frac{5}{2}$

    (D) 3

    (E) $\frac{7}{2}$

89. $f(x) = |3x - 3|$. Which of the following are true?

    I. $f(x)$ is differentiable at $x = 1$

    II. $f(x)$ is continuous at $x = 1$

    III. $\lim_{x \to 1} f(x) = 3$

    (A) II only

    (B) III only

    (C) I and II only

    (D) I and III only

    (E) I, II, and III

90. What is the slope of the line tangent to $y = \sin^2(5x + \pi)$ at $x = \frac{\pi}{4}$?

    (A) 1

    (B) 2

(C)   3

(D)   4

(E)   5

91.   If the rate of πr^2 increases at three times the rate that $2\pi r$ increases what is the value of r?

(A)   2

(B)   3

(C)   4

(D)   5

(E)   6

92.

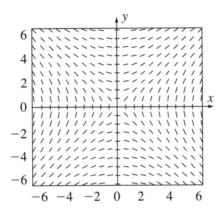

The slope field shown in the figure above is for which one of the following differential equations?

(A) $\dfrac{dy}{dx} = \dfrac{x}{y}$

(B) $\dfrac{dy}{dx} = \dfrac{y}{x}$

(C) $\dfrac{dy}{dx} = e^x$

(D) $\dfrac{dy}{dx} = \dfrac{x^2}{y}$

(E) $\dfrac{dy}{dx} = xy$

STOP

This is the end of Section I, Part B.

If time still remains, you may check your work only in this section.

Do not begin Section II, Part A until instructed to do so.

Section II

PART A

Time: 45 minutes
3 free-response problems

DIRECTIONS: Show all your work in your exam booklet. Grading is based on the methods used to solve the problems as well as the accuracy of your final answers.

Calculators MAY be used for this section of the exam.

---

1. Let R be a region in the first quadrant bounded above by $y = x + 2$ and below by $y = e^x$.

    (a) Find the area of R.

    (b) If the line $x = c$ divides R into two equal areas, find the value of c.

    (c) Find the volume of the solid generated when R is rotated about the line $y = -2$.

2. Let the growth rate (in grams/sec) of the weight of a plant culture be directly proportional to the weight, w, (in grams) of the plant culture present at the same instant.

    (a) Write an equation for the rate of growth of the plant culture in terms of its weight, w.

    (b) Solve the differential equation in part (a) to find the weight of the plant culture as a function of time ($t \geq 0$).

    (c) If the weight of the culture at the beginning of the experiment ($t = 0$) is 10 grams, and the weight after one second ($t = 1$) is 100 grams, find the weight of the culture after 0.5 seconds.

    (d) Find the difference between the instantaneous rate of growth when t is one second and the average rate of growth for the first second.

3. (a) Determine the constants a and b in order for the function $f(x) = x^3 + ax^2 + bx + c$ to have a relative minimum at $x = 4$ and a point of inflection at $x = 1$.

    (b) Using the results from part (a), at what value of x does $f(x)$ have a relative maximum point?

STOP

This is the end of Section II, Part A.

If time still remains, you may check your work only in this section.

Do not begin Section II, Part B until instructed to do so.

Section II

PART B

Time: 45 minutes
 3 free-response problems

DIRECTIONS: Show all your work in your exam booklet. Grading is based on the methods used to solve the problems as well as the accuracy of your final answers.

Calculators MAY NOT be used for this section of the exam.

(During the timed portion for Part B, you may continue to work on the problems in Part A without the use of a calculator.)

4.

t (seconds)	0	2	4	6	8	10	12	14	16	18	20
$v(t)$ feet per second)	2	4	7	9	12	15	11	9	6	5	3

Based on the data in the chart above, estimate $\int_0^{20} v(t)\,dt$ by using five subintervals of equal length

(a) by left-hand Riemann sums

(b) by right-hand Riemann sums

(c) by the midpoint rule

(d) Based on the midpoint rule, find an estimate of the average velocity over the time interval 0 to 20 inclusive.

5. A particle moves along a number line such that its position s at any time t, $t \geq 0$, is given by $s(t) = 2t^3 - 15t^2 + 24t + 1$.

(a) Find the average velocity over the time interval $1 \leq t \leq 2$.

(b) Find the instantaneous velocity at $t = 2$.

(c) When is the particle at rest?

(d) What is the total distance traveled by the particle over the time interval $0 \leq t \leq 5$?

6. Consider the differential equation $\frac{1}{2}yy' - x = 0$, and let $y = f(x)$ be a solution.

   (a) On the axes provided, sketch a slope field at the 14 points indicated.

   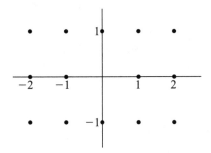

   (b) For the particular solution with the initial condition $f(2) = -1$, write the equation of the tangent line to the graph f at $x = 2$.

   (c) Write the particular solution to the given differential equation with initial condition $f(1) = 1$.

END OF EXAM

PRACTICE EXAM 1

AP Calculus AB

Answer Key

Part A		Part B
Part A		**Part B**

Part A

1. (C)	15. (C)
2. (E)	16. (E)
3. (D)	17. (D)
4. (B)	18. (A)
5. (A)	19. (E)
6. (C)	20. (B)
7. (B)	21. (E)
8. (D)	22. (C)
9. (E)	23. (E)
10. (B)	24. (C)
11. (B)	25. (D)
12. (A)	26. (A)
13. (A)	27. (D)
14. (B)	28. (B)

Part B

76. (C)
77. (E)
78. (A)
79. (C)
80. (A)
81. (B)
82. (E)
83. (B)
84. (B)
85. (D)
86. (A)
87. (C)
88. (C)
89. (A)
90. (E)
91. (B)
92. (A)

Free-Response Answers

1.
(a) 0.803
(b) 0.415
(c) 20.349

2.
(a) $\dfrac{dw}{dt} = kw$
(b) $w = Ae^{kt}$
(c) $10\sqrt{10}$, or 31.623
(d) 140.259 gm/sec

3.
(a) $a = -3, b = -24$
(b) $x = -2$

4.
(a) 152
(b) 156
(c) 168
(d) 8.4

5.
(a) -7
(b) -12
(c) $t = 1$ and $t = 4$
(d) 49

6.
(a) See detailed explanation.
(b) $y + 1 = 4(x - 2)$
(c) $y = \sqrt{2x^2 - 1}$

PRACTICE EXAM 1

AP Calculus AB

Detailed Explanations of Answers

Section 1

Part A

1.**(C)**

Step 1: Move the constant outside the integration symbol:

$$\int_{-2}^{-1} \sqrt{2}x^{-2}\, dx = \sqrt{2}\int_{-2}^{-1} x^{-2}\, dx$$

Step 2: Use $\int u^n du = \dfrac{u^{n+1}}{n+1}$; then $\int x^{-2}dx = \dfrac{x^{-1}}{-1} = -\dfrac{1}{x}$

$$\therefore \sqrt{2}\int_{-2}^{-1} x^{-2}dx = \sqrt{2}\left(-\frac{1}{x}\right)\Bigg|_{-2}^{-1}$$

Step 3: Substitute the integration limits:

$$\sqrt{2}\left(-\frac{1}{x}\right)\Bigg|_{-2}^{-1} = \sqrt{2}\left[\left(\frac{-1}{-1}\right)-\left(\frac{-1}{-2}\right)\right] = \sqrt{2}\left[\frac{1}{2}\right] = \boxed{\frac{\sqrt{2}}{2}}$$

2. **(E)**

Step 1: π is a constant; therefore so is π^3.

Step 2: $\dfrac{d}{dx}[\text{constant}] = 0 \ \therefore f'(1) = \boxed{0}$

3. **(D)**

Step 1: Rewrite the function in exponential form:

$$y = \frac{1}{\sqrt[3]{e^x}} = e^{-\frac{x}{3}}$$

Step 2: Use $\dfrac{d}{dx}[e^u] = e^u \dfrac{d}{dx}[u]$ and $\dfrac{d}{dx}[cx] = c$.

$$\therefore y' = \frac{d}{dx}\left[e^{-\frac{x}{3}}\right] = e^{-\frac{x}{3}}\frac{d}{dx}\left[-\frac{x}{3}\right] = e^{-\frac{x}{3}}\left(-\frac{1}{3}\right) = -\frac{1}{3}e^{-\frac{x}{3}}$$

Step 3: Substitute $x = 1$.

$$y'(1) = \boxed{-\frac{1}{3}e^{-\frac{1}{3}}}$$

4. **(B)**

Step 1: $\displaystyle\lim_{h\to 0}\dfrac{f(x+h)-f(x)}{h}$ is the definition of the derivative of $f(x)$.

$\therefore \displaystyle\lim_{h\to 0}\dfrac{\sin(\pi+h)-\sin\pi}{h}$ is the definition of the derivative

for $\sin x$ with $x = \pi$.

Step 2: $\dfrac{d}{dx}[\sin x] = \cos x$

$$\frac{d}{dx}[\sin x]_{x=\pi} = \cos x\big|_{x=\pi} = \cos\pi = \boxed{-1}$$

5. **(A)**

Step 1: Take the derivative of each side of the equation. (This problem uses implicit differentiation.)

$$\frac{d}{dx}(y^3 + x^2y^2 - 3x^3) = \frac{d}{dx}(9)$$

Step 2: $\dfrac{d}{dx}(y^3) = 3y^2\dfrac{dy}{dx}$; $\dfrac{d}{dx}(-3x^3) = -9x^2$; $\dfrac{d}{dx}(9) = 0$;

and by the product rule, $\dfrac{d}{dx}(x^2y^2) = x^2\left(2y\dfrac{dy}{dx}\right) + y^2(2x)$.

$$\therefore 3y^2\frac{dy}{dx} + x^2\left(2y\frac{dy}{dx}\right) + y^2(2x) - 9x^2 = 0.$$

Step 3: Solve for $\dfrac{dy}{dx}$

$$\frac{dy}{dx}(3y^2 + x^2 \cdot 2y) + 2xy^2 - 9x^2 = 0$$

$$\frac{dy}{dx} = \frac{9x^2 - 2xy^2}{3y^2 + 2x^2 y}$$

Step 4: Let $x = 1$, $y = 2$:

$$\frac{dy}{dx} = \frac{9(1)^2 - 2(1)(2)^2}{3(2)^2 + 2(1)^2(2)} = \boxed{\frac{1}{16}}$$

6. **(C)**

Step 1: To get $f(x)$ given $f'(x)$, integrate $f'(x)$:

$$f(x) = \int \sin x \, dx = -\cos x + C$$

Step 2: Use $f(\pi) = 3$ to calculate the value of C

$$f(\pi) = -\cos \pi + C = 3$$

$$1 + C = 3$$

$$C = 2$$

$$\therefore f(x) = -\cos x + 2 = \boxed{2 - \cos x}$$

7. **(B)**

Step 1: Acceleration is the second derivative of position.

$$s(t) = 2t^3 - 4t^2 + 2t - 1$$

$$\frac{ds}{dt} = 6t^2 - 8t - 2$$

$$a(t) = \frac{d^2 s}{dt^2} = 12t - 8$$

Step 2: Evaluate $a(2)$

$$a(2) = 12(2) - 8 = \boxed{16}$$

8. **(D)**

Step 1:
$$\frac{d}{dx}[a^u] = a^u \frac{d}{dx}[u] \cdot \ln a$$

$$\therefore \frac{d}{dx}[3^{2x}] = 3^{2x} \frac{d}{dx}[2x] \cdot \ln 3$$

$$= 3^{2x}(2)(\ln 3)$$

$$= 3^{2x}(2\ln 3)$$

Step 2: Using the log rule that states $\ln a^b = b \ln a, \quad \therefore 2 \ln 3 = \ln 3^2 = \ln 9.$

$$\therefore \frac{d}{dx}[3^{2x}] = 3^{2x}(\ln 9)$$

$$= \boxed{9^x(\ln 9)}$$

9. **(E)**

Step 1: Horizontal asymptotes are $y = \begin{cases} \lim\limits_{x \to -\infty} f(x) \\ \text{and} \\ \lim\limits_{x \to \infty} f(x) \end{cases}$

or

$$y = \lim_{x \to -\infty} \frac{1 - |x|}{x}, \, y = \lim_{x \to \infty} \frac{1 - |x|}{x}$$

Step 2: For negative numbers $|x| = -x$

For positive numbers $|x| = x$

$$\therefore y = \lim_{x \to -\infty} \frac{1 - |x|}{x} = \lim_{x \to -\infty} \frac{1 - (-x)}{x} = \lim_{x \to -\infty} \frac{1}{x} + 1 = 1$$

$$y = \lim_{x \to \infty} \frac{1 - |x|}{x} = \lim_{x \to \infty} \frac{1 - (x)}{x} = \lim_{x \to \infty} \frac{1}{x} - 1 = -1$$

$$\boxed{y = 1, y = -1}$$

10. **(B)**

Step 1: $\lim\limits_{x \to -4^-} f(x) = 5, \quad \lim\limits_{x \to -4^+} f(x) = -1 \quad \therefore \lim\limits_{x \to -4} f(x) = $ does not exist

$\therefore$ Choice I is incorrect.

Step 2: The value of the function at $x = -4$ is 3, so $f(-4) = 3$

∴ Choice II is correct.

Step 3: $\lim\limits_{x \to 4^-} f(x) = 3$, $\quad \lim\limits_{x \to 4^+} f(x) = 3$, $\quad$ so $\lim\limits_{x \to 4} f(x) = 3$

∴ Choice III is incorrect.

Note: $f(4) = 5$, not $\lim\limits_{x \to 4} f(x)$.

Step 4: The true statement is $\boxed{\text{II only}}$.

11. **(B)**

Step 1: Change $\ln x^2$ to $2 \ln x$ and bring the 2 outside the integral.

$$\int_1^{e^2} \frac{\ln x^2}{2} \, dx = \int_1^{e^2} \frac{2 \ln x}{x} \, dx = 2 \int_1^{e^2} \frac{\ln x}{x} \, dx$$

Step 2: Perform the integration. Let $u = \ln x$ and $du = \frac{1}{x} dx$.

$$2 \int \frac{\ln x}{x} \, dx = 2 \int \ln x \left(\frac{1}{x} dx \right) = 2 \int u \, du = 2 \left(\frac{u^2}{2} \right) = 2 \left[\frac{(\ln x)^2}{2} \right] = (\ln x)^2$$

Step 3: Evaluate the integral

$$2 \int_1^{e^2} \frac{\ln x}{x} \, dx = 2 \quad = (\ln x)^2 \Big|_1^{e^2}$$
$$= (\ln e^2)^2 - (\ln 1)^2$$
$$= (2)^2 - (0)^2 = \boxed{4}$$

12. **(A)**

The trapezoidal method estimates the area as follows:

$$A \ = \ \frac{1}{2} (\Delta x) \Big[h(x_1) + 2h(x_2) + 2h(x_3) + 2h(x_4) + h(x_5) \Big]$$

$$\therefore \ A \ = \ \frac{1}{2} (2)[2 + 2(3) + 2(3) + 2(4) + 5]$$

$$= \ \boxed{27}$$

13. **(A)**

Step 1: Simplify the trigonometric expression with the identity
$\sin^2 x + \cos^2 x = 1$.

$$\cos^4 x - \sin^4 x = (\cos^2 x + \sin^2 x)(\cos^2 x - \sin^2 x)$$
$$= 1 (\cos^2 x - \sin^2 x)$$
$$= \cos^2 x - \sin^2 x$$

Step 2: Simplify $\cos^2 x - \sin^2 x$ to its trigonometric identity $\cos 2x$.

$$\therefore \cos^4 x - \sin^4 x = \cos^2 x - \sin^2 x = \cos 2x$$

Step 3: Simplify $\arccos(\cos 2x) = \cos^{-1}(\cos 2x) = \pm 2x + 2\pi k$,

where k is an integer.

Step 4: Restate the problem in simplified form and differentiate:

$$y = \arccos(\cos^4 x - \sin^4 x)$$
$$= \pm 2x + 2\pi k$$
$$\frac{dy}{dx} = \frac{d}{dx}(\pm 2x + 2\pi k) = \pm 2$$
$$\frac{d^2 y}{dx^2} = \frac{d}{dx}(\pm 2) = \boxed{0}$$

14. **(B)**

Step 1: To find the min/max points, we first find the critical values. Critical values occur when $f'(x) = 0$ or $f'(x)$ does not exist.

$$f(x) = x^3 - x$$
$$f'(x) = 3x^2 - 1$$

Step 2: Set $f'(x) = 0$ and solve for x.

$$f'(x) = 3x^2 - 1 = 0$$
$$x^2 = \frac{1}{3}$$
$$x = \pm \frac{\sqrt{3}}{3}$$

Step 3: Test these values for relative minimum/maximum by using the second derivative test:

If $f''(c)$ is $+ \Rightarrow c$ is a relative minimum

If $f''(c)$ is $-$ $\Rightarrow$ c is a relative maximum

x	$f''(x) = 6x$	result
$\dfrac{\sqrt{3}}{3}$	$2\sqrt{3}$	relative minimum
$-\dfrac{\sqrt{3}}{3}$	$-2\sqrt{3}$	relative maximum

$\therefore$ There is a relative minimum at $x = \dfrac{\sqrt{3}}{3}$.

15. (C)

Step 1: Split $\sin^2 2\theta$ into $(\sin 2\theta)(\sin 2\theta)$, and use $\displaystyle\lim_{\theta \to 0} \frac{\sin \theta}{\theta} = 1$.

$$\lim_{\theta \to 0} \frac{\sin^2 2\theta}{2\theta} = \lim_{\theta \to 0} \left(\frac{\sin 2\theta}{2\theta} \right) (\sin 2\theta)$$
$$= (1) \left(\lim_{\theta \to 0} \sin 2\theta \right)$$

Step 2: $\displaystyle\lim_{\theta \to 0} \sin 2\theta = 0$.

$$\therefore \lim_{\theta \to 0} \frac{\sin^2 2\theta}{2\theta} = \boxed{0}$$

16. (E)

Step 1: Take the log of both sides of the equation, and then use the identity $\ln a^b = b \ln a$.

$$y = (3x)^x$$
$$\ln y = \ln (3x)^x = x \ln (3x)$$

Step 2: Differentiate each side implicitly. Note that $x \ln (3x)$ is a product.

$$\frac{d}{dx} (\ln y) = \frac{d}{dx} (x \ln (3x))$$
$$\frac{1}{y} y' = x \left(\frac{1}{3x} (3) \right) + \ln (3x) (1)$$
$$\frac{1}{y} y' = 1 + \ln (3x)$$
$$y' = y(1 + \ln (3x))$$

Step 3: Replace y with $(3x)^x$

$$y' = y(1 + \ln(3x))$$

$$= \boxed{(3x)^x (1 + \ln(3x))}$$

17. **(D)**

The average rate of change for a function g on the closed interval $[a, b]$ is

$$\frac{g(b) - g(a)}{b - a}$$

Given: $g(x) = 3x^2 - 4$

$$g(3) = 3(3)^2 - 4 = 23$$

$$g(-1) = 3(-1)^2 - 4 = -1$$

$\therefore$ Average rate of change $= \dfrac{23 - (-1)}{3 - (-1)} = \dfrac{24}{4} = \boxed{6}$

18. **(A)**

Step 1: The average value of a function f over the interval $[a, b]$ is given by:

$$\text{average value} = \frac{1}{b-a} \int_a^b f(x)\,dx$$

For $f(x) = 2e^{\frac{x}{4}}$ on $[0, 4]$,

$$\text{average value} = \frac{1}{4-0} \int_0^4 2e^{\frac{x}{4}}\,dx$$

Step 2: $\displaystyle \int_0^4 2e^{\frac{x}{4}}\,dx = 2\int_0^4 e^{\frac{x}{4}}\,dx = 8e^{\frac{x}{4}}\Big|_0^4 = 8\left[e^{\frac{4}{4}} - e^{\frac{0}{4}}\right] = 8(e-1)$

$\therefore$ Average value $= \dfrac{1}{4}(8)(e-1) = \boxed{2(e-1)}$

19. **(E)**

Step 1: The $\displaystyle \int_{-7}^6 f(x)$ represents the area between the function and the x-axis.

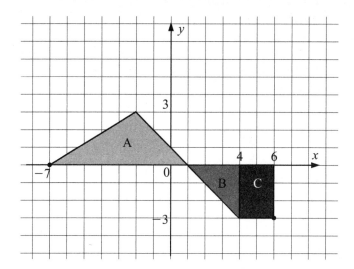

Areas above the x-axis contribute positive values.
Areas below the x-axis contribute negative values.

$$\text{Area } A \ = \ \frac{1}{2}bh \ = \ \frac{1}{2}(8)(3) \ = \ 12 \ \Rightarrow \ +12$$

$$\text{Area } B \ = \ \frac{1}{2}bh \ = \ \frac{1}{2}(3)(3) \ = \ \frac{9}{2} \ \Rightarrow \ -\frac{9}{2}$$

$$\text{Area } C \ = \ bh \ \ = \ 2(3) \ \ = \ 6 \ \Rightarrow \ -6$$

$$\text{Net} \ = \frac{3}{2}$$

$$\therefore \int_{-7}^{6} f(x)\,dx = \boxed{\frac{3}{2}}$$

20. **(B)**

Step 1: Substitute $x = 9$.

$$\frac{x-9}{3-\sqrt{x}} = \frac{9-9}{3-\sqrt{9}} = \frac{0}{0} \text{; this is indeterminate.}$$

Step 2: Rationalize the function.

$$\frac{(x-9)}{(3-\sqrt{x})}\frac{(3+\sqrt{x})}{(3+\sqrt{x})} = \frac{(x-9)(3+\sqrt{x})}{(9-x)} = -(3+\sqrt{x})$$

$$\therefore \lim_{x\to 9} \frac{x-9}{3-\sqrt{x}} = \lim_{x\to 9} -(3+\sqrt{x}) = -(3+\sqrt{9}) = \boxed{-6}$$

21. **(E)**

Step 1: The MVT states that if a function f is differentiable on (a, b) and continuous on $[a, b]$, then there exists at least one value of c in (a, b) such that:

$$f'(c) = \frac{f(b) - f(a)}{b - a}$$

Given: $f(x) = x^3$, $[1, 3]$

$f(3) = 3^3 = 27$ $\qquad$ $f'(x) = 3x^2$

$f(1) = 1^3 = 1$ $\qquad$ $f'(c) = 3c^2$

$f'(c) = \dfrac{f(b) - f(a)}{b - a}$

$3c^2 = \dfrac{27 - 1}{3 - 1} = \dfrac{26}{2} = 13$

Step 2: Solve for c.

$3c^2 = 13$

$c = \pm\sqrt{\dfrac{13}{3}}$

Step 3: To satisfy the MVT, c must be in (a, b).

$$\therefore \boxed{c = \sqrt{\dfrac{13}{3}}}$$

22. **(C)**

Step 1: A particle is at rest when its velocity is zero. Velocity is the first derivative of position.

Given: $\qquad s(t) = \dfrac{2t^3}{3} - \dfrac{5t^2}{2} + 2t - 54$

$\qquad v(t) = \dfrac{ds}{dt} = 2t^2 - 5t + 2$

Step 2: Set the $v(t) = 0$ and solve for t.

$v(t) = 2t^2 - 5t + 2 = 0$

$(2t - 1)(t - 2) \qquad = 0$

$$t = \frac{1}{2} \Bigg| \; t = 2$$

$$\boxed{t = \frac{1}{2} \text{ or } t = 2}$$

23. **(E)**

The fundamental theorem of calculus states:

$$\frac{d}{dx}\left[\int_a^u f(t)\, dt \right] = f(u)\frac{d}{dx}(u)$$

where a is a constant and $u = f(x)$

$$\therefore \frac{d}{dx}\left[\int_{153}^{x^2} t^3\, dt \right] = (x^2)^3 \frac{d}{dx}(x^2) = x^6 \cdot 2x = \boxed{2x^7}$$

24. **(C)**

Step 1: To evaluate whether a function is increasing or decreasing, analyze the first derivative. When $f'(x) > 0$, the function is increasing; when $f'(x) < 0$, the function is decreasing.

Begin by finding the critical values by setting the derivative equal to zero.

Given: $f(x) = 8x^3 + 18x^2 - 24x + 11$

$$f'(x) = 24x^2 + 36x - 24 = 0$$
$$12(2x^2 + 3x - 2) = 0$$
$$(2x - 1)(x + 2) = 0$$
$$x = \frac{1}{2} \Bigg| \; x = -2$$

Step 2: Analyze $f'(x)$ on a number line, using sample values of x in each interval. Determine whether $f'(x)$ is positive or negative.

$$f'(x)\underset{\underset{\displaystyle -2 \qquad \frac{1}{2}}{\big| \qquad\qquad \big|}}{\underrightarrow{+\,+\,+\,+\,+ \quad -\,-\,-\,-\,- \quad +\,+\,+\,+}}\; x$$

Since $f'(x)$ is negative over the interval $\boxed{\left(-2, \dfrac{1}{2}\right)}$, this is where the function is decreasing.

25. **(D)**

This problem requires knowledge of the basic definite integral rules.

Refer to the review section for integral properties.

There is no rule to split the integral of a product (as shown in III) or a quotient.

$\therefore$ Choices $\boxed{\text{I and II only}}$ are properties of definite integrals.

26. **(A)**

Use a vertical rectangle perpendicular to the axis of rotation, and employ the disk and washer method:

$$\text{Volume} = \pi \int_a^b \left[(r_{\text{outer}})^2 - (r_{\text{inner}})^2 \right] dx$$

where r_{outer} is the outer radius and r_{inner} is the inner radius

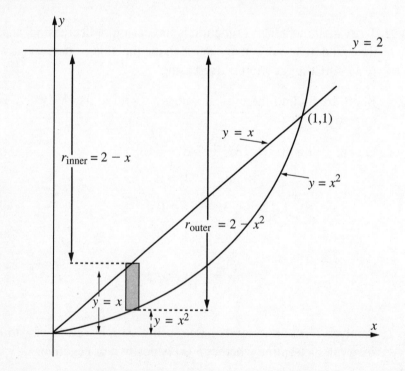

$$\therefore \boxed{\text{Volume} = \pi \int_0^1 \left[(2-x^2)^2 - (2-x)^2 \right] dx}$$

27. **(D)**

Step 1: Use the chain rule:

$$\frac{d}{dx}\big[f(g(x))\big] = f'(g(x)) \cdot g'(x).$$
$$\frac{d}{dx}\big[f(g(2))\big] = f'(g(2)) \cdot g'(2)$$

Step 2: From the table, $g(2) = 3, f'(3) = 5$, and $g'(2) = 4$

$$\therefore f'(g(2)) \cdot g'(2)$$
$$= f'(3) \cdot g'(2)$$
$$= 5(4)$$
$$= \boxed{20}$$

28. **(B)**

Simply stated: To be continuous at $x = 1$, the value of the piecewise function coming from the left must equal the value of the piecewise function coming from the right.

$$\therefore x + 1 = 3 + ax^2 \text{ when } x = 1$$
$$2 = 3 + a$$
$$a = \boxed{-1}$$

Section I

PART B

76. **(C)**

Step 1: the area enclosed between two functions, f and g (where f is the upper function) from the point when $x = a$ to where $x = b$ ($b > a$) is given by:

$$\text{Area} = \int_a^b \left[f(x) - g(x) \right] dx$$

Step 2: To find the a and b limits of integration, it is necessary to identify the x-values at the points of intersection.

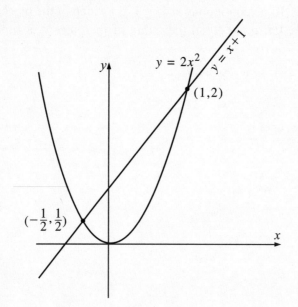

$$2x^2 = x + 1$$

$$2x^2 - x - 1 = 0$$

$$(2x + 1)(x - 1) = 0$$

$$x = -\frac{1}{2} \ \bigg| \ x = 1$$

$$\text{Area} = \int_{-\frac{1}{2}}^{1} [(x+1) - (2x^2)]\, dx = \int_{-\frac{1}{2}}^{1} (-2x^2 + x + 1)\, dx$$

$$= \left. \frac{-2x^3}{3} + \frac{x^2}{2} + x \right|_{-\frac{1}{2}}^{1} \qquad = \frac{5}{6} - \left(\frac{-7}{24} \right) = \boxed{\frac{9}{8}}$$

77. (E)

Step 1: Differentiate implicitly. Note that xy is a product.

$$3y^2 - 2x^2 = 5xy$$

$$6y\frac{dy}{dx} - 4x = 5\left[x\frac{dy}{dx} + y(1) \right]$$

Step 2: Solve for $\dfrac{dy}{dx}$

$$6y\frac{dy}{dx} - 5x\frac{dy}{dx} = 5y + 4x$$

$$\frac{dy}{dx} = \frac{5y + 4x}{6y - 5x}$$

Step 3: Substitute $x = 1$, $y = 2$.

$$\frac{dy}{dx} = \frac{5(2) + 4(1)}{6(2) - 5(1)} = \frac{14}{7} = \boxed{2}$$

78. (A)

Step 1: $f(2)$ asks the question: "Does $f(x)$ have a value at $x = 2$?"

The answer is yes, $f(2) = 2$.

$\therefore$ I is correct.

Step 2: $\lim_{x \to 2} f(x) = 2$ asks the question: "Does $f(x)$ have a limit at $x = 2$?"

To determine the answer, first substitute $x = 2$ into the function

$$\left. \frac{x^2 - 4}{x - 2} \right|_{x=2} = \frac{0}{0}$$

This is indeterminate.

Step 3: To answer the limit question with an indeterminate form, try factoring $f(x)$.

$$\lim_{x \to 2} \frac{x^2 - 4}{x - 2} = \lim_{x \to 2} \frac{(x+2)(x-2)}{x-2} = \lim_{x \to 2}(x+2) = 4$$

$$\lim_{x \to 2} \frac{x^2 - 4}{x - 2} = 4$$

$\therefore$ II is not correct.

Step 4: To be continuous at $x = 2$, $\lim\limits_{x \to 2} f(x) = f(2)$

Since $4 \neq 2$, III is not correct.

$\boxed{\text{I only}}$ is correct.

79. **(C)**

Step 1: For $f(x)$ to be negative, the graph must be below the x-axis. All 5 points meet this requirement.

Step 2: For $f'(x)$ to be negative, the slope of the line tangent to the function should be negative.

Points C and D meet this requirement.

Step 3: For $f''(x)$ to be negative, the curve must be concave down

Only point C meets this requirement.

Only point $\boxed{C}$ meets all three requirements.

80. **(A)**

Step 1: Integrate $g(x)$ by using u-substitution.

Let $u = 1 - e^x$; therefore, $du = -e^x \, dx$

$$
\begin{aligned}
h(x) = \int e^x \sqrt{1 - e^x}\,dx &= \int \sqrt{1 - e^x}\, e^x dx &&= -\int (\sqrt{1 - e^x})(-e^x dx) \\
&&&= -\int \sqrt{u}\, du = -\int u^{\frac{1}{2}} du \\
&&&= -\frac{2}{3} u^{\frac{3}{2}} + C \\
&&&= -\frac{2}{3}(1 - e^x)^{\frac{3}{2}} + C
\end{aligned}
$$

Step 2: Use $h\left(\ln \dfrac{3}{4}\right) = \dfrac{11}{12}$ to calculate the value of C

$$h(x) = -\frac{2}{3}(1-e^x)^{\frac{3}{2}} + C$$

$$h\left(\ln\frac{3}{4}\right) = -\frac{2}{3}\left(1-e^{\ln\frac{3}{4}}\right)^{\frac{3}{2}} + C = \frac{11}{12}$$

$$-\frac{2}{3}\left(1-\frac{3}{4}\right)^{\frac{3}{2}} + C = \frac{11}{12}$$

$$C = 1$$

Step 3: Find $h(-2)$

$$h(x) = -\frac{2}{3}(1-e^x)^{\frac{3}{2}} + 1$$

$$h(-2) = -\frac{2}{3}(1-e^{-2})^{\frac{3}{2}} + 1 = \boxed{.464}$$

81. (B)

Step 1: To develop the distance function, first integrate $a(t)$ to get $v(t)$

$$v(t) = \int (t^{-\frac{1}{2}} + 3t^{\frac{1}{2}})dt$$

$$= 2t^{\frac{1}{2}} + 2t^{\frac{3}{2}} + C$$

Step 2: Since the particle is at rest at time $t = 0$, $v(0) = 0$.

Solve for c

$$v(t) = 2t^{\frac{1}{2}} + 2t^{\frac{3}{2}} + C$$

$$0 = 2(0)^{\frac{1}{2}} + 2(0)^{\frac{3}{2}} + C$$

$$C = 0$$

$$\therefore v(t) = 2t^{\frac{1}{2}} + 2t^{\frac{3}{2}}$$

Step 3: To develop the distance function $s(t)$, integrate $v(t)$

$$s(t) = \int (2t^{\frac{1}{2}} + 2t^{\frac{3}{2}})dt$$

$$s(t) = \frac{4}{3}t^{\frac{3}{2}} + \frac{4}{5}t^{\frac{5}{2}} + C$$

Note: To be sure the particle does not backtrack, be sure that $v(t) \neq 0$ for any value t in the interval [0, 3.61].

Since $v(t) = 0$ yields $t = -1$, $t = 0$, the particle does not backtrack in the given interval.

Step 4: Evaluate $s(3.61)$ and $s(0)$, and subtract to find the distance traveled.

$$s(3.61) = 28.954 + C, \, s(0) = C$$

$$\therefore \text{ Distance traveled } = 28.954 \Rightarrow \boxed{28.95}$$

82. (E)

Step 1: The slope is given by the first derivative, $\dfrac{dy}{dx} = 3x^2(y-6)$. Separate the variables and integrate both sides of the equation to find the equation of the curve.

$$\frac{dy}{dx} = 3x^2(y-6)$$

$$\frac{dy}{y-6} = 3x^2 dx$$

$$\int \frac{dy}{y-6} = \int 3x^2 dx$$

$$\ln|y-6| = x^3 + C$$

$$y-6 = e^{x^3+C}$$

$$y = e^{x^3} \cdot e^C + 6$$

Step 2: Let $e^c = a$ (this is just replacing a constant with a simpler one).

$$y = ae^{x^3} + 6$$

Step 3: Let $x = 0$, $y = 7$, and solve for a

$$7 = ae^0 + 6$$
$$1 = a$$
$$\therefore \boxed{y = e^{x^3} + 6}$$

83. (B)

Step 1: To find $g'(x)$, use the quotient rule:

$$g(x) = \frac{-x - f(x)}{f(x)},$$

$$g'(x) = \frac{f(x)\frac{d}{dx}(-x - f(x)) - (-x - f(x))\frac{d}{dx}(f(x))}{[f(x)]^2}$$

$$= \frac{f(x)[-1 - f'(x)] - (-x - f(x))[f'(x)]}{[f(x)]^2}$$

Step 2: Substitute the given values.

$$g'(1) = \frac{f(1)[-1 - f'(1)] - [-1 - f(1)][f'(1)]}{[f(1)]^2}$$

$$= \frac{4(-1 - 2) - (-1 - 4)(2)}{(4)^2} = \boxed{-\frac{1}{8}}$$

84. (B)

The rate of change in volume is $\frac{dV}{dt}$. Differentiate the given volume function and evaluate $\frac{dV}{dt}$ at $t = 40$.

$$V(t) = 2000 - 40t + 0.2t^2$$

$$\frac{dV}{dt} = -40 + .4t$$

at $t = 40$, $\quad \frac{dV}{dt} = -40 + .4(40) = \boxed{-24\,\text{in}^3/\text{sec}}$

85. (D)

Step 1: Integrate $f(x)$ to find the antiderivative. First, bring the constants outside the integral, then let $u = \ln x$ and $du = \frac{1}{x}dx$

$$F(x) = \int \frac{3}{2}\frac{\ln^2 x}{x}dx$$

$$= \frac{3}{2}\int \frac{(\ln x)^2}{x}dx$$

$$= \frac{3}{2}\int (\ln x^2)\left(\frac{1}{x}dx\right)$$

Let $\quad u = \ln x, \quad du = \dfrac{1}{x} dx$

$$F(x) = \frac{3}{2} \int u^2 \, du = \frac{3}{2} \frac{u^3}{3} + C = \frac{u^3}{2} + C$$

$$F(x) = \frac{(\ln x)^3}{2} + C \implies \frac{\ln^3 x}{2} + C$$

Step 2:

If $C = 0$, $\qquad \dfrac{\ln^3 x}{2} + C \implies \dfrac{\ln^3 x}{2} \qquad$ Choice I is correct.

If $C = \dfrac{11}{2}$, $\quad \dfrac{\ln^3 x}{2} + C \implies \dfrac{\ln^3 x + 11}{2} \quad$ Choice III is correct.

No value of C will achieve choice II.

$\therefore$ Only choices $\boxed{\text{I and III}}$ are correct.

86. **(A)**

Analyze the function intuitively:

1. The second derivative relates to concavity.

2. $f(x)$ first is concave down $\implies$

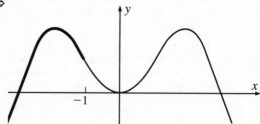

$\therefore f''(x)$ is negative.

3. then switches to concave up $\implies$

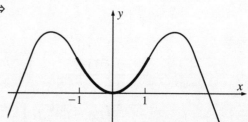

$\therefore f''(x)$ is positive.

4. then switches to concave down $\Rightarrow$

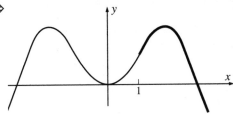

$\therefore f''(x)$ is negative.

This pattern is reflected only in choice $\boxed{A}$.

87. **(C)**

Step 1: If $g(x)$ is the inverse function of $f(x)$, then:

$$g'(x) = \frac{1}{f'(g(x))}$$

Step 2: Calculate $f'(x)$.

$$f(x) = \frac{1}{2}x^3 - x + 5$$

$$f'(x) = \frac{3}{2}x^2 - 1$$

Step 3: Find $g'(x)$ at $x = 7$.

$$g'(7) = \frac{1}{f'(g(7))}$$

Note: If $f(2) = 7$, then $g(7) = 2$

and $g'(7) = \dfrac{1}{f'(2)}$

Step 4: Calculate $f'(2)$ and substitute

$$f'(2) = \frac{3}{2}(2)^2 - 1 = 5$$

$$\therefore g'(7) = \boxed{\frac{1}{5}}$$

88. (C)

The graph of $f(x) = |x + 1|$ shows that the area under the function and above the x-axis between $x = -2$ and $x = 1$ is basically two triangles.

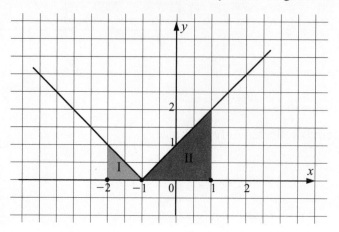

$$\int_{-2}^{1} |x+1|\, dx \quad = \quad A_{\Delta I} + A_{\Delta II}$$

$$= \quad \frac{1}{2}(1)(1) + \frac{1}{2}(2)(2) = \boxed{\frac{5}{2}}$$

89. (A)

Step 1: Graphing $f(x)$ is useful; see the graph below.

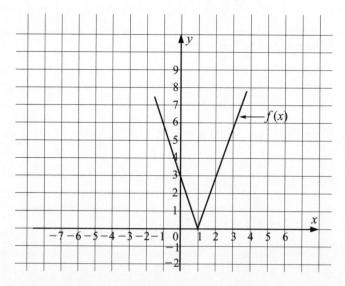

Step 2: The graph is not differentiable at $x = 1$ because

$f'(x)$ coming from the left of $x = 1$ is -3 and

$f'(x)$ coming from the right of $x = 1$ is $+3$

∴ Choice I is not true.

Step 3: the graph is continuous at $x = 1$.

∴ Choice II is true.

Step 4: $\lim_{x \to 1} f(x) = 3$.

∴ Choice III is not true.

∴ Only choice $\boxed{\text{II}}$ is true.

90. **(E)**

Step 1: First find the slope of the curve at $x = \dfrac{\pi}{4}$.

To do this, apply the power rule: $\dfrac{d}{dx}(u^n) = nu^{n-1}\dfrac{d(u)}{dx}$

$$\begin{aligned} y &= \sin^2(5x + \pi) \\ &= [\sin(5x + \pi)]^2 \end{aligned}$$

Then $\dfrac{dy}{dx} = 2[\sin(5x + \pi)]\dfrac{d}{dx}[\sin(5x + \pi)]$

Step 2: Find the derivative of $\sin(5x + \pi)$ using $\dfrac{d}{dx}(\sin u) = \cos u \dfrac{d}{dx}(u)$

$$\therefore \dfrac{d}{dx}[\sin(5x + \pi)] = \cos(5x + \pi)\dfrac{d}{dx}(5x + \pi)$$

Step 3: $\dfrac{d}{dx}(5x + \pi) = 5$

Step 4: Make the substitutions and evaluate at $x = \dfrac{\pi}{4}$:

$$\begin{aligned} \dfrac{dy}{dx} &= 2[\sin(5x + \pi)][\cos(5x + \pi)][5] \\ &= 2\left[\dfrac{\sqrt{2}}{2}\right]\left[\dfrac{\sqrt{2}}{2}\right](5) \\ &= \boxed{5} \end{aligned}$$

91. **(B)**

The rate of increase is the derivative with respect to t.

$$\frac{d}{dt}(\pi r^2) = 3\left[\frac{d}{dt}(2\pi r)\right]$$

$$2\pi r \frac{dr}{dt} = 3\left[2\pi \frac{dr}{dt}\right]$$

$$r = \boxed{3}$$

92. **(A)**

Step 1: Notice that there are horizontal tangents at $x = 0$. $\therefore \frac{dy}{dx} = 0$ when $x = 0$

Also, there are vertical tangents at $y = 0$. $\therefore$ There is a division by y^n

This eliminates choices B, C, and E.

Step 2: Pick a 2nd-quadrant point such as $(-2, 1)$.

Choice A indicates $\frac{dy}{dx} = -2$

Choice D indicates $\frac{dy}{dx} = 4$

The actual slope field shows a negatively sloped line at $(-2, 1)$, so choice D is eliminated.

Step 3: $\therefore$ By elimination, choice A, $\boxed{\frac{dy}{dx} = \frac{x}{y}}$ is the equation for the given slope field.

Section II

PART A

1. Note: Use the calculator.

   Step 1: Make a sketch

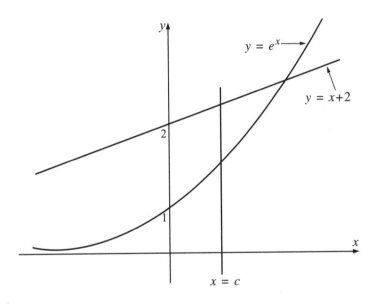

   Step 2: Find the point of intersection:

   $x + 2 = e^x$

   $x = 1.14619 \therefore y = 3.14619$

   (a) Area $= \displaystyle\int_{x=0}^{1.14619} [(x+2)-(e^x)]\,dx = \boxed{0.803}$

   (b) Set the area from $x = 0$ to $x = c$ equal to $\dfrac{1}{2}$ the area of the region
   and solve for c

   $$\int_0^c \left[(x+2)-e^x\right] dx = \frac{.803}{2}$$

   $\boxed{c = 0.415}$

   (c) Employ the disk and washer method. See the sketch

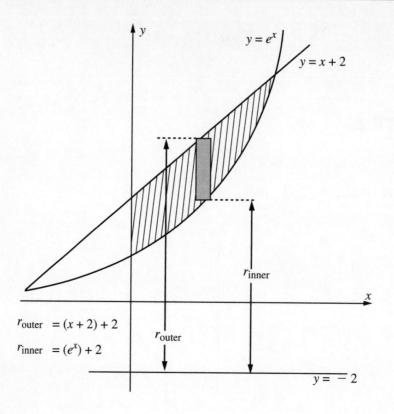

$$V = \pi \int_a^b (r^2_{\text{outer}} - r^2_{\text{inner}})\,dx$$

$$= \pi \int_0^{1.14619} [(x+4)^2 - (e^x+2)^2]\,dx$$

$$= \boxed{20.349}$$

2.

Step 1: The growth rate is proportional to its weight.

(a) $\dfrac{dw}{dt} \propto w \Rightarrow \boxed{\dfrac{dw}{dt} = kw}$, where k is the constant of proportionality.

Step 2: Separate the variables and integrate.

(b) $\dfrac{d\dot{w}}{dt} = kw \quad \Rightarrow \quad \dfrac{dw}{w} = k\,dt$

$$\int \frac{dw}{w} = \int k\,dt$$

$$\ln|w| = kt + C$$

$$w = e^{kt+c} = A^{kt}, \text{where } A \text{ is a constant.}$$

$$\boxed{w = Ae^{kt}}$$

Step 3: Use the initial conditions $w(0) = 10$ and $w(1) = 100$ to find the values of A and k.

$$10 = Ae^{k(0)} \Rightarrow A = 10$$

$$100 = 10e^{k(1)} \Rightarrow k = \ln 10$$

$$\therefore w = 10e^{(\ln 10)t} = 10[e^{\ln 10}]^t = 10 \cdot 10^t = 10^{t+1}$$

$$\therefore w(t) = 10^{t+1}$$

Step 4: Determine $w\left(\dfrac{1}{2}\right)$.

(c) $\quad w\left(\dfrac{1}{2}\right) = 10^{\frac{1}{2}+1} = 10^{\frac{3}{2}} = \boxed{10\sqrt{10} \text{ or } 31.623}$

Step 5:

- The average rate of growth for the first second, from $t = 0$ to $t = 1$:

$$\text{Average Rate of Growth} = \frac{w(1) - w(0)}{1-0} = \frac{10^2 - 10^1}{1-0} = 90 \text{ gm/sec}$$

- The instantaneous rate of growth at $t = 1$:

Instantaneous Rate of Growth $= w'(1) = \dfrac{d(10^{t+1})}{dt}$ evaluated at $t = 1$

$$= 10^{t+1} \cdot \ln 10 \big|_{t=1} = 10^2 \ln 10 = 230.259 \text{ gm/sec}$$

(d) $230.259 - 90 = \boxed{140.259 \text{ gm/sec}}$

3.

Step 1: Find $f'(x)$ and $f''(x)$

$$f(x) = x^3 + ax^2 + bx + c$$

$$f'(x) = 3x^2 + 2ax + b$$

$$f''(x) = 6x + 2a$$

Step 2: To have a relative minimum at $x = 4$, $x = 4$ must be a root of $f'(x)$, or $f'(4) = 0$.

Eq. 1: $f'(4) = 48 + 8a + b = 0$

Step 3: To have an inflection point at $x = 1$, $x = 1$ must be a root of $f''(x)$, or $f''(1) = 0$.

Eq. 2: $f''(1) = 6 + 2a = 0$

Step 4: (a) Find a from Eq. 2:

$6 + 2a = 0 \Rightarrow \boxed{a = -3}$

Find b from Eq. 1 with $a = -3$:

$48 + 8a + b = 0 \Rightarrow \boxed{b = -24}$

$\therefore f(x) = x^3 - 3x^2 - 24x + c$

Step 5: Find the critical points by solving $f'(x) = 0$, and evaluate $f'(x)$ on a number line:

$f(x) = x^3 - 3x^2 - 24x + c$

$f'(x) = 3x^2 - 6x - 24$

$f'(x) = 3x^2 - 6x - 24 = 0$

at $x = -2$ or $x = 4$

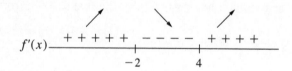

(b) $\therefore$ There is a relative maximum point at $\boxed{x = -2}$

Section II

PART B

4.

Step 1: Approximate $\int_0^{20} v(t)dt$ as the area between the graph of $y = v(t)$ and the x-axis.

Step 2: The interval length with five subintervals will be $\dfrac{20-0}{5} = 4.$

Step 3: Left-hand Riemann sums use the left endpoint of each subinterval

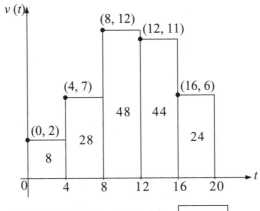

(a) $A = 8 + 28 + 48 + 44 + 24 = \boxed{152}$

Step 4: Right-hand Riemann sums use the right endpoint of each subinterval

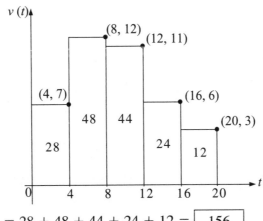

(b) $A = 28 + 48 + 44 + 24 + 12 = \boxed{156}$

Step 5: The midpoint rule uses the midpoint of each subinterval

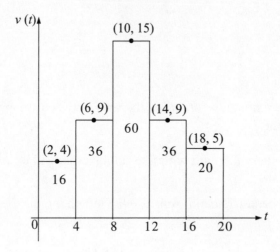

(c) $A = 16 + 36 + 60 + 36 + 20 = \boxed{168}$

Step 6: Average velocity $= \dfrac{1}{20-0}\displaystyle\int_0^{20} v(t)dt$

(d) $\qquad\qquad\qquad = \dfrac{1}{20}[168] = \boxed{8.4}$

5. $s(t) = 2t^3 - 15t^2 + 24t + 1$

Step 1: Average velocity $= \dfrac{\Delta s}{\Delta t} = \dfrac{s(2)-s(1)}{2-1} = \dfrac{5-12}{1} = -7$

(a) So the average velocity is $\boxed{-7}$ or 7 and moving left

Step 2: Instantaneous velocity $= \dfrac{ds}{dt} = 6t^2 - 30t + 24$

(b) $v(t) = \dfrac{ds}{dt}\Big|_{t=2} = \boxed{-12}$ or 12 and moving left

Step 3: The particle is at rest when the velocity is zero.

(c) $v(t) = 6t^2 - 30t + 24 = 0$

$$\boxed{t = 1 \text{ and } t = 4}$$

Step 4: Because the particle stops and turns to go in the other direction at $t = 1$ and $t = 4$, examine its position at $t = 0$, $t = 1$, $t = 4$ and $t = 5$ to determine its total distance. A diagram of the particle's motion is shown below.

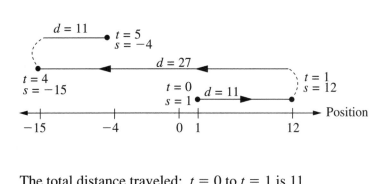

The total distance traveled: $t = 0$ to $t = 1$ is 11

$t = 1$ to $t = 4$ is 27

$t = 4$ to $t = 5$ is 11

$$11 + 27 + 11 = \boxed{49}$$

6.

Step 1: Rewrite the differential equation as $\dfrac{dy}{dx}$ equals

$$\frac{1}{2}yy' - x = 0$$

$$y' = \frac{dy}{dx} = \frac{2x}{y}$$

Step 2: To create the slope field:

- Make a table of values

- Plot a line segment with slope $\dfrac{dy}{dx}$ at each (x, y) coordinate pair

(a)

x	y	$\dfrac{dy}{dx}$
−2	−1	4
−2	0	infinite
−2	1	−4
−1	−1	2
−1	0	infinite
−1	1	−2
0	−1	0
0	1	0
1	−1	−2
1	0	infinite
1	1	2
2	−1	−4
2	0	infinite
2	1	4

Step 3: At the point $(2, -1)$, $\dfrac{dy}{dx} = -4$

(b) $\therefore$ $\boxed{y + 1 = -4(x - 2)}$

Step 4: Solve the differential equation using separation of variables (general solution).

$$\frac{dy}{dx} = \frac{2x}{y}$$

$$y\,dy = 2x\,dx$$

$$\int y\,dy = \int 2x\,dx$$

$$\frac{y^2}{2} = 2\frac{x^2}{2} + C$$

$$\frac{y^2}{2} - x^2 = C$$

Step 5: If $f(1) = 1$, find the value of C

$$\frac{1^2}{2} - (1)^2 = C$$

$$C = -\frac{1}{2}$$

$$\therefore \frac{y^2}{2} - x^2 = -\frac{1}{2}$$

Step 6: Write the particular solution to the differential equation. (Solve for y.)

$$y^2 = 2x^2 - 1$$

(c) Since the particular solution goes through the point $(1, 1)$

$$\boxed{y = \sqrt{2x^2 - 1}}$$

PRACTICE EXAM 2

This exam is also on CD-ROM in our
special interactive AP Calculus TESTware®

AP Calculus AB

Section I

PART A

Time: 55 minutes
28 questions

(Answer sheets appear in the back of this book.)

DIRECTIONS: Solve each of the following problems, select the best answer choice, and fill in the corresponding oval on the answer sheet.

Calculators may NOT be used for this section of the exam.

NOTES:

(1) Unless otherwise specified, the domain of a function f is assumed to be the set of all real numbers x for which $f(x)$ is a real number.

(2) The inverse of a trigonometric function f may be indicated by using the inverse function notation f^{-1} or with the prefix "arc" (e.g., $\sin^{-1}x = \arcsin x$).

1. If $y = (3x^2 - 1)^3$, find $\dfrac{dy}{dx}$.

   (A) $18x(3x^2 - 1)^2$

   (B) $9x(3x^2 - 1)^2$

   (C) $18(3x^2 - 1)^2$

   (D) $9(3x^2 - 1)^2$

   (E) $3(3x^2 - 1)^2$

2. $\int_0^3 xe^{-2x^2} dx =$

(A) $-\dfrac{3}{4}\left[e^{-18} - 1\right]$

(B) $-\dfrac{1}{4}\left[e^{-18} - 1\right]$

(C) $-\dfrac{3}{4}\left[e^{-18} + 1\right]$

(D) $\dfrac{1}{4}\left[e^{-18} - 1\right]$

(E) $-\dfrac{1}{4}\left[e^{-18} + 1\right]$

3. $\displaystyle\lim_{x\to\infty} \dfrac{8x^4 - 3x^2 + 2}{9x^5 + 7x^4 - 3x^2 + 2} =$

(A) -1

(B) $\dfrac{8}{7}$

(C) $\dfrac{8}{9}$

(D) 0

(E) does not exist

4. $\int_0^{\frac{\pi}{2}} \sin(x)\cos^2(x)\, dx =$

(A) $\dfrac{\pi}{3}$

(B) $\dfrac{2\pi}{3}$

(C) $-\dfrac{\pi}{3}$

(D) $\dfrac{1}{3}$

(E) $\dfrac{2}{3}$

5. If $f(t)=\ln(1+t+e^{5t})$, then $f'(0)=$

(A) $\dfrac{1}{3}$

(B) $\dfrac{1}{2}$

(C) 1

(D) 2

(E) 3

6. I.

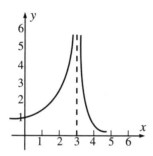

II.

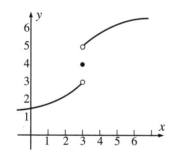

III.

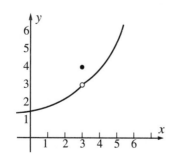

For which of the functions f shown above does $\displaystyle\lim_{x\to 3} f(x)$ exist?

(A)   I only

(B)   II only

(C)   I and II only

(D)   I and III only

(E)   II and III only

7.

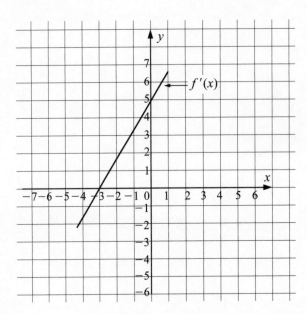

The graph of $f'(x)$ is shown above. If the point $(6, 10)$ lies on $f(x)$, then $f(-6)=$

(A)   50

(B)   20

(C) -20

(D) -30

(E) -50

8. $\lim\limits_{n\to\infty}\left(1+\dfrac{1}{n}\right)^{n+2} =$

(A) e^2+e

(B) e^2

(C) $2e$

(D) e

(E) $e+2$

9. If $f(x) = \dfrac{1}{x-2}$, $(f \cdot g)'(1) = 6$ and $g'(1) = -1$, then $g(1) =$

(A) -7

(B) -5

(C) 5

(D) 7

(E) 8

10. For $x \neq 0$, $\displaystyle\lim_{h \to 0} \frac{1}{h}\left(\frac{1}{x+h} - \frac{1}{x} \right) =$

(A) $-\dfrac{2}{x^2}$

(B) $-\dfrac{2}{x}$

(C) $-\dfrac{1}{x^2}$

(D) 0

(E) $\dfrac{1}{x}$

11. If $\arctan(x) = \ln(y^2)$, then in terms of x and y, $\dfrac{dy}{dx} =$

(A) $\dfrac{1}{1-x^2}$

(B) $\dfrac{-1}{1-x^2}$

(C) $\dfrac{y}{1-x^2}$

(D) $\dfrac{y}{1+x^2}$

(E) $\dfrac{y}{2(1+x^2)}$

12. If $\int_a^b f(x)\,dx = 8$, $a=2$, f is continuous, and the average value of f on $[a, b]$ is 4, then $b=$

   (A) 0

   (B) 2

   (C) 3

   (D) 4

   (E) 5

13. If $0 \le x \le 1$, then $\dfrac{d}{dx}\left[\displaystyle\int_x^0 \dfrac{dt}{2+t}\right] =$

   (A) $\dfrac{1}{x+2}$

   (B) $-\dfrac{1}{x+2}$

   (C) $3\ln|x+2|+C$

   (D) $\ln|x+2|+C$

   (E) $-\ln|x+2|+C$

14.

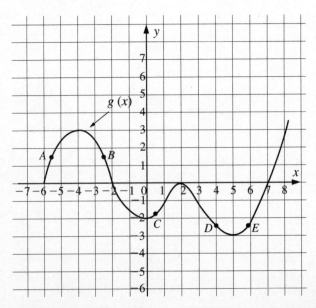

   The function g is represented on the graph above. At which lettered point is $g(x)$ concave down and $g'(x) < 0$?

(A) *A*

(B) *B*

(C) *C*

(D) *D*

(E) *E*

15.

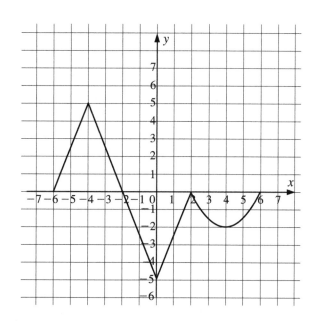

For the graph of $f(x)$ shown above, which of the following integral state-ments must be true?

I. $\displaystyle\int_{-6}^{-4} f(x)\,dx = \int_{-4}^{-2} f(x)\,dx$

II. $\displaystyle\int_{-6}^{-2} f(x)\,dx = \int_{-2}^{2} f(x)\,dx$

III. $\displaystyle\int_{-6}^{6} f(x)\,dx > \int_{-6}^{2} f(x)\,dx$

(A) I only

(B) I and II only

(C) I and III only

(D) II and III only

(E) I, II, and III

16. The sum of a number and twice another number is 12. What is their maximum product?

    (A) 16

    (B) 18

    (C) 20

    (D) 24

    (E) 36

17. The function f has a slope of $3x-2$ at each point. If $f(4)=10$, which of the following is an equation for $f(x)$?

    (A) $\dfrac{3x^2}{2} - 2x - 6$

    (B) $\dfrac{3x^2}{2} - 2x - 2$

    (C) $\dfrac{3x^2}{2} - 6x + 3$

    (D) $3x^2 - 4x + 20$

    (E) $\dfrac{3x^2}{2} - 2x + 10$

18. Which of the following correctly describes the discontinuities associated with $f(x) = \dfrac{x^2 - 2x - 3}{x^2 - 9}$?

    (A) A hole at $x=-3$, a vertical asymptote at $x=3$

    (B) Holes at $x=-3$ and $x=3$

    (C) A hole at $x=3$, a vertical asymptote at $x=-3$

    (D) Vertical asymptotes at $x=3$ and $x=-3$

    (E) No discontinuities

19. When is the function $h(x) = x^3 - 3x^2 - 19x + 4$ concave up?

    (A) $(-\infty, 3)$

    (B) $(-4, 3]$

    (C) $(-3, 3)$

    (D) $(1, \infty)$

    (E) $(3, \infty)$

20. Given the piecewise function $f(x) = \begin{cases} 2x + a & x \le 1 \\ bx^2 - 1 & x > 1 \end{cases}$,

for what values of a and b is $f(x)$ differentiable at $x=1$?

(A) $a = 2, b = -3$

(B) $a = 1, b = -2$

(C) $a = -2, b = 1$

(D) $a = 3, b = -1$

(E) $a = 5, b = 8$

21. A collapsible spherical tank is being relieved of air at the rate of 2 in³/min. At what rate is the radius of the tank changing when the surface area is 12 in²?

(Note: $V_{\text{sphere}} = \dfrac{4}{3}\pi r^3$ and $\text{S.A.}_{\text{sphere}} = 4\pi r^2$)

(A) $\dfrac{1}{6}$ in/min

(B) $\dfrac{\pi}{6}$ in/min

(C) $-\dfrac{1}{6}$ in/min

(D) $-\dfrac{\pi}{6}$ in/min

(E) $-\dfrac{1}{12}$ in/min

22. The rate of growth of the mass of a tumor, m, with respect to time t, is inversely proportional to the square of the mass. The differential equation that best describes this relationship is which of the following?

(A) $\dfrac{dm}{dt} = km^2$

(B) $\dfrac{dm}{dt} = \dfrac{k}{m^2}$

(C) $\dfrac{dm}{dt} = k\sqrt{m}$

(D) $\dfrac{dm}{dt} = \dfrac{k}{\sqrt{m}}$

(E) $\dfrac{dm}{dt} = (km)^2$

23.   A function f is differentiable for all values of x, and $f'(x) < 0$ and $f''(x) < 0$ for all values x. If $f(3)=27$ and $f(5)=17$, which of the following could be $f(7)$?

   I.   3

   II.   7

   III.   11

   (A)   I only

   (B)   I and II only

   (C)   II only

   (D)   II and III only

   (E)   I, II, and III

24.   An ellipse with semiaxes a and b has an area πab.

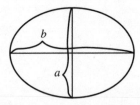

If the area is held constant at 9π, how fast is b increasing when $a=1$ and a is decreasing at $\dfrac{1}{2}$ unit/minute?

   (A) $\dfrac{9}{2}$ units/min

   (B)   3 units/min

   (C)   1 units/min

   (D) $\dfrac{2}{9}$ units/min

   (E) $\dfrac{1}{3}$ unit/min

25. The area between the line $y=x$ and curve $y=\dfrac{1}{2}x^2$ can be which of the following?

   I. $\pi\displaystyle\int_0^2 (x)^2 - \left(\dfrac{1}{2}x^2\right)^2 \, dx$

   II. $\displaystyle\int_0^2 \left(x - \dfrac{1}{2}x^2\right) dx$

   III. $\displaystyle\int_0^2 \left(\sqrt{2y} - y\right) dy$

   (A) I only

   (B) II only

   (C) III only

   (D) I and II only

   (E) II and III only

26. What is the value of the circumference of a circle at the instant when the radius is increasing at $\dfrac{1}{6}$ the rate the area is increasing?

   (A) 3

   (B) $\dfrac{3}{\pi}$

   (C) 6

   (D) $\dfrac{6}{\pi}$

   (E) 2π

27. Which of the following is (are) true about the function $f(x) = x^{\frac{1}{3}}$?

   I. It is continuous at $x = 0$.

   II. It is differentiable at $x = 0$.

   III. $\displaystyle\lim_{x \to 0} f(x) = 0$.

   (A) I only

   (B) II only

   (C) I and III only

   (D) II and III only

   (E) I, II, and III

28. The tangent line to the function $h(x)$ at $(6, -1)$ intercepts the y-axis at $y = 4$. Find $h'(6)$.

(A) $-\dfrac{1}{6}$

(B) $-\dfrac{2}{3}$

(C) $-\dfrac{4}{5}$

(D) -1

(E) $-\dfrac{5}{6}$

STOP
This is the end of Section I, Part A.
If time still remains, you may check your work only in this section.
Do not begin Section I, Part B until instructed to do so.

Section I

PART B

Time: 50 minutes
17 questions

(Answer sheets appear in the back of this book.)

NOTES:

(1) The exact numerical value of the correct answer does not always appear among the choices given. When this happens, select the number from among the choices that best approximates the exact numerical value.

(2) Unless otherwise specified, the domain of a function f is assumed to be the set of all real numbers x for which $f(x)$ is a real number.

(3) The inverse of a trigonometric function f may be indicated by using the inverse function notation f^{-1} or with the prefix "arc" (e.g., $\sin^{-1}x$ = arcsin x).

76. The radius of a circle is measured to be 3 cm correct to within .02 cm. Estimate the propagated error in the area of the circle.

   (A)   .183 cm

   (B)   .213 cm

   (C)   .285 cm

   (D)   .377 cm

   (E)   .427 cm

77. The base of a solid is the region in the first quadrant enclosed by the *x*-axis, *y*-axis, and the line $y = -2x + 6$. The cross sections are squares perpendicular to the *x*-axis. Find the volume of the resulting solid.

    (A) 18

    (B) 24

    (C) 30

    (D) 34

    (E) 36

78. To apply either the Mean Value theorem or Rolle's theorem to a function *f*, certain requirements regarding the continuity and differentiability of the function must be met. Which of the following states the requirements correctly?

    (A) *f* is continuous on (a, b) and differentiable on (a, b)

    (B) *f* is continuous on (a, b) and differentiable on $[a, b]$

    (C) *f* is continuous on (a, b) and differentiable on $[a, b)$

    (D) *f* is continuous on $[a, b]$ and differentiable on (a, b)

    (E) *f* is continuous on $[a, b]$ and differentiable on $[a, b]$

79. If the length of a rectangle is increasing at the rate of 7 cm/sec and the width of the rectangle is decreasing at the rate of 7 cm/sec, then which of the following best describes the change in area when the length is greater than the width?

    (A) none (it remains constant)

    (B) always increasing

    (C) always decreasing

    (D) decreasing then increasing

    (E) increasing then decreasing

80.

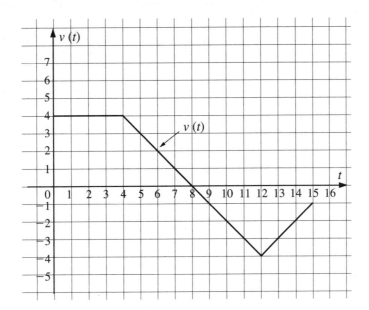

The graph above displays $v(t)$ for a moving object. What is the total distance traveled by the object during the time interval $0 \le t \le 12$?

(A) 8

(B) 16

(C) 20

(D) 24

(E) 32

81. If $\dfrac{dy}{dt} = 4(y+5)t^3$ and $y(0) = 8$, which of the following is an expression for $y(t)$?

(A) $y(t) = 8e^{t^4} - 5$

(B) $y(t) = 13e^{t^4} - 5$

(C) $y(t) = \ln|8t^4 - 5|$

(D) $y(t) = 13t^4 - 5$

(E) $y(t) = 12t^2 - 8$

82.

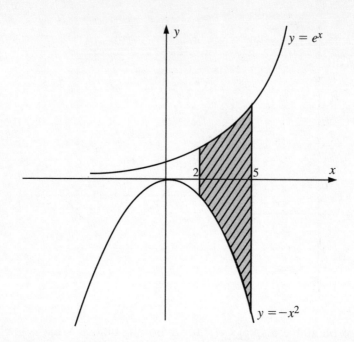

Based on the graph above, find the shaded area to the nearest integer.

(A)   140

(B)   160

(C)   180

(D)   200

(E)   220

83.   Let $f(x) = \begin{cases} ax^2 + bx & x \le 2 \\ ax + 5 & x > 2 \end{cases}$.

If $f(x)$ is differentiable at $x = 2$, what is the value of a?

(A) $-\dfrac{5}{4}$

(B) $-\dfrac{4}{5}$

(C) $-\dfrac{2}{3}$

(D)   3

(E)   cannot be determined

84. The area of an equilateral triangle can be expressed in terms of a side s as $A = \dfrac{s^2}{4}\sqrt{3}$. If the area is increasing at five times the rate that the sides are increasing, what is the perimeter of the triangle?

    (A) 3

    (B) $\dfrac{8\sqrt{3}}{5}$

    (C) $\dfrac{8\sqrt{3}}{3}$

    (D) $\dfrac{10\sqrt{3}}{3}$

    (E) $10\sqrt{3}$

85. Find the approximate volume generated by revolving the first quadrant area enclosed by $y = 3x + 4$, $y = e^{2x}$ and the y-axis about the x-axis.

    (A) 56

    (B) 68

    (C) 70

    (D) 73

    (E) 85

86. A ball is thrown from the top of a 1200-foot building. The position function expressing the height h of the ball above the ground at any time t is given as $h(t) = -16t^2 - 10t + 1200$.

    Find the average volocity for the first 6 seconds of travel.

    (A) -202 ft/sec

    (B) -106 ft/sec

    (C) -86 ft/sec

    (D) -74 ft/sec

    (E) 74 ft/sec

87. Over which interval is the function $f(x) = 3x^5 - 20x^3 - 12$ increasing?

    (A) $(-\infty, -2)$ only

    (B) $(-\infty, 2)$ only

(C) $(-\infty, -2)$ and $(2, \infty)$

(D) $(-2, 2)$

(E) $(-2, 0)$ and $(0, 2)$

88. For the ellipse $2x^2 + y^2 = 11$, what is the value of $\dfrac{d^2y}{dx^2}$ at the point in the third quadrant where $x = -1$?

(A) $-\dfrac{14}{17}$

(B) $-\dfrac{11}{27}$

(C) $\dfrac{4}{5}$

(D) $\dfrac{22}{27}$

(E) $\dfrac{8}{9}$

89. The normal line to the graph $y = x^4 + 1$ at $x = 1$ also intersects the graph at which one of the following values of x?

(A) -1.18

(B) -1.11

(C) -1.06

(D) $-.98$

(E) $-.86$

90. If the function g is defined as $g(x) = \displaystyle\int_0^x (t^2 - 3t - 4)\,dt$ on the interval $[-7, 5]$, then $g(x)$ has a local minimum at $x =$

(A) -7

(B) -4

(C) -1

(D) 1

(E) 4

91. If $\dfrac{dy}{dx} = \dfrac{x+1}{y+1}$, which one of the following best describes the relationship between x and y?

(A) line

(B) parabola

(C) circle

(D) ellipse

(E) hyperbola

92.

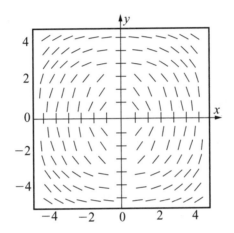

The figure shown above is the slope field for which one of the following differential equations?

(A) $\dfrac{dy}{dx} = \dfrac{x^2}{y}$

(B) $\dfrac{dy}{dx} = \dfrac{y}{x}$

(C) $\dfrac{dy}{dx} = xy$

(D) $\dfrac{dy}{dx} = -\dfrac{x}{y}$

(E) $\dfrac{dy}{dx} = -\dfrac{y}{x}$

STOP

This is the end of Section I, Part B.

If time still remains, you may check your work only in this section.

Do not begin Section II, Part A until instructed to do so.

Section II

PART A

Time: 45 minutes
   3 free-response problems

(Answer sheets appear in the back of this book.)

DIRECTIONS: Show all your work in your exam booklet. Grading is based on the methods used to solve the problems as well as the accuracy of your final answers.

Calculators MAY be used for this section of the exam.

1. Let R be the region in the first quadrant bounded above by $y = 4x + 3$ and below by $y = x^2 + 3$.

    (a) Find the area of R.

    (b) The line $x = c$ divides R into two regions. If the area of region R to the left of $x = c$ is $\frac{2}{3}$ the area of the region, find the value of c.

    (c) The line $y = a$ divides R into two regions of equal area. Find the value of a.

2. For the 18-hour time period beginning at midnight, the temperature F (in degree Fahrenheit) in a particular room is given by the function $F(t) = -12\sin\left(\frac{t}{3}\right) + 78$, where t is measured in hours.

    (a) To the nearest degree, what is the temperature in °F at 9 A.M.?

    (b) During which two consecutive hours does the temperature reach a maximum?

    (c) To the nearest tenth, what is the average temperature for the 18-hour period?

    (d) If the air conditioning turns on when the temperature is 83°F or higher, at what time interval(s) is the air conditioning operating?

3. Make a rain gutter from a long strip of sheet metal of width *w* inches by bending the metal in the middle to form a *V*-shape (see figure below). Find the value of *x*, in terms of *w*, that maximizes the amount of water the gutter can handle by maximizing the cross-sectional area of the gutter.

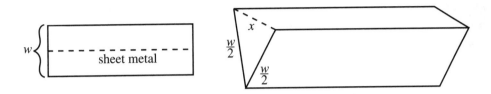

STOP
This is the end of Section II, Part A.
If time still remains, you may check your work only in this section.
Do not begin Section II, Part B until instructed to do so.

Section II

PART B

Time: 45 minutes
  3 free-response problems

(Answer sheets appear in the back of this book.)

DIRECTIONS: Show all your work in your exam booklet. Grading is based on the methods used to solve the problems as well as the accuracy of your final answers.

Calculators MAY NOT be used for this section of the exam.

(During the timed portion for Part B, you may continue to work on the problems in Part A without the use of a calculator.)

4.

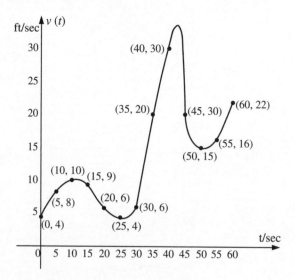

(a) Based on the graph above, estimate $\int_0^{60} v(t)\,dt$ using six subintervals of equal length. Use the trapezoid rule.

(b) Using the result in part (a), what is the average velocity over the interval $0 \leqslant t \leqslant 60$?

(c)   What is the average acceleration over the interval $0 \leqslant t \leqslant 60$?

(d)   Using the result in part (a), estimate the total distance traveled over the interval $0 \leqslant t \leqslant 60$.

5.   Assume the volume V of a cube is increasing at a constant rate of $3\,\text{cm}^3$ per second. Let t_0 be the instant $(t > 0)$ when the rate of change of the volume (cm^3/sec) is numerically equal to the rate of change of the surface area (cm^2/sec) for the cube. Assume $V = 0$ when $t = 0$.

(a)   Find the rate of change of the length of a side when $t = t_0$.

(b)   Find the rate of change of the surface area when $t = t_0$.

(c)   Find the value of t_0.

6.   Consider the differential equation $x\dfrac{dy}{dx} = 2y$, and let $f(x)$ be a solution to that equation.

(a)   On the axes provided, sketch a slope field for the given differential equation at the 12 indicated points.

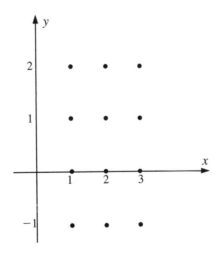

(b)   For the particular solution with an initial condition of $f(2) = 1$, find the equation of the line tangent to f at $x = 2$.

(c)   Use the tangent line in part (b) to estimate $f(2.1)$.

(d)   Find the particular solution to the given diffrential equation with an initial condition of $f(1) = 5$.

END OF EXAM

PRACTICE EXAM 2
AP Calculus AB

Answer Key

Part A

1. (A)
2. (B)
3. (D)
4. (D)
5. (E)
6. (D)
7. (E)
8. (D)
9. (B)
10. (C)
11. (E)
12. (D)
13. (B)
14. (B)
15. (C)
16. (B)
17. (A)
18. (C)
19. (D)
20. (C)
21. (C)
22. (B)
23. (A)
24. (A)
25. (E)
26. (C)
27. (C)
28. (E)

Part B

76. (D)
77. (E)
78. (D)
79. (C)
80. (E)
81. (B)
82. (C)
83. (A)
84. (E)
85. (A)
86. (B)
87. (C)
88. (D)
89. (B)
90. (E)
91. (E)
92. (D)

Free-Response Answers

1.
(a) $\frac{32}{3}$, or 10.667
(b) 2.452
(c) 9.038

2.
(a) 76°F
(b) between 2 P.M. and 3 P.M.
(c) 77.9°F
(d) $10.71 \leq t \leq 17.56$

3.
$x = \frac{w\sqrt{2}}{2}$

4.
(a) 800
(b) $\frac{40}{3}$
(c) $\frac{3}{10}$
(d) 800

5.
(a) $\frac{1}{16}$ cm/sec
(b) 3 cm/sec
(c) $21\frac{1}{3}$ sec or $\frac{64}{3}$ sec

6.
(a) See detailed explanation
(b) $y - 1 = x - 2$
(c) 1.1
(d) $y = 5x^2$

PRACTICE EXAM 2

AP Calculus AB

Detailed Explanations of Answers

Section 1

PART A

1. **(A)**

    Use the power rule.

    $$\frac{d}{dx}(u^n) = nu^{n-1}\frac{d}{dx}(u)$$

    $$y = (3x^2 - 1)^3$$

    $$\frac{dy}{dx} = 3(3x^2 - 1)^2\frac{d}{dx}(3x^2 - 1)$$

    $$= 3(3x^2 - 1)^2(6x)$$

    $$= \boxed{18x(3x^2 - 1)^2}$$

2. **(B)**

    Use $\int e^u du = e^u$, and let $u = -2x^2$ $\quad \therefore du = -4x\,dx$

    Step 1:

    $$\int_0^3 xe^{-2x^2}dx = \int_0^3 e^{-2x^2}(x\,dx) = \frac{-1}{4}\int_0^3 (e^{-2x^2})(-4x\,dx)$$

    $$= -\frac{1}{4}\int_{x=0}^3 e^u du = -\frac{1}{4}e^u\Big|_{x=0}^3 = -\frac{1}{4}e^{-2x^2}\Big|_0^3$$

    Step 2: Evaluate the definite integral.

    $$-\frac{1}{4}e^{-2x^2}\Big|_0^3 = -\frac{1}{4}[e^{-18} - e^0] = \boxed{\frac{-1}{4}[e^{-18} - 1]}$$

3. **(D)**

Only the highest powered term in the numerator and the highest powered term in the denominator are significant as $x \to \infty$.

$$\therefore \lim_{x \to \infty} \frac{8x^4 - 3x^2 + 2}{9x^5 + 7x^4 - 3x^2 + 2} = \lim_{x \to \infty} \frac{8x^4}{9x^5} = \boxed{0}$$

4. **(D)**

Use $\int_a^b u^n\,du = \left.\frac{u^{n+1}}{n+1}\right|_a^b$, let $u = \cos(x)$ $\therefore du = -\sin(x)\,dx$

Step 1:

$$\int_0^{\frac{\pi}{2}} \sin(x)\cos^2(x)\,dx = \int_0^{\frac{\pi}{2}} \cos^2(x)\left[\sin x\,dx\right]$$
$$= -\int_0^{\frac{\pi}{2}} \cos^2(x)\left[-\sin(x)\,dx\right]$$
$$= -\int_{x=0}^{\frac{\pi}{2}} u^2\,du = \left.\frac{-u^3}{3}\right|_{x=0}^{\frac{\pi}{2}}$$
$$= \left.\frac{-\cos^3 x}{3}\right|_0^{\frac{\pi}{2}}$$

Step 2: Evaluate the integral

$$\left.\frac{-\cos^3 x}{3}\right|_0^{\frac{\pi}{2}} = -\frac{1}{3}\left[\cos^3\left(\frac{\pi}{2}\right) - \cos^3(0)\right]$$
$$= -\frac{1}{3}\left[0 - (1)^3\right] = \boxed{\frac{1}{3}}$$

5. **(E)**

Step 1: $\dfrac{d}{dt}(\ln u) = \dfrac{1}{u}\dfrac{du}{dt}$

$$\therefore f'(t) = \frac{d}{dt}\left(\ln(1 + t + e^{5t})\right) = \frac{1}{1 + t + e^{5t}}\frac{d}{dt}(1 + t + e^{5t})$$

Step 2: Since $\dfrac{d}{dt}(1) = 0,\quad \dfrac{d}{dt}(t) = 1,\quad \dfrac{d}{dt}(e^{5t}) = 5e^{5t},$

$$\therefore f'(t) = \frac{1}{1+t+e^{5t}}(0+1+5e^{5t}) = \frac{1+5e^{5t}}{1+t+e^{5t}}$$

Step 3: Evaluate $f'(0)$:

$$f'(0) = \frac{1+5e^{5(0)}}{1+0+e^{5(0)}} = \frac{1+5}{2} = \boxed{3}$$

6. **(D)**

$$\lim_{x \to 3} f(x) \text{ exists if } \lim_{x \to 3^-} f(x) = \lim_{x \to 3^+} f(x)$$

Graph 1: $\lim_{x \to 3^-} f(x) = \lim_{x \to 3^+} f(x) = \infty$

Graph 2: $\lim_{x \to 3^-} f(x) = 3, \ \lim_{x \to 3^+} f(x) = 5$

$\therefore$ this limit does not exist

Graph 3: $\lim_{x \to 3^-} f(x) = \lim_{x \to 3^+} f(x) = 3$

The limit exists for $\boxed{\text{I and III only}}$.

7. **(E)**

Step 1: Write the equation of $f'(x)$:

$$f'(x) = \frac{5}{3}x + 5$$

Step 2: To find $f(x)$, integrate $f'(x)$:

$$f(x) = \int \left(\frac{5}{3}x + 5 \right) dx = \frac{5x^2}{6} + 5x + C$$

Step 3: Use the point $(6, 10)$ to find the value of C.

$$f(x) = \frac{5x^2}{6} + 5x + C$$

$$10 = \frac{5(6)^2}{6} + 5(6) + C$$

$$C = -50$$

$$\therefore f(x) = \frac{5x^2}{6} + 5x - 50$$

Step 4: Find $f(-6)$.

$$f(-6) = \frac{5(-6)^2}{6} + 5(-6) - 50$$

$$= \boxed{-50}$$

8. **(D)**

$$\lim_{n \to \infty}\left(1+\frac{1}{n}\right)^n = e, \quad \text{this is the definition of } e.$$

$$\lim_{n \to \infty}\left(1+\frac{1}{n}\right)^2 = 1.$$

$$\therefore \lim_{n \to \infty}\left(1+\frac{1}{n}\right)^{n+2} = \lim_{n \to \infty}\left(1+\frac{1}{n}\right)^n \cdot \lim_{n \to \infty}\left(1+\frac{1}{n}\right)^2$$

$$= e(1)$$

$$= \boxed{e}$$

9. **(B)**

Step 1: Use the product rule for $(f \cdot g)'(1)$:

$$(f \cdot g)'(1) = f(1)\,g'(1) + f'(1)\,g(1)$$

Step 2: $f(x) = \dfrac{1}{x-2} = (x-2)^{-1} \therefore f'(x) = -1(x-2)^{-2}(1)$

Step 3: At $x = 1$, evaluate $f(1)$ and $f'(1)$

$$f(1) = \frac{1}{1-2} = -1,\ f'(1) = (-1)(1-2)^{-2}(1) = -1$$

Step 4: Substituting all of the values into the product rule, solve for $g(1)$.

$$(f \cdot g)'(1) = f(1)\,g'(1) + f'(1)\,g(1)$$

$$6 = (-1)(-1) + (-1)\,g(1)$$

$$g(1) = \boxed{-5}$$

10. **(C)**

Step 1: Rewrite: $\lim\limits_{h \to \infty} \dfrac{1}{h}\left(\dfrac{1}{x+h} - \dfrac{1}{x}\right)$ as $\lim\limits_{h \to 0} \dfrac{\left(\frac{1}{x+h}\right) - \left(\frac{1}{x}\right)}{h}$.

This is the definition of the derivative with $f(x) = \dfrac{1}{x}$.

Step 2: $\dfrac{d}{dx}\left(\dfrac{1}{x}\right) = \dfrac{d}{dx}(x^{-1}) = -1x^{-2} = \boxed{-\dfrac{1}{x^2}}$

11. **(E)**

Step 1: $\dfrac{d}{dx}(\arctan x) = \dfrac{1}{1+x^2},\; \dfrac{d}{dy}\left((\ln(y^2))\right) = \dfrac{1}{y^2}\dfrac{d}{dy}(y^2) = \dfrac{1}{y^2}(2y) = \dfrac{2}{y}$

Step 2: Differentiate the equation implicitly with respect to x.

$$\dfrac{d}{dx}[\arctan x] = \dfrac{d}{dx}[\ln(y^2)]$$

$$\dfrac{1}{1+x^2} = \dfrac{2}{y}\dfrac{dy}{dx}$$

$$\therefore \dfrac{dy}{dx} = \boxed{\dfrac{y}{2(1+x^2)}}$$

12. **(D)**

The average value of f on $[a, b]$ is given by $\dfrac{1}{b-a}\displaystyle\int_a^b f(x)\,dx.$

For $a = 2$, the average value is $\dfrac{1}{b-2}\displaystyle\int_2^b f(x)\,dx$.

According to the given information,

$$4 = \dfrac{1}{b-2}(8),$$

$$b = \boxed{4}$$

13. **(B)**

Step 1: Use $\displaystyle\int_x^0 f(x)\,dx \equiv -\int_0^x f(x)\,dx$

Step 2: The fundamental theorem of calculus states:

$$\frac{d}{dx}\left[\int_a^x f(t)\,dt\right] = f(x)$$

$$\therefore \frac{d}{dx}\left[\int_x^0 \frac{1}{2+t}\,dt\right] = -\frac{d}{dx}\left[\int_0^x \frac{1}{2+t}\,dt\right] = -\left[\frac{1}{2+x}\right] = \boxed{-\frac{1}{x+2}}$$

14. **(B)**

Step 1: A graph is concave down if its shape is either $\Big($ or $\Big)$. For the given graph, this is true for only points B and D.

Step 2: $g'(x)$ is the slope of the graph, which is negative at point B, but positive at point D.

∴ The graph is concave down and $g'(x) < 0$ only at point $\boxed{B}$.

15. **(C)**

Step 1: Divide the graph into five areas, as shown in the figure below.

The signed area when $f(x)$ is above the x-axis is considered $+$

The signed area when $f(x)$ is below the x-axis is considered $-$

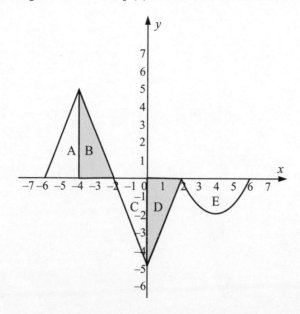

Step 2: $\int_{-6}^{-4} f(x)\,dx$ is the signed area A; $\int_{-4}^{-2} f(x)\,dx$ is the signed area B. Both signed areas are positive and equal. $\therefore$ I is true.

Step 3: $\int_{-6}^{-2} f(x)\,dx$ is the net signed area of A + B; $\int_{-2}^{2} f(x)$ is the net signed area of C + D. Both areas are equal, but A + B is signed positive, and C + D is signed negative. $\therefore$ II is not true.

Step 4: $\int_{-6}^{2} f(x)\,dx = 0$ because the signed areas A and B are cancelled by the signed areas C and D.

$\int_{-6}^{6} f(x)\,dx$ is negative. The net signed area is E, which is below the x-axis.

$\therefore$ III is true.

So choices $\boxed{\text{I and III only}}$ are true.

16. **(B)**

Step 1: If the two numbers are represented by x and y,

$$x + 2y = 12 \quad \Rightarrow \quad x = 12 - 2y$$

Step 2: Express the product xy as a function of a single variable

$$\text{Product} = P = xy = (12 - 2y)(y) = 12y - 2y^2$$

Step 3: To maximize (or minimize) the product, take its derivative and set it equal to zero.

$$P = 12y - 2y^2$$

$$\frac{dP}{dy} = 12 - 4y = 0$$

$\therefore y = 3$, and

$$x = 12 - 2y = 6$$

Step 4: Use the second derivative test to confirm the product is a maximum:

$$\frac{d^2P}{dy^2} = -4$$

Since the second derivative is negative at $y = 3$, the product is a maximum.

$$\therefore P = xy = \boxed{18}.$$

17. **(A)**

Step 1: Integrate the slope to obtain the function.

$$f(x) = \int (3x - 2)\, dx$$

$$f(x) = \frac{3x^2}{2} - 2x + C$$

Step 2: Use $f(4) = 10$ to find the value of C.

$$10 = \frac{3(4)^2}{2} - 2(4) + C$$

$$\therefore C = -6$$

$$f(x) = \boxed{\frac{3x^2}{2} - 2x - 6}$$

18. **(C)**

- Holes in the graph occur when the numerator and denominator have a term that cancels.
- Vertical asymptotes occur for every x that causes the denominator to equal zero after eliminating the holes.

$$f(x) = \frac{x^2 - 2x - 3}{x^2 - 9} = \frac{(x-3)(x+1)}{(x-3)(x+3)} = \frac{(x+1)}{(x+3)}$$

$$\boxed{\text{There is a hole at } x = 3, \text{ a vertical asymptote at } x = -3.}$$

19. **(D)**

Step 1: A graph is concave up when the second derivative is positive.

$$h(x) = x^3 - 3x^2 - 19x + 4$$

$$h'(x) = 3x^2 - 6x - 19$$

$$h''(x) = 6x - 6$$

$$h''(x) = 0 \text{ at } x = 1.$$

Step 2: Analyze the $+/-$ characteristics of $h''(x)$

$$h''(x) \quad \underset{x=1}{\underline{\qquad \overset{-}{\qquad} \overset{0}{+} \overset{+}{\qquad} \qquad}}$$

$\therefore h''(x)$ is positive over the interval $\boxed{(1, \infty)}$.

20. **(C)**

Step 1: Differentiability implies continuity $\therefore 2x + a$ and $bx^2 - 1$ must be equal at $x = 1$.

$$2x + a = bx^2 - 1$$

at $x = 1,$ $2 + a = b - 1,$

$$\therefore a - b = -3$$

Step 2: To be differentiable at $x = 1, \dfrac{d}{dx}(2x + a) = \dfrac{d}{dx}(bx^2 - 1).$

$$2 = 2bx$$

at $x = 1,$ $2 = 2b$

$$1 = b$$

Step 3: Solve for a.

$$a - b = -3$$

$$a - (1) = -3$$

$$a = -2$$

$$\boxed{a = -2, b = 1}$$

21. **(C)**

Step 1: You are given $\dfrac{dV}{dt} = -2$ and asked to find $\dfrac{dr}{dt}$.

Differentiate the volume equation with respect to t.

$$V = \frac{4}{3}\pi r^3$$

$$\frac{dV}{dt} = 4\pi r^2 \frac{dr}{dt}$$

Step 2: Using S.A. $= 4\pi r^2 = 12$, solve for $\dfrac{dr}{dt}$.

$$-2 = (12)\frac{dr}{dt}$$

$$\frac{dr}{dt} = \boxed{-\frac{1}{6} \text{ in/min}}$$

Note that the negative value means it is getting smaller.

22. **(B)**

$$\frac{dm}{dt} \propto \frac{1}{m^2}$$

becomes $\boxed{\dfrac{dm}{dt} = \dfrac{k}{m^2}}$

23. **(A)**

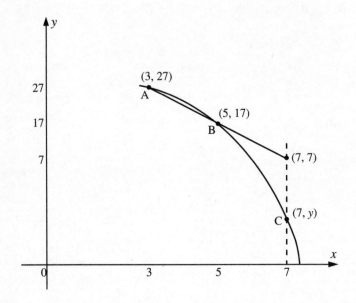

Because the curve is decreasing ($f'(x) < 0$) and concave down ($f''(x) < 0$), point C must have a y-value lower than that of the line connecting points A and B (see figure above).

Only $y = 3$ is possible from the three choices.

Choice $\boxed{\text{I only}}$ is possible.

24. **(A)**

Step 1: Express the area formula as a rate equation.

$$A = \pi ab$$

$$\frac{dA}{dt} = \pi \left[a\frac{db}{dt} + b\frac{da}{dt} \right]$$

Step 2: Given the area A remains constant at 9π,

$$\frac{dA}{dt} = 0.$$

We are given $a = 1$, $\quad \therefore b = 9$.

We are given a is decreasing at $\frac{9}{2}$ units/min $\quad \therefore \quad \frac{da}{dt} = -\frac{1}{2}$.

$$\therefore \quad \frac{dA}{dt} = \pi\left[a\frac{db}{dt} + b\frac{da}{dt}\right] = 0$$

$$0 = \pi\left[(1)\left(\frac{db}{dt}\right) + (9)\left(-\frac{1}{2}\right)\right]$$

$$\frac{db}{dt} = \boxed{\frac{9}{2} \text{ units/min}}$$

25. **(E)**

Step 1: Find the points of intersection.

$$x = \frac{1}{2}x^2$$

$$x^2 - 2x = 0$$

$$x(x - 2) = 0$$

$$x = 0, x = 2$$

Step 2:

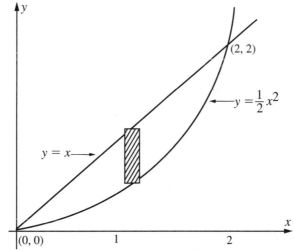

$$A = \int_0^2 \left(x - \frac{1}{2} x^2 \right) dx$$

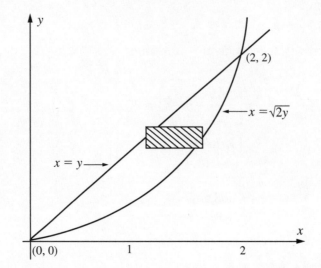

$$A = \int_0^2 \left(\sqrt{2y} - y \right) dy$$

Only choices $\boxed{\text{II and III}}$ are correct.

26. **(C)**

    Step 1: Write the rate equation for the area of a circle.

$$A = \pi r^2$$

    Then $\dfrac{dA}{dt} = 2\pi r \dfrac{dr}{dt}$.

Step 2: Find r when $\dfrac{dr}{dt} = \dfrac{1}{6} \dfrac{dA}{dt}$:

$$r = \frac{3}{\pi}$$

Step 3: Find the circumference of the circle.

$$C = 2\pi r$$
$$= 2\pi \left(\frac{3}{\pi} \right) = \boxed{6}$$

27. **(C)**

Step 1: $f(x) = x^{\frac{1}{3}}$ has a vertical tangent at $x = 0$. The slope at $x = 0$ is undefined, which means the function is NOT differentiable at $x = 0$.

$$f'(x) = \frac{1}{3}x^{-\frac{2}{3}}; \quad \frac{1}{3}x^{-\frac{2}{3}} \text{ is undefined at } x = 0.$$

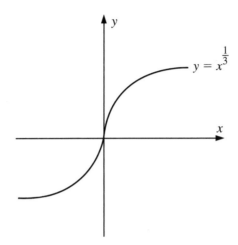

Step 2: The graph has both a limit at $x = 0$ and a value at $x = 0$. Since $\lim_{x \to 0} f(x) = f(0) = 0$, the function is continuous at $x = 0$.

Only choices $\boxed{\text{I and III}}$ are true.

28. **(E)**

The slope of the tangent line to a function h at $x = c$ equals $h'(c)$.

$$h'(6) = \frac{\Delta y}{\Delta x} = \frac{4-(-1)}{0-6} = \frac{5}{-6} = \boxed{-\frac{5}{6}}$$

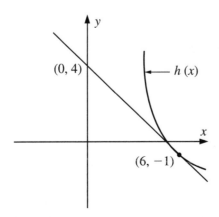

Section I

PART B

76. **(D)**

Step 1: The differential of y is dy, and the differential of x is dx

$$\therefore dy = f'(x)\, dx$$

In many applications, dy can be used to approximate Δy.

$$\therefore \Delta y \approx dy = f'(x)\, dx$$

Step 2: Use differentials to estimate ΔA, with $r = 3$ and $dr = \pm .02$.

The area of a circle is given by

$$A = \pi r^2$$

$$\Delta A \approx dA = 2\pi r\, dr$$

$$= (2\pi)(3)(\pm .02)$$

$$= \pm .376991$$

$$= \boxed{.377}$$

77. **(E)**

Step 1: Draw a diagram

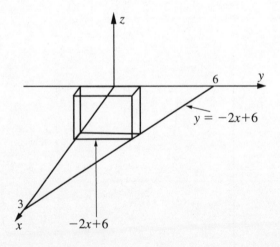

Step 2: Each side of the square is $-2x + 6$.

$$V = \int_0^3 (-2x+6)^2 \, dx = \boxed{36}$$

78. **(D)**

Refer to the review section for Rolle's theorem and the MVT.

79. **(C)**

Step 1: Create a rate equation for the area of a rectangle.

$$A = lw$$

$$\frac{dA}{dt} = l\frac{dw}{dt} + w\frac{dl}{dt}$$

Step 2: Substitute $\dfrac{dl}{dt} = 7, \ \dfrac{dw}{dt} = -7$:

$$\frac{dA}{dt} = -7l + 7w = 7[w - l]$$

Step 3: Since $l > w$, $\dfrac{dA}{dt} < 0$

$$\boxed{\frac{dA}{dt} \text{ is always decreasing}}.$$

80. **(E)**

Divide the graph into three parts, as shown in the sketch.

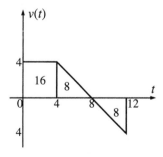

Step 1: The total distance traveled by the object in time $0 \le t \le 12$

is $\displaystyle\int_0^{12} |v(t)| \, dt.$

Step 2: $\int_0^{12}|v(t)|dt = \int_0^4|v(t)|dt + \int_4^8|v(t)|dt + \int_8^{12}|v(t)|dt$

Step 3: $\int_0^4|v(t)|dt = $ area of rectangle $= 4 \times 4 = 16$

$\int_4^8|v(t)|dt = $ area of triangle $= \dfrac{1}{2}(4)(4) = 8$

$\int_8^{12}|v(t)|dt = $ area of triangle $= \dfrac{1}{2}(4)(4) = 8$

Step 4: $\therefore$ Total distance $= 16 + 8 + 8 = \boxed{32}$

81. **(B)**

Step 1: Separate the variables and integrate.

$$\frac{dy}{dt} = 4(y+5)t^3$$

$$\frac{dy}{y+5} = 4t^3dt$$

$$\int\frac{dy}{y+5} = \int 4t^3dt$$

$$\ln|y+5| = t^4 + C$$

Step 2: Solve for y.

$$\ln|y+5| = t^4 + C$$

$$y+5 = e^{t^4+c} \Rightarrow A$$

$$y(t) = Ae^{t^4} - 5$$

Step 3: Use $y(0) = 8$ to find the value of A.

$$8 = A(1) - 5$$

$$13 = A$$

Step 4: $\therefore$ $\boxed{y(t) = 13e^{t^4} - 5}$

82. **(C)**

The area between two curves, $f(x)$ and $g(x)$, as shown in the sketch to the right is $\int_a^b [f(x) - g(x)]\, dx$

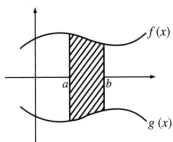

$$\therefore A = \int_2^5 [e^x - (-x^2)]\, dx$$
$$= \int_2^5 [e^x + x^2]\, dx$$
$$= e^x + \frac{x^3}{3}\Big|_2^5 = \boxed{180}$$

83. **(A)**

Step 1: To be differentiable at $x = 2$, the function must also be continuous at $x = 2$.

To be continuous at $x = 2$,

$$ax^2 + bx\big|_{x=2} = ax + 5\big|_{x=2}$$

$$\therefore 4a + 2b = 2a + 5$$

Step 2: To be differentiable at $x = 2$,

$$\frac{d}{dx}[ax^2 + bx] = \frac{d}{dx}[ax + 5],$$

or $2ax + b = a$ at $x = 2$,

$$\therefore 4a + b = a$$

Step 3: Solve $4a + 2b = 2a + 5$ and $4a + b = a$ simultaneously.

$$\boxed{a = \frac{-5}{4}} \text{ and } b = \frac{15}{4}$$

84. **(E)**

Step 1: Change the area equation into a rate equation.

$$A = \frac{s^2}{4}\sqrt{3}$$

$$\frac{dA}{dt} = \frac{2s}{4}\sqrt{3}\frac{ds}{dt}$$

$$= \frac{\sqrt{3}}{2}s\frac{ds}{dt}$$

Step 2: Let $\frac{dA}{dt} = 5\frac{ds}{dt}$ and solve for s.

$$5\frac{ds}{dt} = \frac{\sqrt{3}}{2}s\frac{ds}{dt}$$

$$s = \frac{10}{\sqrt{3}} = \frac{10\sqrt{3}}{3}$$

Step 3: For an equilateral triangle, the perimeter is $3s$.

$$P = \frac{3(10\sqrt{3})}{3} = \boxed{10\sqrt{3}}$$

85. **(A)**

Step 1: Sketch the area as shown to the right.

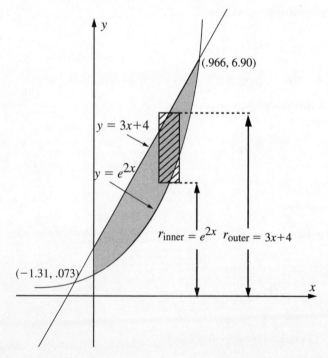

y

$(.966, 6.90)$

$y = 3x+4$

$y = e^{2x}$

$r_{inner} = e^{2x}$ $r_{outer} = 3x+4$

$(-1.31, .073)$

x

Use a calculator to find the x-value of the point of intersection in the first quadrant.

$$3x + 4 = e^{2x}$$

$$x = -1.31 \text{ or } x = .966$$

Step 2: Using the washer method to evaluate (with a calculator)

$$V = \pi \int_0^{.966} \left(r_{\text{outer}}^2 - r_{\text{inner}}^2 \right) dx$$

$$= \pi \int_0^{.966} (3x + 4)^2 - (e^{2x})^2 \, dx$$

$$= 55.59 \sim \boxed{56}$$

86. **(B)**

The average velocity is $\dfrac{\Delta h}{\Delta t} = \dfrac{h(6) - h(0)}{6 - 0}$.

$$h = 16t^2 - 10t + 1200$$

$\therefore \quad h(6) = 564, \text{ and } h(0) = 1200.$

$$\therefore \text{ Average velocity} = \frac{564 - 1200}{6}$$

$$= \frac{-636}{6} = \boxed{-106 \text{ ft/sec}}$$

87. **(C)**

Step 1: A function is increasing if the first derivative is positive.

Find the first derivative, the critical values, and evaluate the first derivative on a number line.

$$f(x) = 3x^5 - 20x^3 - 12$$

$$f'(x) = 15x^4 - 60x^2$$

$$= 15x^2(x^2 - 4) = 15x^2(x + 2)(x - 2)$$

$$f'(x) = 0 \Rightarrow x = 0, -2, 2$$

Step 2: Establish a number line analysis of $f'(x)$.

$$f'(x) \quad \underset{\underset{-2}{} \quad \underset{0}{} \quad \underset{2}{}}{\overset{+ \quad - \quad - \quad +}{\rule{5cm}{0.4pt}}}$$

$\therefore f'(x)$ is increasing in the intervals $\boxed{(-\infty, -2) \text{ and } (2, \infty)}$.

88. (D)

Step 1: Find the value of y that places the point in the third quadrant, when $x = -1$.

$$2x^2 + y^2 = 11$$

$$2(-1)^2 + y^2 = 11$$

$$y^2 = 9$$

$$y = \pm 3$$

$$\therefore x = -1, y = -3$$

Step 2: Find $\dfrac{dy}{dx}$ implicitly.

$$2x^2 + y^2 = 11$$

$$4x + 2y\frac{dy}{dx} = 0$$

$$\frac{dy}{dx} = \boxed{\frac{-2x}{y}} = \frac{-2(-1)}{-3} = \frac{-2}{3}$$

Step 3: Find $\dfrac{d^2y}{dx^2} = \dfrac{d\left(\dfrac{dy}{dx}\right)}{dx} = \dfrac{d\left(\dfrac{-2x}{y}\right)}{dx}$

$$= \frac{y(-2) - (-2x)\dfrac{dy}{dx}}{y^2} = \frac{-3(-2) - (2)\left(\dfrac{-2}{3}\right)}{9} = \boxed{\frac{22}{27}}$$

89. (B)

Step 1: Find $f(1)$ and $f'(1)$. This will give the y value when $x = 1$ and the slope of the tangent line at $x = 1$, respectively.

$$f(x) = x^4 + 1 \qquad f'(x) = 4x^3$$

$$f(1) = 2 \qquad f'(1) = 4$$

Step 2: The slope of the normal line is the negative reciprocal of the slope of the tangent line. Therefore, the slope of the normal line at $x = 1$ is

$$m_{\text{normal line}} = -\frac{1}{4}.$$

Then the equation of the normal line with $m = -\dfrac{1}{4}$ through the point $(1, 2)$ is $y - 2 = -\dfrac{1}{4}(x - 1)$.

Step 3: Find where $x^4 + 1$ intersects the line

$$y - 2 = -\frac{1}{4}(x-1) \Rightarrow y = -\frac{1}{4}(x-1) + 2.$$

Use the calculator to solve:

$$x^4 + 1 = -\frac{1}{4}(x-1) + 2$$

$$x = -1.11, \, x = 1$$

So the other x-value is $\boxed{-1.11}$.

90. **(E)**

Step 1: Use the Fundamental Theorem of Calculus: $\dfrac{d}{dx}\left[\displaystyle\int_0^x f(t)dt\right] = f(x)$

$$g(x) = \int_0^x (t^2 - 3t - 4)\,dt$$

$$g'(x) = \frac{d}{dx}\left[\int_0^x (t^2 - 3t - 4)\,dt\right] = x^2 - 3x - 4$$

Step 2: Locate local min/max points by setting the first derivative equal to zero

$$g'(x) = x^2 - 3x - 4 = 0$$

$$x = 4, \quad x = -1$$

Step 3: Analyze the first derivative on a number line utilizing the critical values

$\therefore$ There is a local minimum at $\boxed{x = 4}$.

91. **(E)**

Step 1: Solve the differential equation by using separation of variables.

$$\frac{dy}{dx} = \frac{(x+1)}{(y+1)}$$

$$(y+1)\,dy = (x+1)\,dx$$

$$\frac{y^2}{2} + y = \frac{x^2}{2} + x + C$$

Step 2: Rearrange the terms.

$$\frac{x^2}{2} + x - \frac{y^2}{2} - y + c = 0$$

Step 3: Identify the equation.

This is the equation of a $\boxed{\text{hyperbola}}$.

92. **(D)**

Step 1: There are horizontal tangent lines at $x = 0$, so $\dfrac{dy}{dx} = 0$ when $x = 0$.

There are vertical tangent lines at $y = 0$, so there is a division by y^n. This eliminates choices B, C, and E.

Step 2: If we pick the first quadrant point (2, 1):

Choice A indicates $\dfrac{dy}{dx} = \dfrac{4}{1} = 4$

Choice D indicates $\dfrac{dy}{dx} = \dfrac{-2}{1} = -2$

the actual slope field shows a negatively sloped line at (2, 1), so choice A is eliminated.

Choice D is the correct equation, $\boxed{\dfrac{dy}{dx} = \dfrac{-x}{y}}$

Section II

PART A

1.

Note: Use the calculator.

Step 1: Make a sketch.

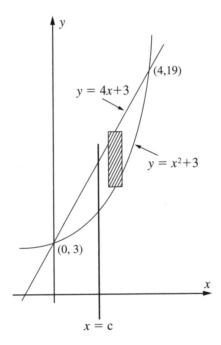

Step 2: Find the point(s) of intersection of the curves.

$$4x + 3 = x^2 + 3$$

$$x = 0, x = 4$$

$(0, 3)$ and $(4, 19)$

(a) $A = \int_0^4 [(4x+3) - (x^2+3)]dx = \boxed{\dfrac{32}{3}, \text{ or } 10.667}$

(b) Set the integral from $x = 0$ to $x = c$ equal to $\dfrac{2}{3}\left(\dfrac{32}{3}\right)$, and solve for c.

$$\int_0^c [(4x+3)-(x^2+3)]\,dx = \frac{2}{3}\left(\frac{32}{3}\right)$$

$\therefore c = \boxed{2.452}$

(c) To answer this question, use horizontal rectangles (see sketch).

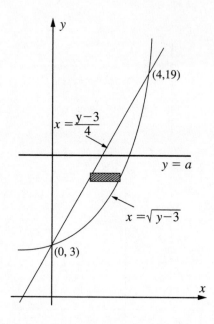

First solve each equation for x: $x = \sqrt{y-3}$ and $x = \dfrac{y-3}{4}$.

Then $\displaystyle\int_{y=3}^{a}\left[\sqrt{y-3}-\left(\frac{y-3}{4}\right)\right]dy = \int_{a}^{19}\left[\sqrt{y-3}-\left(\frac{y-3}{4}\right)\right]dy$

$\therefore a = \boxed{9.038}$

2.

Step 1: A graph is useful, as is the "table" feature of the calculator.

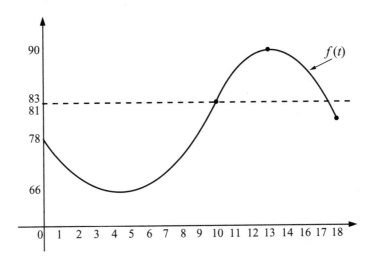

Step 2: 9 A.M. corresponds to $t = 9$.

(a) $F(9) = -12 \sin\left(\dfrac{9}{3}\right) + 78 = 76.306 \Rightarrow \boxed{76°\text{F}}$

Step 3: $F(t)$ achieves a maximum temperature when $\sin\left(\dfrac{t}{3}\right) = -1$.

$\therefore F(t)_{\text{max}}$ is $12 + 78 = 90°$

$$\sin\left(\frac{t}{3}\right) = -1 \implies \frac{t}{3} = \frac{3\pi}{2} \implies t = \frac{9\pi}{2} = 14.137$$

(b) The maximum temperature occurs between the 14th and 15th hour, corresponding to: $\boxed{\text{between 2 P.M. and 3 P.M.}}$.

Step 4:

The average temperature over the 18-hour period

(c) $= \dfrac{1}{18-0} \displaystyle\int_0^{18} \left[-12 \sin\left(\frac{t}{3}\right) + 78 \right] dt = 77.92 \Rightarrow \boxed{77.9°\text{F}}$

Step 5: On the interval $[0, 18]$ when does $F(t) = 83°$ F?

$$-12\sin\left(\frac{t}{3}\right)+78=83$$

$$\sin\left(\frac{t}{3}\right)=-\frac{5}{12}$$

$$t=10.71, t=17.56$$

(d) The air conditioning is on $\boxed{10.71 \le t \le 17.56}$

3.

Step 1: Sketch the cross-sectional area.

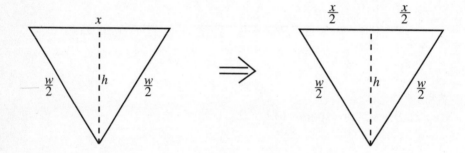

By the Pythagorean Theorem,

$$h^2+\left(\frac{x}{2}\right)^2=\left(\frac{w}{2}\right)^2$$

$$\therefore h=\frac{\sqrt{w^2-x^2}}{2}$$

Step 2: Write an expression that represents the cross-sectional area $A(x)$ in terms of the constant w and the variable x.

$$A=A(x)=\frac{1}{2}(x)\left(\frac{\sqrt{w^2-x^2}}{2}\right)$$

$$A(x)=\frac{1}{4}x\sqrt{w^2-x^2}$$

Step 3: It is easier to use the function $A^2(x)=\dfrac{1}{16}x^2(w^2-x^2)$

$$=\frac{1}{16}[w^2x^2-x^4]$$

Step 4: Differentiate with respect to x, set the derivative equal to zero, and solve for x.

$$A^2 = \frac{1}{16}(w^2x^2 - x^4)$$

$$2A\frac{dA}{dx} = \frac{1}{16}(2w^2x - 4x^3)$$

Set $\frac{dA}{dx} = 0 \Rightarrow 0 = \frac{1}{16}(2w^2x - 4x^3)$

Solve for x:

$$x = 0$$
$$x = \frac{w\sqrt{2}}{2}$$
$$x = \frac{-w\sqrt{2}}{2}$$

Only $x = \dfrac{w\sqrt{2}}{2}$ makes constructive sense.

Step 5: The maximum value of a continuous function in a closed interval occurs either at the endpoints of the intervals or at a critical point. The measurement x has a domain of $[0, w]$. A table of values will help.

	Test value	Area
end point	0	0
critical point	$\dfrac{w\sqrt{2}}{2}$	$\dfrac{w^2}{8}$
end point	w	0

$$\therefore \boxed{x = \frac{w\sqrt{2}}{2}}$$

Section II

PART B

4.

Step 1: Approximate $\int_0^{60} v(t)\,dt$ as the area between the graph of $y = v(t)$ and the x-axis.

Step 2: The interval length with six subintervals will be $\dfrac{60-0}{6} = 10$.

Step 3: Sketch the graph as a set of trapezoids, as shown in the figure below.

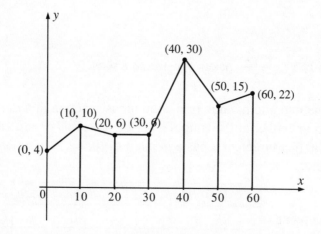

The trapezoid rule for six subintervals gives

(a) $A = \dfrac{1}{2}(10)[4 + 2(10) + 2(6) + 2(6) + 2(30) + 2(15) + 22]$

$= \boxed{800}$

Step 4: (b) Average velocity $= \dfrac{1}{60-0}\int_0^{60} v(t)\,dt = \dfrac{1}{60}(800) = \boxed{\dfrac{40}{3}}$

Step 5: (c) Average acceleration $=$

$\dfrac{\Delta v}{\Delta t} = \dfrac{v(60)-v(0)}{60-0} = \dfrac{22-4}{60} = \dfrac{18}{60} = \boxed{\dfrac{3}{10}}$

Step 6: The $\int_0^{60} v(t) \, dt$ is an estimate of the distance traveled.

$d = 800$ ft

5.

Step 1: Let x = length of the edge of the cube

$\therefore$ volume $= V(x) = x^3$, and surface area $= S(x) = 6x^2$

Step 2: Equate the rates of change $\dfrac{dV}{dt} = \dfrac{dS}{dt}$, and solve for x.

$$\frac{dV}{dt} = 3x^2 \frac{dx}{dt} = \frac{ds}{dt} = 12x \frac{dx}{dt}$$

$$3x^2 \frac{dx}{dt} = 12x \frac{dx}{dt}$$

$$\therefore x = 0, 4$$

Step 3:

Given $\dfrac{dV}{dt} = 3 = 3x^2 \dfrac{dx}{dt}$.

For $x = 4$, $3 = 3(4)^2 \dfrac{dx}{dt}$

(a) $\dfrac{dx}{dt} = \boxed{\dfrac{1}{16}}$ cm/sec

Step 4: (b) $\dfrac{dS}{dt} = 12x \dfrac{dx}{dt} = 12(4)\left(\dfrac{1}{16}\right) = \boxed{3 \text{ cm/sec}}$

Step 5: When $\dfrac{dV}{dt} = \dfrac{dS}{dt}$ we found $x = 4$ $\quad \therefore V = 4^3 = 64$

If $V(0) = 0$ and V grows at the rate of 3 cm^3/sec, it takes $\dfrac{64}{3}$ seconds to grow from a volume of zero to a volume of 64.

$$\frac{64}{3} = \boxed{21\frac{1}{3} \text{ sec}}$$

6.

Step 1: Rewrite the differential equation to determine $\dfrac{dy}{dx}$.

$$x\frac{dy}{dx} = 2y \Rightarrow \frac{dy}{dx} = \frac{2y}{x}$$

Step 2: To create the slope field, create a table of values. Then plot a line segment with a slope of $\dfrac{dy}{dx}$ at each (x, y) coordinate pair.

x	y	$\dfrac{dy}{dx}$
1	−1	−2
1	0	0
1	1	2
1	2	4
2	−1	−1
2	0	0
2	1	1
2	2	2
3	−1	$-\dfrac{2}{3}$
3	0	0
3	1	$\dfrac{2}{3}$
3	2	$\dfrac{4}{3}$

(a)

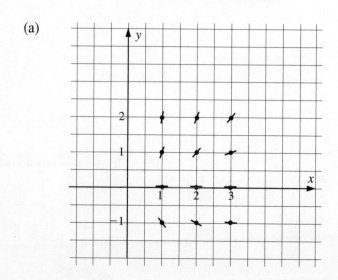

Step 3: At the point $(2, 1)$, $\dfrac{dy}{dx} = \dfrac{2(1)}{2} = 1 =$ slope.

(b) By the point-slope formula,

$$y - 1 = 1(x - 2) \Rightarrow \boxed{y - 1 = x - 2} \text{ or } \boxed{f(x) = x - 1}$$

Step 4: Find $f(2.1)$.

(c) $f(2.1) = 2.1 - 1 = \boxed{1.1}$

Step 5: Solve the differential equation (general solution).

$$\frac{dy}{dx} = \frac{2y}{x} \quad \Rightarrow \quad \frac{dy}{y} = 2\frac{dx}{x}$$

$$\int \frac{dy}{y} = 2 \int \frac{dx}{x}$$

$$\ln|y| = 2\ln|x| + C$$

$$= \ln x^2 + C$$

If we change C to $\ln C$, then $\ln |y| = \ln x^2 + \ln C = \ln Cx^2$

or $\boxed{y = Cx^2}$ (general solution).

Step 6: Find the particular solution at $(1, 5)$.

(d)

$$5 = C(1)^2$$

$$5 = C$$

$$\boxed{y = 5x^2}$$

PRACTICE EXAM 3

AP Calculus AB

Section I

PART A

Time: 55 minutes
      28 questions

(Answer sheets appear in the back of this book.)

> **DIRECTIONS:** Solve each of the following problems, select the best answer choice, and fill in the corresponding oval on the answer sheet.
>
> Calculators may NOT be used for this section of the exam.

NOTES:

(1) Unless otherwise specified, the domain of a function f is assumed to be the set of all real numbers x for which $f(x)$ is a real number.

(2) The inverse of a trigonometric function f may be indicated by using the inverse function notation f^{-1} or with the prefix "arc" (e.g., $\sin^{-1} x = \arcsin x$).

1.   If $y = \left(\sqrt{x} + 1\right)^4$, find $\dfrac{dy}{dx}$.

    (A) $4\left(\sqrt{x} + 1\right)^3$

    (B) $4x\left(\sqrt{x} + 1\right)^3$

    (C) $4\sqrt{x}\left(\sqrt{x} + 1\right)^3$

(D) $\dfrac{2\left(\sqrt{x}+1\right)^{3}}{\sqrt{x}}$

(E) $\dfrac{4\left(\sqrt{x}+1\right)^{3}}{\sqrt{x}}$

2. $\displaystyle\int_{0}^{\pi}\sin(3x)\,dx =$

(A) $-\dfrac{2}{3}$

(B) $-\dfrac{1}{3}$

(C) 0

(D) $\dfrac{1}{3}$

(E) $\dfrac{2}{3}$

3.

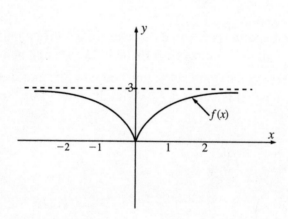

Based on the graph shown above, which of the following is NOT true?

(A) f is continuous at $x = 0$.

(B) $\displaystyle\lim_{x\to 0} f(x) = 0$.

(C) $\displaystyle\lim_{x\to\infty} f(x) = 3$.

(D) $f'(x) < 0$ for $x < 0$.

(E) f is differentiable at $x = 0$.

4. If $y = xe^x$, then $\dfrac{d^2y}{dx^2} =$

(A) xe^x

(B) $(x + 1)e^x$

(C) $(x + 2)e^x$

(D) $(x + 3)e^x$

(E) $xe^x + 3$

5. $\displaystyle\int_{\ln 2}^{\ln 3} e^{3x}\,dx =$

(A) e^4

(B) $e^3 - 1$

(C) $\dfrac{19}{3}$

(D) $\dfrac{15}{8}$

(E) $\dfrac{7}{2}$

6. $\displaystyle\lim_{x \to \infty} \dfrac{-7x^5 + 3x^3 + 7x - 1}{8x^6 + 2x^4 - 5x^2 + 6} =$

(A) $-\dfrac{7}{8}$

(B) 0

(C) $\dfrac{3}{8}$

(D) $\dfrac{7}{8}$

(E) $\dfrac{3}{2}$

7. If $f(x) = \sin(\cos x)$, $f'(x) =$

    (A) $-\sin x[\cos(\cos x)]$

    (B) $2\cos^2(x) - 1$

    (C) $-\sin x \cos^2 x$

    (D) $\cos x \sin^2 x$

    (E) $-\sin x[\sin x(\cos x)]$

8. $\int_{-2}^{-1} |x^3| \, dx =$

    (A) $-\dfrac{7}{8}$

    (B) $\dfrac{1}{3}$

    (C) $\dfrac{3}{5}$

    (D) $\dfrac{15}{4}$

    (E) $\dfrac{17}{4}$

9. For what value(s) of x will the tangent lines to $f(x) = \ln x$ and $g(x) = 2x^2$ be parallel?

    (A) 0

    (B) $\dfrac{1}{4}$

    (C) $\dfrac{1}{2}$

    (D) $\pm\dfrac{1}{2}$

    (E) 2

10.

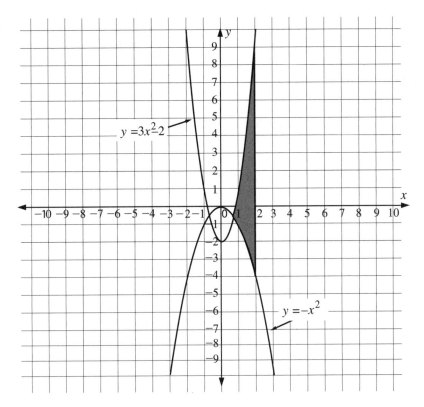

Which one of the following represents the shaded area as shown in the graph above?

(A) $\pi \int_1^2 \left[(3x^2 - 2)^2 - (-x^2)^2 \right] dx$

(B) $\int_1^2 \left[(3x^2 - 2)^2 - (-x^2)^2 \right] dx$

(C) $\int_1^2 \left[(3x^2 - 2) - (-x^2) \right] dx$

(D) $\int_1^2 \left[(-x^2) - (3x^2 - 2) \right] dx$

(E) $\int_1^2 \left[(3x^2 + 2) + (-x^2) \right] dx$

11. If $\sin y = \cos x$, find $\dfrac{dy}{dx}$ at the point $\left(\dfrac{\pi}{2}, \pi \right)$.

(A) $-\dfrac{\pi}{2}$

(B) -1

(C) 0

(D) 1

(E) $\dfrac{\pi}{2}$

12. A square is inscribed in a circle. How fast is the area of the square changing when the area of the circle is increasing at the rate of 1 in²/min?

(A) -1 in²/min

(B) $\dfrac{1}{2}$ in²/min

(C) $\dfrac{2}{\pi}$ in²/min

(D) 1 in²/min

(E) $\dfrac{\pi}{2}$ in²/min

13. For which of the following intervals is the graph of $y = x^4 - 2x^3 - 12x^2$ concave down?

(A) $(-2, 1)$

(B) $(-1, 2)$

(C) $(-2, -1)$

(D) $(-\infty, -1)$

(E) $(-1, \infty)$

14. If $h(x) = \displaystyle\int_a^x (1 - 2t)^3\, dt$, then the second derivative of $h(x)$ at $x = \dfrac{1}{2}$ is which of the following?

(A) 0

(B) $\dfrac{1}{12}$

(C) $\dfrac{1}{8}$

(D) $\dfrac{3}{5}$

(E) $\dfrac{1}{2}$

15. If $f(x) = \ln x$, then $f\left(\dfrac{3}{2}\right) =$

(A) $\dfrac{\ln 3}{\ln 2}$

(B) $\log_2 3$

(C) $\displaystyle\int_{\ln 2}^{\ln 3} e^t\, dt$

(D) $\displaystyle\int_{2}^{3} \ln(t)\, dt$

(E) $\displaystyle\int_{2}^{3} \dfrac{1}{t}\, dt$

16. $\displaystyle\lim_{x \to 0} \dfrac{\dfrac{3}{x^2}}{\dfrac{2}{x^2} + \dfrac{105}{x}} =$

(A) $\dfrac{3}{2}$

(B) 1

(C) $\dfrac{3}{4}$

(D) $\dfrac{3}{107}$

(E) 0

17. If a function f is continuous on $[1, 2]$ and $f(1) = 2$, $f(1.5) = 0.5$, and $f(2) = -3$, then which of the following choices could be false?

(A) The maximum value of f in $[1, 2]$ is 2

(B) $f(c) = 0$ for some real value of c

(C) $\displaystyle\lim_{x \to 2^-} f(x) = -3$

(D) $\left| f(2) \right| - \left| f(1) \right| \le \left| f(2) - f(1) \right|$

(E) $\displaystyle\lim_{x \to \frac{5}{4}} f(x) = f\left(\dfrac{5}{4}\right)$

18. Newton's law of cooling states that the rate of change of the temperature of an object Q is proportional to the difference between its temperature and that of its surroundings. If the surrounding temperature is 40°, which of the following best expresses this relationship?

   (A) $\dfrac{dQ}{dt} = 40Q$

   (B) $\dfrac{dQ}{dt} = k(Q - 40)$

   (C) $\dfrac{dQ}{dt} = kQ - 40$

   (D) $Q(t) = kQ - 40$

   (E) $Q(t) = k(Q - 40)$

19.

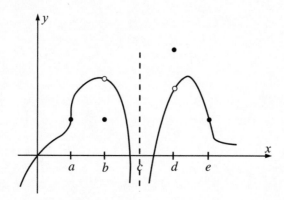

   Based on the graph above, for which value of x is the function continuous but not differentiable?

   (A) a

   (B) b

   (C) c

   (D) d

   (E) e

20.

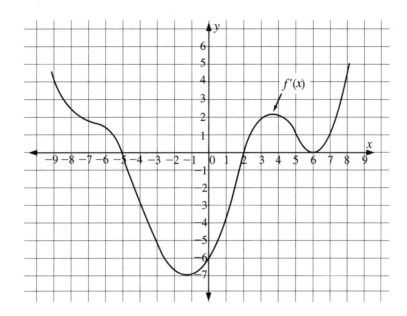

The graph of f' is shown above. Over which interval(s) is the function f decreasing?

(A) $(-\infty, -1)$ and $(4, 6)$

(B) $(-5, 0)$ and $(4, 6)$

(C) $(-5, 2)$

(D) $(-\infty, -1)$ and $(2, 4)$

(E) $(-\infty, -5)$ and $(2, \infty)$

21.   A particle moves along the curve $y = 2x^3 - 4x + 1$. What is the rate of change of its y-coordinate, in cm/sec, when the particle crosses the y-axis if the rate of change of its x-coordinate is constant at 3 cm/sec?

(A)   2 cm/sec

(B) -2 cm/sec

(C) -6 cm/sec

(D) -10 cm/sec

(E) -12 cm/sec

22. The function f is integrable on the interval $[a, b]$. If $f(x) = 2x + 3$ has an average value of 29 over the interval $[a, b]$, what is the value of $a + b$?

   (A) 13

   (B) 19

   (C) 26

   (D) 29

   (E) 34

23.

x	$f(x)$	$g(x)$	$f'(x)$	$g'(x)$
1	7	1	-1	6
2	4	3	6	-1
3	2	2	5	5

   Using the data in the table above, find the value of $h'(3)$ if $h(x) = f(g(x))$.

   (A) 35

   (B) 30

   (C) 25

   (D) 20

   (E) 15

24. If $g(x) = \int_{28}^{x^2} (t+1)\, dt$, then $g'(2) =$

   (A) 20

   (B) 21

   (C) 22

   (D) 23

   (E) 24

25. $\int \dfrac{dx}{x \ln^5 x} =$

    (A) $\dfrac{1}{6} \ln^6 x + C$

    (B) $\dfrac{1}{4} \ln^4 x + C$

    (C) $\dfrac{-1}{4 \ln^4 x} + C$

    (D) $\dfrac{-4}{\ln^4 x} + C$

    (E) $-4 \ln^4 x + C$

26. The equation of the tangent line to the curve $(y + 1) x - x^2 + y = 1$ at $(2, 1)$ is

    (A) $2x - 3y - 1 = 0$

    (B) $3x - 2y - 1 = 0$

    (C) $2x - 3y + 1 = 0$

    (D) $3x - 2y + 1 = 0$

    (E) $2x + 3y - 1 = 0$

27. Find the area in the first quadrant that is enclosed by $y = \sin(3x)$ and the x-axis from $x = 0$ to the first x-intercept on the positive x-axis.

    (A) $\dfrac{1}{3}$

    (B) $\dfrac{2}{3}$

    (C) 1

    (D) 2

    (E) 6

28. At what value of x does $f(x) = \dfrac{x^3}{3} - x^2 - 3x + 5$ have a relative minimum?

   (A) -1 only

   (B)   0 only

   (C)   1 only

   (D)   3 only

   (E) -1 and 3

STOP

This is the end of Section I, Part A.

If time still remains, you may check your work only in this section.

Do not begin Section II, Part A until instructed to do so.

Section I

PART B

Time: 50 minutes
   17 questions

(Answer sheets appear in the back of this book.)

DIRECTIONS: Solve each of the following problems, select the best answer choice, and fill in the corresponding oval on the answer sheet.

Calculators MAY be used for this section of the exam.

NOTES:

(1) The exact numerical value of the correct answer does not always appear among the choices given. When this happens, select the number from among the choices that best approximates the exact numerical value.

(2) Unless otherwise specified, the domain of a function f is assumed to be the set of all real numbers x for which $f(x)$ is a real number.

(3) The inverse of a trigonometric function f may be indicated by using the inverse function notation f^{-1} or with the prefix "arc" (e.g., $\sin^{-1} x = \arcsin x$).

76.   Find the value of c such that the area enclosed by $y = c$ and $y = x^2$ is $\dfrac{1}{48}$.

(A) $\dfrac{1}{512}$

(B) $\dfrac{1}{256}$

(C) $\dfrac{1}{64}$

(D) $\dfrac{1}{32}$

(E) $\dfrac{1}{16}$

77.

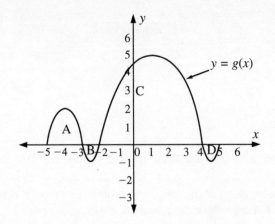

The regions A, B, C, and D in the figure above are each bounded by the x-axis and the function g. If the areas of A, B, C, and D are 2, 1, 4, and 1, respectively, what is the value of $\int_{-5}^{5}(g(x)+2)dx$?

(A) 28

(B) 26

(C) 24

(D) 22

(E) 20

78. A particle moves along a number line at any time $t \geq 0$ with a velocity function described by $v(t) = t + 7.6\sin(3t)$. Find the acceleration of the particle at time $t = 6$.

(A) −4.71

(B) 6.02

(C) 11.02

(D) 16.06

(E) 21.06

79. A ball is thrown vertically upward such that its initial velocity is 100 ft/sec, and at $t = 0$ the ball is 5 ft above the ground. Its height h above the ground at any time ($t \geq 0$) is given by the function $h(t) = -16t^2 + 100t + 5$. What is the maximum height reached by the ball?

(A) 140.50 ft

(B) 148.75 ft

(C)   151 ft

(D)   154.25 ft

(E)   161.25 ft

80.   The function f has a derivative $f'(x) = \dfrac{-x}{e^{\frac{x^2}{2}}}$. What is (are) the x values of its inflection point(s)?

(A) $x = 1$ only

(B) $x = 2$ only

(C) $x = -1$ only

(D) $x = 1$ and $x = -1$

(E) $x = -2$ and $x = 1$

81.   Let $f(x) = \dfrac{\sin x \cos x}{\cos 9x \tan 2x}$. Then $f'(.5) =$

(A) -49.5

(B) -5

(C) -2.5

(D) 3.8

(E) 70.1

82.   Let $f(x) = \dfrac{x}{\sqrt{4-x^2}}$. What is the minimum value of $g(x)$ if $g(x) = f'(x)$?

(A) -1

(B) $-\dfrac{1}{2}$

(C) $\dfrac{1}{2}$

(D) 1

(E) 2

83. The volume generated by revolving $y = x^3$ $(-1 \leqslant x \leqslant 1)$ about the y-axis is:

(A) $\dfrac{2\pi}{5}$

(B) $\dfrac{4\pi}{5}$

(C) π

(D) $\dfrac{6\pi}{5}$

(E) 2π

84.

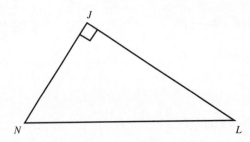

Given right triangle NJL shown above. If $\overline{NJ}$ is growing at the rate of 2 ft/sec and $\overline{JL}$ is shrinking at the rate of 2 ft/sec, then which one of the following is true about $\overline{NL}$ when $\overline{NJ} = 7$ and $\overline{JL} = 24$?

(A) It is growing at the rate of 1.36 ft/sec.

(B) It is growing at the rate of 0.56 ft/sec.

(C) It remains unchanged.

(D) It is shrinking at the rate of 0.56 ft/sec.

(E) It is shrinking at the rate of 1.36 ft/sec.

85. Which one of the following could be the graph of a function h if $\dfrac{1}{4}\displaystyle\int_2^6 h(x)\,dx = 3$?

(A)

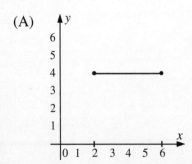

(B)

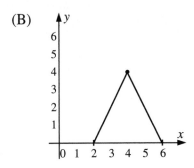

(C)

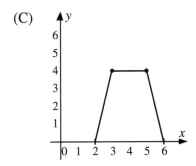

(D)

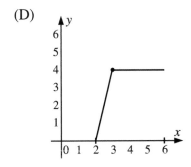

(E)

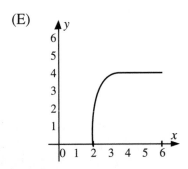

86. If $f(x) = g(x) - \dfrac{1}{g(x)}$ and $g(0) = 3$, $g'(0) = 2$, then $f'(0) =$

    (A) 3.222

    (B) 2.333

    (C) 1.778

    (D) 2.222

    (E) 1.222

87. If $f(x) = 2^{x^3+1}$, then to the nearest thousandth $f'(1) =$

    (A) 2.000

    (B) 2.773

    (C) 4.000

    (D) 6.000

    (E) 8.318

88. Use differentials to approximate the change in y of the curve
    $y = 3x^2 - 6x + 1$ as x changes from 6 to 6.1.

    (A) 3

    (B) 3.01

    (C) 3.02

    (D) 3.03

    (E) 3.04

89. The base of a solid is the region enclosed by $y = \sqrt{x-1}$, the x-axis and
    $x = 5$. Cross sections perpendicular to the x-axis are semicircles with the
    diameter lying in the base. Find the volume of the solid.

    (A) π

    (B) 3.5

    (C) 4.8

    (D) 5.1

    (E) $2\pi + 1$

90. If $f(x) = 5x^2 - 2x + 1$ contains the point $(3, 40)$ and $g(x) = f^{-1}(x)$, find $g'(40)$.

    (A) $\dfrac{1}{5}$

    (B) $\dfrac{1}{6}$

    (C) $\dfrac{1}{12}$

    (D) $\dfrac{1}{15}$

    (E) $\dfrac{1}{18}$

91. Find the x-coordinate on the graph of the equation $y = x^3$ that is closest to the point $(3, 0)$.

    (A) .843

    (B) .929

    (C) 1.042

    (D) 1.135

    (E) 1.419

92.

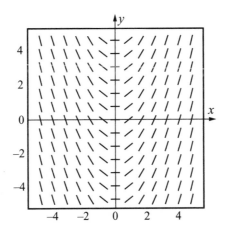

The slope field shown above is for a certain differential equation. Which one of the following could be a specific solution to that differential equation?

(A) $y = \sin x$

(B) $y = \dfrac{1}{2}x^2$

(C) $y = e^x$

(D) $y = \cos x$

(E) $y = 2x^3$

STOP
This is the end of Section I, Part B.
If time still remains, you may check your work only in this section.

Do not begin Section II, Part A until instructed to do so.

Section II

PART A

Time: 45 minutes
   3 free-response problems

DIRECTIONS: Show all your work in your exam booklet. Grading is based on the methods used to solve the problems as well as the accuracy of your final answers.

Calculators MAY be used for this section of the exam.

---

1.   Let R be the region in the first quadrant bounded above by $y = 4 + \ln x$ and below by $y = \dfrac{1}{2}x + 1$.

   (a)   Find the area of region R.

   (b)   Find the volume generated by revolving region R about the x-axis.

   (c)   Find the volume generated by revolving region R about the line $y = -1$.

2.

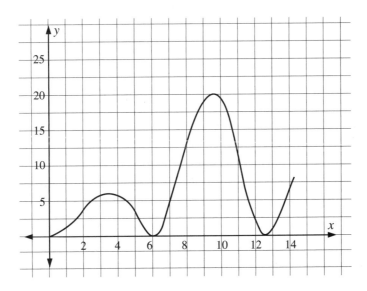

People enter a particular museum exhibit at the rate of $M(t) = 2t \sin^2 \left(\dfrac{t}{2} \right)$ over the time interval $0 \le t \le 14$. The graph shown above displays $y = M(t)$.

(a)   Find the total number of people (to the nearest integer) entering this exhibit during the time interval $0 \leqslant t \leqslant 12$.

(b)   Find the values of t for which $M(t) \geqslant 15$.

(c)   Over the interval determined in part (b), what is the average value of $M(t)$?

(d)   If the museum charges \$7 for each visitor to the exhibit, estimate to the nearest dollar the amount of money the museum will receive in admission fees during the time interval established in part (b).

3.   A conical cup 8 inches across the top and 12 inches deep is leaking water at the rate of 2 in³/min (see figure below).

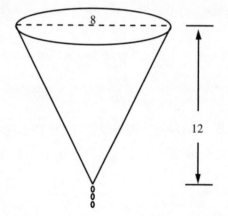

(a)   At what rate is the water level dropping when the water is 6 inches deep?

(b)   At what rate is the water level dropping when the cup is half full?

STOP

This is the end of Section II, Part A.
If time still remains, you may check your work only in this section.
Do not begin Section II, Part B until instructed to do so.

Section II

PART B

Time: 45 minutes
      3 free-response problems

DIRECTIONS: Show all your work in your exam booklet. Grading is based on the methods used to solve the problems as well as the accuracy of your final answers.

Calculators MAY NOT be used for this section of the exam.

(During the timed portion for Part B, you may continue to work on the problems in Part A without the use of a calculator.)

---

4.   The function $y = f(x)$ is twice differentiable and has the following characteristics:

x	$(-\infty, -2)$	-2	$(-2, 0)$	0	$(0, 2)$	2	$(2, \infty)$
$f(x)$	////////	8	////////	4	////////	0	////////
$f'(x)$	$+$	0	$-$	$-$	$-$	0	$+$
$f''(x)$	$-$	$-$	$-$	0	$+$	$+$	$+$

+ is positive, − is negative

   (a)   Determine the interval(s) when $-2f(x)$ is increasing and/or decreasing.

   (b)   Determine the relative minimum and maximum points of $-2f(x)$, if any. Justify your answer.

   (c)   Determine the interval(s) when $-2f(x)$ is concave up and/or concave down.

   (d)   Determine the point(s) of inflection for $-2f(x)$, if any. Justify your answer.

   (e)   Sketch a graph of $-2f(x)$.

5.   Let f be an even function that has a derivative at every value of x in its domain. If $f(2) = 1$ and $f'(2) = 5$, then

   (a)   Find $f'(-2)$ and $f'(0)$.

(b) Let L_1 and L_2 be the tangents to the graph of f at $x = 2$ and $x = -2$, respectively. Find the coordinates of the point p at which L_1 and L_2 intersect.

6. Consider the differential equation $y\dfrac{dy}{dx} = x^2 + 1$, and let $f(x)$ be a solution to the equation.

(a) On the axes provided, sketch a slope field for the given differential equation at the 10 indicated points:

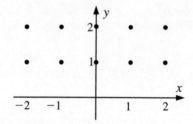

(b) For the particular solution with an initial condition $f(2) = 1$, find a tangent line approximation for $f(2.1)$.

(c) Find the particular solution to the given differential equation with an initial condition of $f(3) = 4$.

END OF EXAM

PRACTICE EXAM 3

AP Calculus AB

Answer Key

Part A		Part B
Part A		**Part B**
1. (D)	15. (E)	76. (E)
2. (E)	16. (A)	77. (C)
3. (E)	17. (A)	78. (D)
4. (C)	18. (B)	79. (E)
5. (C)	19. (A)	80. (D)
6. (B)	20. (C)	81. (A)
7. (A)	21. (E)	82. (C)
8. (D)	22. (C)	83. (D)
9. (C)	23. (B)	84. (E)
10. (C)	24. (A)	85. (C)
11. (D)	25. (C)	86. (D)
12. (C)	26. (A)	87. (E)
13. (B)	27. (B)	88. (A)
14. (A)	28. (D)	89. (A)
		90. (E)
		91. (B)
		92. (B)

Free-Response Answers

1.

(a) 18.190

(b) 468.910

(c) 583.201

2.

(a) 79

(b) $8.672 \le t \le 10.562$

(c) 17.661

(d) $234

3.

(a) $\dfrac{1}{2\pi} = .159$ in./min

(b) .063 in/min

4.

(a) decr. $(-\infty, -2)$ and $(2, \infty)$

   incr. $(-2, 2)$

(b) rel min $(-2, 16)$

   rel max $(2, 0)$

(c) concave up $(-\infty, 0)$

   concave down $(0, \infty)$

(d) $(0, -8)$

(e) See detailed explanation

5.

(a) -5
   0

(b) $(0, -9)$

6.

(a) See detailed explanation

(b) 1.5

(c) $y = \sqrt{\dfrac{2}{3}x^3 + 2x - 8}$

PRACTICE EXAM 3

AP Calculus AB

Detailed Explanations of Answers

Section 1

PART A

1. **(D)**

Use $\dfrac{d}{dx}(u^n) = nu^{n-1}\dfrac{d}{dx}(u)$.

$$y = \left(x^{\frac{1}{2}} + 1\right)^4$$

$$\frac{dy}{dx} = 4\left(x^{\frac{1}{2}} + 1\right)^3 \frac{d}{dx}\left(x^{\frac{1}{2}} + 1\right)$$

$$= 4\left(x^{\frac{1}{2}} + 1\right)^3 \left(\frac{1}{2}x^{-\frac{1}{2}}\right)$$

$$= \boxed{\dfrac{2\left(\sqrt{x} + 1\right)^3}{\sqrt{x}}}$$

2. **(E)**

Use $\displaystyle\int_a^b \sin u \, du = -\cos u \Big|_a^b$

Let $u = 3x \quad \therefore du = 3\,dx$

$$\int_0^\pi \sin(3x)\,dx = \frac{1}{3}\int_0^\pi \sin(3x)\,3\,dx$$

$$= -\frac{1}{3}\cos(3x)\Big|_0^\pi$$

$$= -\frac{1}{3}\big[\cos(3\pi) - \cos(0)\big] = \boxed{\dfrac{2}{3}}$$

3. **(E)**

The graph is NOT differentiable at $x = 0$ because $f'(x)$ from the left of zero does not equal $f'(x)$ from the right of zero. It also appears to have a vertical tangent at $x = 0$. $\therefore f'(x)$ is undefined.

4. **(C)**

Step 1: Use the product rule to find $\dfrac{dy}{dx}$.

$$y = xe^x$$

$$\frac{dy}{dx} = x(e^x) + e^x(1)$$

$$= xe^x + e^x$$

Step 2: Take the derivative of $\dfrac{dy}{dx}$ to find $\dfrac{d^2y}{dx^2}$.

$$\frac{dy}{dx} = xe^x + e^x$$

$$\frac{d^2y}{dx^2} = x(e^x) + e^x(1) + e^x$$

$$= xe^x + 2e^x$$

$$= \boxed{(x+2)e^x}$$

5. **(C)**

Step 1: Use $\displaystyle\int_a^b e^u \, du = e^u \Big|_a^b$

Let $u = 3x$ $\therefore du = 3 \, dx$.

$$\int_{\ln 2}^{\ln 3} e^{3x} dx = \frac{1}{3} \int_{\ln 2}^{\ln 3} e^{3x} \cdot 3 dx = \frac{1}{3} \int_{x=\ln 2}^{\ln 3} e^u \, du$$

$$= \frac{1}{3} e^u \Big|_{x=\ln 2}^{\ln 3}$$

$$= \frac{1}{3} e^{3x} \Big|_{\ln 2}^{\ln 3}$$

Step 2: Evaluate the integral.

$$\frac{1}{3}e^{3x}\Big|_{\ln 2}^{\ln 3}$$

$$=\frac{1}{3}\left[e^{3(\ln 3)}-e^{3(\ln 2)}\right]$$

$$=\frac{1}{3}\left[e^{\ln 27}-e^{\ln 8}\right]$$

$$=\frac{1}{3}[27-8]=\boxed{\frac{19}{3}}$$

6. **(B)**

For limits with $x \to \infty$, only the highest powered term in the numerator and the highest powered term in the denominator control the solution.

$$\therefore \lim_{x\to\infty}\frac{-7x^5+3x^3+7x-1}{8x^6+2x^4-5x^2+6}\approx\lim_{x\to\infty}\frac{-7x^5}{8x^6}$$

$$=\lim_{x\to\infty}\frac{-7}{8x}=\boxed{0}$$

7. **(A)**

This function is of the form $\sin u$, where $u = \cos x$. It is NOT the product of $\sin x$ and $\cos x$.

Use $\dfrac{d}{du}\left[\sin u\right]=\cos u\, du.$

Let $u = \cos x$.

$$\frac{d}{dx}\left[\sin(\cos x)\right]=\cos(\cos x)\frac{d}{dx}(\cos x)$$

$$=\left[\cos(\cos x)\right](-\sin x)$$

$$=\boxed{-\sin x\left[\cos(\cos x)\right]}$$

8. **(D)**

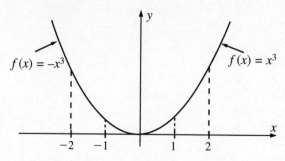

It is useful to sketch the graph of $y = |x^3|$

$$\int_{-2}^{-1} |x^3| \, dx = \int_{1}^{2} x^3 \, dx \quad \text{or} \quad \int_{-2}^{-1} -x^3 \, dx$$

Use

$$\int_{1}^{2} x^3 \, dx = \frac{x^4}{4} \Big|_{1}^{2}$$

$$= \frac{16}{4} - \frac{1}{4} = \boxed{\frac{15}{4}}$$

9. **(C)**

Find the derivatives of $f(x)$ and $g(x)$. Equate them and solve for x.

$$f'(x) = \frac{1}{x}, \quad g'(x) = 4x$$

$$\frac{1}{x} = 4x$$

$$x^2 = \frac{1}{4}$$

$$\therefore \ x = \pm \frac{1}{2}$$

However, $\ln\left(-\frac{1}{2}\right)$ is not defined, so $x = \boxed{\frac{1}{2}}$ only.

10. **(C)**

Step 1: For the shaded region, the graph of $y = 3x^2 - 2$ is always above the graph of $y = -x^2$, similar to the situation in the graph below.

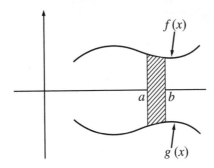

Step 2: For this situation, the shaded area is given by $\int_a^b \left[f(x) - g(x) \right] dx$.

$\therefore$ The shaded region is represented by $\boxed{\int_1^2 \left[(3x^2 - 2) - (-x^2) \right] dx}$.

11. **(D)**

Step 1: Differentiate implicitly:

$$\sin y = \cos x$$

$$\cos y \frac{dy}{dx} = -\sin x$$

$$\frac{dy}{dx} = \frac{-\sin x}{\cos y}$$

Step 2: Evaluate $\dfrac{dy}{dx}$ at $\left(\dfrac{\pi}{2}, \pi \right)$

$$\frac{dy}{dx} = \frac{-\sin \frac{\pi}{2}}{\cos \pi} = \frac{-1}{-1} = \boxed{1}$$

12. **(C)**

Step 1: It is useful to draw a sketch.

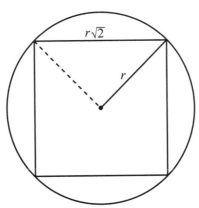

Let A_s = area of the square

A_c = area of the circle

$$A_s = \left(r\sqrt{2}\right)^2 = 2r^2, \quad A_c = \pi r^2$$

Step 2: Create the rate equations for the area of the square and the area of the circle.

$$\frac{d}{dt}(A_s) = 4r\frac{dr}{dt}, \quad \frac{d}{dt}(A_c) = 2\pi r\frac{dr}{dt}$$

$$\therefore \frac{dr}{dt} = \frac{1}{4r}\frac{d(A_s)}{dt} = \frac{1}{2\pi r}\frac{d(A_c)}{dt}$$

Step 3: Solve for $\frac{d(A_s)}{dt}$, and substitute the given information that $\frac{d(A_c)}{dt} = 1$.

$$\frac{d(A_s)}{dt} = \frac{2}{\pi}\frac{d(A_c)}{dt} = \frac{2}{\pi}(1) = \boxed{\frac{2}{\pi}}$$

13. **(B)**

Step 1: Concavity requires analysis of the second derivative.

$$y = x^4 - 2x^3 - 12x^2$$

$$y' = 4x^3 - 6x^2 - 24x$$

$$y'' = 12x^2 - 12x - 24$$

$$= 12(x^2 - x - 2)$$

$$= 12(x - 2)(x + 1)$$

Step 2: $y'' = 0$ at critical points.

$$y'' = 12(x - 2)(x + 1) = 0$$

$$\therefore x = 2, x = -1 \text{ are critical points.}$$

Analyze y'' by using sample points in each interval.

$$y''(x) \underset{\substack{\\-1}}{\overset{+}{\rule{2cm}{0.4pt}}} \underset{\substack{\\2}}{\overset{-}{\rule{2cm}{0.4pt}}} \overset{+}{\rule{2cm}{0.4pt}}$$

The original graph is concave down when $y'' < 0$.
This occurs on the interval $\boxed{(-1, 2)}$

14. **(A)**

Step 1: The fundamental theorem of calculus (part 2) states

$$\frac{d}{dx}\left[\int_a^x f(t)\, dt\right] = f(x)$$

$$h(x) = \int_a^x (1-2t)^3\, dt$$

$$h'(x) = \frac{d}{dx}\left[\int_a^x (1-2t)^3\, dt\right] = (1-2x)^3$$

$$h''(x) = 3(1-2x)^2(-2)$$

Step 2: Evaluate $h''\left(\frac{1}{2}\right)$:

$$h''\left(\frac{1}{2}\right) = -6\left(1-2\left(\frac{1}{2}\right)\right)^2$$

$$= \boxed{0}$$

15. **(E)**

Step 1: Use $\ln\left(\frac{3}{2}\right) = \boxed{\ln 3 - \ln 2}$

Step 2: Use $\int_a^b \frac{1}{x}\, dx = \ln|x|\Big|_a^b$

$$\therefore \int_2^3 \frac{1}{t}\, dt = \ln|t|\Big|_2^3 = \ln 3 - \ln 2$$

16. **(A)**

Multiply the numerator and denominator by x^2.

$$\lim_{x \to 0} \frac{\left(\dfrac{3}{x^2}\right)}{\left(\dfrac{2}{x^2} + \dfrac{105}{x}\right)} \frac{(x^2)}{(x^2)}$$

$$= \lim_{x \to 0} \frac{3}{2+105x} = \boxed{\frac{3}{2}}$$

17. **(A)**

$\boxed{\text{(A) could be FALSE.}}$ There is not enough information to tell where the maximum is

(B) is TRUE because of the intermediate value theorem.

(C)   is TRUE because of the definition of continuity on $[a, b]$.

(D)   is TRUE for any a, b as a consequence of the triangle inequality, $|a| - |b| \leq |a - b|$.

(E)   is TRUE because of the definition of continuity.

18. **(B)**

The law of cooling can be written as $\dfrac{dQ}{dt} \propto (Q - 40)$.

$$\therefore \boxed{\dfrac{dQ}{dt} = k(Q - 40)}$$

19. **(A)**

Step 1: At $x = a$, the function is continuous because $\lim\limits_{x \to a^-} f(x) = \lim\limits_{x \to a^+} f(x)$.

At $x = e$, the function also is continuous because $\lim\limits_{x \to e^-} f(x) = \lim\limits_{x \to e^+} f(x)$.

At $x = b$, c, and d, the function is not continuous.

Step 2: At $x = a$, the function has a vertical tangent; therefore, it is not differentiable at $x = a$. The tangent at $x = e$ has a negative slope, the function is differentiable at $x = e$.

$\therefore$ Only at $x = \boxed{a}$ is the function continuous but not differentiable.

20. **(C)**

Step 1: Convert the graph into a number line, indicating when $f'(x)$ is positive, negative, or zero.

$$f'(x) \quad \overset{\textstyle +}{\underset{\textstyle -5}{\rule{0pt}{0pt}}} \quad \overset{\textstyle 0}{\rule{0pt}{0pt}} \quad \overset{\textstyle -}{\rule{0pt}{0pt}} \quad \overset{\textstyle 0}{\underset{\textstyle 2}{\rule{0pt}{0pt}}} \quad \overset{\textstyle +}{\rule{0pt}{0pt}}$$

Step 2: $f(x)$ is decreasing when $f'(x)$ is negative.

$\therefore \boxed{(-5, 2)}$

21. **(E)**

Step 1: Establish the rate of change of the equation.

$y = 2x^3 - 4x + 1$

$$\frac{dy}{dt} = 6x^2 \frac{dx}{dt} - 4\frac{dx}{dt}$$

Step 2: The particle crosses the y-axis at $(0, 1)$.

The constant rate of change of x is given as $\dfrac{dx}{dt} = 3$.

$$\therefore \quad \frac{dy}{dt} = 6(0)^2(3) - 4(3)$$

$$= \boxed{-12\,\text{cm/sec}}$$

(Note: The minus sign indicates it is decreasing.)

22. **(C)**

Step 1: Average value $= \dfrac{1}{b-a}\displaystyle\int_a^b (2x+3)\,dx = 29$

Step 2: Integrate and simplify the algebra.

$$\frac{1}{b-a}\left[\frac{2x^2}{2} + 3x\right]_a^b = 29$$

$$\frac{1}{b-a}\left[(b^2 + 3b) - (a^2 + 3a)\right] = 29$$

$$\frac{1}{b-a}\left[(b^2 - a^2) + (3b - 3a)\right] = 29$$

$$\frac{1}{b-a}\left[(b+a)(b-a) + 3(b-a)\right] = 29$$

$$b + a + 3 = 29$$

$$a + b = \boxed{26}$$

23. **(B)**

Step 1: Use the chain rule.

If $h(x) = f(g(x))$,

$h'(x) = f'(g(x)) \cdot g'(x)$

Step 2: Evaluate at $x = 3$.

$h'(3) = f'(g(3)) \cdot g'(3)$

$= f'(2) \cdot (5)$

$= 6 \cdot 5 = \boxed{30}$

24. **(A)**

Step 1: Use the fundamental theorem of calculus (part 2).

$$\frac{d}{dx}\left[\int_a^{h(x)} f(t)\,dt\right] = f(h(x)) \cdot h'(x)$$

$$g(x) = \int_{28}^{x^2} (t+1)\,dt$$

$$\therefore g'(x) = \frac{d}{dx}\left[\int_{28}^{x^2} (t+1)\,dt\right] = (x^2+1)\cdot(2x)$$

Step 2: Evaluate $g'(2)$.

$$g'(2) = (2^2 + 1) \cdot (2 \cdot 2)$$
$$= \boxed{20}$$

25. **(C)**

Rearrange the fraction algebraically, and let $u = \ln x \therefore du = \frac{1}{x}dx$.

$$\int \frac{1}{x\ln^5 x}\,dx = \int \frac{(\ln x)^{-5}}{x}\,dx \quad = \quad \int (\ln x)^{-5}\cdot\frac{1}{x}\,dx$$

$$= \quad \int u^{-5}\,du$$

$$= \quad -\frac{1}{4}u^{-4} + C$$

$$= \quad -\frac{1}{4}(\ln x)^{-4} + C$$

$$= \quad \boxed{\frac{-1}{4\ln^4 x} + C}$$

26. **(A)**

Step 1: Differentiate implicitly. Note that $(y+1)(x)$ is a product.

$$(y+1)(x) - x^2 + y = 1$$

$$(y+1)(1) + x\frac{dy}{dx} - 2x + 1\frac{dy}{dx} = 0$$

Step 2: Let $x = 2$ and $y = 1$, and solve for $\frac{dy}{dx}$.

$$(1+1)+(2)\frac{dy}{dx}-2(2)+\frac{dy}{dx}=0$$

$$\frac{dy}{dx}=\frac{2}{3}$$

Step 3: Use the equation of a line $y-y_1=m(x-x_1)$ to write the equation of the tangent line, with $(x_1, y_1)=(2, 1)$ and $m=\frac{dy}{dx}=\frac{2}{3}$.

$$\therefore (y-1)=\frac{2}{3}(x-2)$$

or $\boxed{2x-3y-1=0}$

27. **(B)**

Step 1: The frequency of $y=\sin 3x$ is 3, and the period is $\frac{2\pi}{3}$.

A quick reference sketch is useful.

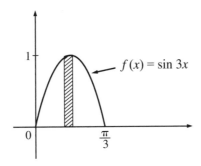

Step 2: Area $=\int_0^{\frac{\pi}{3}}\sin 3x\,dx$

$$=\frac{1}{3}\int_0^{\frac{\pi}{3}}\sin(3x)\cdot 3dx \qquad\qquad \text{let } u=3x$$
$$\qquad\qquad\qquad\qquad\qquad du=3dx$$

$$=\frac{1}{3}\int_{x=0}^{\frac{\pi}{3}}\sin u\,du=\frac{1}{3}(-\cos u)\Big|_{x=0}^{x=\frac{\pi}{3}}$$

$$=-\frac{1}{3}(\cos(3x))\Big|_0^{\frac{\pi}{3}}$$

$$=-\frac{1}{3}[\cos\pi-\cos 0]=-\frac{1}{3}[-1-1]=\boxed{\frac{2}{3}}$$

28. **(D)**

Step 1: Set the first derivative equal to zero and determine the critical values.

$$f(x) = \frac{x^3}{3} - x^2 - 3x + 5$$
$$f'(x) = x^2 - 2x - 3 = 0$$

Critical values are $x = 3$, $x = -1$.

Step 2: Analyze the first derivative on a number line

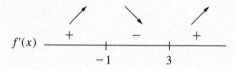

The function has a relative minimum at $x = \boxed{3 \text{ only}}$.

Section I

PART B

76. **(E)**

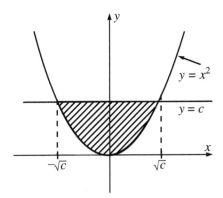

Step 1: It is useful to envision the graphs of $y = x^2$ and $y = c$.

Step 2: The graphs intersect at $\left(-\sqrt{c}, c\right)$ and $\left(\sqrt{c}, c\right)$

$$A = \int_{-\sqrt{c}}^{\sqrt{c}} (c - x^2)\, dx = \frac{1}{48}, \quad \text{or by symmetry,} \quad A = 2\int_{0}^{\sqrt{c}} (c - x^2)\, dx = \frac{1}{48}$$

Step 3: $A = 2\int_{0}^{\sqrt{c}} (c - x^2)\, dx = \frac{1}{48}$

$$2\left[cx - \frac{x^3}{3} \right]_{0}^{\sqrt{c}} = \frac{1}{48}$$

$$c\left(\sqrt{c}\right) - \frac{\left(\sqrt{c}\right)^3}{3} = \frac{1}{96}$$

$$c\sqrt{c} - \frac{c\sqrt{c}}{3} = \frac{1}{96}$$

$$\frac{2c\sqrt{c}}{3} = \frac{1}{96}$$

$$\boxed{c = \frac{1}{16}}$$

77. (C)

Step 1: Split the integral into two integrals.

$$\int_{-5}^{5}[g(x)+2]dx = \int_{-5}^{5}g(x)dx + \int_{-5}^{5}2\,dx$$

Step 2: Assign "signed" values to the indicated areas. Those above the x-axis are positive; those below are negative.

$$A = 2, B = -1, C = 4, D = -1$$

$$\therefore \int_{-5}^{5}g(x)dx = (2)+(-1)+(4)+(-1) = 4$$

Step 3: Evaluate $\int_{-5}^{5}2\,dx = 2x\Big|_{-5}^{5} = 20.$

Step 4: $\therefore \int_{-5}^{5}[g(x)+2]dx = 4+20 = \boxed{24}$

78. (D)

Step 1: Acceleration is $\dfrac{dv}{dt}$.

$$v(t) = t + 7.6\sin(3t)$$

$$a(t) = \frac{d[v(t)]}{dt} = 1+7.6\cos(3t)\cdot 3$$
$$= 1+22.8\cos(3t)$$

Step 2: Evaluate $a(6)$.

$$a(t) = 1 + 22.8\cos(3t)$$
$$a(6) = 1 + 22.8\cos(18)$$
$$= \boxed{16.06}$$

79. (E)

Step 1: When the ball achieves its maximum height, its velocity is zero.

Take the first derivative of $h(t)$ to get $v(t)$ and equate it to zero. Then solve for t to determine the time the ball achieves its maximum height.

$$h(t) = -16t^2 + 100t + 5$$
$$v(t) = h'(t) = -32t + 100$$

$$0 = -32t + 100$$

$$t = 3.125 \text{ sec}$$

Step 2: At time $t = 3.125$, calculate $h(t)$ to obtain the maximum height.

$$h(t) = -16t^2 + 100t + 5$$

$$h(3.125) = \boxed{161.25}$$

80. **(D)**

Step 1: To locate points of inflection, begin by setting the second derivative equal to zero and solving for x.

$$f'(x) = \frac{-x}{e^{\frac{x^2}{2}}} = -xe^{-\frac{x^2}{2}}$$

$$f''(x) = -x\frac{d}{dx}\left(e^{-\frac{x^2}{2}}\right) + e^{-\frac{x^2}{2}}\frac{d}{dx}(-x)$$

$$= -x\left(e^{-\frac{x^2}{2}} \cdot (-x)\right) + e^{-\frac{x^2}{2}}(-1)$$

$$= e^{-\frac{x^2}{2}}[x^2 - 1]$$

Solve

$$e^{-\frac{x^2}{2}}(x^2 - 1) = 0$$

$$e^{-\frac{x^2}{2}} = 0 \quad \bigg| \quad x^2 - 1 = 0$$

No real solution $\bigg| \quad x = \pm 1$

Step 2: Analyze the second derivative on a number line.

Step 3: Since $f''(x)$ changes from positive to negative at $x = -1$ and then from negative to positive at $x = 1$, both $\boxed{x = 1 \text{ and } x = -1}$ are inflection points.

81. (A)

Use the calculator to solve this problem. (A non-calculator solution is too time consuming.)

$$d((\sin(x) \cdot \cos(x))/(\cos(9x) \cdot \tan(2x), x)\,|\,x = .5$$

$$= \boxed{-49.5}$$

82. (C)

Step 1: First find $f'(x)$.

$$f(x) = \frac{x}{\sqrt{4-x^2}} = x(4-x^2)^{-\frac{1}{2}}$$

$$f'(x) = x\frac{d}{dx}\left((4-x^2)^{-\frac{1}{2}}\right) + (4-x^2)^{-\frac{1}{2}}\frac{d}{dx}(x)$$

$$= x\left(-\frac{1}{2}(4-x^2)^{-\frac{3}{2}}(-2x)\right) + (4-x^2)^{-\frac{1}{2}}(1)$$

$$= (4-x^2)^{-\frac{3}{2}}[x^2 + (4-x^2)]$$

$$g(x) = f'(x) = 4(4-x^2)^{-\frac{3}{2}}$$

Step 2: Take the derivative of the function to be minimized, $g(x) = 4(4-x^2)^{-\frac{3}{2}}$ and set it equal to zero and solve for x.

$$g'(x) = 4\left[-\frac{3}{2}(4-x^2)^{-\frac{5}{2}} \cdot (-2x)\right]$$

$$= \frac{12x}{(4-x^2)^{\frac{5}{2}}} = 0$$

$$x = 0$$

Step 3: Confirm this is a minimum by using the first derivative test.

$$g'(x) \underline{}\underset{0}{+}\underline{}$$

$\therefore g'(x)$ has a minimum at $x = 0$.

$$g'(0) = 4(4-0^2)^{-\frac{3}{2}} = 4\left(\frac{1}{8}\right) = \boxed{\frac{1}{2}}$$

83. **(D)**

   Step 1: A quick sketch is useful.

   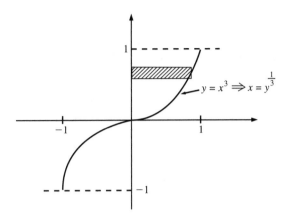

   By symmetry, find the volume generated from $x = 0$ to $x = 1$ and double it.

   This is a washer type problem.

   $$\therefore V = \pi \int_a^b r^2 \, dy$$

   Step 2: Set up the integral and evaluate.

   $$V = 2\left[\pi \int_{y=0}^{y=1} (y^{\frac{1}{3}})^2 \, dy \right] = 2\pi \int_0^1 y^{\frac{2}{3}} = \frac{3}{5}(2\pi)y^{\frac{5}{3}} \Big|_0^1$$

   $$= \frac{3}{5}(2\pi)(1) - 0$$

   $$= \boxed{\frac{6\pi}{5}}$$

84. **(E)**

   Step 1: Label the sides of the triangle x, y, z and write a geometry equation relating the sides.

   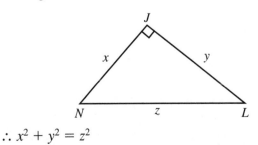

   $$\therefore x^2 + y^2 = z^2$$

Step 2: Create a rate equation (use implicit differentiation with respect to t).

$$2x\frac{dx}{dt}+2y\frac{dy}{dt}=2z\frac{dz}{dt} \Rightarrow x\frac{dx}{dt}+y\frac{dy}{dt}=z\frac{dz}{dt}$$

Step 3: By the Pythagorean Theorem, $z = 25$ when $x = 7$ and $y = 24$.

Substitute $\frac{dx}{dt} = 2$, $\frac{dy}{dt} = -2$, $x = 7$, $y = 24$, $z = 25$, and solve for $\frac{dz}{dt}$.

$$7(2)+24(-2)=25\frac{dz}{dt}$$
$$\frac{dz}{dt}=\frac{-34}{25}=-1.36$$

$\therefore$ $\boxed{dt \text{ is shrinking at the rate of 1.36 ft/sec.}}$

85. **(C)**

Step 1: $\dfrac{1}{b-a}\displaystyle\int_a^b h(x)\,dx = $ average value

$\therefore (b-a)(\text{average value}) = \displaystyle\int_a^b h(x)\,dx$

Since the graphs are all above the x-axis,

$\displaystyle\int_a^b h(x)\,dx$ represents the area bounded by the curve $y = h(x)$ and the x-axis.

Step 2: Using the given data,

$$\frac{1}{4}\int_2^6 h(x)\,dx = 3 \implies \int_2^6 h(x)\,dx = 12$$

The question is asking which graph displays an area of 12 for the region bounded by h and the x-axis on the interval $[2, 6]$.

A

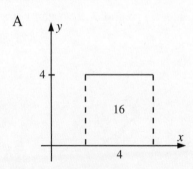

B

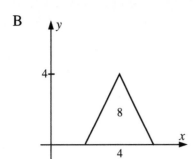

C

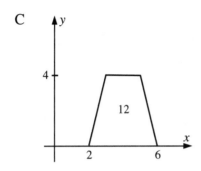

D

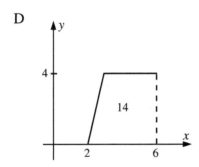

E

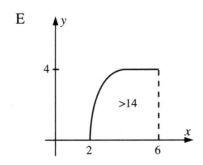

Choice C is correct.

86. **(D)**

   Step 1: Rearrange the given equation and differentiate. Use the chain rule.

   $$f(x) = g(x) - [g(x)]^{-1}$$
   $$f'(x) = g'(x) + [g(x)]^{-2} \cdot g'(x)$$

   Step 2: $f'(0) = g'(0) + [g(0)]^{-2} \cdot g'(0)$

   $$= 2 + [3]^{-2} \cdot 2$$

   $$= 2 + \frac{2}{9} = \boxed{2.222}$$

87. **(E)**

   Step 1: Use $\dfrac{d}{dx}(a^u) = a^u \cdot \dfrac{d}{dx}(u) \cdot \ln a$.

   $$a = 2, u = x^3 + 1$$

   $$\frac{d}{dx}(2^{x^3+1}) = 2^{x^3+1}\frac{d}{dx}(x^3+1) \cdot \ln 2$$

   $$= 3x^2 \cdot 2^{x^3+1} \cdot \ln 2$$

   Step 2: Evaluate at $x = 1$.

   $$3x^2 \cdot 2^{x^3+1} \cdot \ln 2 \Big|_{x=1} = \boxed{8.318}$$

88. **(A)**

   Step 1: Begin with the relationship $y = 3x^2 - 6x + 1$.

   If Δx is a small change in x, Δx can be estimated as dx.

   The change in y (Δy) can be estimated as dy.

   Step 2: $\Delta y \approx dy = (6x - 6)\,dx$

   with $dx = +.1$ and $x = 6$

   $$\Delta y \approx dy = (6(6) - 6)(+.1)$$

   $$= (30)(.1) = \boxed{3}$$

89. **(A)**

Step 1: A sketch will prove helpful.

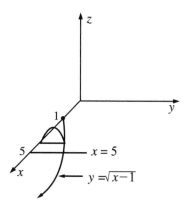

Step 2: The diameter of each semicircle is $\sqrt{x-1}$.

The volume of each semicircular slice

is $\dfrac{1}{2}\pi r^2\, dx$

$$=\frac{1}{2}\pi\left(\frac{\sqrt{x-1}}{2}\right)^2 dx$$

Step 3: Add all the semicircular slices from $x = 1$ to $x = 5$ and evaluate the integral.

$$\int_1^5 \frac{1}{2}\pi\left(\frac{\sqrt{x-1}}{2}\right)^2 dx = \frac{1}{8}\pi\int_1^5 (x-1)\,dx$$

$$=\frac{1}{8}\pi\left(\frac{1}{2}x^2 - x\right)\Big|_1^5 = \frac{1}{8}\pi\left(\frac{15}{2} + \frac{1}{2}\right)$$

$$=\frac{1}{8}\pi(8) = \boxed{\pi}$$

90. **(E)**

Step 1: If $g(x)$ is the inverse of $f(x)$, then

$$g'(x) = \frac{1}{f'(g(x))}$$

Step 2: Calculate $f'(x)$.

$$f(x) = 5x^2 - 2x + 1$$

$$f'(x) = 10x - 2$$

Step 3: Find $g'(x)$ at $x = 40$.

$$g'(40) = \frac{1}{f'(g(40))}$$

Note: If $f(3) = 40$, then $g(40) = 2$.

$$\therefore g'(40) = \frac{1}{f'(2)}$$

Step 4: Calculate $f'(2)$ and substitute.

$$f'(2) = 10(2) - 2 = 18$$

$$g'(40) = \boxed{\frac{1}{18}}$$

91. **(B)**

Step 1: A quick sketch is helpful.

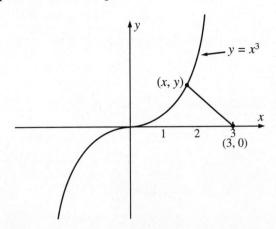

Refer to the point on this curve that satisfies the requirement as (x, y).

Step 2: Write an expression for the distance from (x, y) to $(3, 0)$.

$$d = \sqrt{(x-3)^2 + (y-0)^2}$$
$$= \sqrt{(x-3)^2 + y^2}$$

Step 3: Replace y with x^3 so that d becomes a function of a single variable.

$$d(x) = \sqrt{(x-3)^2 + x^6}$$

Step 4: In problems involving distance, minimizing the square of the distance function gives the same solution but involves an easier function to deal with (no square root). Call the square of the distance function $s(x)$.

$$\therefore s(x) = (x - 3)^2 + x^6$$

Step 5: To minimize $s(x)$, set $s'(x) = 0$ and solve for x.

$$s'(x) = 2(x - 3) + 6x^5 = 0$$

Use a calculator to solve this equation.

$$x = .92859$$

$$\boxed{x = .929}$$

92. **(B)**

The skeleton created by the tangent line segments outlines a parabolic shape. Only choice B $\boxed{y = \frac{1}{2}x^2}$ reflects this outline.

Section II

PART A

1. Note: Use the calculator.

Step 1: Make a sketch.

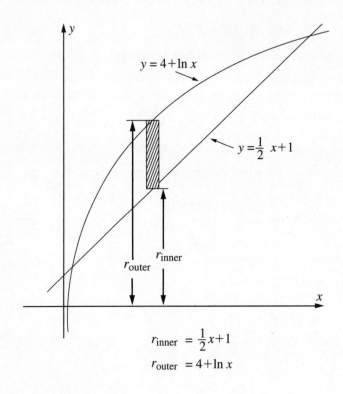

$$r_{inner} = \frac{1}{2}x+1$$

$$r_{outer} = 4+\ln x$$

Step 2: Find the points of intersection.

$$4+\ln x = \frac{1}{2}x+1$$

$$x = 0.051 \text{ and } x = 10.750$$

Step 3:

(a) $A = \int_{.051}^{10.75}\left[(4+\ln x)-\left(\frac{1}{2}x+1\right)\right]dx = \boxed{18.190}$

Step 4:

(b) $V = \pi \int_a^b (r_{outer}^2 - r_{inner}^2) \, dx$

$= \pi \int_{.051}^{10.75} \left[(4 + \ln x)^2 - \left(\frac{1}{2} x + 1 \right)^2 \right] dx$

$= \boxed{468.910}$

Step 5: Make another sketch to show the axis of rotation $y = -1$. Note the new r_{inner} and r_{outer}.

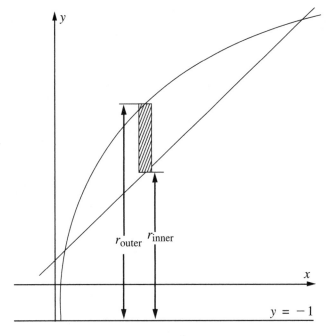

$r_{inner} = \left(\frac{1}{2} x + 1 \right) + 1$

$r_{outer} = (4 + \ln x) + 1$

(c) $V = \pi \int_{.051}^{10.75} \left[(5 + \ln x)^2 - \left(\frac{1}{2} x + 2 \right)^2 \right] dx = \boxed{583.201}$

2. A calculator is required for this problem.

Step 1:

(a) The total number of people entering in the interval $0 \leq t \leq 12$ is given by $\int_0^{12} 2t \sin^2 \left(\frac{t}{2} \right) dt = 78.59 \Rightarrow \boxed{79}$

Step 2: First solve $M(t) \geq 15$ for all values of t in the interval $0 \leq t \leq 14$.

$t \geq 8.672$ and $t \leq 10.562$

or $\boxed{8.672 \leq t \leq 10.562}$

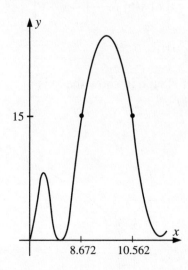

Step 3: Average value $= \dfrac{1}{10.562 - 8.672} \displaystyle\int_{8.672}^{10.562} 2t \sin^2\left(\dfrac{t}{2}\right) dt = \dfrac{1}{1.890}(33.380)$

where $\displaystyle\int_{8.672}^{10.562} 2t \sin^2\left(\dfrac{t}{2}\right) dt = 33.380$ is the total number of people entering in the time interval $[8.672, 10.562]$.

$= \boxed{17.661}$

Step 4: Total admission fees $=$ number of people $\times$ \$7

$= 33.380\,(7) = 233.66$

$\approx \boxed{\$234}$

3.

Step 1: • Volume of a cone is $V = \dfrac{1}{3}\pi r^2 h$.

• Since this equation has 2 variables (r and h), look for a geometric relationship between the variables such that the volume can be expressed in terms of a single variable. (See sketches below.)

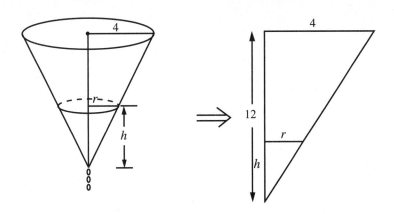

From similar triangles, $\dfrac{r}{4} = \dfrac{h}{12}$ $\therefore h = 3r$ or $r = \dfrac{h}{3}$.

Because the question asks for $\dfrac{dh}{dt}$, replace r with $\dfrac{h}{3}$.

$$\therefore V = \frac{1}{3}\pi\left(\frac{h}{3}\right)^2 h$$

$$= \frac{\pi}{27}h^3$$

Step 2: Create a rate equation.

$$\frac{dV}{dt} = \frac{\pi}{27}\left(3h^2\frac{dh}{dt}\right) = \frac{\pi}{9}h^2\frac{dh}{dt}$$

Step 3: Water leaking at the rate of 2 in²/min means

$$\frac{dV}{dt} = -2 \text{. and At } h = 6,\ -2 = \frac{\pi}{9}(6)^2\frac{dh}{dt}$$

or $\dfrac{dh}{dt} = \dfrac{-1}{2\pi}$

(a) $\therefore$ At $h = 6$, the water is dropping at the rate of $\dfrac{1}{2\pi} = \boxed{.159\,\text{in/min}}$

Step 4: The full volume of the cup $= \dfrac{1}{3}\pi(4)^2(12) = 64\pi$ in³.

Then half the volume $= 32\pi$ in³.

The height at this volume is:

$$V = \frac{\pi}{27}h^3$$

$$32\pi = \frac{\pi}{27}h^3$$

$$h = 6 \cdot \sqrt[3]{4} = 9.524$$

Step 5: At $h = 9.524$,

$$\frac{dV}{dt} = \frac{\pi}{9}h^2\frac{dh}{dt}$$

$$-2 = \frac{\pi}{9}(9.524)^2\frac{dh}{dt}$$

$$\frac{dh}{dt} = -.063 \text{ in/min}$$

(b) $\therefore$ When the cup is half full, the water is dropping at the rate of $\boxed{.063 \text{ in/min}}$

Section II

PART B

4.

Step 1: Modify the characteristics chart to reflect a new function, $g(x)$:

$$g(x) = -2f(x)$$
$$g'(x) = -2f'(x)$$
$$g''(x) = -2f''(x)$$

x	$(-\infty, -2)$	-2	$(-2, 0)$	0	$(0, 2)$	2	$(2, \infty)$
$g(x)$		-16		-8		0	
$g'(x)$	$-$	0	$+$	$+$	$+$	0	$-$
$g''(x)$	$+$	$+$	$+$	0	$-$	$-$	$-$

Step 2: Analyze the first derivative of g on a number line.

$$g'(x) \quad \underset{\text{decreasing} \quad -2 \quad \text{increasing} \quad 2 \quad \text{decreasing}}{\underline{\qquad \overset{\searrow}{----} \quad \overset{\nearrow}{+++++} \quad \overset{\searrow}{---} \qquad}}$$

(a)

> $g(x)$ is decreasing on the interval $(-\infty, -2)$ and $(2, \infty)$.
> $g(x)$ is increasing on the interval $(-2, 2)$.

Step 3: There is a relative minimum point at $x = -2 \Rightarrow (-2, 16)$

because $g'(x)$ changes from negative to positive.

There is a relative maximum point at $x = 2 \Rightarrow (2, 0)$

because $g'(x)$ changes from positive to negative.

(b)

> So $(-2, 16)$ is a relative minimum and $(2, 0)$ is a relative maximum.

Step 4: Analyze the second derivative on a number line.

$$g''(x) \quad \underset{\text{concave up} \quad 0 \quad \text{concave down}}{\underline{\qquad \overset{+++}{\qquad} \quad \overset{----}{\qquad} \qquad}}$$

(c)

> $g(x)$ is concave up on the interval $(-\infty, 0)$
>
> $g(x)$ is concave down on the interval $(0, \infty)$

Step 5: (d) There is an inflection point at $x = 0 \Rightarrow$ $\boxed{(0, -8)}$

because concavity changes from positive to negative.

Step 6: (e)

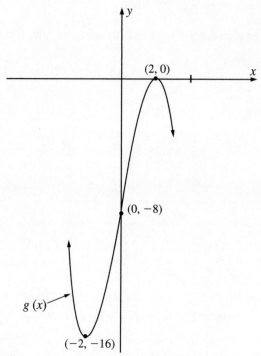

5.

Step 1: An even function has y-axis symmetry,

so $f(x) = f(-x)$.

By the chain rule, $f'(x) = -f'(-x) \Rightarrow f'(-x) = -f'(x)$

(a) $\therefore f'(-2) = -f'(2) = \boxed{-5}$

Step 2: $f'(x) = -f'(-x)$

$f'(0) = -f'(-0) = -f'(0)$

$f'(0) = -f'(0)$

$2f'(0) = 0$

(a) $f'(0) = \boxed{0}$

Step 3: • If $f(2) = 1$ and $f'(2) = 5$,

then $(y - 1) = 5(x - 2)$ is the equation of L_1.

• If $f(-2) = f(2) = 1$ and $f'(-2) = -5$,

then $(y - 1) = -5(x + 2)$ is the equation of L_2.

Step 4: Solve L_1 and L_2 for x and y to find the point of intersection.

$$L_1: (y - 1) = 5(x - 2) \qquad\qquad x = 0$$
$$\Rightarrow$$
$$L_2: (y - 1) = -5(x + 2) \qquad\qquad y = -9$$

(b) $\boxed{(0, -9)}$

6.

Step 1: Rewrite the differential equation.

$$y\frac{dy}{dx} = x^2 + 1 \;\Rightarrow\; \frac{dy}{dx} = \frac{(x^2 + 1)}{y}$$

Step 2: To create the slope field, make a table of values, and plot a line segment with $\text{slope} = \dfrac{dy}{dx}$ at each (x, y) coordinate pair.

x	y	$\dfrac{dy}{dx}$
-2	1	5
-2	2	$\dfrac{5}{2}$
-1	1	2
-1	2	1
0	1	1
0	2	$\dfrac{1}{2}$
1	1	2
1	2	1
2	1	5
2	2	$\dfrac{5}{2}$

(a)

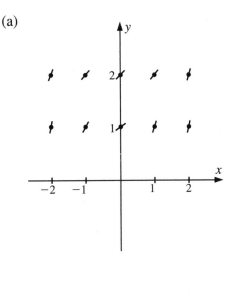

Step 3: At the point $(2, 1)$, $\dfrac{dy}{dx} = 5$,

so the tangent line equation at $x = 2$ is $y - 1 = 5(x - 2)$.

$\therefore y = f(x) = 5(x - 2) + 1$

(b) $f(2.1) = 5(2.1 - 2) + 1$

$= .5 + 1 = \boxed{1.5}$

Step 4: Solve for the general solution.

$$\frac{dy}{dx} = \frac{x^2 + 1}{y} \quad\Rightarrow\quad y\,dy = (x^2 + 1)\,dx$$

$$\int y\,dy = \int (x^2 + 1)\,dx$$

$$\frac{y^2}{2} = \frac{x^3}{3} + x + C$$

$$\text{let } 2C = K \quad y^2 = \frac{2}{3}x^3 + 2x + 2C$$

$$y^2 = \frac{2}{3}x^3 + 2x + K$$

Step 5: Find the particular solution at $(3, 4)$.

$$4^2 = \frac{2}{3}(3)^3 + 2(3) + K$$

$$K = -8$$

$$\therefore y^2 = \frac{2}{3}x^3 + 2x - 8$$

Since $y = 4$ when $x = 3$

(c) $\boxed{y = \sqrt{\dfrac{2}{3}x^3 + 2x - 8}}$

PRACTICE EXAM 4

AP Calculus AB

Section I

PART A

Time: 55 minutes
      28 questions

(Answer sheets appear in the back of this book.)

DIRECTIONS: Solve each of the following problems, select the best answer choice, and fill in the corresponding oval on the answer sheet.

Calculators may NOT be used for this section of the exam.

NOTES:

(1) Unless otherwise specified, the domain of a function f is assumed to be the set of all real numbers x for which $f(x)$ is a real number.

(2) The inverse of a trigonometric function f may be indicated by using the inverse function notation f^{-1} or with the prefix "arc" (e.g., $\sin^{-1} x = \arcsin x$).

1. If $y = (x^5 - 7)^4$, then $\dfrac{dy}{dx} =$

   (A) $4(x^5 - 7)^3$

   (B) $20x(x^5 - 7)^3$

   (C) $4x^4(x^5 - 7)^3$

   (D) $5x^4(x^5 - 7)^3$

   (E) $20x^4(x^5 - 7)^3$

2. $\int_1^5 3e^{-3x} dx =$

   (A) $e^{-15} - e^{-3}$

   (B) $e^{-12} - e^{-3}$

   (C) e^{-12}

   (D) $e^{-3} - e^{-12}$

   (E) $e^{-3} - e^{-15}$

3. $\lim\limits_{x \to 2} \dfrac{x-2}{\sqrt{x-2}} =$

   (A) $-\sqrt{2}$

   (B) 0

   (C) 1

   (D) $\sqrt{2}$

   (E) Limit does not exist.

4. $\int_0^{\frac{\pi}{3}} 3 \sec x \tan x \, dx =$

   (A) -1

   (B) 0

   (C) 1

   (D) 2

   (E) 3

5. If $f(x) = \dfrac{\sin x}{x}$, then $f'(x) =$

   (A) $\dfrac{x \cos x - \sin x}{x^2}$

   (B) $\dfrac{\cos x - x \sin x}{x^2}$

(C) $\dfrac{\cos x - \sin x}{x^2}$

(D) $\dfrac{\sin x - \cos x}{x^2}$

(E) $\dfrac{x^2 \sin x - x \cos x}{x^2}$

6. Given the piecewise function f defined as $f(x) = \begin{cases} 4ax^3 + 7x & x \le 1 \\ (a+2)x^4 - 4 & x > 1 \end{cases}$.

For what value of a is $f(x)$ continuous at $x = 1$?

(A) -3

(B) -2

(C) 1

(D) 2

(E) 3

7. $\displaystyle\int x^5 \sec^2(x^6)\,dx =$

(A) $\dfrac{x^6}{6} \sec^2\left(\dfrac{x^7}{7}\right) + C$

(B) $\dfrac{1}{6}\tan(x^6) + C$

(C) $\dfrac{-x^6}{6} \sec\left(\dfrac{x^7}{7}\right) + C$

(D) $\dfrac{x}{6}\tan(x^6) + C$

(E) $\dfrac{x}{3}\tan(x^6) + C$

8.

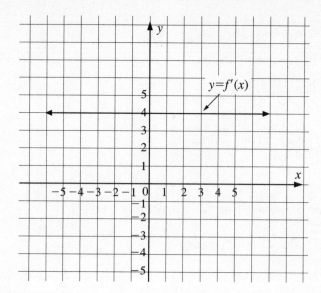

The graph of $y = f'(x)$ is shown above. If $f(0) = 5$, then $f(5) =$

(A) 5

(B) 10

(C) 15

(D) 20

(E) 25

9.

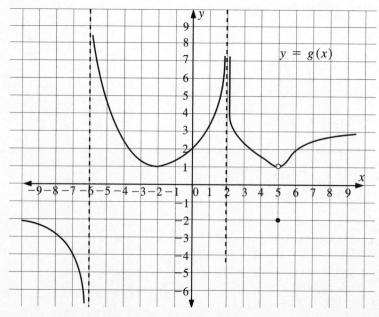

For the graph of g shown above, which of the following statements is NOT true for $g(x)$?

(A) $g(-6)$ is undefined.

(B) $\lim\limits_{x\to\infty} g(x) = 3.$

(C) $\lim\limits_{x\to-6} g(x)$ does not exist.

(D) $f(5) = 1.$

(E) $\lim\limits_{x\to5} g(x) = 1.$

10. If $y = -\dfrac{1}{\sqrt{x^2+1}}$, then $\dfrac{dy}{dx} =$

(A) $\dfrac{x}{\sqrt{x^2+1}}$

(B) $\dfrac{-x}{\sqrt{x^2+1}}$

(C) $\dfrac{-x}{(x^2+1)^{\frac{3}{2}}}$

(D) $\dfrac{x}{(x^2+1)^{\frac{3}{2}}}$

(E) $\dfrac{x}{x^2+1}$

11. If $f(x) = ae^{kx}$ and $\dfrac{f'(x)}{f(x)} = -\dfrac{5}{2}$, then $k =$

(A) -5

(B) $-\dfrac{5}{2}$

(C) $-\dfrac{2}{5}$

(D) $\dfrac{5}{2}$

(E) $\dfrac{2}{5}$

12.

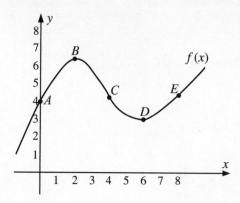

The graph of a function f with point C as an inflection point is shown above. Which of the following statements is true for the graph of g if $g(x) = 2 + f(x)$?

(A) $g(x)$ is concave down on the interval $(2, 6)$.

(B) $g(x)$ is concave up on the interval $(0, 8)$.

(C) $g(x)$ has an inflection point at $x = 5$.

(D) $g(x)$ is concave down on the interval $(0, 3)$.

(E) $g(x)$ is concave down on the interval $(0, 8)$.

13. The volume of a cube is increasing at a rate of 300 in³/min. At the instant when the edge is 20 inches, at what rate is the edge changing?

(A) $\dfrac{1}{4}$ in./min

(B) $\dfrac{1}{3}$ in./min

(C) $\dfrac{1}{2}$ in./min

(D) $\dfrac{3}{4}$ in./min

(E) 1 in./min.

14. If x and y are two positive numbers with a sum of 20, and their product is at a maximum, then which one of the following is true?

(A) $x = 15$ and $y = 5$

(B) $x = 12$ and $y = 8$

(C) $x = 8$ and $y = 12$

(D) $x = 12$ and $y = 10$

(E) $x = 10$ and $y = 10$

15.   If $\lim\limits_{n \to \infty} \dfrac{6n^2}{200 - 4n + kn^2} = \dfrac{1}{2}$, then $k =$

(A)   2

(B)   3

(C)   6

(D)   8

(E)   12

16.   Given the curve $4x^2 + 2xy - xy^3 = 3$, find the values of $\dfrac{dy}{dx}$ at the point $(1, -1)$.

(A)   5

(B)   6

(C)   7

(D)   9

(E)   11

17.

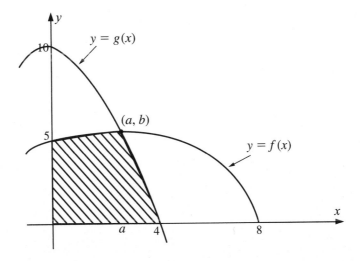

The curves $y = f(x)$ and $y = g(x)$, shown in the figure above, intersect at (a, b). The area of the shaded region, bounded by these curves and the coordinate axes, is given by which of the following?

(A) $\int_0^a (f(x) - g(x))\,dx$

(B) $\int_0^a (g(x) - f(x))\,dx$

(C) $\int_0^a f(x)\,dx - \int_a^4 g(x)\,dx$

(D) $\int_0^a f(x)\,dx + \int_a^4 g(x)\,dx$

(E) $\int_0^4 g(x)\,dx - \int_0^a f(x)\,dx$

18. Let $f(x) = \sqrt{x-1}$. Find all the values of x in the interval $(1, 5)$ guaranteed by the Mean Value Theorem.

   (A) 1 only

   (B) 2 only

   (C) 1 and 2

   (D) 1 and 4

   (E) 4 only

19. If $y = \ln[(x + 1)(x + 2)]$, then $\dfrac{dy}{dx} =$

   (A) $\dfrac{1}{x+1} + (x+2)$

   (B) $\dfrac{1}{x+2} + (x+1)$

   (C) $\dfrac{1}{(x+1)(x+2)}$

   (D) $\dfrac{x+1}{x+2}$

   (E) $\dfrac{1}{x+1} + \dfrac{1}{x+2}$

20.

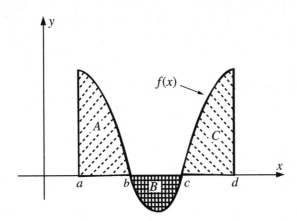

Given the graph of the continuous function f shown above, with:

area of region $A = 3$

area of region $B = 1\frac{1}{2}$

area of region $C = 2$,

Evaluate $\int_a^d f(x)\,dx$.

(A) $\dfrac{2}{5}$

(B) $\dfrac{5}{2}$

(C) $\dfrac{7}{2}$

(D) 5

(E) $\dfrac{13}{2}$

21. Find the equation of the tangent line to the curve $f(x) = \dfrac{\ln x}{e^x}$ at $x = 1$.

(A) $x - ey - 1 = 0$

(B) $x + ey - 1 = 0$

(C) $x - y - 1 = 0$

(D) $ex + y - 1 = 0$

(E) $ex - y - 1 = 0$

22. If $y = A \sin x + B \cos x$, then $y + \dfrac{d^2y}{dx^2} =$

(A) 0

(B) $(A + B) \sin x + (A + B) \cos x$

(C) $(A + B) \sin x - (A + B) \cos x$

(D) $AB \sin x + AB \cos x$

(E) $2 AB \sin x \cos x$

23. Which of the following are antiderivatives of $f(x) = \dfrac{2}{\sec x \csc x}$?

I. $\sin^2 x + C$

II. $-\cos^2 x + C$

III. $\dfrac{-\cos 2x}{2} + C$

(A) I only

(B) II only

(C) I and II only

(D) II and III only

(E) I, II, and III

24. Which of the following is a solution to the differential equation $\dfrac{dy}{dx} = y - 5$?

(A) $y = Ae^x + 5$

(B) $y = Ae^{-x} + 5$

(C) $y = Ae^{x+5}$

(D) $y = Ae^{-x+5}$

(E)　$y = \ln|x+5|$

25.　Data suggest that between the hours of 1:00 P.M. and 3:00 P.M. on Sunday, the speed of traffic along a street is approximately $s(t) = 3t^2 + 10t$ miles per hour, where t is the number of hours past noon. Compute the average speed of the traffic between the hours of 1:00 P.M. and 3.00 P.M.

(A)　22

(B)　33

(C)　44

(D)　66

(E)　70

26.　If the function f is even and $\int_0^a f(x)\,dx = 5m - 1$, then $\int_{-a}^a f(x) =$

(A)　0

(B)　$10m$

(C)　$10m - 1$

(D)　$10m - 2$

(E)　2

27.

x	3	4	5	6	7	8	9
$f(x)$	6	8	9	5	6	8	4

Use the data in the chart above to estimate $\int_4^8 f(x)\,dx$ by using the trapezoidal rule and four equal subintervals.

(A)　29

(B)　28

(C)　27

(D)　26

(E)　25

28.

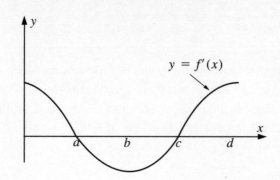

The graph above represents $y = f'(x)$. Which of the following could be the graph of $f(x)$?

(A)

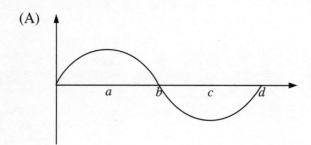

(B)

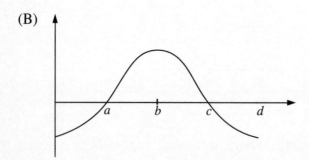

(C)

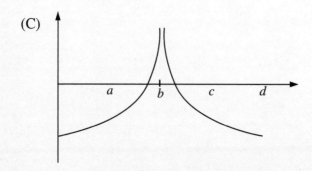

(D)

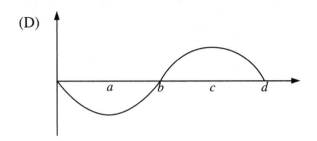

(E)

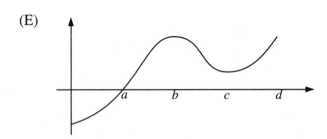

STOP
This is the end of Section I, Part A.
If time still remains, you may check your work only in this section.
Do not begin Section I, Part B until instructed to do so.

Section I

PART B

Time: 50 minutes
     17 questions

(Answer sheets appear in the back of this book.)

> **DIRECTIONS:** Solve each of the following problems, select the best answer choice and fill in the corresponding oval on the answer sheet.
>
> Calculators MAY be used for this section of the exam.

NOTES:

(1) The exact numerical value of the correct answer does not always appear among the choices given. When this happens, select the number from among the choices that best approximates the exact numerical value.

(2) Unless otherwise specified, the domain of a function f is assumed to be the set of all real numbers x for which $f(x)$ is a real number.

(3) The inverse of a trigonometric function f may be indicated by using the inverse function notation f^{-1} or with the prefix "arc" (e.g., $\sin^{-1} x = \arcsin x$).

76.   What is the rate of change of the area A of an equilateral triangle with respect to its side s when $s = 2$?

    (A)   0.43

    (B)   0.50

    (C)   0.87

    (D)   1.73

    (E)   7.00

77.   Find the volume of the solid of revolution generated when the region in the first quadrant enclosed by the graphs $x = y^2$ and $x = 2y$ is revolved about the y-axis.

    (A)   1.269

    (B)   4.114

(C) 4.189

(D) 8.378

(E) 13.404

78. $f(x) = (x^2 - 3)^{\frac{2}{3}}$ is increasing for which of the following interval(s)?

(A) $\left(-\sqrt{3}, \sqrt{3}\right)$

(B) $\left(-\infty, -\sqrt{3}\right)$ or $\left(\sqrt{3}, \infty\right)$

(C) $(-3, 3)$

(D) $\left(-\sqrt{3}, 0\right)$ or $\left(\sqrt{3}, \infty\right)$

(E) $f(x)$ is never increasing

79. What is the slope of the line normal to the graph $y = \dfrac{x^2}{\sqrt[3]{3x^2 + 1}}$ at $x = 1$?

(A) .945

(B) 1.06

(C) -1.06

(D) -2.11

(E) -3.17

80. If $3x\cos y = \sin(x + y)$, then $\dfrac{dy}{dx} =$

(A) $\dfrac{\cos(x + y) - 3x\sin y}{3\cos y - \cos(x + y)}$

(B) $\dfrac{3\cos y + \cos(x + y)}{\cos(x + y) - 3x\sin y}$

(C) $\dfrac{3\cos y + \cos(x + y)}{\cos(x + y) + 3x\sin y}$

(D) $\dfrac{3\cos y - \cos(x + y)}{\cos(x + y) + 3x\sin y}$

(E) $\dfrac{3\cos y - \cos(x + y)}{\cos(x + y) - 3x\sin y}$

81. $\lim\limits_{x\to\frac{3}{2}} \dfrac{8x^3 - 27}{2x - 3} =$

   (A) 1

   (B) 8

   (C) 27

   (D) 28

   (E) 36

82. Point A moves to the right along the positive x-axis at 7 units per second while point B moves upward along the negative y-axis at 2 units per second. At what rate is the distance between A and B changing when A is at $(8, 0)$ and B is at $(0, -6)$?

   (A) $-\dfrac{32}{5}$

   (B) $-\dfrac{22}{5}$

   (C) $\dfrac{22}{5}$

   (D) 5

   (E) $\dfrac{32}{5}$

83. A particle moves along the line $y = 2x + 7$. What is its minimum distance from the origin?

   (A) .32

   (B) 1.40

   (C) 2.80

   (D) 3.13

   (E) 3.50

84. The base of a solid is the region enclosed by the graph of $x = 1 - y^2$ and the y-axis. If all plane cross sections perpendicular to the x-axis are semicircles with diameters parallel to the y-axis, then the volume is:

   (A) $\dfrac{\pi}{8}$

   (B) $\dfrac{\pi}{4}$

(C) $\dfrac{\pi}{2}$

(D) $\dfrac{3\pi}{4}$

(E) $\dfrac{3\pi}{2}$

85. In $\triangle BCD$, let $\overline{BD} = c$ and $\overline{CD} = b$, where b and c are constants and $c > b$. Let angle $BDC = \alpha$. Find the instantaneous rate of change of the area of $\triangle BCD$ when $\alpha = \dfrac{\pi}{3}$ if angle α changes at a constant rate of 2 radians per second. (Note: side $\overline{BC}$ changes length as the measure of α changes.)

(A) $bc\sqrt{2}$

(B) $bc\sqrt{3}$

(C) $\dfrac{bc\sqrt{3}}{2}$

(D) $\dfrac{bc\sqrt{2}}{2}$

(E) $\dfrac{bc}{2}$

86. Suppose a particle moves on a straight line with a position function s such that its position at any time t is given by $s(t) = 3t^3 - 11t^2 + 8t$. In what interval of time is the particle moving to the left?

(A) $(-\infty, 0)$

(B) $(0, 1)$

(C) $\left(1, \dfrac{8}{3}\right)$

(D) $\left(\dfrac{4}{9}, 2\right)$

(E) $(2, \infty)$

87. The population growth P in a certain bacteria colony is best described by the equation $P(t) = t^2 e^{3t^2 + \sqrt{t}}$, where t is in hours. To the nearest integer, what is the rate of population growth at $t = 1$?

    (A) 246

    (B) 300

    (C) 409

    (D) 464

    (E) 546

88. The area bounded by the curve $y = 2\sin\frac{1}{2}x$, the x-axis, lines $x = 0$ and $x = k$ is 0.5. If $0 < k \le 2\pi$, what is the value of k?

    (A) 1.011

    (B) 1.375

    (C) 1.457

    (D) 1.869

    (E) 2.034

89. The acceleration a, in ft/sec^2, of a particle moving along the x-axis is given by the function $a(t) = e^{2t} + t^2 e^t$. What is the average acceleration from time $t = 1$ to $t = 4$?

    (A) 397.42

    (B) 590.43

    (C) 676.68

    (D) 928.61

    (E) 1281.47

90. I

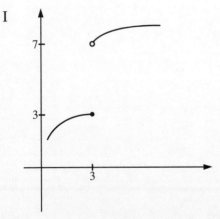

II

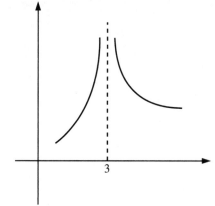

III

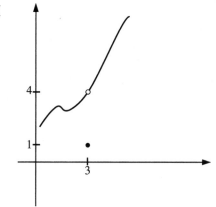

For which of the graphs above does $\lim\limits_{x\to 3} f(x)$ exist?

(A)   I only

(B)   II only

(C)   III only

(D)   I and III only

(E)   II and III only

91.   A particle moves along the *x*-axis so that at any time *t*, its position *s* is given by $s(t) = -2e^t - 3\sin t$, $(t \geq 0)$. What is the particle's acceleration when $t = 6$?

(A)   806.02

(B)   803.98

(C) -803.98

(D) -806.02

(E) -807.70

92.

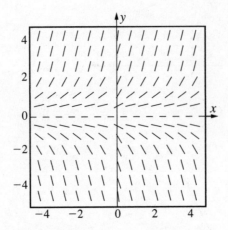

The slope field shown above is for which one of the following differential equations?

(A) $\dfrac{dy}{dx} = x$

(B) $\dfrac{dy}{dx} = y$

(C) $\dfrac{dy}{dx} = x^2$

(D) $\dfrac{dy}{dx} = y^2$

(E) $\dfrac{dy}{dx} = -x$

STOP
This is the end of Section I, Part
If time still remains, you may check your work only in this section.
Do not begin Section II, Part A until instructed to do so.

Section II

PART A

Time: 45 minutes
       3 free-response problems

DIRECTIONS: Show all your work in your exam booklet. Grading is based on the methods used to solve the problems as well as the accuracy of your final answers.

Calculators MAY be used for this section of the exam.

1.

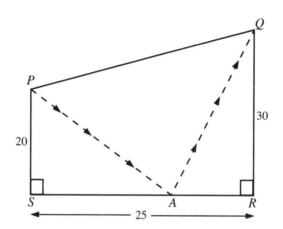

In trapezoid *PQRS* shown above, $\overline{PS} = 20$, $\overline{SR} = 25$, and $\overline{QR} = 30$. Point *A* is located on side $\overline{SR}$. What is the length of the shortest path from *P* to *A* to *Q*?

2.

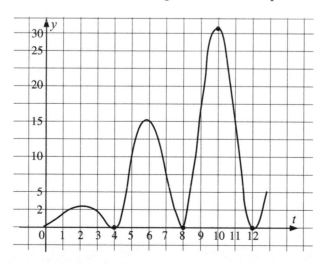

In each successive 4-year cycle of a flowering plant, the plant produces more foliage F than in its previous cycle. The amount of foliage (in pounds of leaves) can be expressed as $F(t) = t^{\frac{3}{2}} \sin^2\left(\dfrac{\pi t}{4}\right)$. The graph shown above depicts $y = F(t)$.

(a) To the nearest pound, how many pounds of leaves were produced during the interval $0 \le t \le 12$?

(b) What is the average number of pounds of leaves produced over the time interval $4 \le t \le 8$?

(c) Consider only the time period $0 \le t \le 12$. During the years when the plant produced at least 20 pounds of leaves, what was its average leaf production (in pounds of leaves)?

3.

A floodlight is on the ground 45 meters from a building. A thief 2 meters tall runs from the floodlight directly toward the building at 6 meters/sec. How rapidly is the length of his shadow on the building changing when he is 15 meters from the building? (See figure above.)

STOP
This is the end of Section II, Part A.
If time still remains, you may check your work only in this section.
Do not begin Section II, Part B until instructed to do so.

Section II

PART A

Time: 45 minutes
   3 free-response problems

DIRECTIONS: Show all your work in your exam booklet. Grading is based on the methods used to solve the problems as well as the accuracy of your final answers.

Calculators MAY NOT be used for this section of the exam.

(During the timed portion for Part B, you may continue to work on the problems in Part A without the use of a calculator.)

---

4.   Let the function g be the line tangent to $f(x) = \dfrac{2}{3}x^{\frac{3}{2}}$ at $x = x_0$. If $g(x) = cx + d$,

   (a)   Find the values of c and d if $x_0 = 2$.

   (b)   Find the values of x_0 and d if $c = 1$.

   (c)   Find the average value of $f(x)$ over the interval $0 \le x \le 3$.

5.   Let f be the function defined by $f(x) = 1 + \dfrac{1}{x} + \dfrac{1}{x^2}$.

   (a)   Determine the x and y intercepts, if any. Justify your answer.

   (b)   Write an equation for each vertical and each horizontal asymptote. Justify your answer.

   (c)   Determine the intervals on which f is increasing or decreasing. Justify your answer.

   (d)   Determine the relative minimum and maximum points, if any. Justify your answer.

   (e)   Determine the intervals on which f is concave up or concave down. Justify your answer.

   (f)   Determine any points of inflection.

6.   Consider the differential equation $\dfrac{dy}{dx} + \dfrac{y}{2} = 1$, and let $y = f(x)$ be a solution.

   (a)   On the axes provided, sketch a slope field at the 20 indicated points.

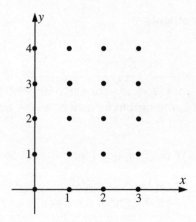

   (b)   Find the general solution $y = f(x)$.

   (c)   Find the particular solution to the differential equation with the initial condition $f(2 \ln 3) = 4$.

END OF EXAM

PRACTICE EXAM 4

AP Calculus AB

Answer Key

Part A		Part B
1. (E)	15. (E)	76. (D)
2. (E)	16. (C)	77. (E)
3. (B)	17. (D)	78. (D)
4. (E)	18. (B)	79. (C)
5. (A)	19. (E)	80. (D)
6. (A)	20. (C)	81. (C)
7. (B)	21. (A)	82. (C)
8. (E)	22. (A)	83. (D)
9. (D)	23. (E)	84. (B)
10. (D)	24. (A)	85. (E)
11. (B)	25. (B)	86. (D)
12. (D)	26. (D)	87. (D)
13. (A)	27. (B)	88. (A)
14. (E)	28. (A)	89. (C)
		90. (E)
		91. (E)
		92. (B)

Free-Response Answers

1.

$25\sqrt{5} \approx 55.902$

2.

(a) 99
(b) 7.389
(c) 27.689

3.

$-\dfrac{3}{5}$ m/sec

4.

(a) $c = \sqrt{2}, \quad d = \dfrac{-2\sqrt{2}}{3}$

(b) $x_0 = 1, \ d = -\dfrac{1}{3}$

(c) $\dfrac{4\sqrt{3}}{5}$

5.

(a) No x-intercepts
     No y-intercepts
(b) $x = 0, y = 1$
(c) decr. $(-\infty, -2)$ and $(0, \infty)$
     incr. $(-2, 0)$
(d) rel min: $(-2, \dfrac{3}{4})$,
     no rel max
(e) concave up: $(-3, 0)$ and
     $(0, \infty)$
     concave down:
     $(-\infty, -3)$
(f) $(-3, \dfrac{7}{9})$ inflection point

6.

(a) See detailed
     explanation

(b) $y = 2 - Ae^{-\frac{1}{2}x}$

(c) $y = 2 + 6e^{-\frac{1}{2}x}$

PRACTICE EXAM 4

AP Calculus AB

Detailed Explanations of Answers

Section 1

PART A

1. **(E)**

    Use

    $$\frac{d}{dx}[u^n] = nu^{n-1}\frac{d}{dx}[u]$$

    $$\frac{d}{dx}(x^5 - 7)^4 = 4(x^5 - 7)^3 \frac{d}{dx}(x^5 - 7)$$

    $$= 4(x^5 - 7)\cdot(5x^4)$$

    $$= \boxed{20x^4(x^5 - 7)^3}$$

2. **(E)**

    Step 1: Use $\int_a^b e^u du = e^u\Big|_a^b$

    Let $u = -3x$; then $du = -3dx$

    $$\int_1^5 3e^{-3x}dx = \int_1^5 e^{-3x}\cdot 3dx = -\int_1^5 e^{-3x}\cdot(-3dx) = -\int_{x=1}^5 e^u du$$

    $$= -e^u\Big|_{x=1}^5 = -e^{-3x}\Big|_1^5$$

    Step 2: Evaluate:

    $$-e^{-3x}\Big|_1^5 = -\left[e^{-3(5)} - e^{-3(1)}\right] = -\left[e^{-15} - e^{-3}\right] = \boxed{e^{-3} - e^{-15}}$$

3. **(B)**

Step 1: Try plugging in $x=2$ to see whether you get a numerical answer.

$$\frac{x-2}{\sqrt{x-2}} = \frac{2-2}{\sqrt{2-2}} = \frac{0}{0} \qquad \Rightarrow \qquad \text{this is an indeterminate form}$$

Step 2: Try rationalizing the denominator.

$$\lim_{x\to 2} \frac{(x-2)}{\sqrt{x-2}} \cdot \frac{\sqrt{x-2}}{\sqrt{x-2}} = \lim_{x\to 2} \frac{(x-2)\sqrt{x-2}}{(x-2)}$$

$$= \lim_{x\to 2} \sqrt{x-2} \qquad = \boxed{0}$$

4. **(E)**

Step 1: Use $\displaystyle\int_a^b \sec x \tan x \, dx = \sec x \Big|_a^b$

$$\int_0^{\frac{\pi}{3}} 3 \sec x \tan x \, dx = 3\int_0^{\frac{\pi}{3}} \sec x \tan x \, dx = 3 \sec x \Big|_0^{\frac{\pi}{3}}$$

Step 2: Evaluate:

$$3 \sec x \Big|_0^{\frac{\pi}{3}} = 3\left[\sec \frac{\pi}{3} - \sec 0 \right] = 3[2-1] = \boxed{3}$$

5. **(A)**

Step 1: Use the quotient rule: $\dfrac{d}{dx}\left(\dfrac{u}{v}\right) = \dfrac{v\dfrac{d(u)}{dx} - u\dfrac{d(v)}{dx}}{v^2}$

$$\frac{d}{dx}\left(\frac{\sin x}{x}\right) = \frac{x\dfrac{d}{dx}(\sin x) - (\sin x)\dfrac{d}{dx}(x)}{x^2}$$

Step 2: Since $\dfrac{d}{dx}(\sin x) = \cos x$ and $\dfrac{d}{dx}(x) = 1$,

$$\therefore \frac{d}{dx}\left(\frac{\sin x}{x}\right) = \frac{x(\cos x) - \sin x}{x^2} = \boxed{\frac{x\cos x - \sin x}{x^2}}$$

6. **(A)**

To be continuous at $x = 1$, the value of $4ax^3 + 7x$ at $x = 1$

should equal the value of $(a+2)x^4 - 4$ at $x = 1$.

$$4ax^3 + 7x\big|_{x=1} = (a+2)x^4 - 4\big|_{x=1}$$

$4a(1)^3 + 7(1) = (a+2)(1)^4 - 4$

$4a + 7 = a - 2$

$a = \boxed{-3}$

7. **(B)**

Use $\int \sec^2 u \ du = \tan u + C$

Let $u = x^6$ $\therefore du = 6x^5 dx$

Then

$$\int x^5 \sec^2(x^6)dx = \int \sec^2(x^6) \cdot x^5 dx = \frac{1}{6}\int \sec^2(x^6) \cdot 6x^5 dx$$

$$= \frac{1}{6}\int \sec^2 u \ du = \frac{1}{6}\tan u + C$$

$$= \boxed{\frac{1}{6}\tan(x^6) + C}$$

8. **(E)**

Step 1: From the graph, $f'(x) = 4$, which means the slope of $f(x)$ is constant and therefore $f(x)$ is linear.

Given $m =$ slope $= 4$ and the point $(0, 5)$,

the equation of f is $f(x) = 4x + 5$.

Step 2: $f(5) = 4(5) + 5 = \boxed{25}$

9. **(D)**

$f(5) = -2$, not 1, so statement $\boxed{(D)}$ is not true.

10. **(D)**

Step 1: Rewrite: $y = -\dfrac{1}{\sqrt{x^2+1}}$ as $y = -(x^2+1)^{-\frac{1}{2}}$

Step 2: Use $\dfrac{d}{dx}(u^n) = nu^{n-1}\dfrac{d(u)}{dx}$.

Let $u = (x^2+1)$ $\quad \therefore\ du = 2xdx$

$$\dfrac{dy}{dx} = -\left[-\dfrac{1}{2}(x^2+1)^{-\frac{3}{2}} \cdot (2x)\right] = \boxed{\dfrac{x}{(x^2+1)^{\frac{3}{2}}}}$$

11. **(B)**

Step 1: $f(x) = ae^{kx}$

Then $f'(x) = a\left[e^{kx} \cdot k\right] = kae^{kx}$

Step 2: Solve $\dfrac{f'(x)}{f(x)} = \dfrac{kae^{kx}}{ae^{kx}} = -\dfrac{5}{2}$ for k.

All the terms cancel except for k. Therefore, $k = \boxed{-\dfrac{5}{2}}$

12. **(D)**

The graph of $g(x) = 2 + f(x)$ is the same shape as $f(x)$. The only difference is a vertical shift upward of 2. In the graph of $g(x)$ below, A', B', C', D', and E' correspond to A, B, C, D, and E shifted upward by 2.

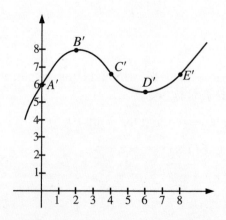

Only statement (D) is true. $\boxed{g(x)\text{ is concave down on the interval }(0, 3).}$

13. **(A)**

Step 1: Begin with $V=x^3$, where V represents the volume of a cube with edge x.

$$V=x^3$$

$$\frac{dV}{dt} = 3x^2 \frac{dx}{dt}$$

Step 2: Given $\frac{dV}{dt} = 300$, $x=20$, find $\frac{dx}{dt}$.

$$300 = 3(20)^2 \frac{dx}{dt}$$

$$\frac{dx}{dt} = \boxed{\frac{1}{4} \text{ in. / min}}$$

14. **(E)**

Step 1: Express the product of x and y in terms of a single variable.

$$P = xy \text{ with } y = 20 - x$$
$$\therefore P = x(20-x) = -x^2 + 20x$$

Step 2: To maximize the product, set its derivative to zero and solve for x.

$$p(x) = -x^2 + 20x$$
$$p'(x) = -2x + 20 = 0$$
$$\therefore x = 10 \quad \Rightarrow \quad y = 10$$

Step 3: To confirm that $x=10$ gives a maximum and not a minimum, use the second derivative test.

$$p''(x) = -2$$
$$p''(10) = -2$$

since $p''(10)$ is negative, $x = 10$ is a maximum.

$$\boxed{x = 10 \text{ and } y = 10}$$

15. **(E)**

Step 1: In a limit problem with $x \to \infty$ only the highest powered polynomial term in the numerator and the highest powered polynomial term in the denominator are significant.

$$\therefore\ \lim_{n\to\infty}\frac{6n^2}{200-4n+kn^2}=\lim_{n\to\infty}\frac{6n^2}{kn^2}$$

The n^2 cancels.

$$\therefore\ \lim_{n\to\infty}\frac{6n^2}{kn^2}=\frac{6}{k}$$

Step 2: $\dfrac{6}{k}=\dfrac{1}{2}$

$$k=\boxed{12}$$

16. **(C)**

Step 1: Do implicit differentiation. Note that xy and xy^3 are products.

$$4x^2+2xy-xy^3=3$$

$$8x+2\left[x\frac{d(y)}{dx}+y(1)\right]-\left[x\frac{d(y^3)}{dx}+y^3(1)\right]=0$$

$$8x+2\left[x\frac{dy}{dx}+y\right]-\left[x\left(3y^2\frac{dy}{dx}\right)+y^3\right]=0$$

Step 2: Let $x=1$, $y=-1$ and solve for $\dfrac{dy}{dx}$.

$$8(1)+2\left[1\frac{dy}{dx}-1\right]-\left[1\left(3\frac{dy}{dx}\right)-1\right]=0$$

$$\frac{dy}{dx}=\boxed{7}$$

17. **(D)**

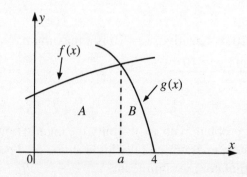

The shaded area consists of two sections, A and B.

$$A = \int_0^a f(x)\,dx \text{ and } B = \int_a^4 g(x)\,dx$$

$\therefore$ Shaded area $= \boxed{\int_0^a f(x)\,dx + \int_a^4 g(x)\,dx}$

18. **(B)**

Step 1: The MVT applies because $f(x) = \sqrt{x-1}$ is continuous on the interval $[1, 5]$ and differentiable on the open interval $(1, 5)$.

The MVT states that there exists at least one number c in $(1, 5)$ such that

$$f'(c) = \frac{f(5) - f(1)}{5 - 1}.$$

Step 2: Calculate $f'(x)$.

$$f(x) = (x-1)^{\frac{1}{2}}$$
$$f'(x) = \frac{1}{2}(x-1)^{-\frac{1}{2}}(1) = \frac{1}{2\sqrt{x-1}}$$
$$f'(c) = \frac{1}{2\sqrt{c-1}}$$

Find $f(5)$: $f(5) = \sqrt{5-1} = 2$

 $f(1)$: $f(1) = \sqrt{1-1} = 0$

Step 3: Employ the MVT and solve for c.

$$f'(c) = \frac{f(5) - f(1)}{5 - 1}$$
$$\frac{1}{2\sqrt{c-1}} = \frac{2-0}{4} = \frac{1}{2}$$
$$\therefore c = \boxed{2} \text{ only.}$$

19. **(E)**

Step 1: Use the log rule: $\ln(ab) = \ln a + \ln b$

$\ln[(x+1) \cdot (x+2)] = \ln(x+1) + \ln(x+2)$

Step 2: Use $\dfrac{d}{dx}(\ln u) = \dfrac{1}{u}\dfrac{d(u)}{dx}$

$$y = \ln(x+1) + \ln(x+2)$$

$$\therefore \frac{dy}{dx} = \boxed{\frac{1}{x+1} + \frac{1}{x+2}}$$

20. **(C)**

Step 1: Areas above the x-axis are signed positive.

Areas below the x-axis are signed negative.

$$\therefore \text{ area } A = +3$$

$$\text{area } B = -1\frac{1}{2}$$

$$\text{area } C = +2$$

Step 2: $\displaystyle\int_a^d f(x)\,dx = $ Sum of the signed areas $A + B + C$

$$= 3 + \left(-1\frac{1}{2}\right) + 2 = 3\frac{1}{2} = \boxed{\frac{7}{2}}$$

21. **(A)**

Step 1: Find $f(1)$.

$$f(1) = \frac{\ln 1}{e^1} = \frac{0}{e} = 0 \text{, so point of tangency is } (1, 0).$$

Step 2: Find $f'(1)$.

Note: It's probably easier to turn the quotient into a product before differentiating. Then use the product rule:

$$f(x) = \frac{\ln x}{e^x} = e^{-x} \cdot \ln x$$

$$f'(x) = e^{-x}\frac{d}{dx}(\ln x) + \ln x \frac{d}{dx}(e^x)$$

$$= e^{-x}\left(\frac{1}{x}\right) + \ln x(e^x)$$

$$f'(1) = e^{-1}(1) + \ln(1) \cdot e^1$$

$$= e^{-1} = \frac{1}{e}$$

Step 3: Write the equation of a line: $y - y_1 = m(x - x_1)$

with slope $m = \dfrac{1}{e}$ through the point $(1, 0)$.

$$y - 0 = \frac{1}{e}(x - 1)$$

$$y = \frac{1}{e}(x - 1) \Rightarrow \boxed{x - ey - 1 = 0}$$

22. (A)

Step 1: Find $\dfrac{dy}{dx}$, then $\dfrac{d^2y}{dx^2}$.

$$y = A \sin x + B \cos x$$

$$\frac{dy}{dx} = A(\cos x) + B(-\sin x)$$

$$= A(\cos x) - B \sin x$$

$$\frac{d^2y}{dx^2} = A(-\sin x) - B(\cos x)$$

$$= -A \sin x - B \cos x$$

Step 2: Evaluate: $y + \dfrac{d^2y}{dx}$:

$$(A \sin x + B \cos x) + (-A \sin x - B \cos x) = \boxed{0}$$

23. (E)

Step 1: Use the identities $\sin x = \dfrac{1}{\csc x}$ and $\cos x = \dfrac{1}{\sec x}$ to rewrite the given trigonometric function.

$$f(x) = \frac{2}{\sec x \csc x} = 2 \sin x \cos x$$

Step 2: Integrate (method 1): Let $u = \sin x$ and $du = \cos x \, dx$.

$$\int 2 \sin x \cos x \, dx = 2 \int (\sin x)(\cos x \, dx) = 2 \int u \, du = \frac{2u^2}{2} + C$$

$$= \sin^2 x + C \quad \text{(Choice I)}$$

Step 3: Integrate (method 2): Let $u = \cos x$ and $du = -\sin x\, dx$.

$$\int 2\sin x \cos x = 2\int (\cos x)(\sin x\, dx) = -2\int (\cos x)(-\sin x\, dx)$$

$$= -2\int u\, du = \frac{-2u^2}{2} = -\cos^2 x\ + C\ \text{(Choice II)}$$

Step 4: Integrate (method 3): Use the identity $2\sin x \cos x = \sin 2x$.

Then $\int 2\sin x \cos x\, dx = \int \sin 2x\, dx$.

Let $u = 2x,\ du = 2dx$

$$\int \sin 2x\, dx = \frac{1}{2}\int \sin 2x \cdot 2dx = \frac{1}{2}\int \sin u\, du$$

$$= \frac{1}{2}(-\cos u) + C = -\frac{1}{2}(\cos 2x) + C$$

$$\boxed{\text{I, II, and III}}$$

$\therefore$ All three are correct.

---

24. (A)

Step 1: Separate the variables.

$$\frac{dy}{dx} = y - 5 \quad \Rightarrow \quad \frac{dy}{y-5} = dx$$

Step 2: Integrate both sides.

$$\int \frac{dy}{y-5} = \int dx$$
$$\ln|y-5| = x + C$$

Step 3: Put into exponential form.

$$y - 5 = e^{x+C} = e^x \cdot e^C$$

Let $A = e^C$.

$$\therefore \boxed{y = Ae^x + 5}$$

---

25. (B)

$$\text{Average value} = \frac{1}{b-a}\int_a^b f(x)\, dx$$

$$\therefore \text{ Average speed} = \frac{1}{3-1}\int_1^3 (3t^2 + 10t)\,dt$$

$$= \frac{1}{2}(t^3 + 5t^2)\Big|_1^3$$

$$= \boxed{33}$$

26. **(D)**

An even function is symmetric with respect to the *y*-axis. This means the area to the right of the *y*-axis equals the corresponding area to the left of the *y*-axis, as shown in the figure below.

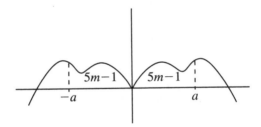

Therefore, $\displaystyle\int_{-a}^{a} f(x)\,dx = 2\int_0^a f(x)\,dx = 2(5m-1)$

$$= \boxed{10m - 2}$$

27. **(B)**

The trapezoidal rule states

$$\int_a^b f(x)\,dx \approx \frac{b-a}{2n}\Big[f(x_0) + 2f(x_1) + 2f(x_2)\ldots 2f(x_{n-1}) + f(x_n)\Big]$$

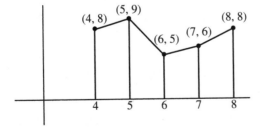

A sketch of the problem shows that $b = 8$, $a = 4$, $n = 4$ intervals, and that

$$\int_4^8 f(x)\,dx = \frac{8-4}{2(4)}\left[f(4)+2f(5)+2f(6)+2f(7)+f(8)\right]$$

$$= \frac{1}{2}\left[8+2(9)+2(5)+2(6)+8\right]$$

$$= \frac{1}{2}[56] = \boxed{28}$$

28. **(A)**

Step 1: Convert the $f'(x)$ graphical information to a number line.

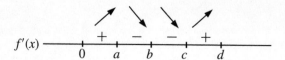

Step 2: This shows that $f(x)$ increases from 0 to a, decreases from a to b, and there is a relative maximum at $x = a$.

Also, $f(x)$ decreases from b to c, increases from c to d, and there is a relative minimum point at $x = c$.

Only graph $\boxed{A}$ exhibits all of these characteristics.

Note: $y = f'(x)$ resembles a cosine graph; therefore, $f(x)$ should resemble a sine graph.

Section I

PART B

76. **(D)**

   Step 1: The area of an equilateral triangle of side s is

   $$A = \frac{s^2}{4}\sqrt{3} = \frac{\sqrt{3}}{4}s^2.$$

   Step 2: Differentiate with respect to s.

   $$\frac{d(A)}{ds} = \frac{\sqrt{3}}{4}(2s)$$
   $$= \frac{\sqrt{3}}{2}s$$

   Step 3: When $s=2$, $\dfrac{dA}{ds} = \sqrt{3} = \boxed{1.73}$

77. **(E)**

   Step 1: Make a sketch.

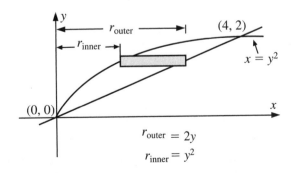

$$r_{outer} = 2y$$
$$r_{inner} = y^2$$

Step 2: Find where the graphs intersect.

$$2y = y^2$$

$$y^2 - 2y = 0$$

$$y(y-2) = 0$$

The graphs intersect at $(0, 0)$ and $(4, 2)$.

Step 3: Using the "washer" method,

$$V = \pi \int_a^b (r_{outer}^2 - r_{inner}^2) \, dy$$

$$= \pi \int_0^2 [(2y)^2 - (y^2)^2] \, dy$$

$$= \pi \left[\frac{4y^3}{3} - \frac{y^5}{5} \right]_0^2 = \frac{64\pi}{15} = \boxed{13.404}$$

78. **(D)**

Step 1: Find $f'(x)$ by using $\dfrac{d}{dx}(u^n) = nu^{n-1}\dfrac{d(u)}{dx}$.

$$f(x) = (x^2 - 3)^{\frac{2}{3}}$$

$$f'(x) = \frac{2}{3}(x^2 - 3)^{-\frac{1}{3}}(2x)$$

$$= \frac{4x}{3\sqrt[3]{x^2 - 3}}$$

Step 2: Find the critical values:

- where $f'(x) = 0$

- where $f(x)$ is not differentiable

$$f'(x) = \frac{4x}{3\sqrt[3]{x^2 - 3}} = 0 \quad \Rightarrow \quad x = 0.$$

$f(x)$ is not differentiable when $x = \pm\sqrt{3}$.

Step 3: Do a number line analysis of $f'(x)$.

$f(x)$ is increasing $\boxed{(-\sqrt{3}, 0) \text{ or } (\sqrt{3}, \infty)}$

79. (C)

Step 1: Use the quotient rule to find $y'(x)$.

$$y(x) = \frac{x^2}{\sqrt[3]{3x^2+1}}$$

$$\therefore\ y'(x) = \frac{(\sqrt[3]{3x^2+1})(2x) - (x^2)\left(\frac{1}{3}(3x^2+1)^{-\frac{2}{3}}\right)(6x)}{(\sqrt[3]{3x^2+1})^2}$$

Step 2: Find $y'(1) = \dfrac{(\sqrt[3]{4}\cdot 2) - (1)\left(\frac{1}{3}\right)(4)^{-\frac{2}{3}}(6)}{(\sqrt[3]{4})^2}$

$$= .945$$

This is the slope of the tangent line at $x = 1$.

Step 3: The slope of the normal line is the negative reciprocal of the tangent line slope, or

$$-\frac{1}{.945} = \boxed{-1.06}.$$

80. (D)

$$3\,x \cos y = \sin(x+y)$$

Step 1: Use implicit differentiation to find $\dfrac{dy}{dx}$. Note that $x \cos y$ is a product.

$$3x\frac{d}{dx}(\cos y) + \cos y\frac{d}{dx}(3x) = \frac{d}{dx}(\sin(x+y))$$

$$3x\left(-\sin y\frac{dy}{dx}\right) + (\cos y)(3) = \cos(x+y)\frac{d}{dx}[x+y]$$

$$-3x\sin y\frac{dy}{dx} + 3\cos y = \cos(x+y)\left[1 + \frac{dy}{dx}\right]$$

Step 2: Solve for $\dfrac{dy}{dx}$.

$$\frac{dy}{dx} = \boxed{\frac{3\cos y - \cos(x+y)}{\cos(x+y) + 3x\sin y}}$$

81. **(C)**

   Step 1: Replace x with $\dfrac{3}{2}$ and see if the limit gives a value.

$$\lim_{x \to \frac{3}{2}} \frac{8x^3 - 27}{2x - 3} \cdot$$

$$\frac{8\left(\dfrac{3}{2}\right)^3 - 27}{2\left(\dfrac{3}{2}\right) - 3} = \frac{0}{0} \quad \Rightarrow \quad \text{this is an indeterminate form.}$$

   Step 2: Try factoring. Recall that $a^3 - b^3 = (a - b)(a^2 + ab + b^2)$.

$$\therefore \ \lim_{x \to \frac{3}{2}} \frac{8x^3 - 27}{2x - 3} = \lim_{x \to \frac{3}{2}} \frac{(2x - 3)(4x^2 + 6x + 9)}{(2x - 3)}$$

$$= \lim_{x \to \frac{3}{2}} 4x^2 + 6x + 9 = \boxed{27}$$

82. **(C)**

   Step 1: A sketch would be useful.

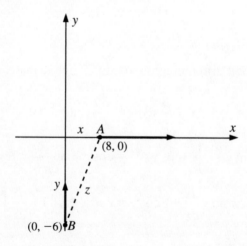

   Step 2: Express the geometric relationship (Pythagorean Theorem).

$$x^2 + y^2 = z^2$$

Given $\dfrac{dx}{dt} = 7$ and $\dfrac{dy}{dt} = -2$, find $\dfrac{dz}{dt}$ when $x = 8$, $y = 6$, and $z = 10$.

Step 3: Write the rate equation and solve for $\dfrac{dz}{dt}$.

$$2x\frac{dx}{dt} + 2y\frac{dy}{dt} = 2z\frac{dz}{dt}$$

Divide by 2, substitute and solve for $\dfrac{dz}{dt}$.

$$x\frac{dx}{dt} + y\frac{dy}{dt} = z\frac{dz}{dt}$$

$$8(7) + 6(-2) = 10\frac{dz}{dt}$$

$$\frac{dz}{dt} = \boxed{\frac{22}{5}}$$

83. **(D)**

Step 1: A quick sketch is helpful.

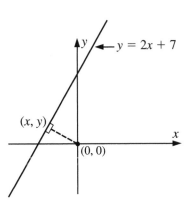

Refer to the point on the line that satisfies the requirement as (x, y).

Step 2: Write an expression for the distance d from (x, y) to $(0, 0)$.

$$d = \sqrt{(x-0)^2 + (y-0)^2}$$
$$= \sqrt{x^2 + y^2}$$

Step 3: Replace y with $2x+7$ so that d becomes a function of a single variable.

$$d(x) = \sqrt{x^2 + (2x+7)^2}$$

Step 4: In problems involving distance, by minimizing the *square* of the distance function, the solution is the same but the function is easier to deal with (no square roots). Call the square of the distance function $s(x)$.

$$\therefore s(x) = x^2 + (2x + 7)^2$$

Step 5: To minimize $s(x)$, set $s'(x) = 0$ and solve for x.

$$s'(x) = 2x + 2(2x + 7)(2) = 0$$

$$x = \frac{-14}{5} = -2.8$$

Step 6: Calculate d when $x = -2.8$. The use of a calculator is helpful.

$$d = \sqrt{(-2.8)^2 + (-5.6 + 7)^2} = \boxed{3.13}$$

84. **(B)**

Step 1: A graph will prove helpful.

Step 2: The radius r of each semicircle is y.

$$\therefore r = y$$

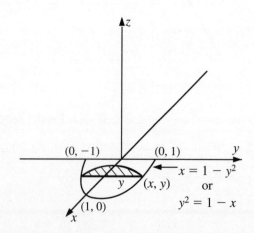

The volume of each semicircular slice is

$$\frac{1}{2}\pi r^2\, dx$$

$$=\frac{1}{2}\pi y^2\, dx$$

$$=\frac{1}{2}\pi(1-x)\, dx$$

Step 3: Add all the semicircular slices from $x = 0$ to $x = 1$ to get the total volume.

$$\text{Volume} = \int_0^1 \frac{1}{2}\pi(1-x)\, dx$$

Step 4: Evaluate the integral.

$$\text{Volume} = \frac{1}{2}\pi\int_0^1 (1-x)\, dx = \boxed{\dfrac{\pi}{4}}$$

85. **(E)**

Step 1: Draw a diagram.

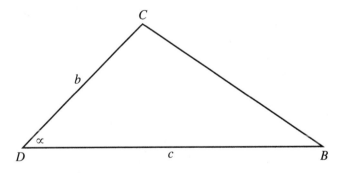

Step 2: $\text{Area} = A = \dfrac{1}{2}bc\sin\alpha$

Step 3: Create a rate equation.

$$\frac{d}{dt}(A) = \frac{1}{2}bc\frac{d}{dt}(\sin\alpha)$$

$$\frac{dA}{dt} = \frac{1}{2}bc\cos\alpha\frac{d\alpha}{dt}$$

Step 4: Find $\dfrac{dA}{dt}$ when $\dfrac{d\alpha}{dt} = 2$ and $\alpha = \dfrac{\pi}{3}$.

$$\frac{dA}{dt} = \frac{1}{2}bc\left(\cos\frac{\pi}{3}\right)(2) = \boxed{\frac{bc}{2}}$$

86. **(D)**

Step 1: The particle is moving to the left when $v(t) < 0$.

$$v(t) = s'(t) = 9t^2 - 22t + 8$$

$$= (9t - 4)(t - 2)$$

Step 2 Find the critical values by setting $v(t) = 0$ and solving for t.

$$v(t) = (9t - 4)(t - 2) = 0$$
$$t = \frac{4}{9} \ \bigg| \ t = 2$$

Step 3: Evaluate $v(t)$ across a number line.

$$\therefore v(t) < 0 \text{ on the interval } \boxed{\left(\frac{4}{9}, 2\right)}$$

87. **(D)**

Step 1: The growth rate of P is represented by $\dfrac{dP}{dt}$. Note that $P(t)$ is a product.

$$\frac{dP}{dt} = t^2 \frac{d}{dt}\left(e^{3t^2 + t^{\frac{1}{2}}}\right) + e^{3t^2 + t^{\frac{1}{2}}} \frac{d}{dt}(t^2)$$

$$= t^2\left[e^{3t^2 + t^{\frac{1}{2}}} \cdot \left(6t + \frac{1}{2}t^{-\frac{1}{2}}\right)\right] + e^{3t^2 + t^{\frac{1}{2}}} \cdot (2t)$$

Step 2: Evaluate $\dfrac{dP}{dt}\bigg|_{t=1}$

$$= 1 \left[e^{3+1} \cdot \left(6 + \frac{1}{2} \right) \right] + e^{3+1} \cdot (2) = \frac{13}{2} (e^4) + 2e^4$$

$$= \boxed{464}$$

Note: The use of a calculator for the derivative function is strongly recommended.

88. **(A)**

Step 1: A sketch is useful.

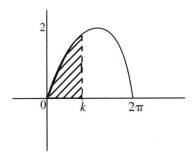

Step 2: Area $= \displaystyle\int_0^k 2\sin\frac{1}{2}x\,dx$

Integrate: let $u = \dfrac{1}{2}x$ and $du = \dfrac{1}{2}dx$.

$$\int_0^k 2\sin\frac{1}{2}x\,dx = 2\cdot 2\int_0^k \left(\sin\frac{1}{2}x\right)\left(\frac{1}{2}dx\right) = 4\int_{x=0}^k \sin u\,du = -4\cos\left(\frac{1}{2}x\right)\Big|_0^k$$

Step 3: Set the integral equal to 0.5 and solve for k.

$$-4\cos\left(\frac{1}{2}x\right)\Big|_0^k = .5$$

$$-4\left[\cos\frac{k}{2} - \cos 0\right] = .5$$

$$\cos\frac{k}{2} = \frac{7}{8}$$

$$\frac{k}{2} = \cos^{-1}\frac{7}{8} = .50536$$

$$\therefore k = \boxed{1.011}$$

Note: A calculator solution is advised.

89. **(C)**

   Step 1: The average value of $a(t)$ from $t = 1$ to $t = 4$

   $$= \frac{1}{4-1} \int_1^4 a(t)\, dt$$

   Step 2: Average $= \frac{1}{3} \int_1^4 (e^{2t} + t^2 e^t)\, dt$

   Step 3: Use a calculator function to evaluate the integral.

   Average acceleration $= \boxed{676.68}$

90. **(E)**

   Step 1: I $\lim_{x \to 3^-} f(x) = 3, \quad \lim_{x \to 3^+} f(x) = 7$

   $\therefore \lim_{x \to 3} f(x)$ DOES NOT EXIST

   Step 2: II $\lim_{x \to 3^-} f(x) = \infty, \quad \lim_{x \to 3^+} f(x) = \infty$

   $\therefore \lim_{x \to 3} f(x) = \infty$

   Step 3: III $\lim_{x \to 3^-} f(x) = 4, \quad \lim_{x \to 3^+} f(x) = 4$

   $\therefore \lim_{x \to 3} f(x) = 4$

   so $\lim_{x \to 3} f(x)$ exists for $\boxed{\text{II and III only}}$.

91. **(E)**

   Step 1: Acceleration is the second derivative of position:
   $$s(t) = -2e^t - 3\sin t$$
   $$v(t) = \frac{d(s)}{dt} = -2e^t - 3\cos t$$
   $$a(t) = \frac{d^2 s}{dt^2} = -2e^t + 3\sin t$$

   Step 2: Evaluate $a(6)$.

   $$a(6) = -2e^t + 3\sin t \big|_{t=6} = \boxed{-807.70}$$

92. **(B)**

Step 1: The slope field has horizontal tangents at $y = 0$ $\therefore \dfrac{dy}{dx} = 0$ when $y = 0$, which eliminates choices A, C, and E.

Step 2: At $y = -1$:

choice B indicates $\dfrac{dy}{dx} = -1$

choice D indicates $\dfrac{dy}{dx} = 1$

The slope field shows a negatively sloped line at $y = -1$, so choice D is eliminated.

Therefore, choice B, $\boxed{\dfrac{dy}{dx} = y}$ is the differential equation for the given slope field.

Section II

PART A

1. Use of a calculator is advised.

   Step 1: Write an expression for the length of the path from P to A to Q.

   Let $\overline{SA} = x$ (see figure below).

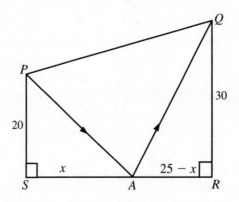

   By the Pythagorean Theorem,

   $$f(x) = \overline{PA} + \overline{AQ} = \sqrt{20^2 + x^2} + \sqrt{(25 - x)^2 + 30^2}$$

   Step 2: Differentiate $f(x)$

   $$f'(x) = \frac{x}{\sqrt{400 + x^2}} + \frac{x - 25}{\sqrt{900 + (25 - x)^2}}$$

   Step 3: Set $f'(x) = 0$ to find critical points, and solve for x.

   $x = 10$ and $x = -50$

   $\therefore x = 10$

   Step 4: Confirm that $x = 10$ is a minimum by using the first derivative test.

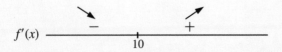

Step 5: Calculate $\overline{PA} + \overline{AQ}$ with $x=10$.

$$\overline{PA} + \overline{AQ} = \sqrt{500} + \sqrt{1125} = \boxed{25\sqrt{5} \approx 55.902}$$

2. A calculator is required for this problem.

Step 1: The total number of pounds of leaves produced is

$$F(t) = \int_0^{12} t^{\frac{3}{2}} \sin^2\left(\frac{\pi t}{4}\right) dt$$

(a) $\quad = 98.86 \Rightarrow \boxed{99}$

Step 2: Average $= \dfrac{1}{8-4} \displaystyle\int_4^8 t^{\frac{3}{2}} \sin^2\left(\frac{\pi t}{4}\right) dt$

(b) $\quad = \boxed{7.389}$

Step 3: First, find the times in the interval $0 \le t \le 12$ when $F(t)=20$.

$$t^{\frac{3}{2}} \sin^2\left(\frac{\pi t}{4}\right) = 20$$

$t = 9.273$ and $t = 10.932$

$$\text{Average} = \frac{1}{10.932 - 9.273} \int_{9.273}^{10.932} t^{\frac{3}{2}} \sin^2\left(\frac{\pi t}{4}\right) dt$$

(c) $\quad = \boxed{27.689}$

3.

Step 1: Draw a diagram.

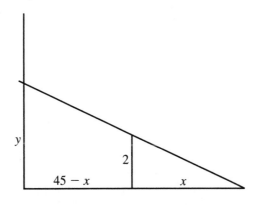

Step 2: Use similar triangles to create a proportion.

$$\frac{y}{2} = \frac{45}{x} \quad \Rightarrow \quad y = \frac{90}{x} = 90x^{-1}$$

Step 3: Create a rate equation.

$$\frac{dy}{dt} = -90x^{-2}\frac{dx}{dt} = -\frac{90}{x^2}\frac{dx}{dt}$$

Step 4: Solve for $\dfrac{dy}{dt}$ with $x = 30$ because the thief is 15 m from the wall.

$$\frac{dx}{dt} = 6 \text{ meters/sec, as given in the problem.}$$

$$\therefore \frac{dy}{dt} = -\frac{90}{(30)^2}(6) = \boxed{-\frac{3}{5} \text{ m/sec}}$$

Section II

PART B

4.

Step 1: Given $f(x) = \frac{2}{3}x^{\frac{3}{2}}$ and $g(x) = cx + d$,

at the point of tangency: $f(x) = g(x)$ and $f'(x) = g'(x)$.

Step 2: If the tangency occurs when $x = 2$:

(a) • $f(2) = g(2) \Rightarrow \frac{2}{3}(2)^{\frac{3}{2}} = c(2) + d$

• $f'(2) = g'(2) \Rightarrow x^{\frac{1}{2}} = c \Rightarrow 2^{\frac{1}{2}} = c$

$$\therefore \boxed{c = \sqrt{2},\, d = \frac{-2\sqrt{2}}{3}}$$

Step 3: If $c=1$, then $g(x)= x+d$.

At the point of tangency:

(b) • $f(x)=g(x) \Rightarrow \frac{2}{3}x^{\frac{3}{2}} = x+d$

• $f'(x)=g'(x) \Rightarrow x^{\frac{1}{2}} = 1$

$$\therefore \boxed{x_0 = 1,\, d = -\frac{1}{3}}$$

Step 4: The average value over the interval $0 \leq x \leq 3$ is

(c)   Average $= \frac{1}{3-0}\int_0^3 \frac{2}{3}x^{\frac{3}{2}}\, dx = \frac{1}{3}\cdot\frac{2}{3}\left[\frac{2}{5}x^{\frac{5}{2}}\right]_0^3$

$$= \boxed{\frac{4\sqrt{3}}{5}}$$

5.

Step 1: Write $f(x)$ in different forms.

$$f(x) = 1 + \frac{1}{x} + \frac{1}{x^2} = \frac{x^2 + x + 1}{x^2} = 1 + x^{-1} + x^{-2}$$

Step 2: To find the x-intercept(s), set the numerator equal to zero.

$x^2 + x + 1 = 0$

(a) This has no real solutions $\therefore$ There are no x-intercepts.

Step 3: To find the y-intercept, set $x = 0$ and solve for y.

$$f(x) = y = \frac{0^2 + 0 + 1}{0^2}; \text{ this is undefined.}$$

(a) $\therefore$ There is no y-intercept.

Step 4: To find the vertical asymptote, set the denominator equal to zero.

$x^2 = 0$

(b) $\therefore$ $x = 0$ is a vertical asymptote.

Step 5: To find the horizontal asymptote(s), take the limit of $f(x)$ as x goes to ∞.

$$\lim_{x \to \infty} 1 + \frac{1}{x} + \frac{1}{x^2} = 1$$

(c) $\therefore$ $y = 1$ is a horizontal asymptote.

Step 6: To determine the critical values, analyze the first derivative.

$$f(x) = 1 + x^{-1} + x^{-2} = \frac{x^2 + x + 1}{x^2}$$

$$f'(x) = -x^{-2} - 2x^{-3} = -\left(\frac{x + 2}{x^3} \right)$$

The function is undefined at $x = 0$. (It has a vertical asymptote.)

The first derivative is zero at $x = -2$.

See the sketch of $f'(x)$.

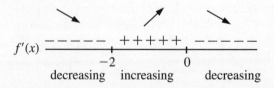

The first derivative analysis indicates a relative minimum point at $x = -2$.

$$f(x) = 1 + (-2)^{-1} + (-2)^{-2} = 1 - \frac{1}{2} + \frac{1}{4} = \frac{3}{4}.$$

(c) | $f(x)$ is decreasing for $(-\infty, -2)$ and $(0, \infty)$.
 $f(x)$ is increasing for $(-2, 0)$. (See the sketch.)

(d) | $\left(-2, \dfrac{3}{4}\right)$ is a relative minimum point.

(e) | There is no relative maximum point <br> because the function is undefined at $x = 0$.

Step 7: For concavity and points of inflection, analyze the second derivative.

$$f''(x) = \frac{2(x+3)}{x^4}$$

The function $f(x)$ is undefined at $x = 0$.

$f''(x) = 0$ at $x = -3$.

See the sketch of $f''(x)$.

The second derivative analysis indicates a point of inflection at $x = -3$.

$$f(x) = 1 + \frac{1}{(-3)} + \frac{1}{(-3)^2} = 1 + \frac{1}{3} + \frac{1}{9} = \frac{7}{9}$$

$$f''(x) \underset{\substack{-3 \\ \text{concave} \\ \text{down}}}{\underline{\quad----- \quad}} \underset{\substack{0 \\ \text{concave} \\ \text{up}}}{\underline{\quad+++++ \quad}} \overset{\substack{+++++ \\ \text{concave} \\ \text{up}}}{}$$

(f) | $f(x)$ is concave down for $(-\infty, -3)$.
 $f(x)$ is concave up for $(-3, 0)$ and $(0, \infty)$.

(g) | $\left(-3, \dfrac{7}{9}\right)$ is an inflection point.

6.

Step 1: Rewrite the differential equation.

$$\frac{dy}{dx} + \frac{y}{2} = 1 \quad \Rightarrow \quad \frac{dy}{dx} = 1 - \frac{y}{2}, \text{ or } \frac{2-y}{2}$$

Step 2: To create the slope field:

- Make a table of values.

- Plot a line segment with slope $= \dfrac{dy}{dx}$ at each (x, y) coordinate pair.

(a)

x	y	$\dfrac{dy}{dx}$
0	0	1
	1	$\dfrac{1}{2}$
	2	0
	3	$-\dfrac{1}{2}$
	4	-1
1	0	1
	1	$\dfrac{1}{2}$
	2	0
	3	$-\dfrac{1}{2}$
	4	-1
2	0	1
	1	$\dfrac{1}{2}$
	2	0
	3	$-\dfrac{1}{2}$
	4	-1
3	0	1
	1	$\dfrac{1}{2}$
	2	0
	3	$-\dfrac{1}{2}$
	4	-1

(a)

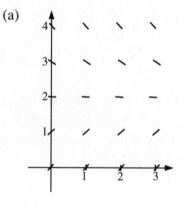

Step 3: Separate the variables and integrate.

$$\frac{dy}{dx} = \frac{2-y}{2} \Rightarrow \frac{dy}{2-y} = \frac{1}{2}dx$$

$$\int \frac{dy}{2-y} = \int \frac{1}{2}dx$$

$$-\ln|2-y| = \frac{1}{2}x + C$$

$$\ln|2-y| = -\frac{1}{2}x + C$$

(b) $\therefore \boxed{y = 2 - Ae^{-\frac{1}{2}x}}$, where A is a constant.

Step 4: Solve for A at the point $(2 \ln 3, 4)$.

$$4 = 2 - Ae^{-\frac{1}{2}(2\ln 3)}$$

$$4 = 2 - Ae^{\ln \frac{1}{3}}$$

$$4 = 2 - A\left(\frac{1}{3}\right)$$

$$A = -6$$

(c) $\therefore \boxed{y = 2 + 6e^{-\frac{1}{2}x}}$

PRACTICE EXAM 5

AP Calculus AB

Section I

PART A

Time: 55 minutes
28 questions

(Answer sheets appear in the back of this book.)

DIRECTIONS: Solve each of the following problems, select the best answer choice and fill in the corresponding oval on the answer sheet.

Calculators may NOT be used for this section of the exam.

NOTES:

(1) Unless otherwise specified, the domain of a function f is assumed to be the set of all real numbers x for which $f(x)$ is a real number.

(2) The inverse of a trigonometric function f may be indicated by using the inverse function notation f^{-1} or with the prefix "arc" (e.g., $\sin^{-1} x = \arcsin x$).

1. $\int_{-1}^{2} (4x^2 - 2)\, dx =$

    (A)   10

    (B)   8

    (C)   6

    (D)   4

    (E)   2

2. If $f(x) = \dfrac{x}{x^2 + 1}$, then $f'(x) =$

(A) $\dfrac{1-x}{(x^2+1)^2}$

(B) $\dfrac{x-1}{(x^2+1)^2}$

(C) $\dfrac{x^2-1}{(x^2+1)^2}$

(D) $\dfrac{1-x^2}{(x^2+1)^2}$

(E) $\dfrac{(x-1)^2}{(x^2+1)^2}$

3. $\displaystyle\lim_{x\to\frac{\pi}{4}}\dfrac{\sin(x)-\sin\left(\dfrac{\pi}{4}\right)}{x-\dfrac{\pi}{4}}=$

(A) π

(B) $\sqrt{2}$

(C) $\dfrac{\sqrt{3}}{2}$

(D) $\dfrac{\sqrt{2}}{2}$

(E) $\dfrac{1}{2}$

4. If $g(x) = \csc(2x^2+1)$, then $g'(x) =$

(A) $4x\cot^2(2x^2+1)$

(B) $-4x\cot^2(2x^2+1)$

(C) $4x\csc(2x^2+1)\cot(2x^2+1)$

(D) $(4x+1)\csc(2x^2+1)\cot(2x^2+1)$

(E) $-4x\csc(2x^2+1)\cot(2x^2+1)$

5. $\displaystyle\int(x-1)^2\sqrt{x}\,dx =$

(A) $\dfrac{2}{7}x^{\frac{7}{2}}-\dfrac{4}{5}x^{\frac{5}{2}}+\dfrac{2}{3}x^{\frac{3}{2}}+C$

(B) $\dfrac{2}{7}x^{\frac{7}{2}}-\dfrac{2}{5}x^{\frac{5}{2}}+\dfrac{2}{3}x^{\frac{3}{2}}+C$

(C) $\dfrac{2}{7}x^{\frac{7}{2}}+\dfrac{2}{3}x^{\frac{3}{2}}+\dfrac{1}{2}x^{\frac{1}{2}}+C$

(D) $\dfrac{1}{2}x^{2}-\dfrac{4}{3}x^{\frac{3}{2}}+x+C$

(E) $\dfrac{1}{2}x^{2}+\dfrac{2}{3}x^{\frac{3}{2}}+x+C$

6. Which of the following is the particular solution to the differential equation $\dfrac{dy}{dx}=\dfrac{3x^{2}}{y^{3}}$, if $y=2$ when $x=1$?

(A) $y=\sqrt[4]{4x^{3}}+12$

(B) $y=\sqrt[4]{(4x^{3}+12)}$

(C) $y=\sqrt[4]{(4x^{2}+5)}$

(D) $y=\sqrt[3]{4x^{4}-2}$

(E) $y=\sqrt{4x^{3}+7}$

7.

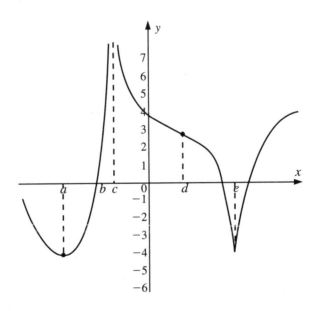

Which one of the following points on the graph contains only critical numbers, also referred to as critical values?

(A) b, c, e

(B) a, c, d

(C)   *a, d, e*

(D)   *a, b, d*

(E)   *a, c, e*

8.   On the interval [1, 3], what is the average rate of change for the function *s*, if $s(t) = 3t^2 - 4t$?

(A)   1

(B)   2

(C)   4

(D)   6

(E)   8

9.   If $f(x) = \tan^2(8 - 2x)$, then $f'(1) =$

(A) $6[\tan(6)][\sec(6)]$

(B) $-4[\tan^2(6)][\sec^2(6)]$

(C) $-4[\tan^2(6)][\sec(6)]$

(D) $-4[\tan(6)][\sec^2(6)]$

(E) $2[\tan(6)][\sec^2(6)]$

10.

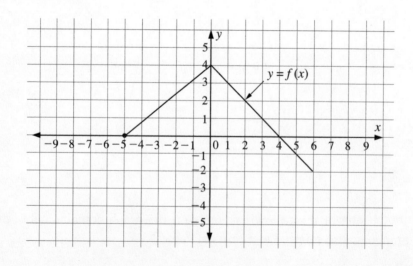

The function *f* shown on the graph above consists of two line segments. Then $\int_{-5}^{6} f(x)\,dx =$

(A)   24

(B)   20

(C)   18

(D)   16

(E)   14

11. $\dfrac{d}{dx}\displaystyle\int_{3}^{2x} f(t)\,dt =$

(A) $2[f(2x) - f(3)]$

(B) $f(2x) - f(3)$

(C) $2x f(2x)$

(D) $2 f(2x)$

(E) $2x f(x)$

12.

x	0	1	2	3
$f(x)$	1	3	2	2
$g(x)$	0	3	1	1
$f'(x)$	3	1	3	5
$g'(x)$	4	5	0	4

Assuming $f(x)$, $g(x)$, and $h(x)$ are continuous and twice differentiable, use the values in the table above to evaluate $h'(1)$ if $h(x) = f^3(g(x))$.

(A)   60

(B)   45

(C)   42

(D)   30

(E)   18

13.   If a number c in the interval $(-1, 2)$ satisfies the conclusion of the Mean Value Theorem for the function $f(x) = 3x^2 + 4x + 1$, then $c =$

(A) $\dfrac{1}{2}$

(B) $\dfrac{1}{3}$

(C) $\dfrac{1}{4}$

(D) $\dfrac{1}{5}$

(E) $\dfrac{1}{6}$

14. If $h(x) = x^2\, g(2x)$, find $h'(x)$.

(A) $2x \cdot g'(2x)$

(B) $4x \cdot g'(2x)$

(C) $x^2 \cdot g'(2x) + 2x \cdot g(2x)$

(D) $2x \cdot g'(2x) + 2x^2 \cdot g(2x)$

(E) $2x^2 \cdot g'(2x) + 2x \cdot g(2x)$

15.

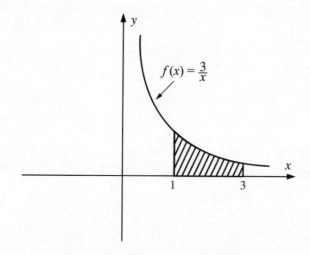

The figure above shows the graph of $y = \dfrac{3}{x}$. What is the area of the shaded region?

(A) $\ln 30$

(B) $\ln 27$

(C) $\ln 21$

(D) $\ln 18$

(E) $\ln 9$

16. Find the equation of the line tangent to the circle $x^2 + y^2 = 25$ at the point $(4, 3)$.

   (A) $(y-3) = \dfrac{3}{4}(x-4)$

   (B) $(y-3) = -\dfrac{3}{4}(x-4)$

   (C) $(y-3) = -\dfrac{4}{3}(x-4)$

   (D) $(y-3) = \dfrac{4}{3}(x-4)$

   (E) $(x-4) = \dfrac{4}{3}(y-3)$

17. For the function f, identify the x-coordinate for each point of inflection if $f'(x) = x^3 - 3x^2 + 4$.

   (A) 0 only

   (B) 2 only

   (C) 3 only

   (D) 0 and 2

   (E) 2 and 3

18.

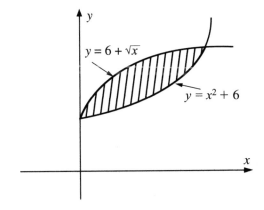

   The figure above shows the graphs of $y = x^2 + 6$ and $y = 6 + \sqrt{x}$. What is the shaded area?

(A) $\dfrac{2}{3}$

(B) $\dfrac{1}{2}$

(C) $\dfrac{1}{3}$

(D) $\dfrac{1}{4}$

(E) $\dfrac{1}{5}$

19.

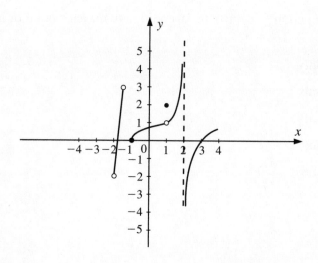

The graph of the function h is shown in the figure above. If the function is not continuous at the value $x = a$ and $\lim\limits_{x \to a} h(x)$ exists, then $a =$

(A) -2 only

(B) 1 only

(C) 2 only

(D) -2 and 1 only

(E) $-2, 1, 2$

20. If $\lim\limits_{n\to\infty}\left(1+\dfrac{1}{n}\right)^{kn} = \dfrac{1}{e^2}$, then $k =$

   (A) -2

   (B) $-\dfrac{1}{e}$

   (C) $\dfrac{1}{e}$

   (D) $\dfrac{1}{2}$

   (E) 1

21. Let R be the region enclosed by the graphs $f(x) = 3x$ and $g(x) = x^2$ when $f(x) > g(x)$. What is the volume of the solid generated when the region R is revolved about the line $y = -2$?

   (A) $\pi\displaystyle\int_0^3\left[(3x+2)^2 - (x^2+2)^2\right]dx$

   (B) $\pi\displaystyle\int_0^3\left[(x^2+2)^2 - (3x+2)^2\right]dx$

   (C) $\pi\displaystyle\int_0^3\left[(3x-2)^2 - (x^2-2)^2\right]dx$

   (D) $\pi\displaystyle\int_0^3\left[(x^2-2)^2 - (3x-2)^2\right]dx$

   (E) $\pi\displaystyle\int_0^3\left[(3x)^2 - (x^2)^2\right]dx$

22. A projectile is fired directly upward from the ground with an initial velocity of 112 ft/sec. Its distance s above the ground after t seconds is given by $s(t) = 112t - 16t^2$. At what time, in seconds, does the projectile achieve its maximum height?

   (A) 3

   (B) $\dfrac{7}{2}$

   (C) 4

   (D) $\dfrac{9}{2}$

   (E) 5

23. Let $f(x) = x^3 + x + 4$ and let $g(x) = f^{-1}(x)$. Find $g'(6)$.

(A) $-\dfrac{1}{4}$

(B) -4

(C) 1

(D) 4

(E) $\dfrac{1}{4}$

24. $\displaystyle\lim_{x\to 0} \frac{\sin 3x}{x} + \lim_{x\to\frac{\pi}{3}} \frac{\sin 3x}{x} =$

(A) 5

(B) 4

(C) 3

(D) 2

(E) 1

25. Which of the following is the graph of the 6th derivative of the function $f(x) = x^5 + x^4 - x^3 + x^2 - x + 1$?

(A)

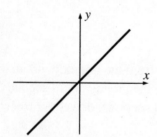

(B)

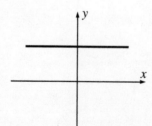

(C)

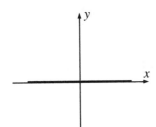

(D)

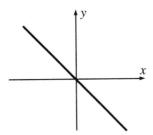

(E)

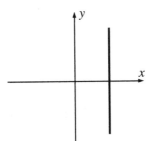

26. Which of the following is a slope field for the differential equation $\dfrac{dy}{dx} = x + y$?

(A)

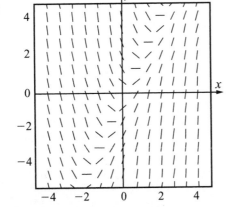

(B)

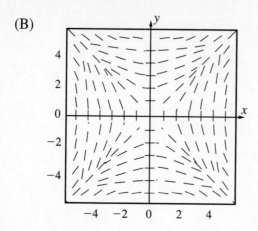

(C)

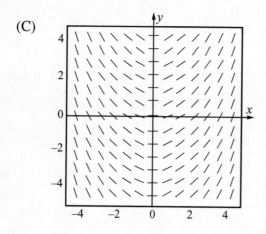

(D)

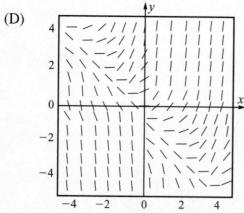

(E)

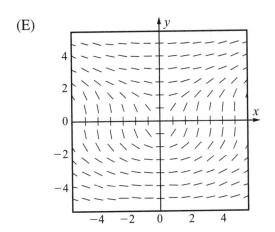

27. Find the area bounded by the curve $xy = 4$, the x-axis, $x = e$ and $x = 2e$.

    (A) 4

    (B) $4 \ln 2$

    (C) $4e^2$

    (D) $4e$

    (E) $\dfrac{e}{4}$

28. Let $f(x) = (x^2 - 3)^2$. If the local minimum of $f'(x)$ occurs at $x = a$, then $a =$

    (A) -2

    (B) -1

    (C) 0

    (D) 1

    (E) 2

STOP
This is the end of Section I, Part A.
If time still remains, you may check your work only in this section.
Do not begin Section I, Part B until instructed to do so.

Section I

PART B

Time: 50 minutes
     17 questions

(Answer sheets appear in the back of this book.)

> **DIRECTIONS:** Solve each of the following problems, select the best answer choice and fill in the corresponding oval on the answer sheet.
>
> Calculators MAY be used for this section of the exam.

NOTES:

(1) The exact numerical value of the correct answer does not always appear among the choices given. When this happens, select the number from among the choices that best approximates the exact numerical value.

(2) Unless otherwise specified, the domain of a function f is assumed to be the set of all real numbers x for which $f(x)$ is a real number.

(3) The inverse of a trigonometric function f may be indicated by using the inverse function notation f^{-1} or with the prefix "arc" (e.g., $\sin^{-1} x = \arcsin x$).

76. On what interval is the graph of $\dfrac{3x^2}{e^x}$ concave down?

    (A) $(-\infty, 3.41)$

    (B) $(-\infty, .58)$

    (C) $(.58, 3.41)$

    (D) $(.58, \infty)$

    (E) $(3.41, \infty)$

77. A point moves along a line such that its velocity at any time t $(t \geq 0)$ is given by $v(t) = 2^t \ln 2$ cm/sec. How many centimeters does the point travel over the time interval $0 \leq t \leq 2.5$?

    (A) 4.657

    (B) 8.121

    (C) 8.882

    (D) 9.882

    (E) 10.003

78. Let $f(x) = e^{bx}$ and $g(x) = e^{ax}$ ($a \ne b$, $a \ne 0$, $a \ne \pm 1$). What is the value of b, expressed in terms of a, such that "the quotient of the derivatives of $f(x)$ and $g(x)$ is equal to the derivative of their quotient"?

(A) $\dfrac{a^2}{a^2 - 1}$

(B) $\dfrac{a^2}{a + 1}$

(C) $\dfrac{a + 1}{a^2}$

(D) $\dfrac{a - 1}{a^2}$

(E) $\dfrac{a^2}{a - 1}$

79. $\displaystyle\lim_{x \to -4^+} \dfrac{4x - 6}{2x^2 + 5x - 12} =$

(A) $-\infty$

(B) 0

(C) 1

(D) $+\infty$

(E) Does not exist

80. Suppose $f(x)$ is a continuous function on $[1, 2]$, and $f(1) = 2, f(1.5) = 0.5$, and $f(2) = -3$. Which one of the following statements can be false?

(A) $\displaystyle\lim_{x \to 2^-} f(x) = -3$.

(B) $|f(2)| - |f(1)| \le |f(2) - f(1)|$.

(C) $\displaystyle\lim_{x \to \frac{5}{4}} f(x) = f\left(\dfrac{5}{4}\right)$.

(D) $f(c) = 0$ for some real value of c.

(E) The maximum value of f in $[1, 2]$ is 2.

81.

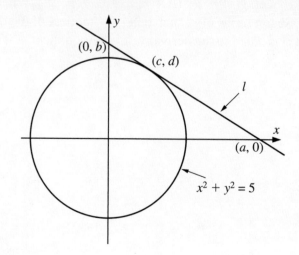

In the figure above, line l is tangent to the circle $x^2 + y^2 = 5$ in the first quadrant at point (c, d) and has a slope of $-\frac{1}{2}$. Line l crosses the x-axis at the point $(a, 0)$. What is the value of a?

(A)   2.9

(B)   3.1

(C)   4.0

(D)   4.3

(E)   5.0

82.   If $f(x) = \int_{3}^{3x^2} \left(\sqrt{e^t + 1} \right) dt$, then $f'(1) =$

(A)   28.41

(B)   27.55

(C)   18.55

(D)   12.41

(E)   4.59

83.   A spherical balloon is deflating at the rate of $\frac{1}{3}$ in³/sec. At what rate is the radius of the sphere decreasing in inches per second when its surface area is 7 in² (surface area of a sphere $= 4\pi r^2$)?

(A)   .035

(B)   .039

(C)   .041

(D)   .048

(E)   .053

84.   Use the trapezoidal rule with four equal intervals to approximate the area of the region bounded by $y = \dfrac{1}{x}$, $y = 0$, $x = 1$, and $x = 9$.

(A)   2.553

(B)   2.463

(C)   2.352

(D)   2.197

(E)   2.005

85.

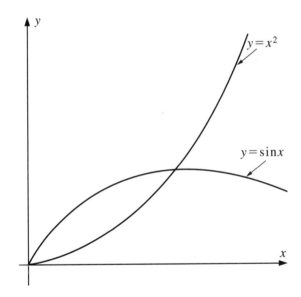

The graph above displays $y = \sin x$ and $y = x^2$. Find the area between the graphs on the interval $[0, 2]$.

(A)   .1357

(B)   1.251

(C)   1.522

(D)   1.647

(E)   1.695

86.   The temperature of an oven is cooling off at the rate of $20e^{-.05t}$ degrees Fahrenheit per minute, where t is measured in minutes. If the oven at time $t = 0$ is $320°$ F, how many minutes, to the nearest tenth, will it take to cool down to $200°$ F?

(A)   6.8

(B)   7.1

(C)   7.6

(D)   7.9

(E)   8.3

87.   If the function h is given by $h(x) = \int_0^x 3\cos\left(\frac{1}{20}t^4\right)dt$ for $-2 \le x \le 3$, on which interval is h decreasing?

(A) $(-2.0, .2815]$

(B) $(-1.405, 1.43)$

(C) $(1.43, 2.815)$

(D) $(2.367, 2.815)$

(E) $(2.367, 3.0]$

88.   The area bounded by the function $g(x) = \dfrac{1}{x\ln^2 x}$, $x = 2$, $x = 3$, and the x-axis is divided in half by the line $x = a$. What is the value of a?

(A)   2.21

(B)   2.34

(C)   2.39

(D)   2.41

(E)   2.47

89.   The base of a solid is the region in the first quadrant bounded by the graph of $y = \dfrac{3}{e^x}$, the x-axis, the y-axis, and the line $x = 2$. Each cross section of this solid perpendicular to the x-axis is a square. What is the volume of the solid?

(A)   2.83

(B)   3.41

(C)   4.42

(D)   4.75

(E)   5.53

90. What is the equation of the line tangent to the graph $x^3 + xy + y^3 = 11$ at the point $(2, 1)$?

   (A) $(y-1) = -\dfrac{13}{5}(x-2)$

   (B) $(y-1) = \dfrac{13}{5}(x-2)$

   (C) $(y-1) = -\dfrac{5}{13}(x-2)$

   (D) $(y-1) = \dfrac{5}{13}(x-2)$

   (E) $(y-1) = -\dfrac{7}{9}(x-2)$

91. The function f is given as $f(x) = 2x^{\frac{2}{3}} - \dfrac{1}{5}x^{\frac{5}{3}}$. What is the x-coordinate of the inflection point of the graph of f?

   (A) -2.34

   (B) -2.0

   (C) -1.85

   (D) 0

   (E) 1.87

92. The acceleration of a particle moving along the x-axis at any time t, $0 \leq t \leq 7$, is given by $a(t) = \dfrac{1}{4+t^2}$. If the particle has a velocity of 7 at $t = 0$, then what is its velocity at time $t = 2$?

   (A)   6.39

   (B)   6.79

   (C)   7.39

   (D)   7.79

   (E)   8.39

STOP
This is the end of Section I, Part B.
If time still remains, you may check your work only in this section.
Do not begin Section II, Part A until instructed to do so.

Section II

PART A

Time: 45 minutes
3 free-response problems

> **DIRECTIONS:** Show all your work in your exam booklet. Grading is based on the methods used to solve the problems as well as the accuracy of your final answers.
>
> Calculators MAY be used for this section of the exam.

1.

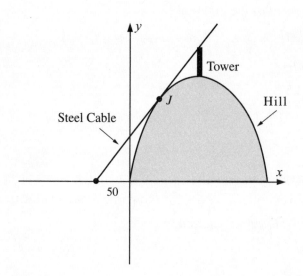

A hill, shown in the figure above, can be described by the equation $y = \dfrac{-x^2 + 200x}{50}$. A rigid, steel cable is attached to the ground 50 ft from the foot of the hill and extends to the top of a vertical tower at the top (apex) of the hill. The cable is supported at point J, where it is tangent to the hill.

(a)   What are the coordinates of point J?

(b)   What is the equation of the line that can be used to represent the cable?

(c)   To the nearest foot, how tall is the tower?

2. A rumor is said to spread at a party at a rate proportional to the number of people at the party who have not heard the rumor. Let R represent the number of people who have heard the rumor at time t minutes ($t \geq 0$). At a party with 200 people: $\dfrac{d(R)}{dt} = k(200 - R)$, where k is constant.

    Suppose at time $t = 0$, one person knows the rumor, and 10 minutes later, 50 people know it.

    (a) Write the equation that expresses the number of people who have heard the rumor R as a function of time.

    (b) To the nearest minute, how long will it take until 80% of the people at the party have heard the rumor?

3.

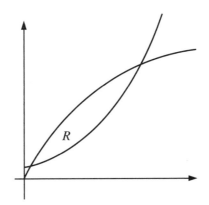

Let R represent the first quadrant region shown in the figure above. Region R is bounded above by $y^2 = 15x$ and below by $y = x^2 + 1$.

(a) Find the area of region R.

(b) Find the volume of the solid generated when region R is rotated about the line $y = 6$.

(c) Find the volume of the solid generated when region R is rotated about the y-axis.

STOP
This is the end of Section II, Part A.
If time still remains, you may check your work only in this section.
Do not begin Section II, Part B until instructed to do so.

Section II

PART B

Time: 45 minutes
   3 free-response problems

DIRECTIONS: Show all your work in your exam booklet. Grading is based on the methods used to solve the problems as well as the accuracy of your final answers.

Calculators MAY NOT be used for this section of the exam.

(During the timed portion for Part B, you may continue to work on the problems in Part A without the use of a calculator.)

---

4.   Consider the differential equation $\dfrac{2}{3}y\dfrac{dy}{dx} = x^2$, where $y \neq 0$.

(a)   Using the axes provided, sketch the slope field for the given differential equation at the 16 indicated points.

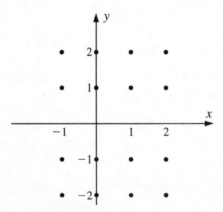

(b)   Find the particular solution $y = f(x)$ to the given differential equation with the initial condition $f(2) = -3$.

5.   The function f is twice-differentiable and satisfies the conditions shown in the table below:

x	$f(x)$	$f'(x)$	$f''(x)$
0	5	3	1
3	0	2	4

Let $g(x) = 3 \sin (2x) + f(x)$

Let $h(x) = e^{f(x)}$

(a)   Find $g(0)$.

(b)   Find $g'(0)$.

(c)   Find h'(3).

(d)   Find h"(3).

(e)   Write an equation for the line tangent to the graph of g at $x = 0$.

6.   A rain gutter is to be made from a long strip of sheet metal of width w inches by bending the metal in two places to form an isosceles trapezoid, as shown in the figure below.

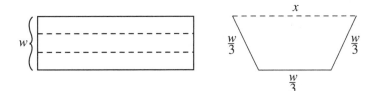

Find the value of x, in terms of w, that will maximize the amount of water the gutter can handle by maximizing the cross-sectional area of the gutter.

END OF EXAM

PRACTICE EXAM 5

AP Calculus AB

Answer Key

Part A

1. (C)	15. (B)
2. (D)	16. (C)
3. (D)	17. (D)
4. (E)	18. (C)
5. (A)	19. (D)
6. (B)	20. (A)
7. (C)	21. (A)
8. (E)	22. (B)
9. (D)	23. (E)
10. (D)	24. (C)
11. (D)	25. (C)
12. (A)	26. (D)
13. (A)	27. (B)
14. (E)	28. (D)

Part B

76. (C)
77. (A)
78. (E)
79. (D)
80. (E)
81. (E)
82. (B)
83. (D)
84. (B)
85. (C)
86. (B)
87. (E)
88. (B)
89. (C)
90. (A)
91. (B)
92. (C)

Free-Response Answers

1.
(a) (61.803, 170.820)
(b) $y = 1.528x + 76.393$
(c) 29 feet

2.
(a) $R(t) = 200 - 199e^{-.0283t}$
(b) 57 minutes

3.
(a) 2.700
(b) 49.176
(c) 17.899

4.
(a) See detailed explanation.
(b) $y = -\sqrt{x^3 + 1}$

5.
(a) 5
(b) 9
(c) 2
(d) 8
(e) $y = 9x + 5$

6.
$x = \dfrac{2w}{3}$

PRACTICE EXAM 5

AP Calculus AB

Detailed Explanations of Answers

Section 1

PART A

1. **(C)**

$$\int_{-1}^{2} (4x^2 - 2)\, dx = \frac{4x^3}{3} - 2x \Big|_{-1}^{2} = \boxed{6}$$

2. **(D)**

Use the quotient rule:

$$f'(x) = \frac{(x^2+1)\dfrac{d}{dx}(x) - x\dfrac{d}{dx}(x^2-1)}{(x^2+1)^2}$$

$$= \frac{(x^2+1) - x(2x)}{(x^2+1)^2} = \boxed{\frac{1-x^2}{(x^2+1)^2}}$$

3. **(D)**

Step 1: One of the definitions of the derivative of a function $f(x)$ at the point $x = a$ is:

$$f'(a) = \lim_{x \to a} \frac{f(x) - f(a)}{x - a}$$

This question is asking for $f'\left(\dfrac{\pi}{4}\right)$ with $f(x) = \sin x$.

Step 2:

$$f(x) = \sin x$$
$$f'(x) = \cos x$$

$$f'\left(\frac{\pi}{4}\right) = \cos\left(\frac{\pi}{4}\right) = \boxed{\frac{\sqrt{2}}{2}}$$

4. **(E)**

Use $\dfrac{d}{dx}(\csc u) = -\csc u \, \cot u \dfrac{d(u)}{dx}$ with $u = 2x^2 + 1$.

$$\dfrac{d}{dx}(\csc(2x^2 + 1)) \;=\; -\csc(2x^2 + 1)\cot(2x^2 + 1)\dfrac{d}{dx}(2x^2 + 1)$$

$$=\; -\csc(2x^2 + 1)\cot(2x^2 + 1)(4x)$$

$$=\; \boxed{-4x\csc(2x^2 + 1)\cot(2x^2 + 1)}$$

5. **(A)**

Step 1: Change:

$$(x - 1)^2 \;\Rightarrow\; x^2 - 2x + 1$$

$$\sqrt{x} \;\Rightarrow\; x^{\frac{1}{2}}$$

Step 2: Carry out the multiplication.

$$(x^2 - 2x + 1)(x^{\frac{1}{2}}) = x^{\frac{5}{2}} - 2x^{\frac{3}{2}} + x^{\frac{1}{2}}$$

Step 3: Integrate. Use $\displaystyle\int u^n du = \dfrac{u^{n+1}}{n+1} + C$

$$\int (x^{\frac{5}{2}} - 2x^{\frac{3}{2}} + x^{\frac{1}{2}})\, dx = \boxed{\dfrac{2}{7}x^{\frac{7}{2}} - \dfrac{4}{5}x^{\frac{5}{2}} + \dfrac{2}{3}x^{\frac{3}{2}} + C}$$

6. **(B)**

Step 1: Separate the variables.

$$\dfrac{dy}{dx} = \dfrac{3x^2}{y^3} \;\Rightarrow\; y^3 dy = 3x^2 dx$$

Step 2: Integrate both sides of the equation.

$$\int y^3 dy = \int 3x^2 dx$$

$$\dfrac{y^4}{4} = x^3 + C_1 \;\Rightarrow\; y^4 = 4x^3 + 4C_1$$

Replace $4C_1$ with C.

$$\therefore y^4 = 4x^3 + C \;\Rightarrow\; y = \pm\sqrt[4]{(4x^3 + C)}$$

Step 3: Since the particular solution goes through the point (1, 2), y must be positive when $x = 1$.

$$y \;=\; +\sqrt[4]{(4x^3 + C)}$$

$$2 \;=\; \sqrt[4]{4 + C}$$

$$C \;=\; 12$$

The particular solution is $\boxed{y = \sqrt[4]{(4x^3 + 12)}}$

7. **(C)**

Step 1: If the value $x = c$ is in the domain of $f(x)$, then it is a critical value if either $f'(c) = 0$ or $f'(c)$ does not exist.

Step 2: Make a table to analyze the points.

Point	Analysis	Critical value?
a	$f'(a)=0$	Yes
b	x-intercept	No
c	c is not in the domain of $f(x)$	No
d	$f'(d)=0$	Yes
e	$f'(e)$ does not exist	Yes

Points $\boxed{a, d, e}$ are critical points.

8. **(E)**

Step 1: Average rate of change $= \dfrac{\Delta s}{\Delta t} = \dfrac{s(3) - s(1)}{3 - 1}$

Step 2: $s(3)=15$

$s(1)=-1$

$\therefore$ Average rate of change $= \dfrac{15-(-1)}{3-1} = \boxed{8}$

9. **(D)**

Step 1: Rewrite $\tan^2(8-2x) \Rightarrow [\tan(8-2x)]^2$

Step 2: Use $\dfrac{d}{dx}(\tan u) = \sec^2 u \dfrac{d(u)}{dx}$ and $\dfrac{d(u^n)}{dx} = n u^{n-1} \dfrac{d(u)}{dx}$

$$\therefore \frac{d}{dx}\left[\tan(8-2x)\right]^2 = 2\left[\tan(8-2x)\right]^1 \frac{d}{dx}\left[\tan(8-2x)\right]$$

$$= 2\left[\tan(8-2x)\right]\sec^2(8-2x)\cdot\frac{d}{dx}(8-2x)$$

$$= 2\left[\tan(8-2x)\right]\left[\sec^2(8-2x)\right]\left[-2\right]$$

$$f'(x) = -4\tan(8-2x)\sec^2(8-2x)$$

$$f'(1) = \boxed{-4\left[\tan(6)\right]\left[\sec^2(6)\right]}$$

10. **(D)**

   Step 1: $\int_a^b f(x)\,dx$ represents the sum of the "signed" areas created between the function and the x-axis. See sketch below.

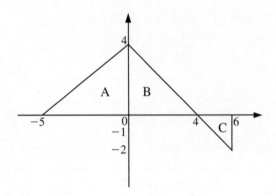

   Those above the x-axis are positive, and those below are negative.

   Step 2: Area $A = \dfrac{1}{2}(5)(4) = 10 \Rightarrow$ signed area $= +10$

   Area $B = \dfrac{1}{2}(4)(4) = 8 \Rightarrow$ signed area $= +8$

   Area $C = \dfrac{1}{2}(2)(2) = 2 \Rightarrow$ signed area $= -2$

   Step 3: $\int_{-5}^{6} f(x)\,dx = 10 + 8 - 2 = \boxed{16}$

11. **(D)**

   Step 1: The fundamental theorem of calculus (part 2) states

   $$\frac{d}{dx}\left[\int_a^{g(x)} f(t)\,dt\right] = f(g(x)) \cdot g'(x)$$

   Step 2: $\dfrac{d}{dx}\left[\int_3^{2x} f(t)\,dt\right] = f(2x) \cdot \dfrac{d}{dx}(2x) = \boxed{2f(2x)}$

12. **(A)**

   Step 1: Rewrite $f^3(g(x))$ as $[f(g(x))]^3$

   Step 2: Apply the chain rule: $h(x) = [f(g(x))]^3$

   $$h'(x) = 3\,[f(g(x))]^2 \cdot g'(x)$$
   $$h'(1) = 3[f(g(1))]^2 \cdot g'(1)$$
   $$h'(1) = 3[f(3)]^2(5)$$
   $$= 3(2)^2(5) = \boxed{60}$$

13. **(A)**

Step 1: The Mean Value Theorem asserts that there exists a value c on the interval (a, b) such that $f'(c) = \dfrac{f(b) - f(a)}{b - a}$.

Step 2: $f(x) = 3x^2 + 4x - 1 \Rightarrow f'(x) = 6x + 4$

$$f(-1) = -2 \qquad\qquad f'(c) = 6c + 4$$

$$f(2) \;\; = 19$$

$$6c + 4 = \frac{19 - (-2)}{2 - (-1)} = \frac{21}{3} = 7$$

$$c = \boxed{\frac{1}{2}}$$

14. **(E)**

Step 1: Use the product rule first.

$$h(x) = x^2 \cdot g(2x)$$
$$h'(x) = x^2 \frac{d}{dx}\big[g(2x)\big] + g(2x) \cdot \big[2x\big]$$

Step 2: $\dfrac{d}{dx}[g(2x)]$ requires the chain rule

$$\frac{d}{dx}\big[g(2x)\big] = g'(2x)\frac{d}{dx}(2x) = 2g'(2x)$$

Step 3:

$$\therefore h'(x) = x^2 \cdot [2g'(2x)] + g(2x) \cdot [2x]$$
$$= \boxed{2\,x^2 \cdot g'(2x) + 2x \cdot g(2x)}$$

15. **(B)**

$$\text{Area} = \int_1^3 \frac{3}{x}\,dx = 3\int_1^3 \frac{1}{x}\,dx = 3\ln|x|\Big|_{x=1}^{3}$$
$$= 3\ln 3 - 3\ln 1 = 3\ln 3 = \boxed{\ln 27}$$

16. **(C)**

Step 1: Use implicit differentiation to find $\dfrac{dy}{dx}$

$$x^2 + y^2 = 25$$

$$2x + 2y\frac{dy}{dx} = 0 \quad \Rightarrow \quad \frac{dy}{dx} = \frac{-x}{y}$$

Step 2: $\dfrac{dy}{dx} = \dfrac{-x}{y} = \dfrac{-4}{3} =$ slope, $(x, y) \Rightarrow (4,3)$

Equation of line: $\boxed{(y-3) = \dfrac{-4}{3}(x-4)}$

17. **(D)**

Step1: Set the second derivative $f''(x) = 0$ and solve for x.

$$f''(x) = 3x^2 - 6x = 0$$
$$3x\,(x-2) = 0$$
$$x = 0 \,|\, x = 2$$

Step 2: Use a number line to verify that $f''(x)$ changes sign as it passes the potential inflection points.

$$f''(x) \underset{\underset{0}{|}\qquad\quad\underset{2}{|}}{\underline{\quad ++++ \quad ---- \quad ++++ \quad}}$$

$\therefore$ $\boxed{0 \text{ and } 2}$ are the x-coordinates of the two points of inflection.

18. **(C)**

Step 1: Find the x values where the two graphs cross by setting them equal in each other.

$$x^2 + 6 = 6 + \sqrt{x} \quad \Rightarrow \quad x^2 = \sqrt{x} \quad \Rightarrow \quad x^4 = x$$

$$x^4 - x = 0 \Rightarrow x\,(x^3 - 1) \,\therefore\, x = 0 \text{ and } x = 1.$$

Step 2: Area $= \displaystyle\int_a^b \big[(\text{top curve}) - (\text{bottom curve})\big]\,dx$

$= \displaystyle\int_0^1 \big[(6 + \sqrt{x}) - (x^2 + 6)\big]\,dx = \int_0^1 (\sqrt{x} - x^2)\,dx$

$= \dfrac{2}{3}x^{\frac{3}{2}} - \dfrac{1}{3}x^3 \Big|_0^1 = \boxed{\dfrac{1}{3}}$

19. **(D)**

Prepare a table as follows.

x-value	Analysis	Meets requirements
-2	$\lim\limits_{x \to -2} h(x) = -2$, not continuous	✓
-1	$\lim\limits_{x \to -1} h(x)$ does not exist	✗
1	$\lim\limits_{x \to 1} h(x) = 1$, not continuous	✓
2	$\lim\limits_{x \to 2} h(x)$ does not exist	✗

$\therefore$ The values of x that meet the requirements are $\boxed{-2 \text{ and } 1 \text{ only.}}$

20. **(A)**

Step 1: Recall that $e = \lim\limits_{n \to \infty} \left(1 + \dfrac{1}{n}\right)^n$.

Step 2: $\lim\limits_{n \to \infty} \left(1 + \dfrac{1}{n}\right)^{kn} = \lim\limits_{n \to \infty} \left[\left(1 + \dfrac{1}{n}\right)^n\right]^k = e^k = \dfrac{1}{e^2}$

$\therefore$ $\boxed{k = -2}$

21. **(A)**

Step 1: Sketch a graph of the region.

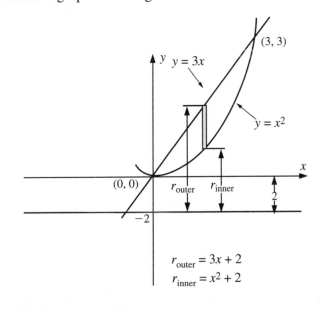

345

Step 2: Volume $= \pi \int_a^b (r^2_{\text{outer}} - r^2_{\text{inner}}) \, dx$

$$= \boxed{\pi \int_0^3 \left[(3x+2)^2 - (x^2+2)^2 \right] dx}$$

22. **(B)**

When the projectile achieves maximum height, its velocity is zero. Find the value of t for which $v(t) = 0$.

$$s(t) = 112t - 16t^2$$

$$v(t) = \frac{d(s(t))}{dt} = 112 - 32t = 0$$

$$t = \frac{112}{32} = \boxed{\frac{7}{2}} \text{ sec}$$

23. **(E)**

Step 1: If $g(x) = f^{-1}(x)$ and $f(a) = b$, then $g(b) = a$

Step 2: $g'(b) = \dfrac{1}{f'(a)} = \dfrac{1}{f'(g(b))}$

Step 3: Then $g'(6) = \dfrac{1}{f'(g(6))} = \dfrac{1}{f'(1)}$

Step 4: $f(x) = x^3 + x + 4$

$$f'(x) = 3x^2 + 1$$
$$f'(1) = 4$$

$$\therefore g'(6) = \boxed{\frac{1}{4}}$$

24. **(C)**

Step 1: Recall: $\lim\limits_{x \to 0} \dfrac{\sin x}{x} = 1$.

Step 2: $\lim\limits_{x \to 0} \dfrac{\sin 3x}{x} = 3 \left[\lim\limits_{x \to 0} \dfrac{\sin 3x}{3x} \right] = 3$

Step 3: $\lim\limits_{x \to \frac{\pi}{3}} \dfrac{\sin 3x}{x} = \dfrac{\sin \pi}{\left(\frac{\pi}{3} \right)} = 0$

Step 4: $\therefore \lim\limits_{x\to 0}\dfrac{\sin 3x}{x}+\lim\limits_{x\to\frac{\pi}{3}}\dfrac{\sin 3x}{x}=3+0=\boxed{3}$

25. **(C)**

$$\dfrac{d^6}{dx^6}(x^5+x^4-x^3+x^2-x+1)=0 \qquad \therefore \dfrac{d^6 f(x)}{dx^6}=0,$$

Graph $\boxed{C}$

26. **(D)**

Plot short line segments using useful (x, y) values. Note that $\dfrac{dy}{dx}$ is the slope. When $y=-x$, $\dfrac{dy}{dx}=0$. Only choice $\boxed{D}$ has zero slope line segments for all $y=-x$.

27. **(B)**

Step 1: A sketch is useful. Note that $y=\dfrac{4}{x}$.

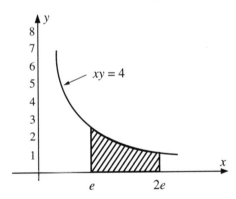

Step 2: Area $=\displaystyle\int_e^{2e}\dfrac{4}{x}\,dx$

$$=4\ln|x|\Big\|_e^{2e}=4\big[\ln 2e-\ln e\big]=4\big[\ln 2\big]=\boxed{4\ln 2}$$

28. **(D)**

Step 1: Note: The question discusses a relative minimum point for $f'(x)$, NOT $f(x)$.

$$f'(x)=2(x^2-3)(2x)=4x^3-12x$$

Call this new function $g(x)$ $\quad \therefore g(x)=4x^3-12x$

347

Step 2: To find a relative minimum/maximum point, set $g'(x) = 0$ and analyze the $g'(x)$ values on a number line.

$$g'(x) = 12x^2 - 12 = 0$$

$$x = \pm 1$$

increasing decreasing increasing

Because $f'(x)$ changes from negative to positive as it crosses $x = 1$, $g(x) = f'(x)$ has a local minimum at $x = \boxed{1}$.

Section I

PART B

76. **(C)** A calculator is required.

Step 1: Analysis of concavity requires analysis of the second derivative.
Solve $\dfrac{d^2}{dx^2}\left(\dfrac{3x^2}{e^x}\right)=0$ either manually or by calculator to find points where concavity changes.
$x = 2 \pm \sqrt{2}$, or $x \approx .586, 3.41$

Step 2: To process manually, change the function to a product and take successive derivatives.

$$f(x) = \frac{3x^2}{e^x} = 3x^2 e^{-x}$$

$$\begin{aligned}
f'(x) &= 3x^2\left[-e^{-x}\right] + e^{-x}\left[6x\right] = e^{-x}(-3x^2 + 6x) \\
f''(x) &= e^{-x}(-6x + 6) + (-3x^2 + 6x)(-e^{-x}) \\
&= e^{-x}\left[-6x + 6 + 3x^2 - 6x\right] \\
&= 3e^{-x}\left[x^2 - 4x + 2\right] = 0
\end{aligned}$$

$x = 2 \pm \sqrt{2}$ or $x \approx .586, 3.41$

Step 3: Analyze the second derivative on a number line.

$$f''(x) \quad \underset{\substack{2-\sqrt{2} \\ (.58)}}{\overset{++++}{\rule{0pt}{0pt}}} \quad \underset{\substack{2+\sqrt{2} \\ (3.41)}}{\overset{---}{\rule{0pt}{0pt}}} \quad \overset{+++}{\rule{0pt}{0pt}}$$

f'' is concave down in the interval $\boxed{(.58, 3.41)}$

77. **(A)**

Step 1: Distance is the antiderivative of velocity. However, we first need to ensure that in the interval $[0, 2.5]$ the particle does not stop and reverse direction.

Determine if there is a time $[0, 2.5]$ such that $v(t) = 0$.
Since $2^t \ln 2$ never equals zero, the particle does not reverse direction.

Step 2: $s(t) = \int v(t) \, dt$

$$s(t) = \int_0^{2.5} 2^t \ln 2 \, dt = 2^t \Big|_0^{2.5} = 2^{2.25} - 2^0 = \boxed{4.657} \text{ cm}$$

78. **(E)**

Step 1: To restate the problem, find b such that

$$\frac{d\left(\dfrac{f(x)}{g(x)}\right)}{dx} = \frac{f'(x)}{g'(x)}$$

Step 2: Find the various components, as shown in the table below.

$f(x) = e^{bx}$	$g(x) = e^{ax}$	$\dfrac{f(x)}{g(x)} = e^{(b-a)x}$
$f'(x) = be^{bx}$	$g'(x) = ae^{ax}$	$\dfrac{d\left(\dfrac{f(x)}{g(x)}\right)}{dx} = (b-a)e^{(b-a)x}$

Step 3: Combine steps 1 and 2.

$$(b-a)e^{(b-a)x} = \frac{be^{bx}}{ae^{ax}} = \frac{b}{a}e^{(b-a)x}$$

$$\therefore \quad b - a = \frac{b}{a}$$

$$b = \boxed{\frac{a^2}{a-1}}$$

79. **(D)**

Step 1: Reduce the rational function $\dfrac{4x-6}{2x^2+5x-12} = \dfrac{2(2x-3)}{(2x-3)(x+4)} = \dfrac{2}{x+4}$.

Step 2: If $x = -4$, this is $\dfrac{2}{0}$, or undefined.

Step 3: Therefore, the limit is headed toward $\pm\infty$. The question is, which one?

Substitute a number near and to the right of -4, such as -3.9. Then $\dfrac{2}{-3.9+4}$ is positive. $\therefore$ The limit approaches $\boxed{+\infty}$.

80. **(E)**

(A) TRUE. This is the definition of continuity on $[1, 2]$.

(B) TRUE. This is the triangle inequality: $|a| - |b| \le |a - b|$.

(C) TRUE. This is the definition of continuity on $[1, 2]$.

(D) TRUE. This is the Intermediate Value Theorem.

(E) FALSE. There is not enough information to tell where the maximum occurs on $[1, 2]$.

The only answer that could be false is

$\boxed{\text{the maximum value of } F \text{ in } [1, 2] \text{ is } 2}$, choice E.

81. **(E)**

Step 1: Determine an expression for the slope of the tangent lines to the circle.

$$x^2 + y^2 = 5$$

$$2x + 2y\frac{dy}{dx} = 0 \quad \Rightarrow \quad \frac{dy}{dx} = -\frac{x}{y} = -\frac{1}{2}$$

Step 2: At the point of tangency (c, d),

$$-\frac{x}{y} = -\frac{1}{2} \Rightarrow y = 2x$$

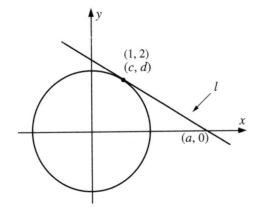

Step 3: Substitute $y = 2x$ into the equation of the circle to determine the values of c and d.

$$x^2 + y^2 = 5 \Rightarrow x^2 + (2x)^2 = 5$$

$$5x^2 = 5$$

$$x = \pm 1$$

In the first quadrant line l is tangent to the circle at $(1, 2)$.

Step 4: The slope of l is $\dfrac{2-0}{1-a} = -\dfrac{1}{2}$ $\therefore a = \boxed{5.0}$

82. (B)

Use the fundamental theorem of calculus (part 2):

$$\frac{d}{dx}\left[\int_a^{g(x)} f(t)\,dt\right] = f(g(x)) \cdot g'(x)$$

$$f(x) = \int_3^{3x^2} (\sqrt{e^t + 1})\,dt$$

$$f'(x) = \frac{d}{dx}\left[\int_3^{3x^2} (\sqrt{e^t + 1})\,dt\right] = \sqrt{e^{3x^2} + 1} \cdot (6x)$$

$$f'(1) = 6\sqrt{e^3 + 1} = \boxed{27.55}$$

83. (D)

Step 1: The volume of a sphere is given by

$$V = \frac{4}{3}\pi r^3$$

Step 2: Create a rate equation: $\dfrac{dV}{dt} = 4\pi r^2 \dfrac{dr}{dt}$

Step 3: $\dfrac{dV}{dt} = -\dfrac{1}{3}$in.^{3}/sec and $4\pi r^2 = 7$ in.^{2}

$$\therefore -\frac{1}{3} = (7)\frac{dr}{dt} \Rightarrow \frac{dr}{dt} = \frac{-1}{21} = -.048 \text{ in/sec}$$

The minus sign designates decreasing, so the radius is decreasing at a rate of $\boxed{.048}$ in./sec.

84. **(B)**

Step 1: Sketch a graph.

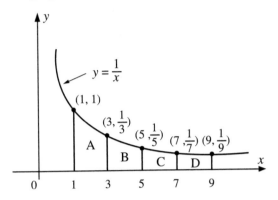

Step 2: The width of each interval $= \dfrac{9-1}{4} = 2$

Step 3: Find the area of each trapezoid.

$$\text{Area A} = \frac{1}{2}(2)\left(1+\frac{1}{3}\right)$$

$$\text{Area B} = \frac{1}{2}(2)\left(\frac{1}{3}+\frac{1}{5}\right)$$

$$\text{Area C} = \frac{1}{2}(2)\left(\frac{1}{5}+\frac{1}{7}\right)$$

$$\text{Area D} = \frac{1}{2}(2)\left(\frac{1}{7}+\frac{1}{9}\right)$$

Add these areas to get the total area.

$$\text{Total area} = \frac{1}{2}(2)\left[1+2\left(\frac{1}{3}\right)+2\left(\frac{1}{5}\right)+2\left(\frac{1}{7}\right)+\frac{1}{9}\right]$$

$$= \frac{776}{315} = \boxed{2.463}$$

85. **(C)**

Step 1: Find the points of intersection of the curves.

$$x^2 = \sin x$$

$$x = 0 \text{ or } x = .8767$$

Sketch the curves.

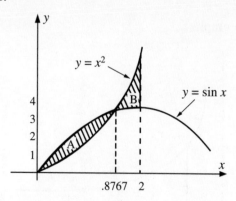

Step 2: Area $= \int_a^b \left[(\text{top curve}) - (\text{bottom curve})\right] dx$

Note: The curves switch top/bottom positions after $x = .8767$.

∴ The area MUST be done as two separate integrals.

$$\text{Area} = \int_0^{.8767} \left[(\sin x) - x^2\right] dx + \int_{.8767}^2 (x^2 - \sin x) dx$$
$$= .1357 + 1.3862$$
$$= \boxed{1.522}$$

86. **(B)** This problem requires a calculator.

Step 1: $\int_0^x 20e^{-.05t} dt$ represents the temperature drop over the time interval $[0, x]$.

Step 2: To find when the temperature drop is $120°$, find x:
$$\int_0^x 20e^{-.05t} dt = 120$$

$$x = 7.13 \Rightarrow \boxed{7.1} \text{ minutes}$$

Note: It is possible to work backward from the answer choices as an alternate approach to finding the correct answer.

87. **(E)**

Step 1: Find the critical values by setting the first derivative equal to zero.

$$\frac{d}{dx}\left(\int_0^x 3\cos\left(\frac{t^4}{20}\right) dt\right) = 0$$

$$3\cos\left(\frac{x^4}{20}\right) = 0$$

This occurs when $\dfrac{x^4}{20} = \dfrac{\pi}{2}$ and $\dfrac{x^4}{20} = \dfrac{3\pi}{2}$.

$\therefore x = -2.367$ | these are not in the
$\quad x = 2.367$ | domain $[-2, 3]$

Only 2.367 is in the domain.

Step 2: Do a first derivative number line analysis.

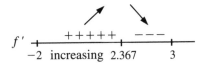

$\therefore$ The function is decreasing in the interval $\boxed{(2.367, 3.0)}$

88. **(B)** A calculator is required.

Step 1: A sketch is useful.

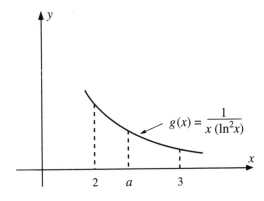

Step 2: The given area is represented by the equation:

$$\int_2^a g(x)\, dx = \int_a^3 g(x)\, dx$$

Step 3: By CAS calculator, $a = \boxed{2.34}$

Step 4: Manually: To find $\int_a^b \frac{1}{x} \cdot \frac{1}{(\ln x)^2} \, dx$, let $u = \ln x$

$$du = \frac{1}{x} \, dx$$

$$\int_a^b \frac{1}{x} \cdot \frac{1}{(\ln x)^2} \, dx = \int_{x=a}^b \frac{1}{u^2} \, du = \left. \frac{u^{-1}}{-1} \right|_{x=a}^b = \left. \frac{-1}{\ln x} \right|_a^b$$

Step 5: Since a divides the area in half

$$\int_2^a \frac{1}{x \ln^2 x} \, dx \quad = \quad \int_a^3 \frac{1}{x \ln^2 x} \, dx$$

$$\left[\frac{-1}{\ln a} - \left(\frac{-1}{\ln 2} \right) \right] \quad = \quad \left[\frac{-1}{\ln 3} - \left(\frac{-1}{\ln a} \right) \right]$$

$$a = \boxed{2.34}$$

89. **(C)**

Step 1: Make a sketch.

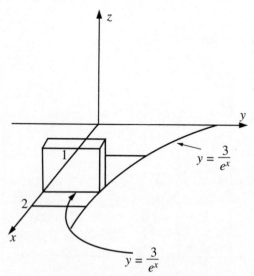

Step 2: The edge of each cross-sectional square is $\frac{3}{e^x}$.

Step 3: The volume of each cross-sectional slice is

$$\left(\frac{3}{e^x} \right)\left(\frac{3}{e^x} \right) dx \quad = \quad \frac{9}{e^{2x}} \, dx$$

$$= \quad 9e^{-2x} \, dx$$

Step 4: The volume of the solid $= \int_0^2 9e^{-2x}\,dx = \boxed{4.42}$

90. **(A)**

Step 1: Find $\dfrac{dy}{dx}$ using implicit differentiation. Note that xy is a product.

$$x^3 + xy + y^3 = 11$$

$$3x^2 + \left[x\frac{dy}{dx} + y\right] + 3y^2\frac{dy}{dx} = 0$$

$$\therefore \quad \frac{dy}{dx} = \frac{-3x^2 - y}{x + 3y^2}$$

Step 2: At the point $(2, 1)$, $x = 2$, $y = 1$, $m = \dfrac{dy}{dx} = \dfrac{-13}{5}$.

Write the equation of the tangent line:

$$\boxed{(y - 1) = -\frac{13}{5}(x - 2)}$$

91. **(B)**

Step 1: To find inflection points, use the second derivative.

$$f(x) = 2x^{\frac{2}{3}} - \frac{1}{5}x^{\frac{5}{3}}$$

$$f'(x) = \frac{4}{3}x^{-\frac{1}{3}} - \frac{1}{3}x^{\frac{2}{3}}$$

$$f''(x) = -\frac{4}{9}x^{-\frac{4}{3}} - \frac{2}{9}x^{-\frac{1}{3}}$$

$$= -\frac{2}{9}x^{-\frac{4}{3}}(2 + x)$$

Step 2: Set the second derivative equal to zero, solve for x, and analyze $f''(x)$.

$$-\frac{2}{9}x^{-\frac{4}{3}}(2 + x) = 0$$

$x = -2$ is the only solution.

Step 3: Do a number line analysis.

$$\overset{++++\quad--\quad-----}{\underset{-2\quad\;\;0}{\rule{6cm}{0.4pt}}}$$

$x = \boxed{-\,2.0}$ is the x-coordinate of the only inflection point.

92. **(C)** A calculator is necessary for this question.

Step 1: Velocity is the antiderivative of acceleration.

$$v(t) = \int \frac{1}{4+t^2}\,dt$$

Step 2: This is an arc tangent $(\tan^{-1})$ type of integral.

$$\int \frac{1}{a^2+t^2}\,dt = \frac{1}{a}\tan^{-1}\!\left(\frac{t}{a}\right)+C$$

$$\therefore\quad v(t) = \int \frac{1}{4+t^2}\,dt = \frac{1}{2}\tan^{-1}\!\left(\frac{t}{2}\right)+C$$

Step 3: Since $v(0) = 7$,

$$7 = \frac{1}{2}\tan^{-1}\!\left(\frac{0}{2}\right)+C \quad\Rightarrow C = 7$$

$$\therefore\quad v(t) = \frac{1}{2}\tan^{-1}\!\left(\frac{t}{2}\right)+7$$

Step 4: $v(2) = \dfrac{1}{2}\tan^{-1}\!\left(\dfrac{2}{2}\right)+7 = \boxed{7.39}$

Section II

PART A

1.

Step 1: Label points in the figure as coordinates.

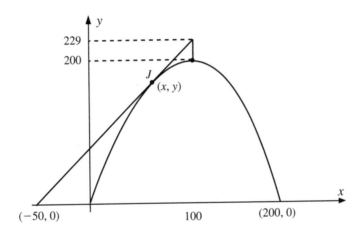

Step 2: At point J,

$$y = \frac{-x^2 + 200x}{50}$$

The slope of the steel cable will equal the derivative of the hill equation.

$$\frac{y-0}{x+50} = \frac{-2x+200}{50}$$

Step 3: Solving the equation simultaneously yields

$$x = 61.803, y = 170.820$$

(a) $\boxed{(61.803, 170.820)}$

Step 4: Using J (61.803, 170.820) and point $(-50, 0)$, the slope $=$

$$m = \frac{y}{x+50} = \frac{170.820}{111.803} = 1.528.$$

∴ The equation of the line used to represent the cable is:

(b)

$$y = 1.528x + 76.393$$
or
$$(y - 170.820) = 1.528\,(x - 61.803)$$

Step 5: The hill peaks at $x = 100$, with a height of $y = 200$. The rigid cable represented by $y = 1.528x + 76.393$ will have a height of 229.193, when $x = 100$.

Therefore, the tower is $(229.193 - 200) = 29.193$ feet tall, which is $\boxed{29\ \text{feet}}$ to the nearest foot.

2.

Step 1: Solve the differential equation $\dfrac{dR}{dt} = k(200 - R)$ by separating the variables.

$$\frac{dR}{200 - R} = k\,dt$$

Step 2: Integrate the equation.

$$\int \frac{dR}{200 - R} = \int k\,dt$$
$$-\ln\left|200 - R\right| = k\,t + C$$

Step 3: Solve for R. Since $R < 200$, $\left|200 - R\right| = 200 - R$.

$$\ln\left|200 - R\right| = -k\,t - C$$
$$200 - R = e^{-kt} \cdot e^{-C}$$
$$R = 200 - Ae^{-kt}, \text{ where } A = e^{-C}$$

Step 4: Use $R(0) = 1$ to find the value of A.

$$1 = 200 - Ae^0 \therefore A = 199$$

The equation is now: $R = 200 - 199e^{-kt}$

Step 5: Use $R(10) = 50$ to find the value of k.

$$50 = 200 - 199\, e^{-k(10)}$$
$$k = .0283$$

(a) $\therefore$ $\boxed{R(t) = 200 - 199\, e^{-.0283t}}$

Step 6: 80% of 200 = 160. Solve for t, when $R(t) = 160$.

$$160 = 200 - 199e^{-.0283t}$$

$$-40 = -199e^{-.0283t}$$

$$\frac{40}{199} = e^{-.0283t}$$

$$-.0283t = \ln\frac{40}{199} = -1.6044$$

(b) $\therefore$ $t = 56.69 \Rightarrow \boxed{57 \text{ minutes}}$

3.

Step 1: Sketch the graph. Locate the intersection points of $y^2 = 15x$ and $y = x^2 + 1$.

$(.067, 1.004)$ or $(2.169, 5.705)$

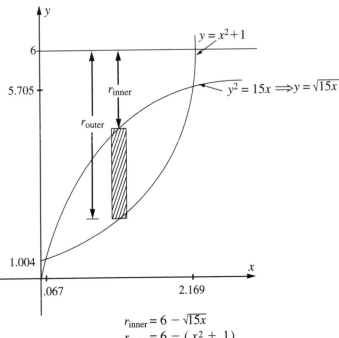

$$r_{inner} = 6 - \sqrt{15x}$$
$$r_{outer} = 6 - (x^2 + 1)$$
$$= 5 - x^2$$

Step 2:

(a) Area $= \int_a^b [(\text{top curve}) - (\text{bottom curve})] dx$

$= \int_{.067}^{2.169} \left[\sqrt{15x} - (x^2 + 1) \right] dx = \boxed{2.700}$

Step 3:

(b) Volume $= \pi \int_a^b (r^2_{\text{outer}} - r^2_{\text{inner}}) dx$

$= \pi \int_{.067}^{2.169} \left[(5 - x^2)^2 - (6 - \sqrt{15x})^2 \right] dx = \boxed{49.176}$

Step 4: To use washers, change the equations from: $y = x^2 + 1$ to

$x = \sqrt{y - 1}$

and $y^2 = 15x$ to $x = \dfrac{y^2}{15}$. See sketch.

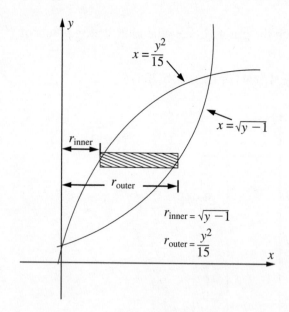

(c) Volume $= \pi \int_{1.004}^{5.705} \left[(\sqrt{y - 1})^2 - \left(\dfrac{y^2}{15} \right)^2 \right] dy$

$= \boxed{17.899}$

Section II

PART B

4.

Step 1 Rewrite the differential equation as

$$\frac{2}{3}y\frac{dy}{dx} = x^2 \quad \Rightarrow \quad \frac{dy}{dx} = \frac{3x^2}{2y}.$$

Step 2: To create the slope field, make a table of values.

Step 3: Plot a line segment with a slope of $\frac{dy}{dx}$ at each (x, y) coordinate pair.

(a)

x	y	$\dfrac{dy}{dx}$
-1	-2	$-\dfrac{3}{4}$
-1	-1	$-\dfrac{3}{2}$
-1	1	$\dfrac{3}{2}$
-1	2	$\dfrac{3}{4}$
0	-2	0
0	-1	0
0	1	0
0	2	0
1	-2	$-\dfrac{3}{4}$
1	-1	$-\dfrac{3}{2}$

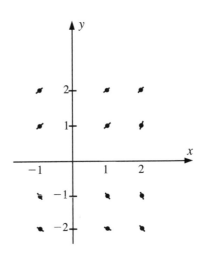

(Continued)

1	1	$\dfrac{3}{2}$
1	2	$\dfrac{3}{4}$
2	-2	-3
2	-1	-6
2	1	6
2	2	3

Step 3: Separate the variables and integrate.

$$\frac{dy}{dx} = \frac{3x^2}{2y} \quad \Rightarrow \quad 2y\,dy = 3x^2 dx$$

$$\int 2y\,dy = \int 3x^2\,dx$$

$$y^2 = x^3 + C$$

$$f(x) = y = \pm\sqrt{x^3 + C}$$

Step 4: Use $f(2) = -3$ to find the value of C.

$$-3 = -\sqrt{(2)^3 + C}$$

$$C = 1$$

(b) $\therefore$ $\boxed{y = -\sqrt{x^3 + 1}}$

Note: Choose the $-\sqrt{x^3 + 1}$, not the $+\sqrt{x^3 + 1}$ because $f(2) = -3$.

5.

Step 1: $g(x) = 3\sin(2x) + f(x)$

$$g(0) = 3\sin(0) + f(0)$$

(a) $\qquad = 0 + 5 = \boxed{5}$

Step 2: $g'(x) = 6\cos(2x) + f'(x)$

$$g'(0) = 6\cos(0) + f'(0)$$

(b) $\qquad = 6 + 3 = \boxed{9}$

Step 3: $h(x) = e^{f(x)}$

$$h'(x) = e^{f(x)} \cdot f'(x)$$

(c) $\qquad h'(3) = e^0 \cdot 2 = \boxed{2}$

Step 4: $h'(x)$ is a product, so use the product rule to find $h''(x)$.

$$h''(x) = e^{f(x)} f''(x) + f'(x) \frac{d}{dx}(e^{f(x)})$$
$$= e^{f(x)} f''(x) + f'(x) \cdot e^{f(x)} \cdot f'(x)$$

(d) $\qquad h''(3) = e^{f(3)} f''(3) + f'(3) \cdot e^{f(3)} \cdot f'(3)$

$$= e^0 \cdot 4 + 2 \cdot e^0 \cdot 2 = \boxed{8}$$

Step 5: $g(0) = 5, g'(0) = 9$

(e) The tangent line equation is

$$\boxed{\begin{array}{l} (y - 5) = 9(x), \\ \text{or} \quad y = 9x + 5 \end{array}}$$

6.

Step 1: A good approach is to find the area of the trapezoid with the aid of trigonometry. Also, let $a = \dfrac{w}{3}$ for simplification. The resulting figure is shown below.

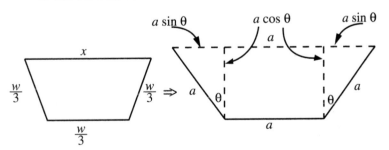

365

Step 2: The area of a trapezoid is given by $\frac{1}{2}h(b_1 + b_2)$.

For this trapezoid: $b_1 = a$
$$b_2 = x = a + 2a \sin \theta$$
$$h = a \cos \theta$$

Step 3:

$$\therefore \text{Area} = \frac{1}{2}h(b_1 + b_2) = \frac{1}{2}(a\cos\theta)(a + a + 2a\sin\theta)$$

$$= \frac{1}{2}(a\cos\theta)(2a + 2a\sin\theta)$$

$$= a^2 \cos\theta(1 + \sin\theta)$$

Step 4: Set $\dfrac{dA}{d\theta} = 0$ and solve for the critical values.

Area $= A = a^2 \cos\theta(1 + \sin\theta)$

$$\frac{dA}{d\theta} = a^2\left[\cos\theta\frac{d}{d\theta}(1+\sin\theta) + (1+\sin\theta)\frac{d}{d\theta}\cos\theta\right]$$

$$= a^2\left[(\cos\theta)(\cos\theta) - (1+\sin\theta)(\sin\theta)\right]$$

$$= a^2\left[\cos^2\theta - \sin^2\theta - \sin\theta\right]$$

Use the identity $\cos^2\theta = 1 - \sin^2\theta$

$$A = a^2\left[1 - 2\sin^2\theta - \sin\theta\right]$$

$$= -a^2\left[2\sin^2\theta + \sin\theta - 1\right]$$

$$= -a^2(2\sin\theta - 1)(\sin\theta + 1) = 0$$

$$\therefore \theta = \frac{\pi}{6} \quad \Big| \quad \theta = \frac{3\pi}{2}$$

$$= 30° \quad \text{reject}$$

Reject $\theta = \dfrac{3\pi}{2}$ because $0 \leq \theta \leq \dfrac{\pi}{2}$.

Step 5: The maximum value of a continuous function in a closed interval occurs at the endpoints or at a critical value. Evaluate the area function at 0, $\dfrac{\pi}{6}$, and $\dfrac{\pi}{2}$ (see the value table).

θ	A
0	a^2
$\dfrac{\pi}{6}$	$\dfrac{3\sqrt{3}}{4}a^2 > a^2$
$\dfrac{\pi}{2}$	0

The maximum area occurs at $\theta = \dfrac{\pi}{6}$.

$\therefore x = a + 2a \sin \theta$, when $a = \dfrac{w}{3}$ and $\theta = \dfrac{\pi}{6}$

$$x = \frac{w}{3} + \frac{2w}{3}\left(\frac{1}{2}\right)$$

$$\boxed{x = \frac{2w}{3}}$$

PRACTICE TESTS

AP Calculus BC

PRACTICE EXAM 1

This exam is also on CD-ROM in our special interactive AP Calculus TEST*ware*®

AP Calculus BC

Section I

PART A

Time: 55 minutes
 28 questions

(Answer sheets appear in the back of this book.)

DIRECTIONS: Solve each of the following problems. Select the best answer choice and fill in the corresponding oval on the answer sheet.

Calculators may NOT be used for this section of the exam.

NOTES:
  (1) Unless otherwise specified, the domain of a function f is assumed to be the set of all real numbers x for which $f(x)$ is a real number.
  (2) The inverse of a trigonometric function f may be indicated by using the inverse function notation f^{-1} or with the prefix "arc" (e.g., $\sin^{-1} x = \arcsin x$).

1. $\displaystyle\lim_{x \to 0} \frac{1 - \cos x}{x^2} =$

    (A) 0

    (B) $\dfrac{1}{2}$

    (C) 1

    (D) 2

    (E) Does not exist

2. What is the equation of the line normal to the graph $f(x) = 7x^4 + 2x^3 + x^2 + 2x + 5$ at the point where $x = 0$?

(A) $x + 2y = 10$

(B) $2x + y = 10$

(C) $5x + 5y = 2$

(D) $2x - y = -5$

(E) $2x + y = -10$

3. $\int_1^2 \dfrac{x^3 + x}{x^2} dx =$

(A) $1 + \ln 2$

(B) $\dfrac{3}{2} + \ln 3$

(C) 2

(D) $\dfrac{3}{2} + \ln 2$

(E) $1 - \ln 2$

4.   For $-1 < x \le 1$, if $f(x) = \displaystyle\sum_{n=1}^{\infty} \dfrac{(-1)^{n+1} x^{3n-2}}{3n-2}$, then $f'(x) =$

(A) $\displaystyle\sum_{n=1}^{\infty} (-1)^{n+1} x^{3n}$

(B) $\displaystyle\sum_{n=1}^{\infty} (-1)^{n+1} x^{3n-3}$

(C) $\displaystyle\sum_{n=1}^{\infty} (-1)^{3n} x^{3n}$

(D) $\displaystyle\sum_{n=1}^{\infty} (-1)^{n} x^{3n-3}$

(E) $\displaystyle\sum_{n=1}^{\infty} (-1)^{n} x^{3n}$

5.   A particle moves in the xy-plane so that at any time, t, its coordinates are $x = t^3 - t^2$ and $y = t^4 - 5t^2$. What is the acceleration vector at $t = 1$?

(A) $\langle -4, -2 \rangle$

(B) $\langle 0, 2 \rangle$

(C) $\langle 0, 4 \rangle$

(D) $\langle 2, 4 \rangle$

(E) $\langle 4, 2 \rangle$

6. If $\int f(x) \cdot e^x dx = f(x) \cdot e^x - \int 2x \cdot e^x dx$, then $f(x)$ could be which of the following?

(A) 2

(B) $2x$

(C) x^2

(D) $-x^2$

(E) e^x

7. $\int \dfrac{1}{x^2 + x - 6} dx =$

(A) $\dfrac{1}{5} \ln\left|\dfrac{x+3}{x-2}\right| + C$

(B) $\dfrac{1}{5} \ln\left|\dfrac{x-2}{x+3}\right| + C$

(C) $\dfrac{1}{5} \ln|(x-2)(x+3)| + C$

(D) $\left(\ln|x-2|\right)\left(\ln|x+3|\right) + C$

(E) $\left(\ln|x+2|\right)\left(\ln|x-3|\right) + C$

8. If A is a constant, what is the general solution for the differential equation $\dfrac{dy}{dx} = xy$ in terms of x and A?

(A) $y = Ae^x$

(B) $y = Ae^{x^2}$

(C) $y = Ax^2$

(D) $y = Ae^{\frac{x^2}{2}}$

(E) $y = Ae^{2x^2}$

9. The movement of a particle in the xy-plane is $x(t) = \sin t$, and $y(t) = \cos^2 t$. If t is in the interval $[0, \pi]$, when is the particle at rest?

(A) 0

(B) $\dfrac{\pi}{4}$

(C) $\dfrac{\pi}{2}$

(D) $\dfrac{3\pi}{4}$

(E) π

10. $\displaystyle\int x\sin(2x^2)\,dx =$

(A) $-\dfrac{1}{4}\cos(2x^2)+C$

(B) $\dfrac{1}{4}\cos(2x^2)+C$

(C) $-\dfrac{2x}{3}\cos(2x^2)+C$

(D) $2x^2\cos(2x^2) + C$

(E) $\dfrac{1}{4}\sin^2(4x)+C$

11. Let $x(t) = \dfrac{e^t + e^{-t}}{2}$ and $y(t) = \dfrac{e^t - e^{-t}}{2}$ generate a curve from $t = -1$ to $t = 1$. What is the length of this arc?

(A) $\sqrt{2}\displaystyle\int_{-1}^{1}\sqrt{e^{2t}+e^{-2t}}\,dt$

(B) $\dfrac{\sqrt{2}}{2}\displaystyle\int_{-1}^{1}(e^t+e^{-t})\,dt$

(C) $\dfrac{\sqrt{2}}{2}\displaystyle\int_{-1}^{1}(e^{2t}-e^{-2t})\,dt$

(D) $\dfrac{\sqrt{2}}{2}\displaystyle\int_{-1}^{1}\sqrt{e^{2t}+e^{-2t}}\,dt$

(E) $\dfrac{\sqrt{2}}{2}\displaystyle\int_{-1}^{1}\sqrt{e^{2t}-e^{-2t}}\,dt$

12. $\displaystyle\int\dfrac{7}{x^2+a^2}\,dx =$

(A) $\dfrac{7}{a}\tan^{-1}(x^2)+C$

(B) $7\tan^{-1}\left(\dfrac{x}{a}\right)+C$

(C) $\dfrac{7}{a}\tan^{-1}\left(\dfrac{7x}{a}\right)+C$

(D) $\dfrac{7}{a}\tan^{-1}\left(\dfrac{x}{a}\right)+C$

(E) $\dfrac{1}{a}\tan^{-1}\left(\dfrac{7x}{a}\right)+C$

13.   Find the shaded arc inside the lemniscate $r^2 = 3\sin 2\theta$.

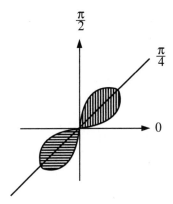

(A) $\dfrac{\pi}{2}$

(B) $\dfrac{3}{2}$

(C) $\dfrac{3\pi}{2}$

(D) $\dfrac{5\pi}{2}$

(E)   3

14. $\lim\limits_{x\to 0} x\cdot\ln x =$

(A)   0

(B)   1

(C)   ln 3

(D) e^3

(E)   does not exist

15. What is the coefficient of the $(x - 1)^3$ term in the Taylor series expansion of $f(x) = \ln x$ expanded about $x = 1$?

   (A) $\dfrac{1}{6}$

   (B) $\dfrac{1}{4}$

   (C) $\dfrac{1}{3}$

   (D) $\dfrac{1}{2}$

   (E) $\dfrac{2}{3}$

16. If $f(x) = \dfrac{x}{\cot x}$, then $f'\left(\dfrac{\pi}{4}\right) =$

   (A) $1 - \dfrac{\pi}{2}$

   (B) $1 + \dfrac{\pi}{2}$

   (C) $\dfrac{\pi}{2} - 1$

   (D) 2

   (E) $\dfrac{3}{4}$

17. If $y = x^2 + 3x + 5$ and $x = \sin t$, what is $\dfrac{dy}{dt}$ when $t = \pi$?

   (A) -3

   (B) 0

   (C) 1

   (D) 2

   (E) 3

18. $\displaystyle\int_1^\infty \dfrac{7}{x^3}\,dx =$

   (A) $-\dfrac{5}{2}$

   (B) $\dfrac{3}{2}$

   (C) $\dfrac{5}{2}$

(D) $\dfrac{7}{2}$

(E) diverges

19. If $y = x^{(x^2)}$, then $\dfrac{dy}{dx} =$

   (A) $x^{(x^2)}(1 + \ln x^2)$

   (B) $x^{(x^2)}(1 + \ln x)$

   (C) $x^{(x^2)}(2 + \ln x)$

   (D) $x^{(x^2+1)}(1 + \ln x^2)$

   (E) $x^{(x^2+1)}(2 + \ln x)$

20. The first four terms of the Maclaurin series approximation for sin .2 =

   (A) $1 - \dfrac{(.2)^3}{3!} + \dfrac{(.2)^5}{5!} - \dfrac{(.2)^7}{7!}$

   (B) $1 - \dfrac{(.2)^3}{3} + \dfrac{(.2)^5}{5} - \dfrac{(.2)^7}{7}$

   (C) $1 - \dfrac{(.2)^2}{2!} + \dfrac{(.2)^4}{4!} - \dfrac{(.2)^6}{6!}$

   (D) $1 - \dfrac{(.2)^2}{2} + \dfrac{(.2)^4}{4} - \dfrac{(.2)^6}{6}$

   (E) $1 - \dfrac{(.2)^2}{2!} + \dfrac{(.2)^3}{3!} - \dfrac{(.2)^4}{4!}$

21. Using the data in the figure, estimate $\int_1^9 f(x)\,dx$ by using the midpoint rule and four equal subintervals.

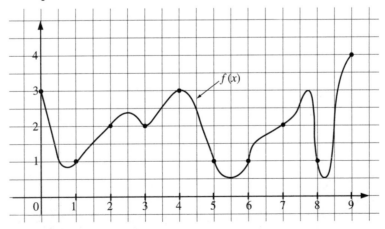

377

(A) 13

(B) 14

(C) 15

(D) 16

(E) 17

22. If $\int_1^7 f(x)\,dx = 4$ and $\int_1^7 g(x)\,dx = 2$, find $\int_1^7 [3f(x) + 2g(x) + 1]\,dx$.

(A) 22

(B) 23

(C) 24

(D) 25

(E) 26

23. The slope field for a differential equation is shown in the graph below. Which of the following could be the differential equation?

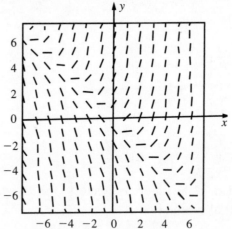

(A) $\dfrac{dy}{dx} + y = x$

(B) $\dfrac{dy}{dx} - y = x$

(C) $\dfrac{dy}{dx} - y + 1 = x$

(D) $y\dfrac{dy}{dx} = x$

(E) $y\dfrac{dy}{dx} = -x$

24. A point (x, y) travels along the graph of the function $y = f(x)$. If the y-coordinate is decreasing at the rate of 7 units per second, at what rate is the x-coordinate changing at the instant the slope of the function is -4?

(A) $-\dfrac{7}{4}$

(B) $-\dfrac{4}{7}$

(C) $\dfrac{4}{7}$

(D) $\dfrac{7}{4}$

(E) 28

25. If the average value of the function $f(x) = 2x^2$ on the interval $[0, c]$ is 6, then $c =$

(A) 2

(B) 3

(C) 4

(D) 5

(E) 6

26. In the diagram below $f(x) = 3x^2 + 3$. What is the average value of $f(x)$ on the interval $[1, 3]$?

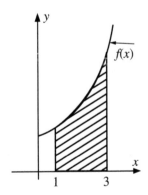

(A) 36

(B) 32

(C) 24

(D) 16

(E) 8

27. The region in the first quadrant between the *x*-axis and $y = x^2$ from $x = 0$ to $x = 4$ is rotated about the line $x = 4$. The volume of the resulting solid is given by which of the following?

(A) $2\pi \int_{y=0}^{4} (4 - \sqrt{y})^2 dy$

(B) $\pi \int_{y=0}^{4} (4 - \sqrt{y})^2 dy$

(C) $\pi \int_{y=0}^{16} (4 - x^2)^2 dy$

(D) $\pi \int_{y=0}^{16} (\sqrt{y} + 4)^2 dy$

(E) $\pi \int_{y=0}^{16} (4 - \sqrt{y})^2 dy$

28. Which of the following intervals best describes all the values of *x* for which the series $\sum_{n=1}^{\infty} \dfrac{x^n}{n}$ coverages?

(A) $(-1, 1)$

(B) $[-1, 1)$

(C) $(-1, 1]$

(D) $[-1, 1]$

(E) $(-\infty, \infty)$

STOP
This is the end of Section I, Part A.
If time still remains, you may check your work only in this section.
Do not begin Section I, Part B until instructed to do so.

Section I

PART B

Time: 50 minutes
    17 questions

(Answer sheets appear in the back of this book.)

> **DIRECTIONS:** Solve each of the following problems. Select the best answer choice and fill in the corresponding oval on the answer sheet.
>
> Calculators MAY be used for this section of the exam.

NOTES:

(1) The exact numerical value of the correct answer does not always appear among the choices given. When this happens, select the number from among the choices that best approximates the exact numerical value.

(2) Unless otherwise specified, the domain of a function f is assumed to be the set of all real numbers x for which $f(x)$ is a real number.

(3) The inverse of a trigonometric function f may be indicated by using the inverse function notation f^{-1} or with the prefix "arc" (e.g., $\sin^{-1} x = \arcsin x$).

76. Let $g(x)$ represent the continuous solution to the differential equation $\dfrac{dy}{dx} = xy$ over the interval $[3, 5]$. Use Euler's method with step-size at 0.1 to approximate $g(3.3)$ if $g(3) = 1$.

    (A) 2.24796

    (B) 2.13478

    (C) 2.01462

    (D) 1.39865

    (E) 1.39721

77. Suppose that $f(x)$ is continuous for $a \le x \le b$, and let $\{a = x_0 < x_1 < x_2 \ldots < x_n = b\}$ be a subdivision of $[a, b]$ into n equal intervals of length $h = \dfrac{b-a}{n}$. Which one of the following approximates $\int_a^b f(x)\,dx$?

(A) $h\,[f(x_0) + 2f(x_1) + 2f(x_2) + \ldots + 2f(x_{n-1}) + f(x_n)]$

(B) $2h\,[f(x_0) + 2f(x_1) + 2f(x_2) + \ldots + 2f(x_{n-1}) + f(x_n)]$

(C) $\dfrac{h}{2}[f(x_0) + 2f(x_1) + 2f(x_2) + \ldots + 2f(x_{n-1}) + f(x_n)]$

(D) $2h\,[f(x_0) + f(x_1) + f(x_2) + \ldots + f(x_n)]$

(E) $\dfrac{h}{3}[f(x_0) + 2f(x_1) + 3f(x_2) + 2f(x_3) + 3f(x_4) + \ldots]$

78. Let $f(x) = x^3$. Find the value c that satisfies the Mean Value Theorem on the closed interval $[1, 3]$.

(A) 1.414

(B) 1.732

(C) 2.000

(D) 2.082

(E) 2.351

79. An object moves along a line with a velocity $v(t) = t^3 + 2t - t - 2 = (t + 1)(t + 2)(t - 1)$ meters/sec. How far in meters does the object travel from $t = 0$ to $t = 3$?

(A) $\dfrac{169}{6}$

(B) 30

(C) $\dfrac{371}{12}$

(D) $\dfrac{218}{7}$

(E) $\dfrac{200}{6}$

80. If $f(x) = \cos(\sin(\cos(2x)))$, find $f'(x)$.

(A) $2\sin(2x)\cos(\cos(2x))\sin(\sin(\cos(2x)))$

(B) $-2\sin(2x)\cos(\cos(2x))\sin(\sin(\cos(2x)))$

(C) $2\cos(2x)\sin(\sin(2x))\cos(\cos(\sin(2x)))$

(D) $-2\cos(2x)\sin(\sin(2x))\cos(\cos(\sin(2x)))$

(E) $2\sin(2x)\sin(\cos(2x))\sin(\cos(\sin(2x)))$

81. $\displaystyle\lim_{h\to 0}\frac{\sqrt{1+h}+\sqrt{1-h}-2}{h} =$

(A) $-\dfrac{1}{4}$

(B) 0

(C) $\dfrac{3}{8}$

(D) $\dfrac{1}{2}$

(E) $\dfrac{3}{4}$

82.   Let $f(x) = \int_0^x (t-t^2)\,dt$ for $x > 0$. What is the maximum value of f?

(A) -1

(B) 0

(C) $\dfrac{1}{6}$

(D) $\dfrac{1}{3}$

(E) 1

83.   What is the length of arc joining $(1, 0)$ to $(0, 1)$ on the curve $x = \cos t$, $y = \sin^2 t$?

(A)   1.628

(B)   1.479

(C)   1.443

(D)   1.391

(E)   .861

84.   How many relative or absolute maximum values does $f(x) = x - \cos x$ have on the interval $[-2\pi, 2\pi]$?

(A)   1

(B)   2

(C)   3

(D)   4

(E)   5

85. $\displaystyle\int_0^4 \frac{dx}{(x-1)^{\frac{2}{3}}} =$

(A)   1.327

(B)   3.000

(C)   4.326

(D)   7.327

(E)   diverges

86.

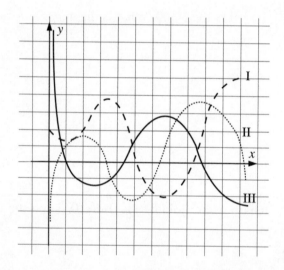

The graphs shown above represent a function $f(x)$, its first derivative $f'(x)$, and its second derivative $f''(x)$. Which of the following correctly identifies each of the three graphs?

	$f(x)$	$f'(x)$	$f''(x)$
(A)	I	II	III
(B)	I	III	II
(C)	II	I	III
(D)	III	II	I
(E)	III	I	II

87. If $\sin x = x - \dfrac{x^3}{3!} + \dfrac{x^5}{5!} - \cdots + \dfrac{(-1)^n x^{2n+1}}{(2n+1)!}$, what is $\cos(3x^2)$?

(A) $\displaystyle\sum_{n=0}^{\infty} \dfrac{x^{4n}}{(2n)!}$

(B) $\displaystyle\sum_{n=0}^{\infty} \dfrac{(-9x)^{2n}}{(2n)!}$

(C) $\displaystyle\sum_{n=0}^{\infty} \dfrac{(-1)^n x^{2n}}{(2n)!}$

(D) $\displaystyle\sum_{n=0}^{\infty} \dfrac{-9x^{4n}}{(2n)!}$

(E) $\displaystyle\sum_{n=0}^{\infty} \dfrac{(-9)^n x^{4n}}{(2n)!}$

88. If f and g are twice differentiable functions such that $g(x) = \ln(f(x))$ and $g''(x) = \dfrac{h(x)}{[f(x)]^2}$, then $h(x) = $

(A) $f(x)f''(x) - 2f'(x)$

(B) $f(x)f''(x) - f'(x)$

(C) $f(x)[f''(x)]^2 - f'(x)$

(D) $f(x)f''(x) - [f'(x)]^2$

(E) $[f(x)f''(x) - f'(x)]^2$

89. If $x = 2\sin\theta$ and $y = 3\cos\theta$, then $\dfrac{d^2y}{dx^2} = $

(A) $-\dfrac{3}{4}\csc^3\theta$

(B) $-\dfrac{3}{4}\sec^3\theta$

(C) $-\dfrac{3}{4}\tan^3\theta$

(D) $-\dfrac{3}{4}\cot^3\theta$

(E) $-\dfrac{4}{3}\tan^2\theta\sec\theta$

90. A particle moves along a line such that its velocity at any time t, $1 \le t < 8$, is given by $v(t) = 10\sin(\ln(t))$. At what time within this interval is the average velocity equal to the instantaneous velocity?

(A) 1.937

(B) 2.756

(C) 3.237 and 4.139

(D) 3.567

(E) 4.139 only

91. Which of the following series converge?

I $\displaystyle\sum_{n=1}^{\infty} \frac{n}{2n+1}$

II $\displaystyle\sum_{n=1}^{\infty} \frac{1}{5+4^n}$

III $\displaystyle\sum_{n=1}^{\infty} \frac{2^n}{n!}$

(A) II only

(B) I and II only

(C) I and III only

(D) II and III only

(E) I, II, and III

92. Solve the differential equation $R^2 + \dfrac{dR}{dt} = -R$ for $R(t)$ under the initial condition that $R(0) = \dfrac{1}{2}$.

(A) $\dfrac{3}{7e^t - 1}$

(B) $\dfrac{2}{5e^t - 1}$

(C) $\dfrac{1}{3e^t - 1}$

(D) $\dfrac{1 + 4e^t}{10}$

(E) $\dfrac{-3}{1 - 7e^{2t}}$

STOP
This is the end of Section I, Part B.
If time still remains, you may check your work only in this section.
Do not begin Section II, Part A until instructed to do so.

Section II

PART A

Time: 45 minutes
    3 free-response problems

DIRECTIONS: Show all your work in your exam booklet. Grading is based on the methods used to solve the problems as well as the accuracy of your final answers.

Calculators MAY be used for this section of the exam.

---

1. Referring to the graph below, let $f(x) = x^3 - 3x + 6$ and $g(x) = \frac{1}{5}x^2 + 2x + 6$.

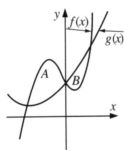

   (a)   Find the area of region A.

   (b)   Find the volume of solid generated when region A is revolved about the x-axis.

   (c)   Find the volume of the solid generated when region B is revolved about the line $y = -1$.

2. All answers that require a series answer can be written in summation notation or with sufficient terms and a general term to clearly identify the pattern unless specified otherwise.

   (a)   Write the Taylor polynomial centered at $x = 0$ for xe^x.

   (b)   Write the Taylor polynomial centered at $x = 0$ for $\int xe^x\,dx$ in polynomial form.

(c) Find the exact value of $\int_0^1 xe^x dx$ using integration by parts.

(d) Use the results of parts (b) and (c) to determine $\sum_{n=1}^{\infty} \dfrac{1}{(n+2)n!}$.

3. Given the equation $r = 1 - \sin\theta$.

(a) Find the θ values at which the horizontal tangents to the cardioid $r = 1 - \sin\theta$ occur.

(b) Find the area inside the cardioid $r = 1 - \sin\theta$.

(c) Find the perimeter of the cardioid $r = 1 - \sin\theta$.

(d) Find the area of the region that lies inside the circle $r = 1$ and outside the cardioid $r = 1 - \sin\theta$.

STOP
This is the end of Section II, Part A.
If time still remains, you may check your work only in this section.
Do not begin Section II, Part B until instructed to do so.

Section II

PART B

Time: 45 minutes
3 free-response problems

DIRECTIONS: Show all your work in your exam booklet. Grading is based on the methods used to solve the problems as well as the accuracy of your final answers.

Calculators MAY NOT be used for this section of the exam.

(During the timed portion for Part B, you may continue to work on the problems in Part A without the use of a calculator.)

---

4. An object starts from point P (5, 1) and moves with an $\vec{a}(t) = \langle\, 2\cos t,\ -3\sin t\, \rangle$. Assume $\vec{v}(0) = \langle 1, 3\rangle$.

   Find:

   (a) the velocity vector.

   (b) the speed of the object at time $t = \dfrac{\pi}{2}$.

   (c) the position vector.

   (d) what is the shortest time for the object to move to point Q $(\pi + 9, 1)$?

5. Consider the differential equation given by $\dfrac{dy}{dx} = \dfrac{2x}{y}$.

   (a) For the 15 points indicated on the axes below, sketch the slope field for the given differential equation.

   (b) Let $f(x)$ be the particular solution such that $f(3) = 5$. Use Euler's method with two steps of equal size to estimate $f(4)$.

   (c) Solve the given differential equation with initial condition $f(3) = 5$, and find the exact value of $f(4)$.

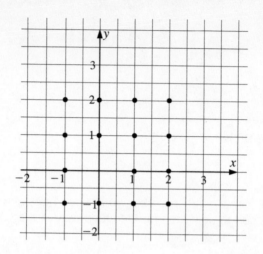

6.   Consider the curve given by $xy^2 - x^2y = 12$.

   (a)   Find $\dfrac{dy}{dx}$ in terms of x and y.

   (b)   Find the equation of the tangent line(s) to the curve at each point where $x = 1$.

   (c)   Find the x-coordinate(s), if any, where the tangent line is horizontal.

   (d)   Find the x-coordinate(s), if any, where the tangent line is vertical.

END OF EXAM

PRACTICE EXAM 1

AP Calculus BC

Answer Key

Part A

1. (B)	15. (C)
2. (A)	16. (B)
3. (D)	17. (A)
4. (B)	18. (D)
5. (E)	19. (D)
6. (C)	20. (A)
7. (B)	21. (B)
8. (D)	22. (A)
9. (C)	23. (B)
10. (A)	24. (D)
11. (D)	25. (B)
12. (D)	26. (D)
13. (E)	27. (E)
14. (A)	28. (B)

Part B

76. (A)
77. (C)
78. (D)
79. (C)
80. (A)
81. (A)
82. (C)
83. (B)
84. (A)
85. (D)
86. (A)
87. (E)
88. (D)
89. (B)
90. (B)
91. (D)
92. (C)

Free-Response Answers

1.

(a) 5.552

(b) 195.733

(c) 355.567

2.

(a) See detailed explanation

(b) See detailed explanation

(c) 1

(d) $\dfrac{1}{2}$

3.

(a) $\dfrac{\pi}{6}, \dfrac{5\pi}{6}, \dfrac{3\pi}{2}$

(b) $\dfrac{3\pi}{2} \approx 4.712$

(c) $\dfrac{8-\pi}{4} \approx 1.215$

4.

(a) $\langle 2\sin t + 1,\ 3\cos t \rangle$

(b) 3

(c) $\langle -2\cos t + t + 7,\ 3\sin t + 1 \rangle$

(d) π

5.

(a) See detailed explanation

(b) 6.225

(c) $\sqrt{39}$

6.

(a) $\dfrac{2xy - y^2}{2xy - x^2}$, or $\dfrac{y(2x - y)}{x(2y - x)}$

(b) $y + 3 = \dfrac{15}{7}(x-1)$

$y - 4 = \dfrac{-8}{7}(x-1)$

(c) $\sqrt[3]{6}$

(d) $\sqrt[3]{-48}$

PRACTICE EXAM 1

AP Calculus BC

Detailed Explanations of Answers

Section 1

PART A

1. **(B)**

   Step 1: Substitute $x=0$. $\lim\limits_{x\to\infty}\dfrac{1-\cos 0}{0^2}\Rightarrow\dfrac{0}{0}$, which is indeterminate. Apply L'Hospital's rule.

   Step 2: $\lim\limits_{x\to 0}\dfrac{1-\cos x}{x^2}=\lim\limits_{x\to 0}\dfrac{\sin x}{2x}\Rightarrow\dfrac{0}{0}$. This is also indeterminate. Apply L'Hospital's rule again.

   Step 3: $\lim\limits_{x\to 0}\dfrac{\sin x}{2x}=\lim\limits_{x\to 0}\dfrac{\cos x}{2}=\boxed{\dfrac{1}{2}}$

2. **(A)**

   Step 1: Find the y value at $x = 0$. Find the slope of the tangent line at $x = 0$.

   $$f(x) = 7x^4+2x^3+x^2+2x+5$$
   $$f(0) = 5$$
   $$f'(x) = 28x^3+6x^2+2x+2$$
   $$f'(0) = 2$$

   Step 2: The slope of the normal line is the negative reciprocal of the slope of the tangent line, $\therefore m=-\dfrac{1}{2}$.

   Step 3: The equation of the line with $m=-\dfrac{1}{2}$ through the point $(0, 5)$ is
   $$y-5=-\dfrac{1}{2}(x-0)\Rightarrow\boxed{x+2y=10}$$

3. **(D)**

Divide by x^2 and integrate

$$\int_1^2 \frac{x^3+x}{x^2}\,dx = \int_1^2 \left(x+\frac{1}{x}\right) dx = \frac{x^2}{2}+\ln|x|\Big|_1^2 = (2+\ln 2)-\left(\frac{1}{2}+\ln 1\right)$$

$$= \boxed{\frac{3}{2}+\ln 2}$$

4. **(B)**

We can differentiate the power series term by term, remembering that the constant term, $(-1)^{n+1}$, remains unchanged.

$$f'(x) = \sum_{n=1}^{\infty}(-1)^{n+1}\left[\frac{d}{dx}\left(\frac{x^{3n-2}}{3n-2}\right)\right] = (-1)^{n+1}\sum_{n=1}^{\infty}\left[\frac{(3n-2)(x)^{3n-3}}{(3n-2)}\right]$$

$$= \boxed{\sum_{n=1}^{\infty}(-1)^{n+1}x^{3n-3}}$$

5. **(E)**

Step 1: Differentiate position, $\vec{s}(t) = \left\langle t^3 - t^2,\ t^4 - 5t^2\right\rangle$

to get velocity, $\vec{v}(t) = \left\langle 3t^2 - 2t,\ 4t^3 - 10t\right\rangle$.

Step 2: Differentiate velocity, to get acceleration, $\vec{a}(t) = \left\langle 6t - 2,\ 12t - 10\right\rangle$
$\vec{a}(1) = \boxed{\langle 4,2\rangle}$

6. **(C)**

Compare the given equation to the process of integration by parts

$$\int u\,dv = uv - \int v\,du$$

$$\int f(x)e^x dx = f(x)\cdot e^x - \int 2x\cdot e^x dx$$

If $\qquad u = f(x)$ and $dv = e^x dx,$
Then $\quad du = f'(x)\,dx \qquad v = e^x$

$\qquad \therefore \quad du = f'(x)\,dx = 2x\,dx$

$\qquad\qquad \text{or } f'(x) = 2x$

$\qquad\qquad \therefore\ f(x) = x^2 + C$

Only answer choice C, $\boxed{x^2}$ is of the correct format.

7. **(B)**

Step 1: Use partial fractions to rearrange the integrand.

$$\frac{1}{x^2+x-6} = \frac{1}{(x+3)(x-2)} = \frac{A}{x+3} + \frac{B}{x-2} \Rightarrow A = -\frac{1}{5}, B = \frac{1}{5}$$

Step 2: Integrate.

$$\int \frac{1}{x^2+x-6}\,dx = \int \left(\frac{-\frac{1}{5}}{x+3} + \frac{\frac{1}{5}}{x-2}\right) dx = -\frac{1}{5}\ln|x+3| + \frac{1}{5}\ln|x-2| + C$$

$$= \frac{1}{5}\ln\left|\frac{x-2}{x+3}\right| + C$$

8. **(D)**

Step 1: Separate the variables.

$$\frac{dy}{dx} = xy \Rightarrow \frac{dy}{y} = x\,dx$$

Step 2: Integrate both sides.

$$\ln|y| = \frac{x^2}{2} + C$$

$$y = \pm e^{\frac{x^2}{2}+c} \Rightarrow Ae^{\frac{x^2}{2}}, \text{ where } A \text{ is a constant}$$

9. **(C)**

Step 1: Write the position vector, $\vec{s}(t) = \left\langle \sin t, \cos^2 t \right\rangle$

Step 2: Differentiate to get the velocity vector $\vec{v}(t) = \frac{d}{dt}(\vec{s}(t))$
$$= \left\langle \cos t, -2\cos t \sin t \right\rangle$$

Step 3: The particle is at rest when $\vec{v}(t) = \left\langle 0,0 \right\rangle$

Step 4: Solve: $\cos t = 0$

$$t = \frac{\pi}{2}$$

Solve $-2\cos t \sin t = 0$

$$t = 0, \frac{\pi}{2}, \pi$$

Step 5: For $\frac{dx}{dt}$ and $\frac{dy}{dt}$ to both be equal to 0 at the same time, $t = \boxed{\dfrac{\pi}{2}}$

10. **(A)**

Use u-substitution. Let $u = 2x^2 \Rightarrow du = 4x\,dx$

$$\int x\sin(2x^2)\,dx = \int (\sin 2x^2) \cdot x\,dx = \tfrac{1}{4}\int (\sin 2x^2) \cdot 4x\,dx$$

$$= \frac{1}{4}\int \sin u\,du = \frac{-1}{4}\cos u + C = \boxed{-\frac{1}{4}\cos(2x^2) + C}$$

11. **(D)**

Step 1: Arc length $= \displaystyle\int_a^b \sqrt{\left(\frac{dx}{dt}\right)^2 + \left(\frac{dy}{dt}\right)^2}\,dt$

$$x = \frac{e^t - e^{-t}}{2} \Rightarrow \frac{dx}{dt} = \frac{e^t - e^{-t}}{2}$$

$$y = \frac{e^t - e^{-t}}{2} \Rightarrow \frac{dy}{dt} = \frac{e^t + e^{-t}}{2}$$

Step 2: $\therefore$ Arc length $= \displaystyle\int_{-1}^1 \sqrt{\left(\frac{e^t - e^{-t}}{2}\right)^2 + \left(\frac{e^t + e^{-t}}{2}\right)^2}\,dt$

$$= \int_{-1}^1 \sqrt{\frac{1}{4}\left(2e^{2t} + 2e^{-2t}\right)}\,dt$$

$$= \int_{-1}^1 \sqrt{\frac{1}{2}\left(e^{2t} + e^{-2t}\right)}\,dt$$

$$= \boxed{\frac{\sqrt{2}}{2}\int_{-1}^1 \sqrt{e^{2t} + e^{-2t}}\,dt}$$

12. **(D)**

Use $\displaystyle\int \frac{dx}{x^2 + a^2} = \frac{1}{a}\tan^{-1}\left(\frac{x}{a}\right) + C.$

$$\therefore \int \frac{7dx}{x^2 + a^2} = 7\int \frac{dx}{x^2 + a^2} = \boxed{\frac{7}{a}\tan^{-1}\left(\frac{x}{a}\right) + C}$$

13. **(E)**

$$A = \frac{1}{2}\int_a^b r^2\,d\theta$$

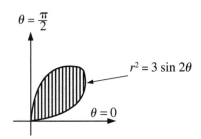

Find the area in one loop and the double the answer.

$$A = 2\left[\frac{1}{2} \cdot \int_0^{\frac{\pi}{2}} 3\sin(2\theta)\, d\theta\right] = 3\int_0^{\frac{\pi}{2}} \sin 2\theta\, d\theta = \frac{3}{2}(-\cos 2\theta)\Big|_0^{\frac{\pi}{2}}$$

$$= \frac{-3}{2}[-1-1] = \boxed{3}$$

14. (A)

Step 1: Substitute $x = 0 \Rightarrow 0 \cdot \ln 0 = 0 \cdot (-\infty)$, which is indeterminate.

Step 2: Rearrange the format to a L'Hospital-compatible form, either $\frac{0}{0}$ or $\frac{\infty}{\infty}$

$$\lim_{x\to 0} x \ln x = \lim_{x\to 0} \frac{\ln x}{\left(\frac{1}{x}\right)} \Rightarrow \frac{-\infty}{\infty}$$

by L'Hospital's rule $= \lim_{x\to 0} \dfrac{\ln x}{\frac{1}{x}} = \lim_{x\to 0} \dfrac{\left(\frac{1}{x}\right)}{\left(\frac{-1}{x^2}\right)} = \lim_{x\to 0}(-x) = \boxed{0}$

15. (C)

Step 1: The general expansion term expanded about $x = a$ is $\dfrac{f^n(a)(x-a)^n}{n!}$.
The coefficient of $(x-1)^3$ is $\dfrac{f^3(1)}{3!}$.

Step 2: $f(x) \quad = \ln x$

$$f'(x) = \frac{1}{x}$$

$$f''(x) = \frac{-1}{x^2}$$

$$f'''(x) = \frac{2}{x^3} \Rightarrow f^3(1) = \frac{2}{1} = 2.$$

$$\therefore \frac{f^3(1)}{3!} = \frac{2}{6} = \boxed{\frac{1}{3}}$$

16. **(B)**

Step 1: Rewrite the quotient as a product: $\dfrac{x}{\cot x} = x \tan x.$

Step 2: Differentiate $f'\left(\dfrac{\pi}{4}\right) = x\left[\sec^2 x\right] + \tan x\big|_{x = \frac{\pi}{4}}$

$$= \dfrac{\pi}{4}\left[\sec^2 \dfrac{\pi}{4}\right] + \tan \dfrac{\pi}{4} = \dfrac{\pi}{4}\left[\left(\sqrt{2}\right)^2\right] + 1 = \boxed{\dfrac{\pi}{2} + 1}$$

17. **(A)**

Step 1: $\dfrac{dy}{dt} = \dfrac{dy}{dx} \cdot \dfrac{dx}{dt}, \ \dfrac{dy}{dx} = 2x + 3 \text{ and } \dfrac{dx}{dt} = \cos t$

$$\therefore \dfrac{dy}{dt} = (2x + 3) \cdot \cos t$$

Step 2: When $t = \pi, x = \sin \pi = 0$

$$\therefore \dfrac{dy}{dx} = (2(0) + 3)\cos \pi = 3(-1) = \boxed{-3}$$

18. **(D)**

$$\int_1^\infty \dfrac{7}{x^3} \, dx = \lim_{b \to \infty} \int_1^b 7x^{-3} dx = \lim_{b \to \infty} \dfrac{7x^{-2}}{-2}\bigg|_1^b$$

$$= \lim_{b \to \infty} \left[\dfrac{-7}{2b^2} + \dfrac{7}{2}\right] = \boxed{\dfrac{7}{2}}$$

19. **(D)**

Step 1: Take the ln of the equation.

$$y = x^{(x^2)}$$

$$\ln y = \ln x^{(x^2)} = x^2 \ln x$$

Step 2: Use implicit differentiation. Note that $x^2 \ln x$ is a product.

$$\ln y = x^2 \ln x$$

$$\dfrac{1}{y}\dfrac{dy}{dx} = x^2\left(\dfrac{1}{x}\right) + (\ln x)(2x) = x(1 + 2\ln x)$$

$$\dfrac{dy}{dx} = y\big(x(1 + 2\ln x)\big)$$

$$= x^{(x^2)} \cdot x \cdot (1 + 2\ln x)$$

$$= \boxed{x^{(x^2 + 1)}(1 + \ln x^2)}$$

20. **(A)**

The Maclaurin series expansion for $\sin x$ about $x = 0$ is

$$\sin(x) = 1 - \frac{x^3}{3!} + \frac{x^5}{5!} - \frac{x^7}{7!} + \cdots.$$

$$\therefore \sin(.2) = \boxed{1 - \frac{(.2)^3}{3!} + \frac{(.2)^5}{5!} - \frac{(.2)^7}{7!}}$$

21. **(B)**

Step 1: Calculate the size of the interval.

$$\frac{b-a}{n} = \frac{9-1}{4} = 2$$

The intervals are $[1, 3]$, $[3, 5]$, $[5, 7]$ and $[7, 9]$.

Step 2: The midpoint rule states that

$$\int_a^b f(x)\, dx \approx \frac{b-a}{n}\left[f\left(\frac{x_0 + x_1}{2}\right) + f\left(\frac{x_1 + x_2}{2}\right) \cdots \right]$$

$$2\left[f(2) + f(4) + f(6) + f(8) \right]$$

$$= 2\left[2 + 3 + 1 + 1\right] = \boxed{14}$$

22. **(A)**

Split the integral and factor out the constant multipliers.

$$\int_1^7 \left[3f(x) + 2g(x) + 1\right] dx = 3\int_1^7 f(x)\,dx + 2\int_1^7 g(x)\,dx + \int_1^7 1\,dx$$

$$= 3(4) + 2(2) + x\big|_1^7$$

$$= 12 + 4 + 6 = \boxed{22}$$

23. **(B)**

Step 1: Rearrange the differential equations in the answer choices in terms of what $\frac{dy}{dx}$ equals:

(A) $\dfrac{dy}{dx} = x - y$

(B) $\dfrac{dy}{dx} = x + y$

(C) $\dfrac{dy}{dx} = x + y - 1$

(D) $\dfrac{dy}{dx} = \dfrac{x}{y}$

(E) $\dfrac{dy}{dx} = \dfrac{-x}{y}$

Step 2: Observe in the slope field that the $y = -x$ coordinate pairs, $(1, -1)$ $(2, -2)$, $(-1, 1)$, $(-2, 2)$, etc., show a slope of zero.

This implies that $x + y = 0$.

The only answer choice for which $\dfrac{dy}{dx} = 0$ at $y = -x$ is choice B, $\boxed{\dfrac{dy}{dx} - y = x}$.

24. **(D)**

Step 1: Use $\dfrac{dx}{dt} = \dfrac{dx}{dy} \cdot \dfrac{dy}{dt}$.

Step 2: From the given data, $\dfrac{dy}{dx} = -4$ and $\dfrac{dy}{dt} = -7$.

$$\therefore \dfrac{dx}{dt} = \left(-\dfrac{1}{4}\right)(-7) = \boxed{\dfrac{+7}{4}}$$

25. **(B)**

Step 1: Average value $= \dfrac{1}{b-a}\displaystyle\int_a^b f(x)\,dx$

$$6 = \dfrac{1}{c-0}\displaystyle\int_a^c 2x^2\,dx$$

$$6 = \dfrac{1}{c}\left[\dfrac{2c^3}{3}\right]$$

$$c^2 = 9$$

$$c = \pm 3$$

Step 2: The interval notation $[0, c]$ implies $c > 0$,

$$\therefore c = \boxed{3}$$

26. **(D)**

Average value $= \dfrac{1}{b-a}\displaystyle\int_a^b f(x)\,dx$

$$= \dfrac{1}{3-1}\displaystyle\int_1^3 \left(3x^2 + 3\right)dx = \boxed{16}$$

27. **(E)**

Step 1: Make a sketch.

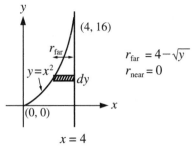

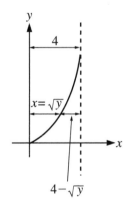

Step 2: Volume $= \pi\int_a^b \left(r_{far}^2 - r_{near}^2\right)dy$

$$= \boxed{\pi\int_{y=0}^{16}\left(4-\sqrt{y}\right)^2 dy}$$

28. **(B)**

Step 1: Use the ratio test.

$$\lim_{n\to\infty}\left|\frac{\frac{x^{n+1}}{n+1}}{\frac{x^n}{n}}\right| = \lim_{n\to\infty}\left|\frac{nx}{n+1}\right| = |x| < 1 \Rightarrow (-1, 1)$$

Step 2: Test these endpoints.

If $x=1$ $\quad \sum_1^\infty \frac{x^n}{n} \Rightarrow \sum_1^\infty \frac{1^n}{n} = \sum_1^\infty \frac{1}{n}$

This is a divergent harmonic.

$$\therefore \sum_{n=1}^{\infty} \frac{x^n}{n} \text{ does NOT converge at } x = 1.$$

If $x = -1$ $\qquad \sum_{n=1}^{\infty} \frac{x^n}{n} \Rightarrow \sum_{n=1}^{\infty} \frac{(-1)^n}{n} \Rightarrow \sum_{n=1}^{\infty} (-1)^n \cdot \frac{1}{n}$

This is a convergent alternating harmonic.

$$\therefore \sum_{n=1}^{\infty} \frac{x^n}{n} \text{ DOES converge at } x = -1.$$

Thus, the series converge in the interval $\boxed{(-1, 1)}$

Section I

PART B

76. **(A)**

Step 1: Euler's method is an iterative process. If $\frac{dy}{dx} = f(x, y)$ with a solution $g(x)$, then $g(x_n) = g(x_{n-1} + \Delta x \cdot f(x_{n-1}, y_{n-1}))$.

Step 2: $\frac{dy}{dx} = f(x, y) = xy$, $g(3) = 1$, $\Delta x = 0.1$

Make an iterative chart:

x_n	$g(x_{n-1} + \Delta x \cdot f(x_{n-1}, y_{n-1}))$	$g(x_n)$
3	Given	1
3.1	$1 + (.1)(3 \times 1)$	1.3
3.2	$1.3 + (.1)(3.1 \times 1.3)$	1.703
3.3	$1.703 + (.1)(3.2 \times 1.703)$	2.24796

$g(3.3) \approx \boxed{2.24796}$

77. **(C)**

The Trapezoidal Rule states that

$$\int_a^b f(x)\, dx \approx \frac{b-a}{2n}\left[f(x_0) + 2f(x_1) \cdots 2f(x_{n-1}) + f(x_n)\right]$$

$$= \boxed{\frac{h}{2}\left[f(x_0) + 2f(x_1)\text{n}2f(x_{n-1}) + f(x_n)\right]}$$

78. **(D)**

Step 1: From the Mean Value Theorem:

$$f'(c) = \frac{f(b) - f(a)}{b - a}$$

Step 2: $f(x) = x^3 \Rightarrow f'(c) = 3c^2$

$$\Rightarrow f(b) = f(3) = 27$$
$$\Rightarrow f(a) = f(1) = 1$$

$$\therefore \quad 3c^2 = \frac{27-1}{3-1}$$

Step 3: Solve for c in the interval $[1, 3]$.

$$c = \frac{\sqrt{39}}{3} = \boxed{2.082}$$

79. **(C)**

Step 1: Determine if the object comes to rest in the interval $[0, 3]$ and reverses direction by checking whether $v(t) = 0$.

$$v(t) = (t + 1)(t + 2)(t - 1) = 0$$
$$\therefore At\ t = +1\ \text{the particle is at rest}$$

Step 2: Analyze the direction of the particle with a diagram.

Step 3: Write the distance function.

$$s(t) = \int v(t)\, dt = \frac{t^4}{4} - \frac{2t^3}{3} - \frac{t^2}{2} - 2t + C$$

$$s(0) = C$$

$$s(1) = -\frac{19}{12} + C$$

$$s(3) = \frac{111}{4} + C$$

Sketch the distance.

Distance traveled: from $t = 0$ to $t = 1$ is $\dfrac{19}{12}$ m

from $t = 1$ to $t = 3$ is $\dfrac{88}{3}$ m

Total distance from $t = 0$ to $t = 3$ is $\dfrac{19}{12} + \dfrac{88}{3} = \dfrac{371}{12}$ m.

80. (A)

Step 1: Use $\dfrac{d}{dx}(\cos u) = -\sin u \dfrac{d}{dx}(u)$, where $u = \sin(\cos(2x))$.

$$\frac{d}{dx}(\cos(\sin(\cos(2x)))) = -\sin(\sin(\cos(2x))) \cdot \frac{d}{dx}(\sin(\cos(2x)))$$

Step 2: Now use $\dfrac{d}{dx}(\sin u) = \cos u \dfrac{du}{dx}$, where $u = \cos(2x)$.

$$\frac{d}{dx}(\sin(\cos(2x))) = \cos(\cos(2x))\frac{d}{dx}(\cos(2x))$$

Step 3: $\dfrac{d}{dx}(\cos 2(x)) = -\sin(2x) \cdot 2 = -2\sin(2x)$

Step 4: Putting it all together yields

$$\frac{d}{dx}(\cos(\sin(\cos(2x)))) = +2\sin(2x)\cos(\cos(2x))\sin(\sin(\cos(2x)))$$

81. (A)

Step 1: Substitute $h = 0$.

$$\left.\frac{\sqrt{1+h}+\sqrt{1-h}-2}{h^2}\right|_{h=0} \Rightarrow \frac{0}{0}, \text{ indeterminate}$$

Step 2: Apply L'Hospital's rule.

$$\lim_{x\to a}\frac{f(x)}{g(x)} = \lim_{x\to a}\frac{f'(x)}{g'(x)}$$

Note: $\dfrac{d}{dh}(\sqrt{1+h}) = \dfrac{1}{2\sqrt{1+h}}$

$$\lim_{h\to 0}\frac{\sqrt{1+h}+\sqrt{1-h}-2}{h^2} = \lim_{h\to 0}\frac{\frac{1}{2\sqrt{1+h}} - \frac{1}{2\sqrt{1-h}}}{2h} \Rightarrow \frac{0}{0}, \text{ indeterminate.}$$

Step 3: Apply L'Hospital's rule again.

$$\lim_{h\to 0}\frac{-\frac{1}{4}(1+h)^{-\frac{3}{2}} - \frac{1}{4}(1-h)^{-\frac{3}{2}}}{2} = \frac{-\frac{1}{4}-\frac{1}{4}}{2} = \boxed{-\frac{1}{4}}$$

82. (C)

Step 1: To maximize, set the derivative equal to zero.

$$f'(x) = \frac{d}{dx}\left(\int_0^x (t-t^2)\,dt\right)$$

$$= x - x^2 = 0$$

$$\therefore x = 0 \quad \text{and} \quad x = 1$$

Step 2: Use the second derivative test to confirm $x = 1$ yields a maximum.

$$f''(1) = 1 - 2x\big|_{x=1} = -1$$

$\therefore x = 1$ maximizes

Step 3: $f(1) = \int_0^1 (t - t^2)\, dt = \boxed{\dfrac{1}{6}}$

83. **(B)**

Step 1: Eliminate the parameter t:

$$x = \cos t \quad \Rightarrow \quad x^2 = \cos^2 t$$

$$\therefore y + x^2 = \sin^2 t + \cos^2 t = 1 \quad \Rightarrow y = 1 - x^2$$

$$y' = -2x$$

Step 2: Arc length $= \displaystyle\int_{x=a}^{b} \sqrt{1 + (y')^2}\, dx$

$$= \int_0^1 \sqrt{1 + 4x^2}\, dx = \boxed{1.479}$$

84. **(A)**

Step 1: Set $f'(x) = 0$ to find the critical values.

$$f'(x) = 1 + \sin x = 0$$

$$x = -\frac{\pi}{2}, \ \frac{3\pi}{2}$$

Step 2: Use the first derivative test to confirm the relative maximums.

$$f'' \quad \frac{+\ +\quad +\ +\quad +\quad +\ +\quad +\ +}{\qquad -\frac{\pi}{2} \qquad\qquad\qquad \frac{3\pi}{2}}$$

Neither point is a relative maximum. The curve is always increasing in the interval $[-2\pi, 2\pi]$.

Step 3: Test the end points.

$$f(x) = x - \cos x$$

$$f(-2\pi) = -7.283$$

$$f(2\pi) = 5.283$$

The absolute maximum occurs at 2π.

$f(x)$ has 0 relative maximum values and 1 absolute maximum value, for a total of $\boxed{1}$.

85. **(D)**

Step 1: Make a sketch of $\dfrac{1}{(x-1)^{\frac{2}{3}}}$

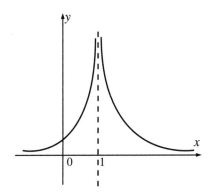

Step 2: Because of the vertical asymptote, split the integral

$$\int_0^4 \frac{dx}{(x-1)^{\frac{2}{3}}} = \lim_{a \to 1^-} \int_0^a \frac{dx}{(x-1)^{\frac{2}{3}}} + \lim_{b \to 1^+} \int_b^4 \frac{dx}{(x-1)^{\frac{2}{3}}}$$

$$= \lim_{a \to 1^-} 3(x-1)^{\frac{1}{3}} \Big|_0^a + \lim_{b \to 1^+} 3(x-1)^{\frac{1}{3}} \Big|_b^4$$

$$= \lim_{a \to 1^-} 3(a-1)^{\frac{1}{3}} + 3 + 3(3)^{\frac{1}{3}} - \lim_{b \to 1^+} 3(b-1)^{\frac{1}{3}}$$

$$= 0 + 3 + 3\sqrt[3]{3} - 0 = \boxed{7.327}$$

86. **(A)**

$f(x) = 0$ at the roots of $f(x)$.
$f'(x) = 0$ at potential minimum/maximum points for $f(x)$.
$f''(x) = 0$ at inflection points for $f(x)$.

The observations above hold true if

$f(x)$ is I
$f'(x)$ is II
$f''(x)$ is III

87. **(E)**

Step 1: $\dfrac{d}{dx}(\sin x) = \cos x$

$$\cos x = \frac{d}{dx}\left(x - \frac{x^3}{3!} + \frac{x^5}{5!} + \dots + \frac{(-1)^n x^{2n+1}}{(2n+1)!} \right)$$

$$\cos x = 1 - \frac{x^2}{2!} + \frac{x^4}{4!} \dots \dots \frac{(-1)^n x^{2n}}{(2n)!}$$

Step 2: Replace x with $3x^2$.

$$\cos 3x^2 = 1 - \frac{(3x^2)^2}{2!} + \frac{(3x^2)^4}{4!} \dots \frac{(-1)^n(3x^2)^{2n}}{(2n)!}$$

$$= \sum_{n=0}^{\infty} \frac{(-1)^n(3x^2)^{2n}}{(2n)!} = \boxed{\sum_{n=0}^{\infty} \frac{(-9)^n x^{4n}}{(2n)!}}$$

88. **(D)**

Differentiate $g(x)$ twice.

$$g(x) = \ln(f(x))$$

$$g'(x) = \frac{1}{f(x)} \cdot f'(x) = \frac{f'(x)}{f(x)}$$

$$g''(x) = \frac{f(x) \cdot f''(x) - f'(x) \cdot f'(x)}{[f(x)]^2}$$

$$= \frac{f(x) \cdot f''(x) - [f'(x)]^2}{[f(x)]^2} = \frac{h(x)}{[f(x)]^2}$$

$$\therefore h(x) = \boxed{f(x) \cdot f''(x) - [f'(x)]^2}$$

89. **(B)**

Step 1: $\dfrac{dy}{dx} = \dfrac{\left(\frac{dy}{d\theta}\right)}{\left(\frac{dx}{d\theta}\right)} = \dfrac{\frac{d}{d\theta}(3\cos\theta)}{\frac{d}{d\theta}(2\sin\theta)} = \dfrac{-3\sin\theta}{2\cos\theta} = -\dfrac{3}{2}\tan\theta$

Step 2: $\dfrac{d^2y}{dx^2} = \dfrac{\frac{d}{d\theta}\left(\frac{dy}{d\theta}\right)}{\frac{dx}{d\theta}} = \dfrac{\frac{d}{d\theta}\left(\frac{-3}{2}\tan\theta\right)}{\frac{d}{d\theta}(2\sin\theta)} = \dfrac{\frac{-3}{2}\sec^2\theta}{2\cos\theta}$

$$= \boxed{\dfrac{-3}{4}\sec^3\theta}$$

90. **(B)**

Step 1: Average velocity $= \dfrac{1}{8-1}\displaystyle\int_1^8 10\sin(\ln(t))\,dt$

Instantaneous velocity $= 10\sin(\ln(t))$

Step 2: Solve for t:

$$\frac{1}{7}\int_1^8 10\sin(\ln(t))\,dt = 10\sin(\ln(t))$$

$$t = \boxed{2.756}$$

91. **(D)**

Step 1: I. $\sum_{n=1}^{\infty} \frac{n}{2n+1}$ Diverges by the nth-term test, $\lim_{n \to \infty} \frac{n}{2n+1} = \frac{1}{2} \neq 0$.

Step 2: II. $\sum_{n=1}^{\infty} \frac{1}{5+4^n}$ Converges by the comparison test to the convergent geometric series $\sum_{n=1}^{\infty} \frac{1}{4^n}$

because $\frac{1}{5+4^n} < \frac{1}{4^n}$

Step 3: III. $\sum_{n=1}^{\infty} \frac{2^n}{n!}$ Converges by the ratio test,

$$\lim_{n \to \infty} \left| \frac{\frac{2^{n+1}}{(n+1)!}}{\frac{2^n}{n!}} \right| = \lim_{n \to \infty} \left| \frac{2}{n+1} \right| = 0 < 1.$$

Step 4: Series $\boxed{\text{II and III only}}$ converge.

92. **(C)**

Step 1: Separate the variables and use partial fractions.

$$R^2 + \frac{dR}{dt} = -R \quad \Rightarrow \frac{-dR}{R(R+1)} = dt \Rightarrow \left(\frac{-1}{R} + \frac{1}{R+1} \right) dR = dt$$

Step 2: Integrate.

$$\int \left(\frac{1}{R+1} - \frac{1}{R} \right) dR = \int dt$$

$$\ln \left| \frac{R+1}{R} \right| = t + C$$

$$\left| \frac{R+1}{R} \right| = e^{t+C} \Rightarrow Ae^t, \text{ where } A \text{ is a constant}$$

Step 3: Solve for R and apply the initial conditions to find the value of A.

$$\frac{R+1}{R} = \pm Ae^t$$

$$R(t) = \pm \frac{1}{Ae^t - 1}$$

Use $R(0) = \frac{1}{2} \quad \therefore A = 3$

$$R(t) = \boxed{\frac{1}{3e^t - 1}}$$

Section II

PART A

1.

Step 1: Make a sketch including all the given information.

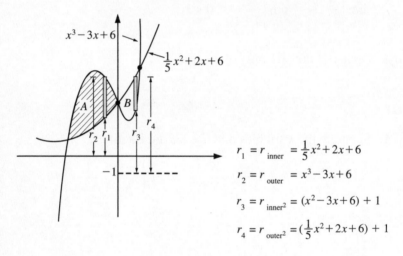

$r_1 = r_{\text{inner}} = \frac{1}{5}x^2 + 2x + 6$

$r_2 = r_{\text{outer}} = x^3 - 3x + 6$

$r_3 = r_{\text{inner2}} = (x^2 - 3x + 6) + 1$

$r_4 = r_{\text{outer2}} = (\frac{1}{5}x^2 + 2x + 6) + 1$

Step 2: Find the points of intersection.

$$x^3 - 3x + 6 = \frac{1}{5}x^2 + 2x + 6$$

$$x = -2.138$$

$$x = 0$$

$$x = 2.338$$

Step 3: Area of region $= \int_{-2.138}^{0} \left[(x^3 - 3x + 6) - \left(\frac{1}{5}x^2 + 2x + 6 \right) \right] dx = \boxed{5.552}$
(a)

Step 4: Volume of region A about the x-axis:

(b) $V = \pi \int_{-2.138}^{0} (r^2_{\text{outer}} - r^2_{\text{inner}}) \, dx$

$$= \pi \int_{-2.138}^{0} \left[(x^3 - 3x + 6)^2 - \left(\frac{1}{5}x^2 + 2x + 6 \right)^2 \right] dx = \boxed{195.733}$$

Step 5: Volume of region B about $y = -1$:

(c) $V = \pi \int_0^{2.338} (r^2_{\text{outer}} - r^2_{\text{inner}}) \, dx$

$$= \pi \int_0^{2.338} \left[\left(\frac{1}{5}x^2 + 2x + 7 \right)^2 - (x^3 - 3x + 7)^2 \right] dx = \boxed{355.567}$$

2.

Step 1: $e^x = 1 + x + \dfrac{x^2}{2!} + \dfrac{x^3}{3!} + \dots \dfrac{x^n}{n!} = \sum_{n=0}^{\infty} \dfrac{x^n}{n!}$

Step 2: $xe^x = \boxed{x + x^2 + \dfrac{x^3}{2!} + \dfrac{x^4}{3!} + \dots \dfrac{x^{n+1}}{n!} = \sum_{n=0}^{\infty} \dfrac{x^{n+1}}{n!}}$

(a)

Step 3: $\int xe^x dx = \boxed{\dfrac{x^2}{2} + \dfrac{x^3}{3} + \dfrac{x^4}{4 \cdot 2!} + \dfrac{x^5}{5 \cdot 3!} + \dots \dfrac{x^{n+2}}{(n+1)n!} + C}$

(b)

$$= \sum_{n=0}^{\infty} \dfrac{x^{n+2}}{(n+2)n!} + C$$

Step 4: $\int_0^1 xe^x dx \quad u = x \quad dv = e^x dx$

$$du = dx \quad v = e^x$$

(c) $\int_0^1 xe^x dx = xe^x - \int e^x dx = xe^x - e^x \Big|_0^1 = \boxed{1}$

Step 5: $\int_0^1 xe^x dx = \dfrac{x^2}{2} + \dfrac{x^3}{3} + \dfrac{x^4}{4 \cdot 2!} + \dfrac{x^5}{5 \cdot 3!} + \dots \dfrac{x^{n+2}}{(n+2)n!} \Bigg]_0^1$

$$= \dfrac{1}{2} + \dfrac{1}{3} + \dfrac{1}{4 \cdot 2!} + \dfrac{1}{5 \cdot 3!} + \dots \dfrac{1}{(n+2)n!}$$

$$= \dfrac{1}{2} + \sum_{n=1}^{\infty} \dfrac{1}{(n+2)n!}$$

But $\int_0^1 xe^x dx = 1$

$$\therefore \sum_{n=1}^{\infty} \dfrac{1}{(n+2)n!} = \boxed{\dfrac{1}{2}}$$

3.

Step 1: To find horizontal tangents, set $\dfrac{dy}{dx} = 0$. Since $\dfrac{dy}{dx} = \dfrac{\left(\frac{dy}{d\theta} \right)}{\left(\frac{dx}{d\theta} \right)}$, you need only find when $\dfrac{dy}{d\theta} = 0$ (assuming $\dfrac{dx}{d\theta} \neq 0$).

Step 2: Represent $r = 1 - \sin\theta$ in parametric form:

$$\begin{matrix} x = r\cos\theta \\ y = r\sin\theta \end{matrix} \Rightarrow \begin{matrix} x = (1-\sin\theta)\cos\theta \\ y = (1-\sin\theta)\sin\theta \end{matrix}$$

Step 3: $\dfrac{dy}{d\theta} = (1-\sin\theta)\cos\theta + \sin\theta(-\cos\theta)$

$$= \cos\theta(1 - 2\sin\theta) = 0$$

$$\theta = \cancel{\dfrac{\pi}{2}}, \dfrac{3\pi}{2} \quad \Big| \quad \theta = \dfrac{\pi}{6}, \dfrac{5\pi}{6}$$

reject

(a) $\therefore \theta = \boxed{\dfrac{\pi}{6}, \dfrac{5\pi}{6}, \dfrac{3\pi}{2}}$

Step 4: Sketch the graph.

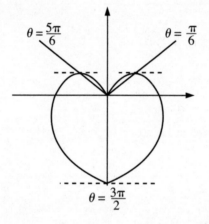

Step 5:

(b) $A = \dfrac{1}{2}\displaystyle\int_a^b r^2\, d\theta = \dfrac{1}{2}\int_0^{2\pi}(1-\sin\theta)^2\, d\theta = \boxed{\dfrac{3\pi}{2}}$ or $\boxed{4.712}$

Step 6: Arc length $= \displaystyle\int_a^b \sqrt{r^2 + \left(\dfrac{dr}{d\theta}\right)^2}\, d\theta$

(c) $= \displaystyle\int_0^{2\pi}\sqrt{(1-\sin\theta)^2 + (-\cos\theta)^2}\, d\theta = \boxed{8}$

Step 7: Sketch cardioid and circle.

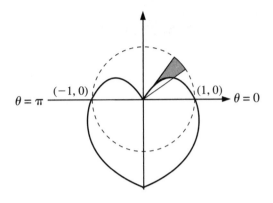

Step 8:

$$A = \frac{1}{2} \int_a^b (r^2{}_{\text{outer}} - r^2{}_{\text{inner}}) \, d\theta$$

$$= \frac{1}{2} \int_0^\pi [(1)^2 - (1 - \sin\theta)^2] \, d\theta = \boxed{\frac{8 - \pi}{4}} \text{ or } \boxed{1.215}$$

Section II

PART B

4.

Step 1: The given information is $\vec{v}(0) = \langle 1, 3 \rangle$ and $\vec{s}(0) = \langle 5, 1 \rangle$.

$$\vec{v}(t) = \int \vec{a}(t)\, dt$$

$$\vec{v}(t) = \langle 2\sin t + C_1,\ 3\cos t + C_2 \rangle$$

$$\vec{v}(0) = \langle C_1,\ 3 + C_2 \rangle = \langle 1, 3 \rangle \quad \therefore C_1 = 1 \text{ and } C_2 = 0$$

(a) $\quad \therefore \vec{v}(t) = \boxed{\langle 2\sin t + 1,\ 3\cos t \rangle}$

Step 2: Speed $= |\vec{v}(t)| = \sqrt{(2\sin t + 1)^2 + (3\cos t)^2}$

(b) $\qquad \left| \vec{v}\left(\dfrac{\pi}{2}\right) \right| = \sqrt{3^2 + 0^2} = \boxed{3}$

Step 3: $\vec{s}(t) = \displaystyle\int \vec{v}(t)\, dt$

$$= \langle -2\cos t + t + c_1,\ 3\sin t + c_2 \rangle$$

$$\vec{s}(0) = \langle -2 + c_1,\ c_2 \rangle = \langle 5, 1 \rangle$$

$$\therefore c_1 = 7 \text{ and } c_2 = 1$$

(c) $\quad \vec{s}(t) = \boxed{\langle -2\cos t + t + 7,\ 3\sin t + 1 \rangle}$

Step 4: $\vec{s}(t) = \langle -2\cos t + t + 7,\ 3\sin t + 1 \rangle = \langle \pi + 9, 1 \rangle$

(d) $\quad \boxed{t = \pi}$

5.

Step 1: Set up a table of values from which to sketch the slope field.

x	y	$\dfrac{dy}{dx}$
-1	-1	$+2$
	0	undefined
	1	-2
	2	-1
0	-1	0
	0	$-$
	1	0
	2	0
1	-1	-2
	0	undefined
	1	2
	2	1
2	-1	-4
	0	undefined
	1	4
	2	2

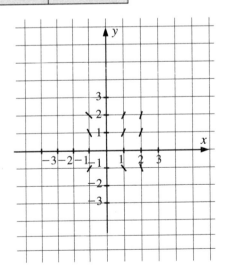

Step 2: Use Euler's method to determine a table of values.

$$\frac{dy}{dx} = f(x, y) = \frac{2x}{y}; \, f(3) = 5; \, \Delta x = .5$$

x_n	$f(x_{n-1}) + \Delta x\, f(x_{n-1},\, y_{n-1}) \approx$	$f(x_n)$
3		5
3.5	$5 + .5\left(\dfrac{6}{5}\right)$	5.6
4	$5.6 + .5\left(\dfrac{7}{5.6}\right) =$ $5.6 + .625$	6.225

$\therefore f(4) \approx \boxed{6.225}$

Step 3: Separate the variables and integrate.

$$\frac{dy}{dx} = \frac{2x}{y} \quad \Rightarrow \quad y\, dy = 2x\, dx$$

$$\int y\, dy = \int 2x\, dx$$

$$\frac{y^2}{2} = x^2 + C_1 \quad \Rightarrow \quad y^2 = 2x^2 + C_2$$

Step 4: Use $f(3) = 5$ to find C.

$$5^2 = 2(3)^2 + C \quad \therefore C = 7$$

$$y^2 = 2x^2 + 7$$

(c) $\qquad \therefore \boxed{y = \sqrt{2x^2 + 7}}$

Step 5:

(c) $\quad f(4) = \sqrt{2(4)^2 + 7} = \boxed{\sqrt{39}}$, which is 6.245.

6.

Step 1: Use implicit differentiation. Note that xy^2 and yx^2 are products.

$$xy^2 - yx^2 = 12$$

$$\left[x\frac{d}{dx}(y^2) + y^2\frac{d}{dx}(x)\right] - \left[y\frac{dy}{dx}(x^2) + x^2\frac{d}{dx}(y)\right] = 0$$

$$\left[x\left(2y\frac{dy}{dx}\right) + y^2\right] - \left[y(2x) + x^2\frac{dy}{dx}\right] \qquad = 0$$

(a) $\qquad \dfrac{dy}{dx} = \boxed{\dfrac{2xy - y^2}{2xy - x^2} = \dfrac{y(2x - y)}{x(2y - x)}}$

Step 2: When $x = 1$,

$$xy^2 - yx^2 = 12 \Rightarrow y^2 - y - 12 = 0$$

$$\therefore y = -3 \text{ or } y = 4$$

Step 3: When $x = 1$, $y = -3$, $m = \dfrac{dy}{dx} = \dfrac{15}{7}$

When $x = 1$, $y = 4$, $m = \dfrac{dy}{dx} = \dfrac{-8}{7}$

$\therefore$ Tangent line equations are $\boxed{y + 3 = \dfrac{15}{7}(x - 1)}$

and $\boxed{y - 4 = \dfrac{-8}{7}(x - 1)}$

Step 4: To find horizontal tangents, set $\dfrac{dy}{dx} = 0$

$\therefore y(2x - y) = 0 \Rightarrow y = 0$ and $y = 2x$

There is no point on the graph where $y = 0$; therefore, reject $y = 0$.

When $y = 2x$,

$$xy^2 - yx^2 = 12$$

$$x(2x)^2 - (2x)x^2 = 12$$

$$4x^3 - 2x^3 = 12$$

(c) $\qquad \therefore \boxed{x = \sqrt[3]{6}}$

Step 5: To find vertical tangents, set the denominator of $\dfrac{dy}{dx}$ to zero.

$x(2y - x) = 0 \Rightarrow x = 0$ or $y = \dfrac{x}{2}$

There is no point on the curve where $x = 0$; therefore, reject $x = 0$.

When $y = \dfrac{x}{2}$,

$$xy^2 - yx^2 = 12$$

$$x\left(\dfrac{x}{2}\right)^2 - \left(\dfrac{x}{2}\right)x^2 = 12$$

$$\dfrac{-x^3}{4} = 12$$

(d) $\qquad \therefore \boxed{x = \sqrt[3]{-48}}$

PRACTICE EXAM 2

AP Calculus BC

Section I

PART A

Time: 55 minutes
28 questions

(Answer sheets appear in the back of this book.)

> **DIRECTIONS:** Solve each of the following problems. Select the best answer choice and fill in the corresponding oval on the answer sheet.
>
> Calculators may NOT be used for this section of the exam.

NOTES:
(1) Unless otherwise specified, the domain of a function f is assumed to be the set of all real numbers x for which $f(x)$ is a real number.
(2) The inverse of a trigonometric function f may be indicated using the inverse function notation f^{-1} or with the prefix "arc" (e.g., $\sin^{-1}x = \arcsin x$).

1. At what value(s) of x does $f(x) = \dfrac{x^3}{3} - x^2 - 3x + 5$ have a relative maximum?

    (A) -1 only

    (B) 0 only

    (C) 1 only

    (D) 3 only

    (E) -1 and 3

2. $\displaystyle\int \dfrac{x}{\sqrt{16+x^2}}\, dx =$

    (A) $\ln\left|16 + x^2\right| + C$

(B) $\left(\frac{1}{2}\ln\left|16+x^2\right|\right)(\ln x)+C$

(C) $x\sqrt{16+x^2}+C$

(D) $\sqrt{16+x^2}+C$

(E) $\frac{1}{2}\sqrt{16+x^2}+C$

3. The length of the arc of $y=\frac{1}{5}x^{\frac{5}{2}}$ from $x=0$ to $x=2$ is given by which of the following?

(A) $\frac{1}{2}\int_0^2 (4+x^3)^{\frac{1}{2}}dx$

(B) $\frac{1}{2}\int_0^2 (4+x^3)dx$

(C) $\int_0^2 (1+x^3)dx$

(D) $\int_0^2 (4+x^3)^{\frac{1}{2}}dx$

(E) $\frac{1}{2}\int_0^2 (1+x^3)^{\frac{1}{2}}dx$

4. $\int_0^2 \left|x^2-x\right|dx =$

(A) $-\frac{2}{3}$

(B) 0

(C) $\frac{1}{2}$

(D) $\frac{2}{3}$

(E) 1

5. What is the equation of the line tangent to the curve $xy = x + y$ at $x = -1$?

(A) $x - 4y = 1$

(B) $4x - y = 1$

(C) $x + y = 4$

(D) $4x + y = 1$

(E) $x + 4y = 1$

6.   If $f(x) = x^2 \ln\left(\dfrac{1}{x^2}\right)$, find $f'(x)$.

(A) $x(x + 2 \ln x)$

(B) $2x^2(x^3 - 2 \ln x)$

(C) $2x(1 + 2 \ln x)$

(D) $-2x^7 + 2x \ln\left(\dfrac{1}{x^2}\right)$

(E) $-2x(1 + 2 \ln x)$

7.   If $y(x) = \displaystyle\int_{t=0}^{x^2} e^{t^2}\, dt$, then $y''(0) =$

(A)   0

(B)   1

(C)   2

(D)   3

(E)   4

8. $\displaystyle\int_0^\infty xe^{-x^2}\, dx =$

(A) $\dfrac{1}{4}$

(B) $\dfrac{1}{3}$

(C) $\dfrac{1}{2}$

(D) $\dfrac{2}{3}$

(E)   1

9.

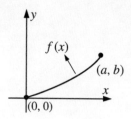

If the function f has the graph shown above, then $\int_0^b f^{-1}(x)dx =$

(A) $\quad ab - \int_0^a f(x)dx$

(B) $\quad \dfrac{1}{\int_0^b f(x)dx}$

(C) $\quad \dfrac{1}{\int_0^a f(x)dx}$

(D) $\quad 1 - \int_0^a f(x)dx$

(E) $\quad \int_0^a \dfrac{1}{f(x)} dx$

10. If $y = x \sin(x + y)$, then $\dfrac{dy}{dx} =$

(A) $\quad \sin(x + y) + x \cos(x + y)$

(B) $\quad \sin(x + y) - x \cos(x + y)$

(C) $\quad \dfrac{\sin(x+y) + x\cos(x+y)}{1 + x\cos(x+y)}$

(D) $\quad \dfrac{\sin(x+y) - x\cos(x+y)}{1 + x\cos(x+y)}$

(E) $\quad \dfrac{\sin(x+y) + x\cos(x+y)}{1 - x\cos(x+y)}$

11. Find all the intervals for which the function $f(x) = 2x^5 - 5x^4 - 10x^3 + 8$ is increasing.

(A) $\quad (-1, 3)$

(B) $\quad (-\infty, -1)$ and $(0, 3)$

(C) $(-1, 0)$ and $(3, \infty)$

(D) $(0, \infty)$

(E) $(-\infty, -1)$ and $(3, \infty)$

12.   Let $f(x) = 2x^3 - x$. Find all the values of c that satisfy the Mean Value Theorem on the interval $[1, 3]$.

(A) $\dfrac{\sqrt{26}}{3}$

(B) $\dfrac{5}{3}$ and $\dfrac{8}{3}$

(C)   2

(D) $\dfrac{\sqrt{39}}{3}$

(E) $\dfrac{\sqrt{26}}{4}$

13.   A particle moves along a curve so that its position at time t is given by the position vector $\left\langle 4e^{3(t-1)}, \cos(t-1) \right\rangle$. What is the speed of the particle when $t = 1$?

(A)   7

(B) $e^2 + 1$

(C)   12

(D) $e^3 - 1$

(E)   15

14. $\displaystyle\int \dfrac{x-8}{x^2 - x - 6}\,dx =$

(A) $\ln\left[(x+2)^2 \cdot |x-3|\right] + C$

(B) $\ln\dfrac{(x+2)^2}{|x-3|} + C$

(C) $\ln\dfrac{|x-3|}{(x+2)^2} + C$

(D) $\ln\left[(x-5)^2 \cdot |x+1|\right] + C$

(E) $\ln\left|\dfrac{(x-8)(x+2)}{(x-3)}\right| + C$

15.

x	$f(x)$	$g(x)$	$f'(x)$	$g'(x)$	$f''(x)$	$g''(x)$
0	3	7	2	0	1	4
1	4	1	5	1	3	0
2	2	3	2	2	4	1
3	1	0	7	2	2	5

Use the data in the table above to evaluate $h''(3)$ if $h(x) = f(g(x))$ and the functions f and g are twice differentiable.

(A) 14

(B) 15

(C) 16

(D) 17

(E) 18

16. What is the x-intercept of the line whose parametric equations are $x = 2t - 1$ and $y = 6t + 11$?

(A) $-\dfrac{2}{3}$

(B) $-\dfrac{5}{3}$

(C) $-\dfrac{7}{3}$

(D) $-\dfrac{13}{4}$

(E) $-\dfrac{14}{3}$

17. If $\dfrac{dy}{dx} = \sec^2 x \tan x$ and if $y = \dfrac{7}{2}$ when $x = \dfrac{\pi}{4}$, what is the value of y when $x = \dfrac{\pi}{3}$?

(A) 5

(B) $\dfrac{9}{2}$

(C) 4

(D) $\dfrac{7}{2}$

(E) 3

18. $\displaystyle\int_1^e \dfrac{x^{\frac{5}{2}} - 3x^{\frac{3}{2}} + x^{\frac{1}{2}}}{\sqrt{x^3}}\, dx =$

(A) $e^2 - 3e + \dfrac{7}{2}$

(B) $\dfrac{3e^2 - 3e + 7}{2}$

(C) $\dfrac{e^2 - 6e + 7}{2}$

(D) $e^2 - \dfrac{1}{e} + 2$

(E) $\dfrac{e^2 + 6e - 5}{2}$

19.

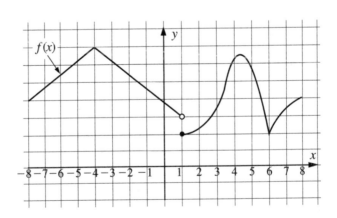

The function f is defined in $[-8, 8]$ and its graph is shown above. Which of the following is a complete list of all the values of x in the interval $(-8, 8)$ for which the function is NOT differentiable?

(A) $-4, 1$

(B) $1, 4, 6$

(C) $-4, 1, 6$

(D) $-4, 6$

(E) $-4, 1, 4, 6$

20. If we use a Maclaurin series for $\ln(x + 1)$ to approximate the value of $\ln(1.2)$, which of the following would reflect the first four terms?

(A) $(.2) - \dfrac{(.2)^2}{2} + \dfrac{(.2)^3}{3} - \dfrac{(.2)^4}{4}$

(B) $1 - \dfrac{(.2)^2}{2!} + \dfrac{(.2)^4}{4!} - \dfrac{(.2)^6}{6!}$

(C) $1 + (.2) + (.2)^2 + (.2)^3$

(D) $1 + (.2) + \dfrac{(.2)^2}{2!} + \dfrac{(.2)^3}{3!}$

(E) $(.2) - \dfrac{(.2)^2}{2!} + \dfrac{(.2)^3}{3!} - \dfrac{(.2)^4}{4!}$

21. $\displaystyle\int \ln x \, dx =$

(A) $x - \ln x + C$

(B) $x \ln x + C$

(C) $x \ln x + x + C$

(D) $x \ln x - x + C$

(E) $x^2 + \ln x + C$

22.

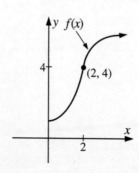

Let the function f be an even function. The graph above shows only the portion of the graph for $x \geq 0$. If $(2, 4)$ is a point of inflection, which of the following is true about the numerical values of the function and its derivatives at $x = -2$? ($-$ is negative, $+$ is positive, 0 is zero)

	$f(-2)$	$f'(-2)$	$f''(-2)$
(A)	$-$	$-$	$-$
(B)	$-$	0	$+$
(C)	$+$	$+$	0
(D)	$-$	$+$	0
(E)	$+$	$-$	0

23. Which of the following series converge?

   I. $\displaystyle\sum_{n=1}^{\infty} \frac{3}{10^n}$

   II. $\displaystyle\sum_{n=1}^{\infty} \frac{2^n}{n}$

   III. $\displaystyle\sum_{n=1}^{\infty} \frac{1}{n!}$

   (A) I only

   (B) II only

   (C) III only

   (D) I and II only

   (E) I and III only

24. The length of the path described by the parametric equations $x = \cos t$ and $y = e^{2t}$, where $0 \leq t \leq \dfrac{\pi}{2}$, is given by

   (A) $\displaystyle\int_0^{\frac{\pi}{2}} \sqrt{1 + (e^{2t} \cdot \cos t)^2}\ dt$

   (B) $\displaystyle\int_0^{\frac{\pi}{2}} \sqrt{\sin^2 t + 4e^{4t}}\ dt$

(C) $\int_0^{\frac{\pi}{2}} \sqrt{\sin^2 t + 2e^{4t}} \, dt$

(D) $\frac{1}{2} \int_0^{\frac{\pi}{2}} 2t\sqrt{\sin^2 t + 2e^{4t}} \, dt$

(E) $\frac{1}{2} \int_0^{\frac{\pi}{2}} 2e^{2t} \cdot \sin t \sqrt{1+t^2} \, dt$

25. The figure below is the slope field for which of the following differential equations?

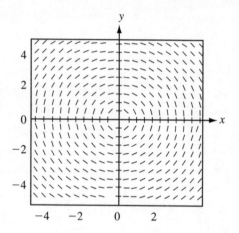

(A) $\dfrac{dy}{dx} = x^2 + y^2$

(B) $\dfrac{dy}{dx} = x + y + 1$

(C) $\dfrac{dy}{dx} = -\dfrac{x}{y}$

(D) $\dfrac{dy}{dx} = x$

(E) $\dfrac{dy}{dx} = \dfrac{y}{x}$

26. If f is a vector-valued function defined by $f(t) = \langle \sin 2t, \cos t \rangle$, then

$f''\left(\dfrac{\pi}{4}\right) =$

(A) $\left\langle -4, -\dfrac{\sqrt{2}}{2} \right\rangle$

(B) $\left\langle -2, -\dfrac{\sqrt{2}}{2} \right\rangle$

(C) $-4 - \dfrac{\sqrt{2}}{2}$

(D) $-2 - \dfrac{\sqrt{2}}{2}$

(E) $\left\langle -1, -\dfrac{\sqrt{2}}{2} \right\rangle$

27. Let the function f be defined as $f(x) = \dfrac{(x-3)(x-1)}{(x-1)(x+4)}$. Which of the following describes the characteristic of f most accurately and completely?

    (A) Vertical asymptotes: $x = 1$ and $x = -4$

        Horizontal asymptote: $y = 0$

    (B) Vertical asymptotes: $x = 1$ and $x = -4$

        Horizontal asymptote: $y = 1$

    (C) Vertical asymptote: $\quad x = -4$

        No horizontal asymptote

        Hole at: $\quad\quad\quad\quad x = 1$

    (D) Vertical asymptote: $\quad x = -4$

        Horizontal asymptote: $y = 0$

        Hole at: $\quad\quad\quad\quad x = 1$

    (E) Vertical asymptote: $\quad x = -4$

        Horizontal asymptote: $y = 1$

        Hole at: $\quad\quad\quad\quad x = 1$

28. The length of a function f from $x = 1$ to $x = 7$ is given by:

$$S = \frac{1}{2}\int_1^7 \sqrt{4+9x^4}\ dx$$

If the curve passes through the point (2, 5), which of the following could be the equation of the function?

(A) $y = \dfrac{1}{2}x^3 + 1$

(B) $y = x^3 - 3$

(C) $y = x^3 + 2x - 7$

(D) $y = \dfrac{1}{2}x^3 + x - 1$

(E) $y = 4x + \dfrac{9}{5}x^5 - \dfrac{303}{5}$

STOP

This is the end of Section I, Part A.
If time still remains, you may check your work only in this section.
Do not begin Section I, Part B until instructed to do so.

Section I

PART B

Time: 50 minutes
 17 questions

(Answer sheets appear in the back of this book.)

DIRECTIONS: Solve each of the following problems. Select the best answer choice and fill in the corresponding oval on the answer sheet.

Calculators MAY be used for this section of the exam.

NOTES:
(1) The exact numerical value of the correct answer does not always appear among the choices given. When this happens, select the number from among the choices that best approximates the exact numerical value.
(2) Unless otherwise specified, the domain of a function f is assumed to be the set of all real numbers x for which $f(x)$ is a real number.
(3) The inverse of a trigonometric function f may be indicated by using the inverse function notation f^{-1} or with the prefix "arc" (e.g., $\sin^{-1}x = \arcsin x$).

76. What is the area inside the circle $r = 4\sin\theta$ and outside the cardioid $r = 1 + \sin\theta$?

(A)   8.142

(B)   8.347

(C)   8.473

(D)   8.743

(E)   9.103

77. If $g(x)$ represents the continuous solution to the differential equation $\dfrac{dy}{dx} = x + y$ over the interval $[0, 2]$, use Euler's method with a step size of 0.1 to approximate $g(.4)$ if $g(0) = 1$.

(A)   2.4079

(B)   1.8634

(C) 1.7952

(D) 1.5282

(E) 1.4983

78. $y = \lim\limits_{x \to \infty} \sqrt[x]{1+x^2} =$

(A) 0

(B) 1

(C) 2

(D) e

(E) diverges

79. What is the interval of convergence for the series $\sum\limits_{n=0}^{\infty} \dfrac{x^{2n}}{(2n)!}$?

(A) $-1 \le x \le 1$

(B) $0 \le x \le 1$

(C) $0 < x < 2$

(D) $-1 < x < 1$

(E) $-\infty < x < \infty$

80. What is the equation of the line tangent to the curve $x(t) = t^2 + 1$, $y(t) = t^3 - 1$ at the point $(5, 7)$?

(A) $x + 2y = 19$

(B) $3x - y = 8$

(C) $3x - 2y = 1$

(D) $4x - y = 13$

(E) $3x + y = 22$

81. Evaluate $\dfrac{d}{dx}\left(e^{\sin 2x}\right)$ when $x = 4°$.

(A) -3.458

(B) -2.276

(C) 1.304

(D) 2.276

(E) 5.389

82. If $\dfrac{dy}{dx} = \dfrac{1}{2t-1}$ and $y = 1$ when $t = 1$, what is the value of y when $t = 5$?

    (A) .7483

    (B) 1.099

    (C) 1.386

    (D) 1.732

    (E) 2.099

83. A particle has a position vector $\langle 2\cos 2t,\ 1+3\sin t \rangle$. What is the speed of the particle at time $t = \dfrac{\pi}{4}$?

    (A) 1.879

    (B) 4.528

    (C) 5.427

    (D) 7.245

    (E) 20.50

84. The graph of the function represented by the series $1+2x+\dfrac{(2x)^2}{2!}+\dfrac{(2x)^3}{3!}\ldots\dfrac{(2x)^n}{n!}$ intersects the function $y = x^2 + 3$ at what value of x?

    (A) -1.873

    (B) -1.227

    (C) $-.607$

    (D) .607

    (E) 1.873

85. The function f is defined as $f(x) = x^2 - 7x + 1$. A tangent line to the function at $x = 3$ is used to approximate values of $f(x)$. For which value of x is the error at most 0.6?

    (A) 0.4

    (B) 1.2

    (C) 1.9

    (D) 2.1

    (E) 3.6

86. What is the volume of the solid formed by rotating the area bounded by $x^2 + y = 1$, $x = 1$, and $y = 1$ about the line $x = 2$?

    (A) $\dfrac{2\pi}{3}$

    (B) $\dfrac{3\pi}{4}$

    (C) $\dfrac{4\pi}{5}$

    (D) $\dfrac{5\pi}{6}$

    (E) $\dfrac{7\pi}{5}$

87. What is the total area enclosed by the polar graph $r = \cos 3\theta$?

    (A) 0.262

    (B) 0.524

    (C) 0.785

    (D) 1.047

    (E) 2.437

88. A particle moves along the x-axis so that its position at time t is given by $x(t) = (1 + t^2)e^{-t}$. For what value of t will the particle be at rest?

    (A) 0

    (B) $\dfrac{1}{2}$

    (C) 1

    (D) 2

    (E) no value

89. Let V be the volume of the region bounded between two expanding concentric spheres. At time $t = 0$ the spheres have radii of 6 cm and 40 cm. The radius of the smaller sphere is increasing at a rate of 8 cm/sec, while the radius of the larger sphere is increasing at a rate of 2 cm/sec. At what value of t $(t > 0)$ will the volume V be a maximum?

    (A) $\dfrac{1}{2}$

(B) 1

(C) $\dfrac{3}{2}$

(D) 2

(E) 3

90. Data suggest that between the hours of 1:00 PM and 3:00 PM on Sunday, the speed of traffic along a street can be expressed by $s(t) = 3t^2 + 10t$ miles per hour, where t is the number of hours past noon. Compute the average speed of the traffic in miles per hour between the hours of 1:00 PM and 3:00 PM on Sunday.

(A) 70

(B) 66

(C) 44

(D) 33

(E) 22

91. If the length of arc from $x = 0$ to $x = 5$ for the curve $y = cx^{\frac{3}{2}}$ is $\dfrac{19}{3}$, then which of the following could be the value of the constant c?

(A) $-\dfrac{1}{4}$

(B) $\dfrac{1}{4}$

(C) $\dfrac{1}{3}$

(D) $\dfrac{2}{3}$

(E) $\dfrac{4}{5}$

92. The coefficient of the x^4 term in the Taylor series for e^{2x} about $x = 0$ is

(A) $\dfrac{1}{24}$

(B) $\dfrac{1}{2}$

(C) $\dfrac{3}{4}$

(D) $\dfrac{2}{3}$

(E) 2

STOP

This is the end of Section I, Part B.
If time still remains, you may check your work only in this section.
Do not begin Section II, Part A until instructed to do so.

Section II

PART A

Time: 45 minutes
3 free-response problems

DIRECTIONS: Show all your work in your exam booklet. Grading is based on the methods used to solve the problems as well as the accuracy of your final answers.

Calculators MAY be used for this section of the exam.

---

1. All answers that require a series answer can be written in summation notation or with sufficient terms and a general term to clearly identify the pattern unless specified otherwise.

    (a) Write a Taylor polynomial for e^{-x^2}.

    (b) Approximate $\int_0^{\frac{1}{2}} e^{-x^2} dx$ with 3 decimal place accuracy, using the power series from part (a).

    (c) Approximate $\int_0^{.1} e^{-x^2} dx$ to within .00001.

2. Let $f(x) = 2 + 3e^{-2x}$ and let region A be the area in the first quadrant bounded by $f(x)$, the x- and y-axes, and $x = 4$.

    (a) Find the area of region A.

    (b) If region A is the base of a solid with each cross-section perpendicular to the x-axis being an equilateral triangle with a side parallel to the y-axis, find the volume of the solid.

    (c) Find the volume of the solid generated when region A is rotated about the x-axis.

3. A virus is spread through a population at a rate given by $r(t) = \dfrac{78}{1 + 3e^{-.15t}}$, where t = number of days.

    (a) At what value of t is there an inflection point?

(b) How many people will have the virus after 10 days?

(c) What is the maximum number of people predicted to have the virus?

STOP

This is the end of Section II, Part A.
If time still remains, you may check your work only in this section.
Do not begin Section II, Part B until instructed to do so.

Section II

PART B

Time: 45 minutes
    3 free-response problems

DIRECTIONS: Show all your work in your exam booklet. Grading is based on the methods used to solve the problems as well as the accuracy of your final answers.

Calculators MAY NOT be used for this section of the exam.

(During the timed portion for Part B, you may continue to work on the problems in Part A without the use of a calculator.)

---

4.   An object starts from point P (2, 1) and moves with an acceleration $\bar{a}(t) = \langle 6t^2, 2t+1 \rangle$.

Assume $\bar{v}(1) = \langle 3, 1 \rangle$.

Find:

   (a)   The velocity vector $\bar{v}(t)$.

   (b)   The speed of the object at time $t = 0$.

   (c)   The position vector $\bar{s}(t)$.

   (d)   The location of the object at time $t = 1$.

5.   Consider the differential equation $\dfrac{dy}{dx} = 3x - y$.

   (a)   For the 15 points indicated on the axes below, sketch the slope field and also the particular solution through (0, 0).

   (b)   Let $f(x)$ be the particular solution such that $f(1) = 1$. Use Euler's method with two steps of equal size to estimate $f(1.6)$.

   (c)   Find $\dfrac{d^2 y}{dx^2}$. Determine whether the Euler's approximation for $f(1.6)$ found in part (b) is greater than or less than the actual value. Explain how you arrived at your conclusion.

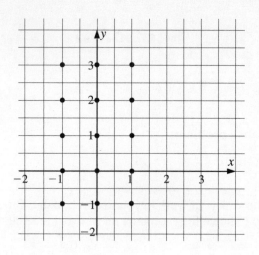

6. Given the curve $y^2 - 6xy + 6x^2 = 1$,

    (a) Find $\dfrac{dy}{dx}$ in terms of x and y.

    (b) Find the equation of the tangent lines to the curve at $x = 1$.

    (c) At what point do the tangent lines in part (b) intersect?

END OF EXAM

PRACTICE EXAM 2

AP Calculus BC

Answer Key

Part A				Part B	
1.	(C)	15.	(A)	76.	(C)
2.	(D)	16.	(E)	77.	(D)
3.	(A)	17.	(B)	78.	(B)
4.	(E)	18.	(C)	79.	(E)
5.	(E)	19.	(C)	80.	(B)
6.	(E)	20.	(A)	81.	(D)
7.	(C)	21.	(D)	82.	(E)
8.	(C)	22.	(E)	83.	(B)
9.	(A)	23.	(E)	84.	(D)
10.	(E)	24.	(B)	85.	(E)
11.	(E)	25.	(C)	86.	(D)
12.	(D)	26.	(A)	87.	(C)
13.	(C)	27.	(E)	88.	(C)
14.	(B)	28.	(A)	89.	(D)
				90.	(D)
				91.	(C)
				92.	(D)

Free-Response Answers

1.
(a) See detailed explanation.
(b) .461459
(c) .099667

2.
(a) 9.499
(b) 10.500
(c) 76.177

3.
(a) 7.324
(b) 47
(c) 78

4.

(a) $\left\langle 2t^3 + 1, \ t^2 + t - 1 \right\rangle$

(b) $\sqrt{2}$

(c) $\left\langle \dfrac{t^4}{2} + t + 2, \dfrac{t^3}{3} + \dfrac{t^2}{2} - t + 1 \right\rangle$

(d) $\left\langle \dfrac{7}{2}, \dfrac{5}{6} \right\rangle$

5.
(a) See detailed explanation.
(b) 2.290

(c) $\dfrac{d^2 y}{dx^2} = 3 - 3x + y$ also see detailed explanation.

6.
(a)

$\dfrac{3y - 6x}{y - 3x}$ or $\dfrac{6x - 3y}{3x - y}$

(b) $y - 1 = \dfrac{3}{2}(x - 1)$

$y - 5 = \dfrac{9}{2}(x - 1)$

(c) $\left(-\dfrac{1}{3}, -1 \right)$

PRACTICE EXAM 2

AP Calculus BC

Detailed Explanations of Answers

Section 1

PART A

1. **(C)**

Step 1: Find the critical values.
$$f(x) = \frac{x^3}{3} - x^2 - 3x + 5$$
$$f'(x) = x^2 - 2x - 3 = 0$$
$$x = 3 \text{ or } x = -1$$

Step 2: Do a second derivative test to determine relative minimum versus maximum.

$$f''(x) \quad = 2x - 2$$
$$f''(-1) = -3 \qquad \therefore x = 1 \text{ is a relative maximum}$$
$$f''(3) \quad = 4 \qquad \therefore x = 3 \text{ is a relative minimum}$$
So $f(x)$ has a relative maximum at $\boxed{1 \text{ only}}$.

2. **(D)**

Use u-substitution with $u = 16 + x^2 \therefore du = 2x dx$
$$\int \frac{x}{\sqrt{16+x^2}} dx = \int x(16+x)^{-\frac{1}{2}} dx = \frac{1}{2}\int (16+x)^{-\frac{1}{2}} \cdot 2x dx$$

$$= \frac{1}{2}\int u^{-\frac{1}{2}} du = u^{\frac{1}{2}} + C = \boxed{\sqrt{16+x^2} + C}$$

3. **(A)**

$$\text{Arc length} = \int_a^b \sqrt{1 + \left[f'(x) \right]^2}\, dx$$

$$= \int_0^2 \sqrt{1 + \left[\frac{1}{2} x^{\frac{3}{2}} \right]^2}\, dx$$

$$= \int_0^2 \sqrt{1 + \frac{1}{4} x^3}\, dx$$

$$= \boxed{\frac{1}{2} \int_0^2 \sqrt{4 + x^3}\, dx \ \text{ or } \ \frac{1}{2} \int_0^2 \left(4 + x^3 \right)^{\frac{1}{2}}\, dx}$$

4. **(E)**

Step 1: Make a sketch.

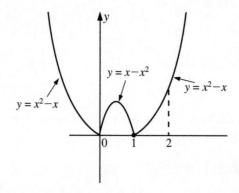

Step 2: Split the integral.

$$\int_0^1 (x - x^2)\, dx + \int_1^2 (x^2 - x)\, dx$$

$$\frac{1}{6} + \frac{5}{6} = \boxed{1}$$

5. **(E)**

Step 1: Find y when $x = -1$:

$$(-1)y = -1 + y \Rightarrow y = \frac{1}{2}$$

Step 2: Find the slope of the curve by using implicit differentiation.

$$xy = x + y$$

$$x\frac{dy}{dx} + y = 1 + \frac{dy}{dx} \implies \frac{dy}{dx} = \frac{y-1}{1-x} = \text{slope}$$

Step 3: At $x = -1$, $y = \frac{1}{2} \implies \frac{dy}{dx} = \frac{\frac{1}{2}-1}{1-(-1)} = -\frac{1}{4}$.

Step 4: The equation of the tangent line is:

$$y - \frac{1}{2} = -\frac{1}{4}(x+1) \implies \boxed{x + 4y = 1}$$

6. **(E)**

Use the product rule.

$$f(x) = x^2 \ln\left(\frac{1}{x^2}\right)$$

$$f'(x) = x^2 \frac{d}{dx}\left[\ln\left(\frac{1}{x^2}\right)\right] + \ln\left(\frac{1}{x^2}\right) \cdot \frac{d}{dx}(x^2)$$

$$= x^2[x^2(-2x^{-3})] + \ln\left(\frac{1}{x^2}\right) \cdot 2x$$

$$= -2x + 2x\ln\left(\frac{1}{x^2}\right) = -2x(1 - \ln(x^{-2}))$$

$$= \boxed{-2x(1 + 2\ln x)}$$

7. **(C)**

Step 1: Use the identity

$$\frac{d}{dx}\left[\int_0^{f(x)} g(t)\,dt\right] = g(f(x)) \cdot f'(x).$$

$$\therefore y(x) = \int_{t=0}^{x^2} e^{t^2}\,dt$$

$$y'(x) = e^{(x^2)^2} \cdot (2x) = e^{x^4} \cdot 2x$$

Step 2: Note that $2xe^{x^4}$ is a product.

$$y''(x) = 2x\frac{d}{dx}[e^{x^4}] + e^{x^4}d[2x]$$

$$= 2xe^{x^4} \cdot 4x^3 + e^{x^4} \cdot 2$$

$$y''(0) = 0 + 2 = \boxed{2}$$

8. **(C)**

Step 1: $\displaystyle\int_0^\infty xe^{-x^2}\,dx = \lim_{b\to\infty}\int_0^b xe^{-x^2}\,dx$

Step 2: Use u-substitution with $u = -x^2 \Rightarrow du = -2x\,dx$

$$\lim_{b\to\infty}\int_0^b xe^{-x^2}\,dx = \lim_{b\to\infty} -\frac{1}{2}\int_0^b e^{-x^2}\cdot(-2)x\,dx$$

$$= \lim_{b\to\infty} -\frac{1}{2}\int_{x=0}^b e^u\,du$$

$$= \lim_{b\to\infty} -\frac{1}{2}\left[e^{-x^2}\right]_0^b$$

$$= \lim_{b\to\infty} -\frac{1}{2}\left[e^{-b^2} - e^0\right]$$

$$= -\frac{1}{2}[0-1] = \boxed{\frac{1}{2}}$$

9. **(A)**

Step 1: The graph of $f^{-1}(x)$ is the reflection of $f(x)$ over the line $y = x$

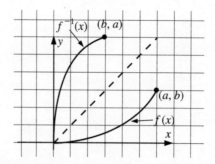

In the lower region:

Step 2: Region $S = \displaystyle\int_0^a f(x)\,dx$

Region $R = ab - \displaystyle\int_0^a f(x)\,dx$

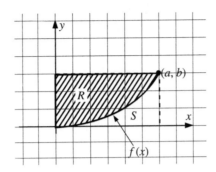

In the upper region:

Step 3: Region $T = \int_0^b f^{-1}(x)\,dx$

Region $V = ab - \int_0^b f^{-1}(x)\,dx$

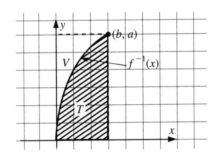

Step 4: By symmetry, Region R = Region T and Region S = Region V

$$\int_0^b f^{-1}(x)\,dx = \text{Region } T = \text{Region } R = \boxed{ab - \int_0^a f(x)\,dx}$$

10. **(E)**

Step 1: Use implicit differentiation. Note that $x \cdot \sin(x + y)$ is a product.

$$y = x \cdot \sin(x + y)$$

$$\frac{dy}{dx} = x \frac{d}{dx}[\sin(x+y)] + \sin(x+y)\frac{d(x)}{dx}$$

$$\frac{dy}{dx} = x\left[\cos(x+y)\frac{d}{dx}(x+y)\right] + \sin(x+y)$$

$$\frac{dy}{dx} = x\cos(x+y)\left[1 + \frac{dy}{dx}\right] + \sin(x+y)$$

Step 2: Solve for $\dfrac{dy}{dx}$

$$\frac{dy}{dx}(1 - x\cos(x+y)) = \sin(x+y) + x\cos(x+y)$$

$$\therefore \quad \boxed{\frac{dy}{dx} = \frac{\sin(x+y) + x\cos(x+y)}{1 - x\cos(x+y)}}$$

11. **(E)**

Step 1: Set $f'(x) = 0$ to find the critical values.

$$f(x) = 2x^5 - 5x^4 - 10x^3 + 8$$
$$f'(x) = 10x^4 - 20x^3 - 30x^2 = 0$$
$$10x^2(x^2 - 2x - 3) = 0$$
$$x = -1, x = 0, x = 3$$

Step 2: Do a first derivative analysis

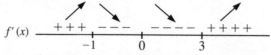

$$f'(x) \quad \underset{\substack{-1 \quad\quad 0 \quad\quad 3}}{+\!+\!+ \quad -\!-\!- \quad -\!-\!-\!- \quad +\!+\!+\!+}$$

increasing decreasing decreasing   increasing

$f(x)$ is increasing on the intervals $\boxed{(-\infty, -1) \text{ and } (3, \infty)}$

12. **(D)**

Step 1: The MVT states that for a point c in (a, b),

$$f'(c) = \frac{f(b) - f(a)}{b - a}$$

Step 2: $f(x) = 2x^3 - x \Rightarrow f'(x) = 6x^2 - 1$

$$f(3) = 51 \qquad\qquad f'(c) = 6c^2 - 1$$
$$f(1) = 1$$

Step 3: Solve for c, using the MVT.

$$6c^2 - 1 = \frac{51 - 1}{3 - 1} = 25$$

$$c = \pm\frac{\sqrt{39}}{3}$$

Only $\boxed{\dfrac{\sqrt{39}}{3}}$ is in the interval $[1, 3]$.

13. **(C)**

$$\vec{s}(t) = \left\langle 4e^{3(t-1)}, \cos(t-1) \right\rangle$$

Step 1: $\vec{v}(t) = \dfrac{d}{dt}(\vec{s}(t)) = \left\langle 12e^{3(t-1)}, -\sin(t-1) \right\rangle$

Step 2: Speed $= |\vec{v}(t)| = \sqrt{(12e^{3(t-1)})^2 + (-\sin(t-1))^2}$

$$|\vec{v}(1)| = \sqrt{(144e^0) + (0)^2} = \boxed{12}$$

14. **(B)**

Step 1: Use partial fractions

$$\frac{x-8}{x^2-x-6} = \frac{x-8}{(x+2)(x-3)} = \frac{A}{(x+2)} + \frac{B}{(x-3)}$$

$$A = 2, B = -1$$

Step 2: $\displaystyle\int \frac{x-8}{x^2-x-6}\,dx = \int \frac{2}{x+2}\,dx + \int \frac{-1}{(x-3)}\,dx$

$$= 2\ln|x+2| - \ln|x-3| + C$$

$$\boxed{= \ln\frac{(x+2)^2}{|x-3|} + C}$$

$$\text{or} \quad \ln\left|\frac{(x+2)^2}{x-3}\right| + C$$

15. **(A)**

Step 1: Differentiate to find $h'(x)$. Remember to use the chain rule.

$$h(x) = f(g(x))$$
$$h'(x) = f'(g(x)) \cdot g'(x)$$

Step 2: Differentiate again to find $h''(x)$. Remember to also use the product rule.

$$h''(x) = f'(g(x)) \cdot g''(x) + g'(x)f''(g(x)) \cdot g'(x)$$
$$h''(3) = f'(g(3)) \cdot g''(3) + g'(3)f''(g(3)) \cdot g'(3)$$

From the table: $g(3) = 0, g''(3) = 5, g'(3) = 2$

$\therefore h''(3) = f'(0) \cdot 5 + 2f''(0) \cdot 2$

From the table: $f'(0) = 2, f''(0) = 1$

$\therefore h''(3) = 2\,(5) + 2(1)(2) = \boxed{14}$

16. **(E)**

Method 1

Step 1: Eliminate the parameter t.

$$x = 2t - 1 \qquad 3x = 6t - 3 \qquad 6t = 3x + 3$$
$$y = 6t + 11 \Rightarrow \quad y = 6t + 11 \Rightarrow \quad 6t = y - 11$$
$$\therefore y - 11 = 3x + 3 \Rightarrow y = 3x + 14$$

Step 2: To get the x-intercept, let $y = 0$.

$$\therefore y = 3x + 14$$
$$\Rightarrow x = \boxed{-\dfrac{14}{3}}$$
$$0 = 3x + 14$$

Method 2

Step 1: To get the x-intercept, let $y = 0$.

$$y = 6t + 11$$
$$0 = 6t + 11 \Rightarrow t = -\dfrac{11}{6}$$

Step 2: Find x when $t = -\dfrac{11}{6}$

$$x = 2t - 1 = \boxed{-\dfrac{14}{3}}$$

17. **(B)**

Step 1: Separate the variables and integrate

$$\frac{dy}{dx} = \sec^2 x \tan x$$
$$dy = (\sec^2 x \tan x)dx$$
$$y = \int dy = \int (\sec^2 x \tan x)dx$$

Step 2: Continue the integration using u-substitution.

Let $u = \tan x \Rightarrow du = \sec^2 x \, dx$

$$y = \int \sec^2 x \tan x \, dx = \int \tan x \cdot \sec^2 x \, dx = \int u \, du = \frac{u^2}{2} + C$$

$$y = \frac{\tan^2 x}{2} + C$$

Step 3: Substitute the initial conditions to find the value of C.

$$\frac{7}{2} = \frac{\tan^2\left(\frac{\pi}{4}\right)}{2} + C \Rightarrow C = 3$$

Step 4: $y = \dfrac{\tan^2 x}{2} + 3$

$$y = \frac{\tan^2\left(\frac{\pi}{3}\right)}{2} + 3 = \boxed{\frac{9}{2}}$$

18. **(C)**

Step 1: Simplify the algebra and integrate.

$$\int_1^e \frac{x^{\frac{5}{2}} - 3x^{\frac{3}{2}} + x^{\frac{1}{2}}}{x^{\frac{3}{2}}} \, dx = \int_1^e \left(x - 3 + \frac{1}{x}\right) dx = \frac{x^2}{2} - 3x + \ln|x| \Big|_{x=1}^{e}$$

Step 2: Evaluate:

$$\left(\frac{e^2}{2} - 3e + \ln e\right) - \left(\frac{1^2}{2} - 3(1) + \ln 1\right)$$

$$= \left(\frac{e^2}{2} - 3e + 1\right) - \left(\frac{1}{2} - 3\right) = \frac{e^2}{2} - 3e + \frac{7}{2}$$

$$= \boxed{\frac{e^2 - 6e + 7}{2}}$$

19. **(C)**

The function is NOT differentiable at:

Corners	$x = -4$
Discontinuities	$x = 1$
Cusps	$x = 6$

$x = \boxed{-4, 1, 6}$

20. (A)

The Maclaurin polynomial for $\ln(x+1)$ is

Step 1: $\ln(x+1) = x - \dfrac{x^2}{2} + \dfrac{x^3}{3} - \dfrac{x^4}{4} + \ldots \dfrac{(-1)^{n+1} x^n}{n}, \; -1 < x \le 1$

Step 2: $\ln(1.2) = \ln(.2+1) = \boxed{(.2) - \dfrac{(.2)^2}{2} + \dfrac{(.2)^3}{3} - \dfrac{(.2)^4}{4}}$

21. (D)

Use integration by parts.

$$\int \ln x \, dx$$

Let $u = \ln x$ and $dv = 1 \, dx$

$$\therefore du = \frac{1}{x} \, dx \qquad v = x$$

$$\int u \, dv = uv - \int v \, du$$

$$\int (\ln x)(1 \, dx) = (\ln x)(x) - \int x\left(\frac{1}{x}\right) dx$$

$$= x \ln x - \int dx$$

$$= x \ln x - x + C$$

22. (E)

Step 1: Sketch the graph. An even function has y-axis symmetry.

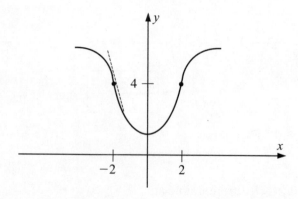

Step 2: $f(-2) = 4 \quad \therefore f(-2) > 0$

$f'(-2)$ is negative because the graph has a negatively sloped tangent at $x = -2$

$$f''(-2) = 0 \text{ because it is an inflection point}$$

$$\therefore \boxed{\begin{array}{l} f(-2) = + \\ f'(-2) = - \\ f''(-2) = 0 \end{array}} \text{ and choice E is correct.}$$

23. **(E)**

Step 1: Series I,

$$\sum_{n=1}^{\infty} \frac{3}{10^n} = \sum_{n=1}^{\infty} \frac{3}{10}\left(\frac{1}{10}\right)^{n-1}, \text{ is a geometric series with } a = \frac{3}{10} \text{ and } r = \frac{1}{10}.$$

$$\therefore \text{ It converges.}$$

Step 2: Check series II, $\displaystyle\sum_{n=1}^{\infty} \frac{2^n}{n}$, by using a ratio test.

$$\lim_{n\to\infty} \left| \frac{\left(\frac{2^{n+1}}{n+1}\right)}{\left(\frac{2^n}{n}\right)} \right| = \lim_{n\to\infty} \left| \frac{2n}{n+1} \right| = 2,$$

which is greater than 1.

$$\therefore \text{ It diverges.}$$

Step 3: Check series III, $\displaystyle\sum_{n=1}^{\infty} \frac{1}{k!}$, by using a ratio test.

$$\lim_{n\to\infty} \left| \frac{\left(\frac{1}{(n+1)!}\right)}{\left(\frac{1}{n!}\right)} \right| = \lim_{n\to\infty} \frac{1}{n+1} = 0,$$

which is less than 1.

$$\therefore \text{ It converges.}$$

Thus, series $\boxed{\text{I and III only}}$ converge.

24. **(B)**

The path is an arc.

$$\text{Arc length} = \int_a^b \sqrt{\left(\frac{dx}{dt}\right)^2 + \left(\frac{dy}{dt}\right)^2} \, dt$$

$$= \int_0^{\frac{\pi}{2}} \sqrt{(-\sin t)^2 + (2e^{2t})^2} \, dt$$

$$= \boxed{\int_0^{\frac{\pi}{2}} \sqrt{(\sin^2 t + 4e^{4t})} \, dt}$$

25. **(C)**

Step 1: The vertical tangents at $y = 0$ indicate that there is a division by y.

Step 2: The horizontal tangents at $x = 0$ indicate that there is a multiplication by x in the numerator.

Step 3: Note that the slopes are negative in the first quadrant. $\therefore$ There is a minus sign in the differential equation.

Only choice $\boxed{\text{C}}$ $\boxed{\dfrac{dy}{dx} = \dfrac{-x}{y}}$ has all of these characteristics.

26. **(A)**

Step 1: Find $f''(t)$.

$$f(t) = \langle \sin 2t, \cos t \rangle$$
$$f'(t) = \langle 2 \cos 2t, -\sin t \rangle$$
$$f''(t) = \langle -4 \sin 2t, -\cos t \rangle$$

Step 2: Find $f''\left(\dfrac{\pi}{4}\right)$.

$$f''\left(\frac{\pi}{4}\right) = \left\langle -4\sin\left(\frac{\pi}{2}\right), -\cos\left(\frac{\pi}{4}\right) \right\rangle$$

$$= \left\langle -4, \frac{-\sqrt{2}}{2} \right\rangle$$

27. **(E)**

Step 1: $f(x) = \dfrac{(x-3)(x-1)}{(x+4)(x-1)} \Rightarrow \dfrac{(x-3)}{(x+4)}$

Step 2: The factor $(x - 1)$ cancels. Therefore, there is a hole at $x = 1$.

Step 3: When the denominator $= 0$, there is a vertical asymptote.

Therefore, there is a vertical asymptote at $x = -4$.

Step 4: $\displaystyle\lim_{x \to \infty} \dfrac{(x-3)}{(x+4)} = 1$ Therefore, there is a horizontal asymptote at $y = 1$.

$\therefore$ Answer choice E,

Vertical asymptote:	$x = -4$
Horizontal asymptote:	$y = 1$
Hole at:	$x = 1$

is correct.

28. **(A)**

The length of a function $f(x)$ from $x = a$ to $x = b$ is:

Step 1: $S = \int_a^b \sqrt{1 + [f'(x)]^2}\ dx$

Algebraically rearrange the given integral by bringing the $\dfrac{1}{2}$ inside the integral and inside the square root (change it to $\dfrac{1}{4}$).

$$S = \frac{1}{2}\int_1^7 \sqrt{4 + 9x^4}\ dx$$

$$S = \int_1^7 \sqrt{\frac{1}{4}(4 + 9x^4)}\ dx$$

$$= \int_1^7 \sqrt{1 + \frac{9}{4}x^4}\ dx$$

$$= \int_1^7 \sqrt{1 + \left(\frac{3}{2}x^2\right)^2}\ dx$$

Step 2: $f'(x) = \dfrac{3}{2}x^2 \Rightarrow \dfrac{dy}{dx} = \dfrac{3x^2}{2} \Rightarrow dy = \dfrac{3x^2}{2}\,dx$

Step 3: Integrate and substitute the given point $(2, 5)$ to find the value of C.

$$\int dy = \int \frac{3x^2}{2}\,dx$$

$$y = \frac{1}{2}x^3 + C$$

$$5 = \frac{1}{2}(2)^3 + C$$

$$\therefore C = 1$$

Thus, $\boxed{y = \dfrac{1}{2}x^3 + 1}$ could be the equation.

Section I

PART B

76. **(C)**

Step 1: Draw the graph of the equations and find the intersection.

$$4 \sin \theta = 1 + \sin \theta$$

$$\theta = .3398 \text{ and } 2.802$$

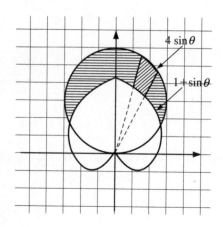

Step 2: $\text{Area} = \dfrac{1}{2} \displaystyle\int_a^b (r_{\text{outer}}^2 - r_{\text{inner}}^2)\, d\theta$

$$= \dfrac{1}{2} \int_{.3398}^{2.802} [(4 \sin \theta)^2 - (1 + \sin \theta)^2]\, d\theta$$

$$= \boxed{8.473}$$

77. **(D)**

Step 1: Euler's method is an iterative process. If $\dfrac{dy}{dx} = f(x, y)$ with a solution $g(x)$, then $g(x_n) = g(x_{n-1}) + \Delta x \cdot f(x_{n-1}, y_{n-1})$

Step 2: $\dfrac{dy}{dx} = x + y = f(x, y);\ g(0) = 1;\ \Delta x = 0.1$

Make an iterative chart.

x_n	$g(x_{n-1}) + \Delta x \cdot f(x_{n-1}, y_{n-1})$	$g(x_n)$
0	Given	1
.1	$1 + .1\,(0 + 1)$	1.1
.2	$1.1 + .1\,(.1 + 1.1)$	1.22
.3	$1.22 + .1\,(.2 + 1.22)$	1.362
.4	$1.362 + .1\,(.3 + 1.362)$	1.5282

Therefore, $g(.4) = \boxed{1.5282}$

78. **(B)**

Step 1: Convert the equation into logarithmic form.

$$y = \lim_{x \to \infty} \sqrt[x]{1 + x^2} \Rightarrow \ln y = \lim_{x \to \infty} \frac{1}{x} \ln(1 + x^2)$$

$$= \lim_{x \to \infty} \frac{\ln(1 + x^2)}{x} \Rightarrow \frac{\infty}{\infty}, \text{ indeterminate}$$

Step 2: Apply L'Hospital's rule.

$$\ln y = \lim_{x \to \infty} \frac{\ln(1 + x^2)}{x} = \lim_{x \to \infty} \frac{\frac{2x}{1+x^2}}{1} = \lim_{x \to \infty} \frac{2x}{1 + x^2} \Rightarrow \frac{\infty}{\infty}, \text{ indeterminate}$$

Step 3: Apply L'Hospital's rule a second time.

$$\ln y = \lim_{x \to \infty} \frac{2}{2x} = 0$$

$$\therefore y = \boxed{1}$$

79. **(E)**

Step 1: Do the ratio test.

$$\lim_{n \to \infty} \left| \frac{\left(\frac{x^{2(n+1)}}{(2(n+1))!} \right)}{\left(\frac{x^{2n}}{(2n)!} \right)} \right| = \lim_{n \to \infty} \left| \frac{x^2}{(2n+2)(2n+1)} \right| = 0$$

The series converges for all values of x.

$$\therefore \boxed{-\infty < x < \infty}$$

457

80. **(B)**

Step 1: Determine the corresponding value of t.

$$t^2 + 1 = 5$$
$$t^3 - 1 = 7$$
$$\therefore t = 2$$

Step 2: Find $\dfrac{dy}{dx} = \dfrac{\frac{dy}{dt}}{\frac{dx}{dt}} = \dfrac{3t^2}{2t} = \dfrac{3t}{2}$.

Step 3: At $t = 2$:

$$m = \frac{dy}{dx} = \frac{3t}{2}\bigg|_{t=2} = 3$$

$$x = 5$$
$$y = 7$$

Step 4: The equation of the tangent line is:

$$y - 7 = 3(x - 5) \Rightarrow \boxed{3x - y = 8}$$

81. **(D)**

Step 1: Convert $4°$ to radians $= \dfrac{\pi}{45} = .0698$.

(Hint: Always do calculus in radians.)

Step 2: Using the calculator, evaluate

$$\frac{d}{dx}(e^{\sin 2x})\bigg|_{x=\frac{\pi}{45}} = \boxed{2.276}$$

82. **(E)**

Step 1: Separate the variables.

$$\frac{dy}{dt} = \frac{1}{2t-1} \Rightarrow dy = \frac{dt}{2t-1} \Rightarrow \int dy = \int \frac{dt}{2t-1}$$

Step 2: Integrate by using u-substitution.

$$u = 2t - 1 \Rightarrow du = 2\, dt$$

$$\int \frac{dt}{2t-1} = \frac{1}{2}\int \frac{2\,dt}{2t-1} = \frac{1}{2}\int \frac{du}{u} = \frac{1}{2}\ln|u| + C = \frac{1}{2}\ln|2t-1| + C$$

Step 3: $\displaystyle\int dy = \int \frac{dt}{2t-1}$

$$y = \frac{1}{2}\ln|2t-1| + C$$

Step 4: Use $y = 1$ when $t = 1$ to find the value of C.

$$1 = \frac{1}{2}\ln 1 + C \quad \therefore C = 1$$

$$y = \frac{1}{2}\ln|2t - 1| + 1$$

Step 5: Find y when $t = 5$.

$$y = \frac{1}{2}\ln|9| + 1$$
$$= \boxed{2.099}$$

83. **(B)**

Step 1: Determine the velocity vector at time $t = \frac{\pi}{4}$.

$$\bar{s}(t) = \langle 2\cos 2t, 1 + 3\sin t \rangle$$

$$\bar{v}(t) = \langle -4\sin 2t, 3\cos t \rangle$$

$$\bar{v}\left(\frac{\pi}{4}\right) = \left\langle -4, \frac{3\sqrt{2}}{2} \right\rangle$$

Step 2: Speed $= |\bar{v}(t)| = \sqrt{(-4)^2 + \left(\frac{3\sqrt{2}}{2}\right)^2}$

$$= \frac{\sqrt{82}}{2} = \boxed{4.528}$$

84. **(D)**

Step 1: By definition,

$$e^x = 1 + x + \frac{x^2}{2!} + \frac{x^3}{3!} \cdots \frac{x^n}{n!}.$$

$$\therefore e^{2x} = 1 + (2x) + \frac{(2x)^2}{2!} + \frac{(2x)^3}{3!} \cdots \frac{(2x)^n}{n!}$$

Step 2: Solve

$$e^{2x} = x^2 + 3$$
$$x = \boxed{.607}$$

85. **(E)**

   Step 1: $f(x) = x^2 - 7x + 1$

   $$f'(x) = 2x - 7$$
   at $x = 3$: $y = (3)^2 - 7(3) + 1 = -11$
   $$m = 2(3) - 7 = -1$$

   Step 2: The tangent line at $x = 3$ is:

   $$y + 11 = -1(x - 3) \Rightarrow y = -x - 8$$

   Step 3: $\left|(x^2 - 7x + 1) - (-x - 8)\right| \leq .6$

   $$2.2254 \leq x \leq 3.7746$$

   The only answer choice in this range is E, $\boxed{3.6}$.

86. **(D)**

   Step 1: Rewrite the curve in terms of x.

   $$x^2 + y = 1 \Rightarrow x = \sqrt{1 - y}$$

   Step 2: Draw a graph.

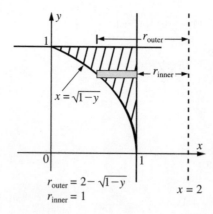

$r_{outer} = 2 - \sqrt{1 - y}$
$r_{inner} = 1$

$x = 2$

   Step 3: Volume $= \pi \int_a^b \left(r_{outer}^2 - r_{inner}^2\right) dy$

   $$= \pi \int_{y=0}^1 [(2 - \sqrt{1 - y})^2 - (1)^2]\, dy$$

   $$= \boxed{\dfrac{5\pi}{6}}$$

87. **(C)**

   Step 1: Make a sketch.

   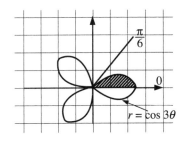

   Step 2: Using symmetry, find the area of half a petal and multiply by 6.

   $$\text{Half petal area} = \frac{1}{2}\int_a^b r^2 d\theta = \frac{1}{2}\int_0^{\frac{\pi}{6}}(\cos 3\theta)^2\, d\theta = \frac{\pi}{24}$$

   $$\text{Total area} = 6\left(\frac{\pi}{24}\right) = \frac{\pi}{4} = .7853 \Rightarrow \boxed{0.785}$$

88. **(C)**

   Step 1: $x(t) = (1+t^2)e^{-t}$

   $$v(t) = x'(t) = (1+t^2)\frac{d}{dt}(e^{-t}) + e^{-t}\frac{d}{dt}(1+t^2)$$
   $$= -(1+t^2)e^{-t} + 2t\,e^{-t}$$

   Step 2: The particle is at rest when $v(t) = 0$.

   $$-(1 + t^2)e^{-t} + 2t\,e^{-t} = 0$$
   $$\therefore t = \boxed{1}$$

89. **(D)**

   Step 1: The radius of the smaller sphere $= 6 + 8t$.

   The radius of the larger sphere $= 40 + 2t$.

   Step 2: Volume of a sphere $= \frac{4}{3}\pi r^3$

   Let $V(t) =$ volume of region between the spheres.

   $$\therefore V(t) = \frac{4}{3}\pi(40+2t)^3 - \frac{4}{3}\pi(6+8t)^3$$
   $$= \frac{4}{3}\pi[(40+2t)^3 - (6+8t)^3]$$

Step 3: To maximize $V(t)$, set its derivative to zero and solve for t.

$$V'(t) = \frac{4}{3}\pi\,[3(40+2t)^2(2) - 3(6+8t)^2(8)] = 0$$

$$t = 2$$

Step 4: Use a first derivative test to confirm this is a maximum.

$$v'(t) \quad \underrightarrow{\qquad +++ \quad \overset{\displaystyle |}{\underset{2}{}} \quad ---- \qquad}$$

increasing   decreasing

$$\therefore t = \boxed{2}$$

90. **(D)**

Average value $= \dfrac{1}{b-a}\displaystyle\int_a^b f(t)\,dt$

$$= \frac{1}{3-1}\int_1^3 (3t^2 + 10t)\,dt$$

$$= \frac{1}{2}\int_1^3 (3t^2 + 10t)\,dt = \boxed{33}$$

91. **(C)**

Step 1: $f(x) = cx^{\frac{3}{2}} \;\therefore\; f'(x) = \dfrac{3}{2}cx^{\frac{1}{2}}$

Step 2: Arc length $= \displaystyle\int_a^b \sqrt{1 + [f'(x)]^2}\;dx$

$$= \int_0^5 \sqrt{1 + \left(\frac{3}{2}cx^{\frac{1}{2}}\right)^2}\;dx = \frac{19}{3}$$

$$= \frac{1}{2}\int_0^5 \sqrt{4 + 9c^2 x}\;dx = \frac{19}{3}$$

Step 3: Let $u = 4 + 9c^2 x \;\therefore\; du = 9c^2\,dx$

Rewrite the arc length as

$$\frac{1}{9c^2} \cdot \frac{1}{2}\int_{x=0}^5 \sqrt{4 + 9c^2 x}\cdot 9c^2\,dx$$

$$= \frac{1}{18c^2}\int_{x=0}^5 \sqrt{u}\,du = \frac{1}{27c^2}[4 + 9c^2 x]^{\frac{3}{2}}\Big|_0^5 = \frac{19}{3}$$

$$c = \boxed{\frac{1}{3}} \text{ or } -\frac{1}{3}.$$

92. **(D)**

Method 1

$$e^x = 1 + x + \frac{x^2}{2!} + \frac{x^3}{3!} + \frac{x^4}{4!} + \dots$$

$$\therefore e^{2x} = 1 + (2x) + \frac{(2x)^2}{2!} + \frac{(2x)^3}{3!} + \frac{(2x)^4}{4!} + \dots$$

The x^4 term is $\dfrac{(2x)^4}{4!} = \dfrac{16x^4}{24} = \dfrac{2x^4}{3}$

$\therefore$ The coefficient is $\boxed{\dfrac{2}{3}}$.

Method 2

The Taylor series expanded about $x = a$ is:

$$\sum_{n=0}^{\infty} \frac{f^n(a)}{n!}(x-a)^n$$

For e^{2x} about $x = 0$:

$$f(x) = e^{2x}, \qquad f(0) = 1$$
$$f'(x) = 2e^{2x}, \qquad f'(0) = 2$$
$$f''(x) = 4e^{2x}, \qquad f''(0) = 4$$
$$f'''(x) = 8e^{2x}, \qquad f'''(0) = 8$$
$$f^4(x) = 16e^{2x}, \qquad f^4(0) = 16$$

$\therefore$ The x^4 term has the coefficient $\dfrac{f^4(0)}{4!} = \dfrac{16}{24} = \boxed{\dfrac{2}{3}}$.

Section II

PART A

1.

The general form of the Taylor polynomial is

Step 1: $e^x = 1 + x + \dfrac{x^2}{2!} + \dfrac{x^3}{3!} + \ldots \dfrac{x^n}{n!} = \displaystyle\sum_{n=0}^{\infty} \dfrac{x^n}{n!}$

Thus,

$$e^{-x^2} = 1 + (-x^2) + \frac{(-x^2)^2}{2!} + \frac{(-x^2)^3}{3!} + \ldots \frac{(-x^2)^n}{n!} = \sum_{n=0}^{\infty} \frac{(-x^2)^n}{n!}$$

(a)
$$= \boxed{1 - x^2 + \frac{x^4}{2!} - \frac{x^6}{3!} + \ldots \frac{(-1)^n x^{2n}}{n!} = \sum_{n=0}^{\infty} \frac{(-1)^n x^{2n}}{n!}}$$

Step 2: $\displaystyle\int_0^{\frac{1}{2}} e^{-x^2}\,dx = \int_0^{\frac{1}{2}} \left[1 - x^2 + \frac{x^4}{2!} - \frac{x^6}{3!} + \ldots + \frac{(-1)^n x^{2n}}{n!} \right] dx$

$$= \int_0^{\frac{1}{2}} \left[\sum_{n=0}^{\infty} \frac{(-1)^n x^{2n}}{n!} \right] dx$$

$$= x - \frac{x^3}{3} + \frac{x^5}{5 \cdot 2!} - \frac{x^7}{7 \cdot 3!} + \ldots \frac{(-1)^n x^{2n+1}}{(2n+1)n!} \Bigg]_0^{\frac{1}{2}}$$

$$= \frac{1}{2} - \frac{\left(\frac{1}{2}\right)^3}{3} + \frac{\left(\frac{1}{2}\right)^5}{10} - \frac{\left(\frac{1}{2}\right)^7}{42} + \ldots$$

$$= .5 - .041666 + .003125 - .000186$$

Step 3: Three decimal accuracy means the error should be a maximum of .0005. Since the fourth term is .000186, this would be the maximum error (which is less than .0005) if we use only the three terms:

(b) $.5 - .041666 + .003125 = \boxed{.461459}$

Step 4: $\displaystyle\int_0^{.1} e^{-x^2}\,dx = x - \frac{x^3}{3} + \frac{x^5}{5 \cdot 2!} - \frac{x^7}{7 \cdot 3!} + \ldots + \frac{(-1)^n x^{2n+1}}{(2n+1)n!} \Bigg]_0^{.1}$

$$= (.1) - \frac{(.1)^3}{3} + \frac{(.1)^5}{10} - \frac{(.1)^7}{42} + \ldots$$

$$= .1 - .000333 + .000001\ldots$$

Step 5: Since this is a decreasing alternating series, the error is bounded by the first term not used. Since .000001 < .00001, only two terms are needed.

(c) $\therefore \int_0^{.1} e^{-x^2}\,dx = .1 - .000333 = \boxed{.099667}$

2.

Step 1: Sketch the graph.

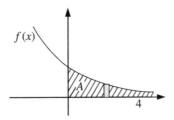

Step 2: $A = \int_0^4 2 + 3e^{-2x}\,dx = \boxed{9.499}$

(a)

Step 3: Sketch the graph.

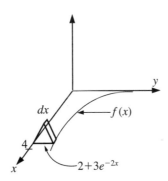

Step 4: Area of an equilateral triangle of side S is $\dfrac{S^2}{4}\sqrt{3}$.

$\therefore$ Volume of the equilateral triangular slice is $\dfrac{(2+3e^{-2x})^2}{4}\sqrt{3}\,dx$

(b) $V = \int_0^4 \dfrac{(2+3e^{-2x})^2}{4}\sqrt{3}\,dx = \boxed{10.500}$

Step 5: Sketch the graph.

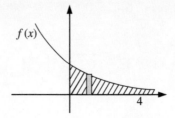

Step 6:

(c) $V = \pi \int_0^4 (2+3e^{-2x})^2 \, dx = \boxed{76.177}$

3.

Step 1: $r(t) = \dfrac{78}{1+3e^{-.15t}}$

(a) Solve : $r''(t) = 0 \;\Rightarrow\; t = \boxed{7.324}$

Note: Referring to the Special Differential Equation section, the point of inflection is $\dfrac{\ln 3}{.15} = 7.324$.

Step 2:

(b) $r(10) = \dfrac{78}{1+3e^{-.15(10)}} = 46.7 \quad \boxed{47} \text{ people}$

Step 3: The maximum number of people is the limit of $r(t)$ *as* $t \rightarrow \infty$,

$$\lim_{t \to \infty} \frac{78}{1+3e^{-.15t}} = \boxed{78}$$

Section II

PART B

4.

Step 1: From the given information, $\vec{a}(t) = \langle 6t^2, 2t+1 \rangle$,

$\vec{v}(1) = \langle 3, 1 \rangle$, and $\vec{s}(0) = \langle 2, 1 \rangle$.

$\vec{v}(t) = \int \vec{a}(t)\, dt$

$= \left\langle \dfrac{6t^3}{3} + C_1, \dfrac{2t^2}{2} + t + C_2 \right\rangle$

Step 2: $\vec{v}(1) = \langle 2 + C_1, 2 + C_2 \rangle = \langle 3, 1 \rangle$

$\therefore C_1 = 1$ and $C_2 = -1$

(a) $\qquad \therefore \vec{V}(t) = \boxed{\langle 2t^3 + 1, t^2 + t - 1 \rangle}$

Step 3: Speed $= |\vec{v}(t)| = \sqrt{(2t^3 + 1)^2 + (t^2 + t - 1)^2}$

(b) $\qquad$ speed $= |\vec{v}(0)| = \sqrt{1^2 + (-1)^2} = \boxed{\sqrt{2}}$

Step 4: $\vec{s}(t) = \int \vec{v}(t)\, dt$

$= \left\langle \dfrac{2t^4}{4} + t + C_1, \dfrac{t^3}{3} + \dfrac{t^2}{2} - t + C_2 \right\rangle$

$\vec{s}(0) = \langle C_1, C_2 \rangle = \langle 2, 1 \rangle \qquad\qquad \therefore C_1 = 2$ and $C_2 = 1$

(c) $\qquad \therefore \vec{s}(t) = \boxed{\left\langle \dfrac{t^4}{2} + t + 2, \dfrac{t^3}{3} + \dfrac{t^2}{2} - t + 1 \right\rangle}$

Step 5: $\vec{S}(1) = \left\langle \dfrac{7}{2}, \dfrac{5}{6} \right\rangle$

(d) $\qquad$ The particle is at the point $\boxed{\left(\dfrac{7}{2}, \dfrac{5}{6}\right)}$ at time $t = 1$.

5.

Step 1: Set up a table of values from which to sketch the slope field.

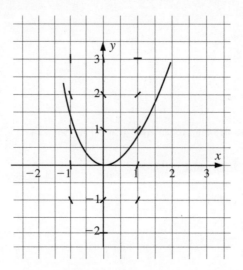

x	y	$\dfrac{dy}{dx}$
−1	−1	−2
	0	−3
	1	−4
	2	−5
	3	−6
0	−1	1
	0	0
	1	−1
	2	−2
	3	−3
1	−1	4
	0	3
	1	2
	2	1
	3	0

Step 2: Use Euler's method to determine a table of values.

$$\frac{dy}{dx} = f(x, y) = 3x - y;\; f(1) = 1;\; \Delta x = .3$$

x_n	$f(x_{n-1}) + \Delta x f(x_{n-1}, y_{n-1})$	$f(x_n)$
1		1
1.3	$1 + .3(3 \times 1 - 1)$	1.6
1.6	$1.6 + .3(3 \times 1.3 - 1.6)$ $1.6 + .69$	2.29

(b) $\therefore f(1.6) \approx \boxed{2.29}$

Step 3: $\dfrac{d^2 y}{dx^2} = \dfrac{d}{dx}(3x - y) = 3 - \dfrac{dy}{dx}$

$$= 3 - (3x - y)$$

(c) $\qquad\qquad\qquad = \boxed{3 - 3x + y}$

Step 4: At the point estimated in part (b), (1.6, 2.29),

$$\frac{d^2 y}{dx^2} = 3 - 3(1.6) + 2.29 = 1.1$$

Since $\dfrac{d^2 y}{dx^2}$ is positive at (1.6, 2.29), the actual graph is concave up and the tangent line approximation based on Euler's method is below the actual curve.

(c) $\boxed{f(1.6) > 2.29}$

6.

Step 1: Use implicit differentiation. Remember that $6xy$ is a product.

$$y^2 - 6xy + 6x^2 = 1$$

$$2y\frac{dy}{dx} - 6\left[x\frac{dy}{dx} + y\right] + 12x = 0$$

(a) $\dfrac{dy}{dx} = \dfrac{6y - 12x}{2y - 6x} = \boxed{\dfrac{3y - 6x}{y - 3x}}$,   or $\boxed{\dfrac{6x - 3y}{3x - y}}$

Step 2: At $x = 1$:

$$y^2 - 6xy + 6x^2 = 1$$
$$y^2 - 6y + 5 = 0$$
$$\therefore y = 5 \text{ or } y = 1$$

Step 3: At $x = 1, y = 1 \Rightarrow m = \dfrac{3}{2}$ $\quad \therefore \boxed{y - 1 = \dfrac{3}{2}(x - 1)}$

(b) $\qquad x = 1, y = 5 \Rightarrow m = \dfrac{9}{2}$ $\quad \therefore \boxed{y - 5 = \dfrac{9}{2}(x - 1)}$

Step 4: Solve the two equations simultaneously to find the point of intersection.

$$\begin{aligned} y - 1 &= \frac{3}{2}(x - 1) \\ y - 5 &= \frac{9}{2}(x - 1) \end{aligned} \Rightarrow x = -\frac{1}{3},\, y = -1$$

$\therefore$ The tangent lines intersect at $\left(-\dfrac{1}{3}, -1 \right)$.

PRACTICE EXAM 3

AP Calculus BC

Section I

PART A

Time: 55 minutes
   28 questions

(Answer sheets appear in the back of this book.)

DIRECTIONS: Solve each of the following problems. Select the best answer choice and fill in the corresponding oval on the answer sheet.

Calculators may NOT be used for this section of the exam.

NOTES:

 (1) Unless otherwise specified, the domain of a function f is assumed to be the set of all real numbers x for which $f(x)$ is a real number.

 (2) The inverse of a trigonometric function f may be indicated by using the inverse function notation f^{-1} or with the prefix "arc" (e.g., $\sin^{-1}x = \arcsin x$).

1. What are all the values of x for which the function $f(x) = 4x^3 - 3x^2 - 18x + 6$ is decreasing?

 (A) $-1 < x < \dfrac{3}{2}$

 (B) $-\dfrac{3}{2} < x < 1$

 (C) $x < -1$ or $x > \dfrac{3}{2}$

 (D) $x < -\dfrac{3}{2}$ or $x > 1$

 (E) $x < -3$ or $x > 2$

2. What is the equation of the line, in the xy-plane, passing through the point (6, 4) and parallel to the line with parametric equations $x = 5t + 4$ and $y = t - 7$.

    (A) $5y - x = 14$

    (B) $x - 5y = 14$

    (C) $5y - x = 39$

    (D) $x - 5y = 39$

    (E) $5x - y = 11$

3. Find the slope of the line tangent to the curve $y = \sqrt{3x + y}$ at the point (1, 6).

    (A) $-\dfrac{3}{4}$

    (B) $-\dfrac{2}{5}$

    (C) $\dfrac{1}{3}$

    (D) $\dfrac{1}{2}$

    (E) $\dfrac{3}{5}$

4. $\displaystyle \int \frac{dx}{x^2 + x} =$

    (A) $\ln\left|x^2 + x\right| + C$

    (B) $\ln\left|\dfrac{x}{x+1}\right| + C$

    (C) $\ln\left|\dfrac{x+1}{x}\right| + C$

    (D) $\ln\left|\dfrac{1}{x^2 + x}\right| + C$

    (E) $2\ln\left|x^2 + x\right| + C$

5. Let $f(x) = e^{\sin 2x}$ and $g(x)$ be differentiable and have the values shown in the table below. If $h(x) = g(f(x))$, then $h'(0) =$

x	$g(x)$	$g'(x)$
0	5	9
1	4	3

(A) 4

(B) 6

(C) 7

(D) 8

(E) 10

6. $\int_e^{e^2} \dfrac{1}{x \ln x}\,dx =$

(A) $e^2 - e$

(B) $e^2 \ln 3$

(C) $\ln 2$

(D) $\ln 3 + e^2$

(E) $3 \ln 2$

7. If $\dfrac{dy}{dx} = \csc^2 x \cot^2 x$, and if $y = 3$ when $x = \dfrac{\pi}{4}$, then the particular solution to the differential equation is which of the following?

(A) $y = \dfrac{6 - 3\cot^2 x}{4}$

(B) $y = \dfrac{\tan^2 x - 5}{4}$

(C) $y = \dfrac{\csc^3 x}{3} + 6$

(D) $y = \dfrac{10 - \cot^3 x}{3}$

(E) $y = -\cot^3 x + 10$

8. A particle moves on the xy-plane so that at any time t its coordinates are $x = t^3 + t$ and $y = t^5 - 2t^2$. The acceleration vector of the particle at $t = 2$ is:

(A) $\langle 12, 156 \rangle$

    (B) $\langle 12, 164 \rangle$

    (C) $\langle 6, 156 \rangle$

    (D) $\langle 6, 164 \rangle$

    (E) $\langle 13, 72 \rangle$

9.   If the function f is differentiable at $x = 1$ and

$$f(x) = \begin{cases} a^2 x^2 + bx - 6 & x < 1 \\ ax + b & x \geq 1 \end{cases}.$$

    What is the value of $a - b$ if $a > 0$?

    (A)   14

    (B)   16

    (C)   18

    (D)   20

    (E)   22

10.   What is the third-degree Taylor polynomial approximation for $\sqrt{e}$ about $x = 0$?

    (A) $1 + \dfrac{1}{2} + \dfrac{1}{8} + \dfrac{1}{48}$

    (B) $1 + \dfrac{1}{2} + \dfrac{1}{8} + \dfrac{1}{24}$

    (C) $1 + \dfrac{1}{2} + \dfrac{1}{4} + \dfrac{1}{8}$

    (D) $1 - \dfrac{1}{2} + \dfrac{1}{8} - \dfrac{1}{24}$

    (E) $1 + \dfrac{1}{2} + \dfrac{1}{6} + \dfrac{1}{10}$

11. $\int x e^{-2x}\, dx =$

    (A) $e^{-2x}\left(x - \dfrac{1}{2}\right) + C$

    (B) $\dfrac{e^{-2x}}{2}\left(x - \dfrac{1}{2}\right) + C$

(C) $\quad -e^{-2x}\left(x+\dfrac{1}{2}\right)+C$

(D) $\quad \dfrac{-e^{-2x}}{2}\left(x+\dfrac{1}{2}\right)+C$

(E) $\quad \dfrac{e^{-2x}}{2}\left(x+\dfrac{1}{2}\right)+C$

12. Which of the following series converges?

I $\quad \displaystyle\sum_{n=1}^{\infty}\dfrac{4n}{3n+1}$

II $\quad \displaystyle\sum_{n=1}^{\infty}\dfrac{\ln n}{n}$

III $\quad \displaystyle\sum_{n=1}^{\infty}\dfrac{n^n}{n!}$

(A) None

(B) II only

(C) II and III only

(D) I and II only

(E) III only

13. The area of the region inside the polar curve $r = 2\cos\theta$ and outside the circle $r = 1$ is given by which of the following?

(A) $\quad \dfrac{1}{2}\displaystyle\int_0^{\pi}(2\cos\theta-1)^2\,d\theta$

(B) $\quad \dfrac{1}{2}\displaystyle\int_{-\frac{\pi}{3}}^{\frac{\pi}{3}}(2\cos\theta-1)^2\,d\theta$

(C) $\quad \dfrac{1}{2}\displaystyle\int_0^{\frac{\pi}{3}}\left[2\cos^2\theta-1\right]d\theta$

(D) $\quad \dfrac{1}{2}\displaystyle\int_{-\frac{\pi}{3}}^{\frac{\pi}{3}}\left[4\cos^2\theta-1\right]d\theta$

(E) $\quad \displaystyle\int_{-\frac{\pi}{3}}^{\frac{\pi}{3}}\left[4\cos^2\theta-1\right]d\theta$

14. What is the equation of the line tangent to the curve described parametrically by $x=\dfrac{9}{t}$ and $y=t^{\frac{1}{2}}$ at the point $(1, 3)$?

(A) $2x - 3y = 9$

(B) $3x - 2y = 9$

(C) $3x + 2y = 9$

(D) $2x + 3y = 9$

(E) $2x + y = 4$

15.   What is the arc length for the spiral $r = e^{2\theta}$ from $\theta = 0$ to $\theta = 2\pi$?

(A) $\displaystyle\int_0^{2\pi} e^{2\theta}d\theta$

(B) $\displaystyle\int_0^{2\pi} \sqrt{5e^{2\theta}}d\theta$

(C) $\displaystyle\int \sqrt{1+2e^{4\theta}}\,d\theta$

(D) $\displaystyle\int_0^{2\pi} \sqrt{1+e^{4\theta}}\,d\theta$

(E) $\displaystyle\int_0^{2\pi} 5e^{4\theta}d\theta$

16.

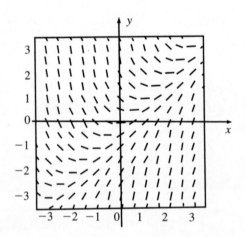

The slope field shown above represents which of the following differential equations?

(A) $\dfrac{dy}{dx} = x + y$

(B) $\dfrac{dy}{dx} = y - x$

(C) $\dfrac{dy}{dx} = x - y$

(D) $\dfrac{dy}{dx} = \ln y$

(E) $\dfrac{dy}{dx} = x + 1$

17. $\displaystyle\int_0^\infty 2e^{-3x}\,dx =$

(A) $-\dfrac{3}{4}$

(B) $\dfrac{2}{3}$

(C) $\dfrac{3}{4}$

(D) $\dfrac{4}{5}$

(E) diverges

18. If the position vector for a particle is $\left\langle \dfrac{1}{2}t^2 + 2t,\ 2t^2 \right\rangle$, then the speed of the particle is

(A) $\dfrac{5}{2}t^2 + 2t$

(B) $\sqrt{\dfrac{5}{2}t^2 + 2t}$

(C) $\sqrt{15t^2 - 4t - 4}$

(D) $15t^2 - 4t - 4$

(E) $\sqrt{17t^2 + 4t + 4}$

19. What is the length of the arc for the curve given parametrically as $x = 4\cos^3 t$ and $y = 4\sin^3 t$ on the interval $\left[0, \dfrac{\pi}{2}\right]$?

(A) $\dfrac{\pi}{2}$

(B) $\dfrac{3\pi}{2}$

(C)   3

(D)   6

(E) 3π

20. A function f has the Maclaurin series $\dfrac{x^4}{3!} - \dfrac{x^6}{5!} + \dfrac{x^8}{7!} - \dfrac{x^{10}}{9!} + \dots$ Which of the following is $f(x)$?

(A) $-x\cos x + x$

(B) $x^2 \ln(x+1) - x^3$

(C) $x^2 e^x - x^2 - x^3$

(D) $-x^2 e^x + x^2 + x^3$

(E) $-x\sin x + x^2$

21. The growth rate of a particular animal population P is modeled against time t by the differential equation $\dfrac{dP}{dt} = .3P\left(1 - \dfrac{P}{150}\right)$. If the initial population at $t = 0$ is 37, what is $\lim\limits_{t\to\infty} p(t)$?

(A)   37

(B)   45

(C)   120

(D)   150

(E)   500

22. $\lim\limits_{x\to 0} \dfrac{1 - \cos x}{3x^4 + x^2} =$

(A)   0

(B) $\dfrac{1}{3}$

(C) $\dfrac{1}{4}$

(D) $\dfrac{1}{2}$

(E)   1

23. What is the coefficient of the x^3 in the Taylor series polynomial for $\dfrac{1}{1+2x}$ about $x = 0$?

(A) -8

(B) -4

(C) 4

(D) 8

(E) 16

24. If $f(x) = |\sin x|$, which of the following is a graph of $f'(x)$?

(A)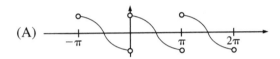

(B)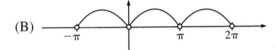

(C)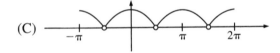

(D)

(E)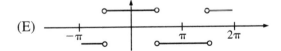

25. At each point on a curve, the slope of the curve is $4x^3y$. If the curve contains the point $(0, 5)$, which of the following is the equation of the curve?

(A) $y = x^4 + 5$

(B) $y = 5e^{x^4}$

(C) $y = e^{x^4} + 5$

(D) $y = \ln(x + 1) + 5$

(E) $y^2 = x^3 + 5$

26.   The position of a particle moving along the x-axis at any time t is given by $x(t) = 2t^3 - 4t^2 + 2t - 1$. What is the slowest velocity achieved by the particle?

(A) $\dfrac{17}{4}$

(B)   3

(C) $\dfrac{1}{2}$

(D) $-\dfrac{2}{3}$

(E) $-\dfrac{3}{2}$

27.   What are all the values of x for which the series $1+\dfrac{x}{4}+\left(\dfrac{x}{4}\right)^2+\left(\dfrac{x}{4}\right)^3+\ldots$ $+\left(\dfrac{x}{4}\right)^n$ converges?

(A) $[-4, 4)$

(B) $[-4, 4]$

(C) $(-4, 4)$

(D) $(-4, 4]$

(E)   all values of x

28.

t (min)	1	4	7	10
$a(t)$ (ft/min^2)	3	1	4	7

The acceleration a of a particle for particular times t is shown in the table above. If $v(1) = 9$ ft/min, what is the approximate value of the velocity v at $t = 10$, using a right-hand Riemann sum with three equal subintervals?

(A)   11

(B)   18

(C)   23

(D)   37

(E)   45

STOP

This is the end of Section I, Part A.
If time still remains, you may check your work only in this section.
Do not begin Section I, Part B until instructed to do so.

Section I

PART B

Time: 50 minutes
17 questions

(Answer sheets appear in the back of this book.)

DIRECTIONS: Solve each of the following problems. Select the best answer choice and fill in the corresponding oval on the answer sheet.

Calculators MAY be used for this section of the exam.

NOTES:

(1) The exact numerical value of the correct answer does not always appear among the choice given. When this happens, select the number from among the choices that best approximates the exact numerical value.

(2) Unless otherwise specified, the domain of a function f is assumed to be the set of all real numbers x for which $f(x)$ is a real number.

(3) The inverse of a trigonometric function f may be indicated by using the inverse function notation f^{-1} or with the prefix "arc" (e.g., $\sin^{-1}x = \arcsin x$).

76. Find $\dfrac{dy}{dx}$ at $x = 2$ if $y = x^{2^x}, x > 0$.

   (A) 62.749

   (B) 32.000

   (C) 22.181

   (D) 17.374

   (E) 15.374

77. What is the rate of change of $\sqrt{1+x^2}$ with respect to $\dfrac{x}{1+x^2}$?

   (A) $\dfrac{\sqrt{1+x^2}}{\left(\frac{x}{1+x}\right)}$

   (B) $\dfrac{x\left(\sqrt{1+x^2}\right)^3}{(1-x)^2}$

(C) $\dfrac{x\left(\sqrt{1+x^2}\right)^3}{1-x^2}$

(D) $\dfrac{x^2\left(\sqrt{1+x^2}\right)^3}{1-x}$

(E) $\dfrac{x^2\sqrt{1+x^2}}{1-x^2}$

78. The graph of the function represented by the series $(3x)-\dfrac{(3x)^2}{2}+\dfrac{(3x)^3}{3}$ $-\dfrac{(3x)^4}{4}+\ldots+\dfrac{(-1)^{n+1}(3x)^n}{n}$ intersects the line $y=-3x+8$ at what value of x?

(A) 1.955

(B) 2.016

(C) 2.103

(D) 2.272

(E) 2.371

79. The function f is defined as $f(x) = x^3 + 4x - 1$. A tangent line to the function at $x = 1$ is used to approximate the value of $f(x)$. For which interval $(x \geq 0)$ is the error at most 0.4?

(A) [.608, 1.346]

(B) [.591, .753]

(C) [.608, 2.105]

(D) [.591, 1.034]

(E) [1.346, 2.105]

80. What is the volume of the solid whose base is the area enclosed by the graphs of $x = 1 - y^2$ and the y-axis, and whose cross sections perpendicular to the x-axis are semicircles with diameters parallel to the y-axis?

(A) $\dfrac{\pi}{8}$

(B) $\dfrac{\pi}{4}$

(C) $\dfrac{\pi}{2}$

(D) $\dfrac{3\pi}{4}$

(E) $\dfrac{3\pi}{2}$

81. Point A moves to the right along the positive x-axis at 7 units per second while point B moves upward along the negative y-axis at 2 units per second. At what rate is the distance between A and B changing when A is at $(8, 0)$ and B is at $(0, -6)$?

(A) $-\dfrac{32}{5}$

(B) $-\dfrac{22}{5}$

(C) $\dfrac{22}{5}$

(D) $\dfrac{32}{5}$

(E) 5

82. A square is inscribed in a circle. How fast is the area between the square and the circle changing when the area of the circle is increasing at the rate of one square inch per minute?

(A) -0.135

(B) 0.179

(C) 0.363

(D) 0.843

(E) cannot be determined.

83. Last year, a fundraiser sold 500 tickets at $4 each. Based on a marketing survey, it was determined that for every $1 increase in ticket price they will lose 10 purchases of tickets. What dollar amount should the fundraiser charge this year per ticket to maximize revenue?

(A) 6

(B) 12

(C) 18

(D) 27

(E) 36

84. A wildlife preserve can support a maximum of 200 buffalo; currently there are 25. The logistic population growth model gives an estimate of $\dfrac{1}{P}\dfrac{dP}{dt} = .001(200 - P)$, where t is given in years. To the nearest number of years, in how many years will the buffalo population be 100?

(A)   5

(B)   10

(C)   15

(D)   20

(E)   25

85.

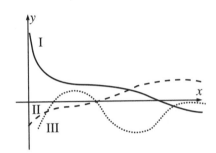

The three graphs shown above represent a function $f(x)$ and its first and second derivatives. Which of the following correctly associates the graphs?

	$f(x)$	$f'(x)$	$f''(x)$
(A)	I	II	III
(B)	I	III	II
(C)	II	I	III
(D)	II	III	I
(E)	III	II	I

86.

t (min)	0	10	20	30	40	50	60
$r(t)$ (gal/min)	35	40	38	42	50	35	40

The table above represents the rate r in gal/min that water is being pumped through a pipe at 10-minute intervals for one hour. Use the trapezoidal method with six equal intervals to estimate the total gallons of water pumped during the hour.

(A) 2,425

(B) 2,524

(C) 2,542

(D) 2,615

(E) 2,638

87. Given the ellipse represented in parametric form by the equations $x = 8\cos\theta$ and $y = \sqrt{2}\sin\theta$, which of the following is the equation of the line tangent to the ellipse at $\theta = 45°$?

(A) $x + y = 7$

(B) $8x - y = \sqrt{2}$

(C) $4x - \sqrt{2}y = 5$

(D) $\sqrt{2}x + 8y = 16$

(E) $2x + 8\sqrt{2}y = 16$

88. If $e^x = \sum_{n=0}^{\infty} \dfrac{x^n}{n!}$, then $\sum_{n=1}^{\infty} \dfrac{(-1)^n x^{2n}}{n!} =$

(A) e^{-x^2}

(B) $\cos x$

(C) $1 - e^{-x^2}$

(D) $e^{-x^2} - 1$

(E) $e^{2x} + 1$

89. If y is a function of x, and $y' = y^2$ and $y(1) = 1$, then $y =$

(A) $\dfrac{1}{x}$

(B) $\dfrac{1}{2-x}$

(C) $\dfrac{1}{1-x}$

(D) $\dfrac{1}{x^2}$

(E) $\dfrac{2}{1+x}$

90. As a particle moves along the line $y = 2x + 7$, what is its minimum distance from the origin?

(A) $\dfrac{7}{5}$

(B) $\dfrac{7}{5}\sqrt{5}$

(C) $\dfrac{14}{5}$

(D) $\dfrac{\sqrt{5}}{7}$

(E) $\dfrac{7}{3}\sqrt{5}$

91. A money market account with an initial deposit of $2,000 is compounded continuously for 12 years at an annual rate of 8% per year. To the nearest ten dollars, what is the average amount of money in the account over the 12-year period?

(A) $2,440
(B) $2,490
(C) $3,250
(D) $3,310
(E) $3,360

92. If $f(x) = x^5 + 3x - 1$ contains the point $(1, 3)$, and $g(x) = f^{-1}(x)$, then $g'(3) =$

(A) $\dfrac{1}{8}$

(B) $\dfrac{1}{7}$

(C) $\dfrac{1}{6}$

(D) $\dfrac{1}{5}$

(E) $\dfrac{1}{4}$

STOP

This is the end of Section I, Part B.
If time still remains, you may check your work only in this section.
Do not begin Section II, Part A until instructed to do so.

Section II

PART A

Time: 45 minutes
   3 free-response problems

DIRECTIONS: Show all your work in your exam booklet. Grading is based on the methods used to solve the problems as well as the accuracy of your final answers.

Calculators MAY be used for this section of the exam.

1.

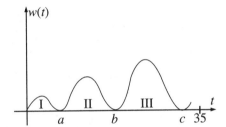

The graph of $w(t) = 20t^{\frac{4}{5}} \cos^2\left(\dfrac{t}{4}\right)$ shown above represents the number of widgets per day manufactured over the time interval $0 \le t \le 35$ days. The arches of the graph are numbered I, II, and III.

(a) What are the values of t, $0 < t \le 35$, where $w(t) = 0$, represented by a, b, and c in the diagram?

(b) How many widgets are produced from time b to time c?

(c) What is the maximum rate at which widgets are produced during the time period $a < t < b$, and what is the corresponding value of t?

(d) What is the average value of $w(t)$ over the time interval from a to c?

(e) If the vertical line $x = d$ splits the areas under all three arches into two equal regions, one from $0 \le t \le d$ and another from $d < t \le c$, between which two integer values of t is the value of d?

2. All answers that require a series answer can be written in summation notation or with sufficient terms and a general term to clearly identify the pattern unless specified otherwise.

    (a) Write the Maclaurin series for xe^{-x}.

    (b) Estimate the value of $\int_0^1 xe^{-x}dx$ by using a Maclaurin series of degree 5.

    (c) Find the exact value of $\int_0^1 xe^{-x}dx$ using integration by parts.

    (d) Verify that the error between the answers from parts (b) and (c) is consistent with the error bound for a decreasing alternating series.

3. Given the ellipse $\dfrac{x^2}{a^2}+\dfrac{y^2}{b^2}=1$, where a and b are positive constants,

    (a) Find the first quadrant area.

    (b) Find the volume when the region representing the first quadrant area is revolved about the x-axis.

    (c) Find the volume when the region representing the first quadrant area is revolved about the y-axis.

STOP
This is the end of Section II, Part A.
If time still remains, you may check your work only in this section.
Do not begin Section II, Part B until instructed to do so.

Section II

PART B

Time: 45 minutes
3 free-response problems

> **DIRECTIONS:** Show all your work in your exam booklet. Grading is based on the methods used to solve the problems as well as the accuracy of your final answers.
>
> Calculators MAY NOT be used for this section of the exam.
>
> (During the timed portion for Part B, you may continue to work on the problems in Part A without the use of a calculator.)

4. Consider the curve given by $4x^3y + 3y^4 = 4$.

   (a) Show that $\dfrac{dy}{dx} = \dfrac{-y}{3(x+y)}$

   (b) Show that $\dfrac{d^2y}{dx^2} = \dfrac{4}{9y^2(x+y)^3}$

5. A population P is modeled by the logistics differential equation:
   $$\frac{1}{P}\frac{dP}{dt} = \frac{1}{5}(1000 - P),\ P \geqslant 0$$

   (a) If $P(0) = 7$, find $\lim\limits_{t \to \infty} P(t)$.

   (b) If $P(0) = 12$, find the horizontal asymptote of $P(t)$ as $t \to \infty$.

   (c) What is the inflection point of $P(t)$ if $P(0) = 100$?

   (d) If $P(0) = 100$, find $P(t)$.

6. The graph of the function f shown in the figure consists of one line, two quarter circles and a semicircle.

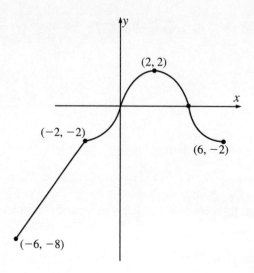

(a)   Let $g(x) = \int_{-6}^{x} f(t)\,dt$.

Find the value of: $g(-6)$, $g(-2)$, $g'(-2)$, and $g''(-2)$.

If the value does not exist, so state.

(b)   For the function g defined in part (a), find the x-coordinate of each relative minimum/maximum point on the interval $(-6, 6)$. Justify your answer.

(c)   For the function g defined in part (a), find the x-coordinate of each inflection point on the interval $(-6, 6)$.

(d)   If $h(x) = \int_{x}^{6} f(t)\,dt$, find all the values of x on the interval $[-6, 6]$ for which $h(x) = 0$.

(e)   For $h(x)$ defined in part (d), find $h'(2)$.

END OF EXAM

PRACTICE EXAM 3

AP Calculus BC

Answer Key

Part A

1. (A)	15. (B)
2. (A)	16. (C)
3. (E)	17. (B)
4. (B)	18. (E)
5. (B)	19.. (D)
6. (C)	20. (E)
7. (D)	21. (D)
8. (A)	22. (D)
9. (C)	23. (A)
10. (A)	24. (A)
11. (D)	25. (B)
12. (A)	26. (D)
13. (D)	27. (C)
14. (C)	28. (E)

Part B

76. (A)	
77. (C)	
78. (B)	
79. (A)	
80. (B)	
81. (C)	
82. (C)	
83. (D)	
84. (B)	
85. (C)	
86. (A)	
87. (D)	
88. (D)	
89. (B)	
90. (B)	
91. (E)	
92. (A)	

Free-Response Answers

1.

(a) $2\pi, 6\pi, 10\pi$

(b) 1,656

(c) $153.87, t = 13.05$

(d) 131.80

(e) $23 < d < 24$

2.

(a) See detailed explanation.

(b) $\dfrac{31}{120} = .25833$

(c) $1 - \dfrac{2}{e} = .26424$

(d) See detailed explanation.

3.

(a) $\dfrac{\pi ab}{4}$

(b) $\dfrac{2\pi ab^2}{3}$

(c) $\dfrac{2\pi a^2 b}{3}$

4.

(a) See detailed explanation.

(b) See detailed explanation.

5.

(a) 1,000

(b) 1,000

(c) $\left(\dfrac{\ln 9}{200}, 500 \right)$

(d) $P(t) = \dfrac{1000}{1 + 9e^{-200t}}$

6.

(a) $0, -20, -2,$ DNE

(b) relative minimum: $x = 0$
relative maximum: $x = 4$

(c) $x = 2$

(d) $-2, 2, 6$

(e) -2

PRACTICE EXAM 3

AP Calculus BC

Detailed Explanations of Answers

Section 1

PART A

1. **(A)**

   Step 1: Find the critical values by setting $f'(x) = 0$.

   $$f(x) = 4x^3 - 3x^2 - 18x + 6$$

   $$f'(x) = 12x^2 - 6x - 18 = 0$$

   $$x = -1 \text{ or } x = \frac{3}{2}$$

   Step 2: Do a first derivative number line analysis.

   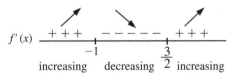

   $$f'(x) \quad \underset{\text{increasing}}{+ + +} \quad \underset{-1}{\big|} \quad \underset{\text{decreasing}}{- - - - -} \quad \underset{\frac{3}{2}}{\big|} \quad \underset{\text{increasing}}{+ + +}$$

   The graph is decreasing in the interval $\left(-1, \frac{3}{2}\right)$.

   $$\therefore \quad \boxed{-1 < x < \frac{3}{2}}$$

2. **(A)**

   Step 1: First find the slope of the given line.

   $$x = 5t + 4 \qquad y = t - 7$$

   $$\frac{dx}{dt} = 5 \qquad \frac{dy}{dt} = 1$$

$$\text{slope} = \frac{dy}{dx} = \frac{\frac{dy}{dt}}{\frac{dx}{dt}} = \frac{1}{5}$$

Step 2: The equation of the line parallel through (6, 4) has $x = 6$, $y = 4$, $m = \frac{1}{5}$.

$$y - 4 = \frac{1}{5}(x - 6) \Rightarrow \boxed{5y - x = 14}$$

3. **(E)**

Step 1: Use implicit differentiation.

$$y = \sqrt{3x + y} = (3x + y)^{\frac{1}{2}}$$

$$\frac{dy}{dx} = \frac{1}{2}(3x + y)^{-\frac{1}{2}} \frac{d}{dx}(3x + y)$$

$$\frac{dy}{dx} = \frac{1}{2}(3x + y)^{-\frac{1}{2}}(3 + \frac{dy}{dx})$$

Step 2: Substitute $x = 1$ and $y = 6$ to find $\frac{dy}{dx}$.

$$\frac{dy}{dx} = \frac{1}{2}(9)^{-\frac{1}{2}}\left(3 + \frac{dy}{dx}\right) = \frac{1}{6}\left(3 + \frac{dy}{dx}\right)$$

$$\frac{dy}{dx} = \boxed{\frac{3}{5}}$$

4. **(B)**

Step 1: Rewrite $\frac{1}{x^2 + x}$ by using partial fractions.

$$\frac{1}{x^2 + x} = \frac{1}{x(x+1)} = \frac{A}{x} + \frac{B}{x+1} \Rightarrow A = 1 \text{ and } B = -1$$

Step 2: $\int \frac{dx}{x^2 + x} = \int \left(\frac{1}{x} - \frac{1}{x+1}\right) dx = \ln|x| - \ln|x+1| + C$

$$= \boxed{\ln\left|\frac{x}{x+1}\right| + C}$$

5. **(B)**

Differentiate by using the chain rule.

$$h(x) = g(f(x)) = g(e^{\sin 2x})$$

$$h'(x) = g'(e^{\sin 2x}) \frac{d}{dx}(e^{\sin 2x})$$

$$= g'(e^{\sin 2x}) \cdot (e^{\sin 2x})(\cos 2x)(2)$$

$$h'(0) = [g'(e^0)] \, (e^0) \, (\cos 0) \, (2)$$

$$= [g'(1)](2)$$

$$= 3(2) = \boxed{6}$$

6. (C)

Step 1: Integrate by using u-substitution.

Let $u = \ln x \Rightarrow \quad du = \dfrac{1}{x} dx$

$$\int_e^{e^2} \frac{1}{x \ln x} dx = \int_e^{e^2} \frac{1}{\ln x} \cdot \frac{1}{x} dx = \int_{x=e}^{e^2} \frac{1}{u} du = \ln|u| \Big\|_{x=e}^{e^2}$$

$$= \ln|\ln x| \Big\|_e^{e^2} = \ln(\ln e^2) - \ln(\ln e)$$

$$= \ln 2 - \ln 1 = \boxed{\ln 2}$$

7. (D)

Step 1: Separate the variables. Integrate by using u-substitution.

Let $u = \cot x \quad \therefore du = -\csc^2 x \, dx$

$$\int dy = \int \csc^2 x \cdot \cot^2 x \, dx = -\int (\cot x)^2 \cdot (-\csc^2 x \, dx)$$

$$y = -\int u^2 du = -\frac{u^3}{3} + C$$

$$\therefore y = -\frac{(\cot^3 x)}{3} + C$$

Step 2: Find C. If $y = 3$ when $x = \dfrac{\pi}{4}$.

$$3 = -\frac{\left(\cot^3 \left(\frac{\pi}{4}\right)\right)}{3} + C$$

$$3 = -\frac{1}{3} + C \Rightarrow C = \boxed{\frac{10}{3}}$$

$$\therefore y = \boxed{\frac{10 - \cot^3 x}{3}}$$

8. **(A)**

Step 1: The position vector is:

$$\vec{s}(t) = \left\langle t^3 + t, t^5 - 2t^2 \right\rangle.$$

The velocity vector is:

$$\vec{v}(t) = \left\langle 3t^2 + 1, 5t^4 - 4t \right\rangle.$$

The acceleration vector is:

$$\vec{a}(t) = \left\langle 6t, 20t^3 - 4 \right\rangle.$$

Step 2: $\vec{a}(2) = \boxed{\left\langle 12, 156 \right\rangle}$

9. **(C)**

Step 1: To be differentiable at $x = 1$, the function must be continuous at $x = 1$.

$$a^2x^2 + bx - 6 = ax + b \qquad \text{at} \quad x = 1$$

$$\therefore a^2 + b - 6 = a + b$$

$$\therefore a^2 - a - 6 = 0$$

$$a = 3 \quad \text{or} \quad a = -2$$

Only $a = 3$ is greater than 0.

Step 2: To be differentiable, the derivative coming from the left should equal the derivative coming from the right.

$$2a^2x + b = a \qquad \text{at} \quad x = 1$$

$$\therefore 2a^2 + b = a$$

Step 3: Solve for b, with $a = 3$.

$$2(3)^2 + b = 3$$

$$b = -15$$

$$\therefore a - b = 3 - (-15) = \boxed{18}$$

10. **(A)**

The Taylor approximation for e^x is

$$e^x = \sum_{n=0}^{\infty} \frac{x^n}{n!} = 1 + x + \frac{x^2}{2!} + \frac{x^3}{3!}$$

$$\therefore e^{\frac{1}{2}} = 1 + \left(\frac{1}{2}\right) + \frac{\left(\frac{1}{2}\right)^2}{2!} + \frac{\left(\frac{1}{2}\right)^3}{3!}$$

$$= \boxed{1 + \frac{1}{2} + \frac{1}{8} + \frac{1}{48}}$$

11. **(D)**

Use integration by parts.

$$u = x \qquad dv = e^{-2x} dx$$

$$du = dx \qquad v = -\frac{1}{2} e^{-2x}$$

$$\int u \, dv = uv - \int v \, du$$

$$\int x e^{-2x} dx = x\left(-\frac{1}{2} e^{-2x}\right) - \int -\frac{1}{2} e^{-2x} dx$$

$$= -\frac{x}{2} e^{-2x} + \frac{1}{2}\left[-\frac{1}{2} e^{-2x}\right] + C$$

$$= \boxed{-\frac{e^{-2x}}{2}\left(x + \frac{1}{2}\right) + C}$$

12. **(A)**

Step 1: I. $\displaystyle\sum_{n=1}^{\infty} \frac{4n}{3n+1}$.

Use the nth-term test.

$$\lim_{n \to \infty} \frac{4n}{3n+1} = \frac{4}{3} \neq 0$$

$\therefore$ diverges

Step 2: II. $\displaystyle\sum_{n=1}^{\infty} \frac{\ln n}{n}$.

Use the comparison test.

$$\frac{\ln n}{n} > \frac{1}{n} \text{ for } n \geq 3$$

Since $\sum_{n=1}^{\infty} \frac{1}{n}$ is a divergent p-series, $\sum \frac{\ln n}{n}$ diverges

Step 3: III. $\sum_{n=1}^{\infty} \frac{n^n}{n!}$.

Use the ratio test.

$$\lim_{n \to \infty} \left| \frac{\frac{(n+1)^{n+1}}{(n+1)!}}{\frac{n^n}{n!}} \right| = \lim_{n \to \infty} \left| \frac{\frac{(n+1)(n+1)^n}{(n+1)(n!)}}{\frac{n^n}{n!}} \right| = \lim_{n \to \infty} \left| \frac{(n+1)^n}{n^n} \right|$$

$$= \lim_{n \to \infty} \left(\frac{n+1}{n} \right)^n = \lim_{n \to \infty} \left(1 + \frac{1}{n} \right)^n = e > 1$$

$\therefore$ diverges

$\therefore$ $\boxed{\text{None}}$ of the series converges.

13. **(D)**

Step 1: Sketch a graph.

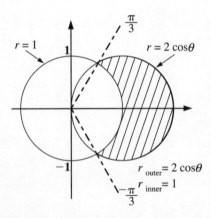

Step 2: Find the points of intersection.

$$r = 1 = 2\cos\theta \Rightarrow \cos\theta = \frac{1}{2}$$

$$\therefore \ \theta = -\frac{\pi}{3}, \frac{\pi}{3}$$

Step 3: $A = \dfrac{1}{2}\displaystyle\int_a^b (r^2_{\text{outer}} - r^2_{\text{inner}})\, d\theta$

$$= \dfrac{1}{2}\int_{-\frac{\pi}{3}}^{\frac{\pi}{3}} \left[(2\cos\theta)^2 - (1)^2 \right] d\theta$$

$$= \boxed{\dfrac{1}{2}\int_{-\frac{\pi}{3}}^{\frac{\pi}{3}} \left[4\cos^2\theta - 1 \right] d\theta}$$

14. **(C)**

Step 1: $\dfrac{dy}{dx} = \dfrac{\left(\dfrac{dy}{dt}\right)}{\left(\dfrac{dx}{dt}\right)} = \dfrac{\dfrac{1}{2\sqrt{t}}}{\dfrac{-9}{t^2}} = -\dfrac{t^{\frac{3}{2}}}{18}$

Step 2: At the point $(1, 3)$, $t = 9$ and $\dfrac{dy}{dx} = -\dfrac{3}{2}$.

Step 3: The tangent line equation is:

$$y - 3 = -\dfrac{3}{2}(x - 1) \;\Rightarrow\; \boxed{3x + 2y = 9}$$

15. **(B)**

$$S = \int_a^b \sqrt{r^2 + \left(\dfrac{dr}{d\theta}\right)^2}\; d\theta, \text{ with } r = e^{2\theta}$$

$$S = \int_0^{2\pi} \sqrt{\left(e^{2\theta}\right)^2 + \left(2e^{2\theta}\right)^2}\; d\theta$$

$$S = \int_0^{2\pi} \sqrt{e^{4\theta} + 4e^{4\theta}}\; d\theta$$

$$\boxed{\int_0^{2\pi} \sqrt{5}\,e^{2\theta}\; d\theta}$$

16. **(C)**

Step 1: When $x = y$, $\dfrac{dy}{dx} = 0$. This eliminates answer choices A, D, and E.

Step 2: In the second quadrant, y is larger than x, and all the slopes are negative. This eliminates answer choice B.

Only answer choice C, $\boxed{\dfrac{dy}{dx} = x - y}$ is possible.

17. **(B)**

$$\int_0^\infty 2e^{-3x}dx = \lim_{b\to\infty}\int_0^b 2e^{-3x}dx = \lim_{b\to\infty}\left(-\frac{2}{3}e^{-3x}\right)\Big|_0^b$$

$$= \lim_{b\to\infty}\left[-\frac{2}{3}e^{-3b} - \left(-\frac{2}{3}e^{-3(0)}\right)\right]$$

$$= \lim_{b\to\infty}\left[-\frac{2}{3e^{3b}} + \frac{2}{3}\right] = 0 + \frac{2}{3} = \boxed{\frac{2}{3}}$$

18. **(E)**

$$\vec{s}(t) = \left\langle \frac{1}{2}t^2 + 2t, 2t^2 \right\rangle$$

$$\vec{v}(t) = \left\langle t + 2, 4t \right\rangle$$

$$\text{Speed} = |\vec{v}(t)| = \sqrt{(t+2)^2 + (4t)^2}$$

$$= \sqrt{t^2 + 4t + 4 + 16t^2}$$

$$= \boxed{\sqrt{17t^2 + 4t + 4}}$$

19. **(D)**

Step 1: Arc length $= S = \int_a^b \sqrt{\left(\frac{dx}{dt}\right)^2 + \left(\frac{dy}{dt}\right)^2}\, dt$

$$x = 4\cos^3 t \qquad\qquad y = 4\sin^3 t$$

$$\frac{dx}{dt} = (12\cos^2 t)(-\sin t) \qquad \frac{dy}{dt} = (12\sin^2 t)(\cos t)$$

$$= -12\cos^2 t \sin t \qquad\qquad = 12\sin^2 t \cos t$$

Step 2: $\left(\frac{dx}{dt}\right)^2 + \left(\frac{dy}{dt}\right)^2 = \left(144\cos^4 t \sin^2 t\right) + \left(144\sin^4 t \cos^2 t\right)$

$$= 144\sin^2 t \cos^2 t\, [\cos^2 t + \sin^2 t]$$

$$= 144\sin^2 t \cos^2 t$$

Step 3: $S = \int_0^{\frac{\pi}{2}} \sqrt{144\sin^2 t \cos^2 t}\, dt = \int_0^{\frac{\pi}{2}} 12\sin t \cos t\, dt$

Step 4: Use u-substitution.

$$u = \sin t \Rightarrow du = \cos t \, dt$$

$$S = 12 \int_0^{\frac{\pi}{2}} u \, du = 12 \frac{u^2}{2} \Bigg|_{t=0}^{\frac{\pi}{2}} = 6 \sin^2 t \Bigg|_0^{\frac{\pi}{2}}$$

$$= 6 \left[\sin^2 \left(\frac{\pi}{2} \right) - \sin^2 (0) \right] = 6(1-0) = \boxed{6}$$

20. **(E)**

Recognize that the series for $\sin x$ is:

$$\sin x = x - \frac{x^3}{3!} + \frac{x^5}{5!} - \frac{x^7}{7!} + \frac{x^9}{9!} - \cdots$$

$$\text{Then} - x \sin x = -x^2 + \frac{x^4}{3!} - \frac{x^6}{5!} + \frac{x^8}{7!} - \frac{x^{10}}{9!} + \cdots$$

$$\therefore \boxed{-x \sin x + x^2} = \frac{x^4}{3!} - \frac{x^6}{5!} + \frac{x^8}{7!} - \frac{x^{10}}{9!} + \cdots$$

21. **(D)**

Step 1: For differential equations of the form:

$$\frac{dP}{dt} = kP \left(1 - \frac{P}{N} \right),$$

the solution $P(t) = \dfrac{N}{1 + \left(\frac{N}{P_0} - 1 \right) e^{-kt}}$,

where $P(0) = P_0$ and $\lim\limits_{t \to \infty} P(t) = N$.

Step 2: If $\dfrac{dP}{dt} = .3P \left(1 - \dfrac{P}{150} \right)$, then $\lim\limits_{t \to \infty} P(t) = N = \boxed{150}$

22. **(D)**

Step 1: $\lim\limits_{x \to \infty} \dfrac{1 - \cos x}{3x^4 + x^2} \Rightarrow \dfrac{0}{0}$, indeterminate

Step 2: Use L'Hospital's rule.

$$\lim\limits_{x \to 0} \frac{1 - \cos x}{3x^4 + x^2} = \lim\limits_{x \to 0} \frac{\sin x}{12x^3 + 2x} \Rightarrow \frac{0}{0}, \text{ indeterminate}$$

Step 3: Use L'Hospital's rule again.

$$\lim_{x \to 0} \frac{\sin x}{12x^3 + 2x} = \lim_{x \to 0} \frac{\cos x}{36x^2 + 2} = \boxed{\frac{1}{2}}$$

23. **(A)**

Step 1: The series for $\dfrac{1}{1-x}$ is:

$$\frac{1}{1-x} = \sum_{n=0}^{\infty} x^n = 1 + x + x^2 + x^3 + x^4 + \ldots -1 < x < 1$$

Step 2: Replace x with $-2x$.

$$\frac{1}{1+2x} = \sum_{n=0}^{\infty} \left(-2x\right)^n = 1 - 2x + 4x^2 - 8x^3 + 16x^4 - \ldots -1 < x < 1$$

The coefficient of the x^3 term is $\boxed{-8}$.

24. **(A)**

Step 1: Sketch $f(x) = |\sin x|$.

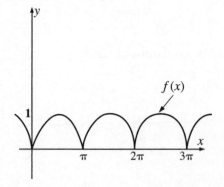

Step 2: The derivative of each arch is $\cos x$. Also note that the derivative is not defined at a cusp. The graph shown in answer choice A is correct.

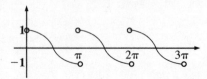

25. **(B)**

Step 1: Slope $= \dfrac{dy}{dx} = 4x^3 y$

Step 2: Separate the variables and integrate.

$$\frac{dy}{y} = 4x^3 \; dx$$

$$\int \frac{dy}{y} = \int 4x^3 dx \Rightarrow \ln|y| = x^4 + C$$

$$|y| = e^{x^4 + c}$$

$$|y| = Ae^{x^4}, \text{ where } A = e^c$$

Step 3: If $y = 5$, when $x = 0$ then $5 = Ae^0$, so $A = 5$.

$$\therefore y = 5 \, e^{x^4}$$

26. **(D)**

Step 1: $x(t) = 2t^3 - 4t^2 + 2t - 1$

$v(t) = 6t^2 - 8t + 2$

Step 2: To minimize $v(t)$, set its derivative to zero and solve for t.

$$v'(t) = 12t - 8 = 0 \Rightarrow t = \frac{2}{3}$$

Step 3: Use the second derivative test to confirm that $t = \frac{2}{3}$ achieves a minimum.

$$v''(t) = 12$$

$$v''\left(\frac{2}{3}\right) = 12 > 0$$

$$\therefore t = \frac{2}{3} \text{ provides a minimum.}$$

Step 4: At $t = \frac{2}{3}$, $v(t) = 6\left(\frac{2}{3}\right)^2 - 8\left(\frac{2}{3}\right) + 2 = \boxed{-\frac{2}{3}}$

27. **(C)**

Step 1: Perform the ratio test.

$$\lim_{n \to \infty} \left| \frac{\left(\frac{x}{4}\right)^{n+1}}{\left(\frac{x}{4}\right)^n} \right| = \lim_{n \to \infty} \left| \frac{x}{4} \right|$$

To converge, $\left|\dfrac{x}{4}\right| < 1$. Therefore, the range is $(-4, 4)$.

Step 2: Test the end points

At $x = -4$, $\sum (-1)^n$ diverges.

At $x = 4$, $\sum (1)^n$ diverges.

$\therefore$ The interval of convergence is $\boxed{(-4, 4)}$

28. **(E)**

Step 1: The Riemann sum gives

$$\int_1^{10} a(t)\, dt \approx \frac{10-1}{3}\left[f(x_1) + f(x_2) + f(x_3)\right] = 3\left[f(4) + f(7) + f(10)\right]$$

$$= 3\,[1 + 4 + 7] = 36$$

Step 2: $v(10) = v(1) + \displaystyle\int_1^{10} a(t)\, dt$

$$= 9 + 36 = \boxed{45}$$

Section I

PART B

76. **(A)**

Step 1: Recognize that $\ln(y) = \ln(x^{2^x}) = 2^x \ln x$.

Step 2: Differentiate, using the product rule.

$$\ln y = 2^x \ln x$$

$$\frac{1}{y}\frac{dy}{dx} = 2^x \frac{d}{dx}(\ln x) + \ln x \frac{d}{dx}(2^x)$$

$$\frac{1}{y}\frac{dy}{dx} = 2^x \left(\frac{1}{x}\right) + \ln x (2^x) \ln 2$$

Step 3: Solve for $\frac{dy}{dx}$.

$$\frac{dy}{dx} = y\left[2^x\left(\frac{1}{x} + \ln x \ln 2\right)\right]$$

$$= x^{2^x}\left(2^x\right)\left(\frac{1 + x \ln x \ln 2}{x}\right)$$

Step 4: $\left.\frac{dy}{dx}\right|_{x=2} = 2^{2^2}(2^2)\left(\frac{1 + 2(\ln 2)(\ln 2)}{2}\right) = \boxed{62.749}$

77. **(C)**

Step 1: Let $y = \sqrt{1 + x^2}$ and $w = \dfrac{x}{1 + x^2}$

Step 2: $\dfrac{dy}{dw} = \dfrac{\left(\frac{dy}{dx}\right)}{\left(\frac{dw}{dx}\right)} = \dfrac{\frac{1}{2}\left(1 + x^2\right)^{-\frac{1}{2}}(2x)}{\dfrac{\left(1 + x^2\right)(1) - x(2x)}{\left(1 + x^2\right)^2}} = \dfrac{\dfrac{x}{\sqrt{1 + x^2}}}{\dfrac{-x^2 + 1}{\left(1 + x^2\right)^2}}$

$$= \frac{x(1+x^2)^2}{(\sqrt{1+x^2})(1-x^2)} = \boxed{\frac{x(\sqrt{1+x^2})^3}{(1-x^2)}}$$

78. **(B)**

Use the series expansion for $\ln(x+1)$.

Step 1: $\ln(x+1) = x - \dfrac{x^2}{2} + \dfrac{x^3}{3} - \dfrac{x^4}{4} + \ldots \dfrac{(-1)^{n+1} x^n}{n}$

Then $\ln(3x+1) = (3x) - \dfrac{(3x)^2}{2} + \dfrac{(3x)^3}{3} - \dfrac{(3x)^4}{4} + \ldots + \dfrac{(-1)^{n+1}(3x)^n}{n}$

$\therefore$ The problem reduces to a solution of:

Step 2: $\ln(3x+1) = -3x + 8$

$x = \boxed{2.016}$

79. **(A)**

Step 1: $f(x) = x^3 + 4x - 1$

$f'(x) = 3x^2 + 4$

$\therefore$ at $x = 1$,

$y = f(1) = 1^3 + 4(1) - 1 = 4$

$m = f'(1) = 3(1)^2 + 4 = 7$

Step 2: The tangent line at $x = 1$ has the equation

$y - 4 = 7(x-1) \Rightarrow y = 7x - 3$

Step 3: $|(x^3 + 4x - 1) - (7x - 3)| \le 0.4, \qquad$ for $x \ge 0$

$.6084 \le x \le 1.346$

The interval is $\boxed{[.608, 1.346]}$

80. **(B)**

Step 1: Make a drawing.

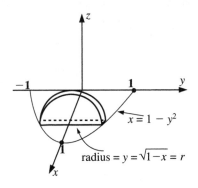

Step 2: $v = \int_a^b \left(\frac{1}{2} \pi r^2 \right) dx$

$$= \frac{\pi}{2} \int_0^1 \left(\sqrt{1-x} \right)^2 dx = \boxed{\frac{\pi}{4}}$$

81. **(C)**

Step 1: Draw a diagram.

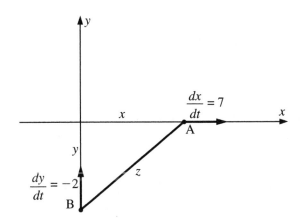

Step 2: By the Pythagorean theorem, $x^2 + y^2 = z^2$

Step 3: Change the equation into a rate equation (differentiate with respect to t):

$$\cancel{2}x\frac{dx}{dt} + \cancel{2}y\frac{dy}{dt} = \cancel{2}z\frac{dz}{dt}$$

Step 4: When $x = 8$ and $y = 6$, then $z = 10$. Note that $\frac{dy}{dt} = -2$.

$$\therefore\ 8(7)+6(-2)=10\frac{dz}{dt}$$

$$\frac{dz}{dt}=\boxed{\frac{22}{5}}$$

82. **(C)**

Step 1: Draw a diagram.

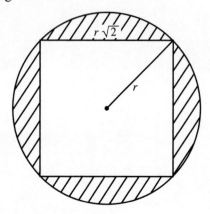

Step 2: Area of the circle $=\pi r^2 = A$

Area of the square $= 2r^2$

Shaded area $= \pi r^2 - 2r^2 = S$

Step 3: Create rate equations.

$$\frac{dA}{dt}=2\pi r\frac{dr}{dt}\Rightarrow 1=2\pi r\frac{dr}{dt}\Rightarrow r\frac{dr}{dt}=\frac{1}{2\pi}$$

$$\frac{dS}{dt}=2\pi r\frac{dr}{dt}-4r\frac{dr}{dt}=2(\pi-2)r\frac{dr}{dt}\Rightarrow 2(\pi-2)\left(\frac{1}{2\pi}\right)$$

$$=\frac{\pi-2}{\pi}=\boxed{.363}$$

83. **(D)**

Step 1: Let revenue $= R$, ticket price $= p$, and number of tickets sold $= n$.

Then $R = np$.

Step 2: Let $x =$ the price increase above \$4.

Then $10x =$ ticket purchases lost for each x increase in cost.

$\therefore R = (500 - 10x)(4 + x)$

Step 3: To maximize R, set $R'(x) = 0$.

$$R(x) = 2000 + 460x - 10x^2$$

$$R'(x) = 460 - 20x = 0$$

$$\therefore x = 23$$

Step 4: Use the second derivative test to confirm, that 23 is a relative maximum.

$$R''(x) = -20$$

$$R''(23) = -20 < 0$$

$\therefore x = 23$ gives a relative maximum.

So the maximum revenue will occur by selling $500 - 230 = 270$ tickets at a price of $\$4 + \$23 = \boxed{\$27}$

84. **(B)**

Step 1: $\dfrac{1}{P}\dfrac{dp}{dt} = .001(200 - P)$ can also be written as:

$$\frac{dP}{dt} = .001P(200 - P) \quad \text{or} \quad \frac{dp}{dt} = .2p\left(1 - \frac{P}{200}\right)$$

Step 2: Integrate to find P.

$$P = \frac{200}{1 + \left(\frac{200}{25} - 1\right)e^{-.2t}}$$

$$P = \frac{200}{1 + 7e^{-.2t}}$$

(See section on Special Differential Equations.)

Step 3: When $P = 100$, $100 = \dfrac{200}{1 + 7e^{-.2t}}$

$$\therefore t = 9.729 \Rightarrow \boxed{10} \text{ years}$$

85. **(C)**

Step 1: Look to see which graph has a value of zero when another graph is at its relative minimum/maximum point. Those graphs will be related as a function and its derivative.

$\therefore$ Graph III is the derivative of graph I and

Graph I is the derivative of graph II

$$\therefore \begin{array}{|l|} f(x) \text{ is II} \\ f'(x) \text{ is I} \\ f''(x) \text{ is III} \end{array}$$

Note: Many other characteristics can also be used to distinguish the graphs.

86. **(A)**

Step 1: Total gallons $= \displaystyle\int_0^{60} r(t)\, dt$

Step 2: Use the trapezoidal rule.

$$\int_a^b f(x)\, dx = \frac{b-a}{2n}\Big[f(x_0)+2f(x_1)+\ldots+2f(x_{n-1})+f(x_n)\Big]$$

$$\int_0^{60} r(t)\, dt \approx \frac{60}{2(6)}\Big[35+2(40)+2(38)+2(42)+2(50)+2(35)+40\Big]$$

$$= \boxed{2{,}425}\ \text{gallons}$$

87. **(D)**

Step 1: $m = \dfrac{dy}{dx} = \dfrac{\left(\frac{dy}{d\theta}\right)}{\left(\frac{dx}{d\theta}\right)} = \dfrac{\sqrt{2}\cos\theta}{-8\sin\theta} = \dfrac{-\sqrt{2}}{8}\cot\theta$

Step 2: At $\theta = 45°$

$$x = 8\cos 45° = 4\sqrt{2}$$

$$y = \sqrt{2}\sin 45° = 1$$

$$m = \frac{-\sqrt{2}}{8}\cot 45° = \frac{-\sqrt{2}}{8}$$

Step 3: The tangent line equation is:

$$y-1 = \frac{-\sqrt{2}}{8}\left(x-4\sqrt{2}\right)$$

$$\text{or}\ \boxed{\sqrt{2}x+8y=16}$$

88. **(D)**

Step 1: $e^x = \displaystyle\sum_{n=0}^{\infty} \frac{x^n}{n!}$

Step 2: Replace x with $-x^2$:

$$e^{-x^2} = \sum_{n=0}^{\infty} \frac{\left(-x^2\right)^n}{n!} = \sum_{n=0}^{\infty} \frac{(-1)^n x^{2n}}{n!}$$

Step 3: $\displaystyle\sum_{n=0}^{\infty} \frac{(-1)^n x^{2n}}{n!} = 1 + \sum_{n=1}^{\infty} \frac{(-1)^n (x)^{2n}}{n!}$

$$\therefore \sum_{n=1}^{\infty} \frac{(-1) x^{2n}}{n!} = \boxed{e^{-x^2} - 1}$$

89. **(B)**

Step 1: $y' = y^2 \Rightarrow \dfrac{dy}{dx} = y^2$

Step 2: Separate the variables and integrate.

$$\int \frac{dy}{y^2} = \int dx$$

$$-\frac{1}{y} = x + C$$

Step 3: If $y(1) = 1$, then $C = -2$

$$\therefore -\frac{1}{y} = x - 2 \Rightarrow \boxed{y = \frac{1}{2-x}}$$

90. **(B)**

Step 1: Make a sketch.

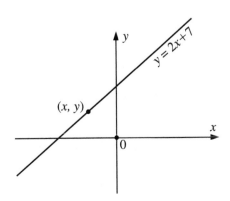

Step 2: $l = \sqrt{(x-0)^2 + (y-0)^2}$ with $y = 2x + 7$

$$l = \sqrt{x^2 + (2x+7)^2}$$

Step 3: (Hint: Use l^2 to minimize, rather than l. It's easier and gives the same answer.)

$$l^2 = x^2 + (2x + 7)^2 = 5x^2 + 28x + 49$$

Step 4: Set the derivative of l^2 with respect to x equal to zero and solve for x.

$$2l\frac{dl}{dx} = 10x + 28 = 0$$

$$x = \frac{-14}{5}$$

$$\therefore \text{Distance} = \sqrt{\left(\frac{-14}{5}\right)^2 + \left(\frac{-28}{5} + 7\right)^2} = \boxed{\frac{7\sqrt{5}}{5}}$$

91. **(E)**

Step 1: Use $P = P_0 e^{rt}$, where P_0 is the initial deposit and r is the interest rate.

$$\therefore P = 2000\, e^{.08t}$$

Step 2: Average value $= \dfrac{1}{12}\displaystyle\int_0^{12} 2000\, e^{.08t}\ dt$

$$= 3{,}357.7 \Rightarrow \boxed{3{,}360}$$

92. **(A)**

Step 1: Sketch the graph.

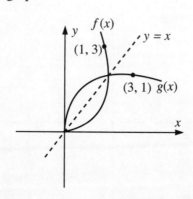

514

Step 2: Find the slope of $f(x)$ at $x = 1$.

$$f(x) = x^5 + 3x - 1$$
$$f'(x) = 5x^5 + 3$$
$$f'(1) = 8$$

Step 3: The slope of $g(x)$ at $(3, 1)$ is the reciprocal of the slope of $f(x)$ at $(1, 3)$.

$$\therefore g'(3) = \boxed{\frac{1}{8}}$$

Section II

PART A

Step 1: For this question, all parts are totally calculator dependent.

$$\text{Solve } 20t^{\frac{4}{5}}\cos^2\left(\frac{t}{4}\right) = 0 \quad 0 < t \le 35$$

(a)

At a, $t = 2\pi$	$= 6.283$ days
At b, $t = 6\pi$	$= 18.850$ days
At c, $t = 10\pi$	$= 31.416$ days

Step 2:

(b) $\displaystyle\int_{6\pi}^{10\pi} w(t)\, dt = \boxed{1,656}$

Step 3: Using graphing functions, find the maximum value of $w(t)$ for arch II:
$$\boxed{w(t) = 153.87}$$

This occurs at time $\boxed{t = 13.05}$

Step 4: Sketch the graph with the known parameters.

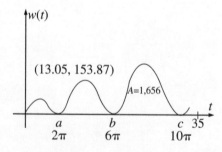

Step 5: Average value $= \dfrac{1}{c-a}\displaystyle\int_{a}^{c} w(t)\, dt$

(d) $\displaystyle = \frac{1}{10\pi - 6\pi}\int_{6\pi}^{10\pi} 20t^{\frac{4}{5}}\cos^2\left(\frac{t}{4}\right) dt = \boxed{131.80}$

Step 6: Sketch how $x = d$ would look.

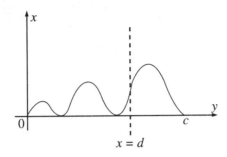

$$\int_0^d w(t)\,dt = \int_d^c w(t)\,dt = \frac{1}{2}\int_0^c w(t)\,dt = \frac{1}{2}\int_0^{31.416} 20t^{\frac{4}{5}}\cos^2\left(\frac{t}{4}\right)dt = 1352.39$$

(e) $\therefore d$ occurs in the interval $\boxed{23 < d < 24}$

(Note: $d = 23.108$.)

2.

The Maclaurin series for e^x is

Step 1: $e^x = 1 + x + \dfrac{x^2}{2!} + \dfrac{x^3}{3!} + \ldots + \dfrac{x^n}{n!} = \displaystyle\sum_{n=0}^{\infty} \dfrac{x^n}{n!}$

Step 2: $e^{-x} = 1 + (-x) + \dfrac{(-x)^2}{2!} + \dfrac{(-x)^3}{3!} + \ldots + \dfrac{(-x)^n}{n!}$

$= 1 - x + \dfrac{(x)^2}{2!} - \dfrac{(x)^3}{3!} + \ldots + \dfrac{(-1)^n x^n}{n!} = \displaystyle\sum_{n=0}^{\infty} \dfrac{(-1)^n x^n}{n!}$

Step 3:

$$\therefore x \cdot e^{-x} = \boxed{x - x^2 + \dfrac{x^3}{2!} - \dfrac{x^4}{3!} + \ldots + \dfrac{(-1)^n x^{n+1}}{n!} = \displaystyle\sum_{n=0}^{\infty} \dfrac{(-1)^n x^{n+1}}{n!}}$$

Step 4: $\displaystyle\int_0^1 xe^{-x} = \dfrac{x^2}{2} - \dfrac{x^3}{3} + \dfrac{x^4}{4 \cdot 2!} - \dfrac{x^5}{5 \cdot 3!}\Big|_0^1 = \boxed{\dfrac{31}{120} = .25833}$

Step 5: $\displaystyle\int_0^1 xe^{-x}\,dx \qquad$ Let $u = x, \qquad dv = e^{-x}\,dx$

$\qquad\qquad\qquad\qquad\qquad\qquad du = dx \qquad v = -e^{-x}$

(c) $\displaystyle\int_0^1 xe^{-x}\, dx = -xe^{-x} - \int_0^1 -e^{-x}\, dx = -xe^{-x} - e^{-x}\Big|_0^1 = \boxed{1 - \dfrac{2}{e} = .26424}$

Step 6: The error bound should be the first omitted term, or $\dfrac{1}{6\cdot 4!} = .00694$

$$|.26424 - .25833| < .00694$$

$$.00591 < .00694$$

3.

Step 1: Sketch a graph of the ellipse.

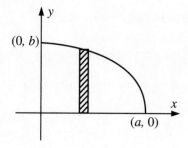

Step 2: Solve for y:

$$\frac{x^2}{a^2} + \frac{y^2}{b^2} = 1$$

$$y = b\sqrt{1 - \frac{x^2}{a^2}}$$

(a) $\displaystyle A = \int_0^a b\sqrt{1 - \frac{x^2}{a^2}}\, dx = \boxed{\dfrac{\pi ab}{4}}$

Step 3:

(b) $\displaystyle V = \pi \int_0^a \left(b\sqrt{1 - \frac{x^2}{a^2}} \right)^2 dx = \boxed{\dfrac{2\pi ab^2}{3}}$

Sketch a graph of the ellipse.

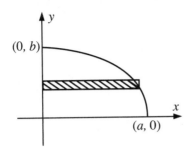

Step 4: Solve: $\dfrac{x^2}{a^2} + \dfrac{y^2}{b^2} = 1$ for x.

$$x = a\sqrt{1 - \frac{y^2}{b^2}}$$

(c) $V = \pi \displaystyle\int_0^b \left(a\sqrt{1 - \frac{y^2}{b^2}} \right)^2 dy = \boxed{\dfrac{2\pi a^2 b}{3}}$

Section II

PART B

4.

Step 1: Use implicit differentiation. Note that xy^3 is a product.

$$4xy^3 + 3y^4 = 4$$

$$\left[4x\frac{d}{dx}(y^3) + y^3\frac{d}{dx}(4x)\right] + 12y^3\frac{dy}{dx} = 0$$

$$4x(3y^2)\frac{dy}{dx} + y^3(4) + 12y^3\frac{dy}{dx} = 0$$

$$\frac{dy}{dx} = \frac{-4y^3}{12xy^2 + 12y^3} = \frac{-y^3}{3xy^2 + 3y^3} = \frac{-y^3}{3y^2(x+y)}$$

(a)
$$\boxed{\frac{dy}{dx} = \frac{-y}{3(x+y)}, \quad y \ne 0, \, y \ne -x}$$

Step 2: $\dfrac{d^2y}{dx^2} = \dfrac{d}{dx}\left(\dfrac{-y}{3(x+y)}\right) = \dfrac{-1}{3}\dfrac{d}{dx}\left(\dfrac{y}{x+y}\right)$

$$= \frac{-1}{3}\left[\frac{(x+y)\frac{dy}{dx} - y\left(1 + \frac{dy}{dx}\right)}{(x+y)^2}\right]$$

$$= -\frac{1}{3}\left[\frac{x\frac{dy}{dx} - y}{(x+y)^2}\right]$$

Step 3: Replace $\dfrac{dy}{dx}$ with $\dfrac{-y}{3(x+y)}$,

$$\frac{d^2y}{dx^2} = \frac{-1}{3}\left[\frac{x\left(\frac{-y}{3(x+y)}\right) - y}{(x+y)^2}\right]$$

$$= \frac{3y^2 + 4xy}{9(x+y)^3}$$

Step 4: Since $4xy^3 + 3y^4 = 4$, then $y^2(4x + 3y^2) = 4$.

$$\therefore 4x + 3y^2 = \frac{4}{y^2}$$

Step 5: Replace $4x + 3y^2$ with $\dfrac{4}{y^2}$

$$\frac{d^2y}{dx^2} = \frac{3y^2 + 4xy}{9(x+y)^3}$$

or $\boxed{\dfrac{d^2y}{dx^2} = \dfrac{4}{9y^2(x+y)^3}}$

5.

Step 1: Equate $\dfrac{1}{P}\dfrac{dP}{dt} = \dfrac{1}{5}(1000 - P)$ with the general form:

$$\frac{1}{P}\frac{dP}{dt} = \frac{k}{N}(N - P), \text{ where } N \text{ is the maximum size of the population.}$$

Step 2:

(a)   Then, regardless of P_0, $\displaystyle\lim_{t\to\infty} P(t) = N = \boxed{1,000}$

Step 3:

(b)   Similarly, the horizontal asymptote is $\displaystyle\lim_{t\to\infty} P(t) = N = \boxed{1,000}$

Step 4: Logistics curves have an inflection point at $\left(\dfrac{\ln\left(\frac{N}{P(0)} - 1\right)}{k}, \dfrac{N}{2} \right)$.

Since $N = 1,000$, $\dfrac{1}{5} = \dfrac{k}{1000}$, so $k = 200$. $P(0) = 100$ is given.

Therefore, the inflection point is

$$\left(\frac{\ln\left(\frac{1000}{100} - 1\right)}{200}, \frac{1000}{2} \right), \text{ or } \boxed{\left(\frac{\ln 9}{200}, 500 \right)}$$

Step 5: If you *must* solve the equation rather than matching the given to the general form, use partial fractions.

$$\frac{dp}{P(1000-P)} = \frac{1}{5}\, dt$$

$$\int \frac{dp}{P(1000-P)} = \int \left(\frac{A}{P} + \frac{B}{1000-p} \right) dp$$

$$= \int \left(\frac{\frac{1}{1000}}{P} + \frac{\frac{1}{1000}}{1000-P} \right) dP = \int \frac{1}{5}\, dt$$

$$\frac{1}{1000} \int \left(\frac{1}{P} + \frac{1}{1000-P} \right) dP = \int \frac{1}{5}\, dt$$

$$\int \left(\frac{1}{P} + \frac{1}{1000-P} \right) dP = \int 200\, dt$$

$$\ln|P| - \ln|1000-P| = 200t + C$$

$$\ln \frac{P}{1000-P} = 200t + C$$

$$\ln \frac{1000-P}{P} = -200t + C$$

$$\frac{1000-P}{P} = Ae^{-200t}$$

$$\frac{1000}{P} - 1 = Ae^{-200t}$$

$$P(t) = \frac{1000}{1+Ae^{-200t}}$$

Step 6: If $P(0) = 100$,

$$100 = \frac{1000}{1+A}, \quad \therefore A = 9$$

$$\boxed{P(t) = \frac{1000}{1+9e^{-200t}}}$$

6.

Step 1: Sketch the graph, dividing it into the four areas.

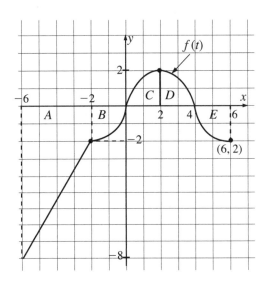

Area $A = 20$ Signed Area $A = -20$
$B = \pi$ $B = -\pi$
$C = \pi$ $C = \pi$
$D = \pi$ $D = \pi$
$E = \pi$ $E = -\pi$

(a) $g(-6) = \int_{-6}^{-6} f(t)\, dt = \boxed{0}$

Step 2: $g(-2) = \int_{-6}^{-2} f(t)\, dt =$ the signed area from

$x = -6$ to $x = -2$. This is a trapezoid with area $= A = \dfrac{1}{2}(4)(2+8)$,

(b)   so $g(-2) = \boxed{-20}$

Step 3: $g'(x) = \dfrac{d}{dx}\left[\int_{-6}^{x} f(t)\ dt\right] = f(x)$

(c) $g'(-2) = f(-2) = \boxed{-2}$

Step 4:

(d) $g''(-2) = f'(-2)$, which $\boxed{\text{does not exist}}$.

The function f has no derivative at $x = -2$.

Step 5: Possible relative minimum/maximum points occur when $g'(x) = 0$.

Find the critical points and do a first derivative analysis.

$g'(x) = f(x) = 0$ at $x = 0$ and $x = 4$

$$g'(x) = f(x) \quad \begin{array}{ccccc} & - - - - & & + + + & - - \\ \hline & -6 \text{ decreasing} & 0 \text{ increasing} & 4 \text{ decreasing} & 6 \end{array}$$

There is a relative $\boxed{\text{minimum point at } x = 0.}$

(b)   There is a relative $\boxed{\text{maximum point at } x = 4.}$

Step 6: Inflection points occur when $g''(x)$ changes sign and $g(x)$ exists. Do a number line analysis of $g''(x)$.

Begin by finding when $g''(x) = 0$ or when $g''(x)$ is undefined.

$g''(x) = f'(x) = 0$ at $x = 2$ (Note: $x = 6$ is not in the domain.)

$g''(x) = f'(x) =$ undefined at $x = -2$

$$g''(x) = f'(x) \quad \begin{array}{cccc} & + + + + + & - - - - - \\ \hline -6 & -2 & +2 & 6 \end{array}$$

There is an inflection point only at $\boxed{x = 2}$.

Step 7: $h(x) = 0$ when $\displaystyle\int_x^6 f(t)\, dt = 0$

That means finding for which values of x the signed area $= 0$.

$\displaystyle\int_{-2}^6 f(t)\, dt = 0 \quad \therefore x = -2$

$\displaystyle\int_2^6 f(t)\, dt = 0 \quad \therefore x = 2$

$\displaystyle\int_6^6 f(t)\, dt = 0 \quad \therefore x = 6$

(d) $\boxed{-2, 2, 6}$

Step 8: $\displaystyle h'(x) = \frac{d}{dx}\left[\int_x^6 f(t)\, dt\right] = -f(x)$

(e) $h'(2) = -f(2) = \boxed{-2}$

ANSWER SHEETS

AP Calculus AB & BC

PRACTICE EXAM 1

AP Calculus AB

Answer Sheet

Part A

1. Ⓐ Ⓑ Ⓒ Ⓓ Ⓔ
2. Ⓐ Ⓑ Ⓒ Ⓓ Ⓔ
3. Ⓐ Ⓑ Ⓒ Ⓓ Ⓔ
4. Ⓐ Ⓑ Ⓒ Ⓓ Ⓔ
5. Ⓐ Ⓑ Ⓒ Ⓓ Ⓔ
6. Ⓐ Ⓑ Ⓒ Ⓓ Ⓔ
7. Ⓐ Ⓑ Ⓒ Ⓓ Ⓔ
8. Ⓐ Ⓑ Ⓒ Ⓓ Ⓔ
9. Ⓐ Ⓑ Ⓒ Ⓓ Ⓔ
10. Ⓐ Ⓑ Ⓒ Ⓓ Ⓔ
11. Ⓐ Ⓑ Ⓒ Ⓓ Ⓔ
12. Ⓐ Ⓑ Ⓒ Ⓓ Ⓔ
13. Ⓐ Ⓑ Ⓒ Ⓓ Ⓔ
14. Ⓐ Ⓑ Ⓒ Ⓓ Ⓔ

15. Ⓐ Ⓑ Ⓒ Ⓓ Ⓔ
16. Ⓐ Ⓑ Ⓒ Ⓓ Ⓔ
17. Ⓐ Ⓑ Ⓒ Ⓓ Ⓔ
18. Ⓐ Ⓑ Ⓒ Ⓓ Ⓔ
19. Ⓐ Ⓑ Ⓒ Ⓓ Ⓔ
20. Ⓐ Ⓑ Ⓒ Ⓓ Ⓔ
21. Ⓐ Ⓑ Ⓒ Ⓓ Ⓔ
22. Ⓐ Ⓑ Ⓒ Ⓓ Ⓔ
23. Ⓐ Ⓑ Ⓒ Ⓓ Ⓔ
24. Ⓐ Ⓑ Ⓒ Ⓓ Ⓔ
25. Ⓐ Ⓑ Ⓒ Ⓓ Ⓔ
26. Ⓐ Ⓑ Ⓒ Ⓓ Ⓔ
27. Ⓐ Ⓑ Ⓒ Ⓓ Ⓔ
28. Ⓐ Ⓑ Ⓒ Ⓓ Ⓔ

Part B

76. Ⓐ Ⓑ Ⓒ Ⓓ Ⓔ
77. Ⓐ Ⓑ Ⓒ Ⓓ Ⓔ
78. Ⓐ Ⓑ Ⓒ Ⓓ Ⓔ
79. Ⓐ Ⓑ Ⓒ Ⓓ Ⓔ
80. Ⓐ Ⓑ Ⓒ Ⓓ Ⓔ
81. Ⓐ Ⓑ Ⓒ Ⓓ Ⓔ
82. Ⓐ Ⓑ Ⓒ Ⓓ Ⓔ
83. Ⓐ Ⓑ Ⓒ Ⓓ Ⓔ
84. Ⓐ Ⓑ Ⓒ Ⓓ Ⓔ
85. Ⓐ Ⓑ Ⓒ Ⓓ Ⓔ
86. Ⓐ Ⓑ Ⓒ Ⓓ Ⓔ
87. Ⓐ Ⓑ Ⓒ Ⓓ Ⓔ
88. Ⓐ Ⓑ Ⓒ Ⓓ Ⓔ
89. Ⓐ Ⓑ Ⓒ Ⓓ Ⓔ
90. Ⓐ Ⓑ Ⓒ Ⓓ Ⓔ
91. Ⓐ Ⓑ Ⓒ Ⓓ Ⓔ
92. Ⓐ Ⓑ Ⓒ Ⓓ Ⓔ

Free-Response Answer Sheet

For the free-response section, write your answers on sheets of blank paper.

PRACTICE EXAM 2

AP Calculus AB

Answer Sheet

Part A

1. Ⓐ Ⓑ Ⓒ Ⓓ Ⓔ
2. Ⓐ Ⓑ Ⓒ Ⓓ Ⓔ
3. Ⓐ Ⓑ Ⓒ Ⓓ Ⓔ
4. Ⓐ Ⓑ Ⓒ Ⓓ Ⓔ
5. Ⓐ Ⓑ Ⓒ Ⓓ Ⓔ
6. Ⓐ Ⓑ Ⓒ Ⓓ Ⓔ
7. Ⓐ Ⓑ Ⓒ Ⓓ Ⓔ
8. Ⓐ Ⓑ Ⓒ Ⓓ Ⓔ
9. Ⓐ Ⓑ Ⓒ Ⓓ Ⓔ
10. Ⓐ Ⓑ Ⓒ Ⓓ Ⓔ
11. Ⓐ Ⓑ Ⓒ Ⓓ Ⓔ
12. Ⓐ Ⓑ Ⓒ Ⓓ Ⓔ
13. Ⓐ Ⓑ Ⓒ Ⓓ Ⓔ
14. Ⓐ Ⓑ Ⓒ Ⓓ Ⓔ

15. Ⓐ Ⓑ Ⓒ Ⓓ Ⓔ
16. Ⓐ Ⓑ Ⓒ Ⓓ Ⓔ
17. Ⓐ Ⓑ Ⓒ Ⓓ Ⓔ
18. Ⓐ Ⓑ Ⓒ Ⓓ Ⓔ
19. Ⓐ Ⓑ Ⓒ Ⓓ Ⓔ
20. Ⓐ Ⓑ Ⓒ Ⓓ Ⓔ
21. Ⓐ Ⓑ Ⓒ Ⓓ Ⓔ
22. Ⓐ Ⓑ Ⓒ Ⓓ Ⓔ
23. Ⓐ Ⓑ Ⓒ Ⓓ Ⓔ
24. Ⓐ Ⓑ Ⓒ Ⓓ Ⓔ
25. Ⓐ Ⓑ Ⓒ Ⓓ Ⓔ
26. Ⓐ Ⓑ Ⓒ Ⓓ Ⓔ
27. Ⓐ Ⓑ Ⓒ Ⓓ Ⓔ
28. Ⓐ Ⓑ Ⓒ Ⓓ Ⓔ

Part B

76. Ⓐ Ⓑ Ⓒ Ⓓ Ⓔ
77. Ⓐ Ⓑ Ⓒ Ⓓ Ⓔ
78. Ⓐ Ⓑ Ⓒ Ⓓ Ⓔ
79. Ⓐ Ⓑ Ⓒ Ⓓ Ⓔ
80. Ⓐ Ⓑ Ⓒ Ⓓ Ⓔ
81. Ⓐ Ⓑ Ⓒ Ⓓ Ⓔ
82. Ⓐ Ⓑ Ⓒ Ⓓ Ⓔ
83. Ⓐ Ⓑ Ⓒ Ⓓ Ⓔ
84. Ⓐ Ⓑ Ⓒ Ⓓ Ⓔ
85. Ⓐ Ⓑ Ⓒ Ⓓ Ⓔ
86. Ⓐ Ⓑ Ⓒ Ⓓ Ⓔ
87. Ⓐ Ⓑ Ⓒ Ⓓ Ⓔ
88. Ⓐ Ⓑ Ⓒ Ⓓ Ⓔ
89. Ⓐ Ⓑ Ⓒ Ⓓ Ⓔ
90. Ⓐ Ⓑ Ⓒ Ⓓ Ⓔ
91. Ⓐ Ⓑ Ⓒ Ⓓ Ⓔ
92. Ⓐ Ⓑ Ⓒ Ⓓ Ⓔ

Free-Response Answer Sheet

For the free-response section, write your answers on sheets of blank paper.

PRACTICE EXAM 3

AP Calculus AB

Answer Sheet

Part A

1. (A) (B) (C) (D) (E)
2. (A) (B) (C) (D) (E)
3. (A) (B) (C) (D) (E)
4. (A) (B) (C) (D) (E)
5. (A) (B) (C) (D) (E)
6. (A) (B) (C) (D) (E)
7. (A) (B) (C) (D) (E)
8. (A) (B) (C) (D) (E)
9. (A) (B) (C) (D) (E)
10. (A) (B) (C) (D) (E)
11. (A) (B) (C) (D) (E)
12. (A) (B) (C) (D) (E)
13. (A) (B) (C) (D) (E)
14. (A) (B) (C) (D) (E)

15. (A) (B) (C) (D) (E)
16. (A) (B) (C) (D) (E)
17. (A) (B) (C) (D) (E)
18. (A) (B) (C) (D) (E)
19. (A) (B) (C) (D) (E)
20. (A) (B) (C) (D) (E)
21. (A) (B) (C) (D) (E)
22. (A) (B) (C) (D) (E)
23. (A) (B) (C) (D) (E)
24. (A) (B) (C) (D) (E)
25. (A) (B) (C) (D) (E)
26. (A) (B) (C) (D) (E)
27. (A) (B) (C) (D) (E)
28. (A) (B) (C) (D) (E)

Part B

76. (A) (B) (C) (D) (E)
77. (A) (B) (C) (D) (E)
78. (A) (B) (C) (D) (E)
79. (A) (B) (C) (D) (E)
80. (A) (B) (C) (D) (E)
81. (A) (B) (C) (D) (E)
82. (A) (B) (C) (D) (E)
83. (A) (B) (C) (D) (E)
84. (A) (B) (C) (D) (E)
85. (A) (B) (C) (D) (E)
86. (A) (B) (C) (D) (E)
87. (A) (B) (C) (D) (E)
88. (A) (B) (C) (D) (E)
89. (A) (B) (C) (D) (E)
90. (A) (B) (C) (D) (E)
91. (A) (B) (C) (D) (E)
92. (A) (B) (C) (D) (E)

Free-Response Answer Sheet

For the free-response section, write your answers on sheets of blank paper.

PRACTICE EXAM 4

AP Calculus AB

Answer Sheet

Part A

1. Ⓐ Ⓑ Ⓒ Ⓓ Ⓔ
2. Ⓐ Ⓑ Ⓒ Ⓓ Ⓔ
3. Ⓐ Ⓑ Ⓒ Ⓓ Ⓔ
4. Ⓐ Ⓑ Ⓒ Ⓓ Ⓔ
5. Ⓐ Ⓑ Ⓒ Ⓓ Ⓔ
6. Ⓐ Ⓑ Ⓒ Ⓓ Ⓔ
7. Ⓐ Ⓑ Ⓒ Ⓓ Ⓔ
8. Ⓐ Ⓑ Ⓒ Ⓓ Ⓔ
9. Ⓐ Ⓑ Ⓒ Ⓓ Ⓔ
10. Ⓐ Ⓑ Ⓒ Ⓓ Ⓔ
11. Ⓐ Ⓑ Ⓒ Ⓓ Ⓔ
12. Ⓐ Ⓑ Ⓒ Ⓓ Ⓔ
13. Ⓐ Ⓑ Ⓒ Ⓓ Ⓔ
14. Ⓐ Ⓑ Ⓒ Ⓓ Ⓔ

15. Ⓐ Ⓑ Ⓒ Ⓓ Ⓔ
16. Ⓐ Ⓑ Ⓒ Ⓓ Ⓔ
17. Ⓐ Ⓑ Ⓒ Ⓓ Ⓔ
18. Ⓐ Ⓑ Ⓒ Ⓓ Ⓔ
19. Ⓐ Ⓑ Ⓒ Ⓓ Ⓔ
20. Ⓐ Ⓑ Ⓒ Ⓓ Ⓔ
21. Ⓐ Ⓑ Ⓒ Ⓓ Ⓔ
22. Ⓐ Ⓑ Ⓒ Ⓓ Ⓔ
23. Ⓐ Ⓑ Ⓒ Ⓓ Ⓔ
24. Ⓐ Ⓑ Ⓒ Ⓓ Ⓔ
25. Ⓐ Ⓑ Ⓒ Ⓓ Ⓔ
26. Ⓐ Ⓑ Ⓒ Ⓓ Ⓔ
27. Ⓐ Ⓑ Ⓒ Ⓓ Ⓔ
28. Ⓐ Ⓑ Ⓒ Ⓓ Ⓔ

Part B

76. Ⓐ Ⓑ Ⓒ Ⓓ Ⓔ
77. Ⓐ Ⓑ Ⓒ Ⓓ Ⓔ
78. Ⓐ Ⓑ Ⓒ Ⓓ Ⓔ
79. Ⓐ Ⓑ Ⓒ Ⓓ Ⓔ
80. Ⓐ Ⓑ Ⓒ Ⓓ Ⓔ
81. Ⓐ Ⓑ Ⓒ Ⓓ Ⓔ
82. Ⓐ Ⓑ Ⓒ Ⓓ Ⓔ
83. Ⓐ Ⓑ Ⓒ Ⓓ Ⓔ
84. Ⓐ Ⓑ Ⓒ Ⓓ Ⓔ
85. Ⓐ Ⓑ Ⓒ Ⓓ Ⓔ
86. Ⓐ Ⓑ Ⓒ Ⓓ Ⓔ
87. Ⓐ Ⓑ Ⓒ Ⓓ Ⓔ
88. Ⓐ Ⓑ Ⓒ Ⓓ Ⓔ
89. Ⓐ Ⓑ Ⓒ Ⓓ Ⓔ
90. Ⓐ Ⓑ Ⓒ Ⓓ Ⓔ
91. Ⓐ Ⓑ Ⓒ Ⓓ Ⓔ
92. Ⓐ Ⓑ Ⓒ Ⓓ Ⓔ

Free-Response Answer Sheet
For the free-response section, write your answers on sheets of blank paper.

PRACTICE EXAM 5

AP Calculus AB

Answer Sheet

Part A

1. Ⓐ Ⓑ Ⓒ Ⓓ Ⓔ
2. Ⓐ Ⓑ Ⓒ Ⓓ Ⓔ
3. Ⓐ Ⓑ Ⓒ Ⓓ Ⓔ
4. Ⓐ Ⓑ Ⓒ Ⓓ Ⓔ
5. Ⓐ Ⓑ Ⓒ Ⓓ Ⓔ
6. Ⓐ Ⓑ Ⓒ Ⓓ Ⓔ
7. Ⓐ Ⓑ Ⓒ Ⓓ Ⓔ
8. Ⓐ Ⓑ Ⓒ Ⓓ Ⓔ
9. Ⓐ Ⓑ Ⓒ Ⓓ Ⓔ
10. Ⓐ Ⓑ Ⓒ Ⓓ Ⓔ
11. Ⓐ Ⓑ Ⓒ Ⓓ Ⓔ
12. Ⓐ Ⓑ Ⓒ Ⓓ Ⓔ
13. Ⓐ Ⓑ Ⓒ Ⓓ Ⓔ
14. Ⓐ Ⓑ Ⓒ Ⓓ Ⓔ

15. Ⓐ Ⓑ Ⓒ Ⓓ Ⓔ
16. Ⓐ Ⓑ Ⓒ Ⓓ Ⓔ
17. Ⓐ Ⓑ Ⓒ Ⓓ Ⓔ
18. Ⓐ Ⓑ Ⓒ Ⓓ Ⓔ
19. Ⓐ Ⓑ Ⓒ Ⓓ Ⓔ
20. Ⓐ Ⓑ Ⓒ Ⓓ Ⓔ
21. Ⓐ Ⓑ Ⓒ Ⓓ Ⓔ
22. Ⓐ Ⓑ Ⓒ Ⓓ Ⓔ
23. Ⓐ Ⓑ Ⓒ Ⓓ Ⓔ
24. Ⓐ Ⓑ Ⓒ Ⓓ Ⓔ
25. Ⓐ Ⓑ Ⓒ Ⓓ Ⓔ
26. Ⓐ Ⓑ Ⓒ Ⓓ Ⓔ
27. Ⓐ Ⓑ Ⓒ Ⓓ Ⓔ
28. Ⓐ Ⓑ Ⓒ Ⓓ Ⓔ

Part B

76. Ⓐ Ⓑ Ⓒ Ⓓ Ⓔ
77. Ⓐ Ⓑ Ⓒ Ⓓ Ⓔ
78. Ⓐ Ⓑ Ⓒ Ⓓ Ⓔ
79. Ⓐ Ⓑ Ⓒ Ⓓ Ⓔ
80. Ⓐ Ⓑ Ⓒ Ⓓ Ⓔ
81. Ⓐ Ⓑ Ⓒ Ⓓ Ⓔ
82. Ⓐ Ⓑ Ⓒ Ⓓ Ⓔ
83. Ⓐ Ⓑ Ⓒ Ⓓ Ⓔ
84. Ⓐ Ⓑ Ⓒ Ⓓ Ⓔ
85. Ⓐ Ⓑ Ⓒ Ⓓ Ⓔ
86. Ⓐ Ⓑ Ⓒ Ⓓ Ⓔ
87. Ⓐ Ⓑ Ⓒ Ⓓ Ⓔ
88. Ⓐ Ⓑ Ⓒ Ⓓ Ⓔ
89. Ⓐ Ⓑ Ⓒ Ⓓ Ⓔ
90. Ⓐ Ⓑ Ⓒ Ⓓ Ⓔ
91. Ⓐ Ⓑ Ⓒ Ⓓ Ⓔ
92. Ⓐ Ⓑ Ⓒ Ⓓ Ⓔ

Free-Response Answer Sheet

For the free-response section, write your answers on sheets of blank paper.

PRACTICE EXAM 1

AP Calculus BC

Answer Sheet

Part A

1. Ⓐ Ⓑ Ⓒ Ⓓ Ⓔ
2. Ⓐ Ⓑ Ⓒ Ⓓ Ⓔ
3. Ⓐ Ⓑ Ⓒ Ⓓ Ⓔ
4. Ⓐ Ⓑ Ⓒ Ⓓ Ⓔ
5. Ⓐ Ⓑ Ⓒ Ⓓ Ⓔ
6. Ⓐ Ⓑ Ⓒ Ⓓ Ⓔ
7. Ⓐ Ⓑ Ⓒ Ⓓ Ⓔ
8. Ⓐ Ⓑ Ⓒ Ⓓ Ⓔ
9. Ⓐ Ⓑ Ⓒ Ⓓ Ⓔ
10. Ⓐ Ⓑ Ⓒ Ⓓ Ⓔ
11. Ⓐ Ⓑ Ⓒ Ⓓ Ⓔ
12. Ⓐ Ⓑ Ⓒ Ⓓ Ⓔ
13. Ⓐ Ⓑ Ⓒ Ⓓ Ⓔ
14. Ⓐ Ⓑ Ⓒ Ⓓ Ⓔ

15. Ⓐ Ⓑ Ⓒ Ⓓ Ⓔ
16. Ⓐ Ⓑ Ⓒ Ⓓ Ⓔ
17. Ⓐ Ⓑ Ⓒ Ⓓ Ⓔ
18. Ⓐ Ⓑ Ⓒ Ⓓ Ⓔ
19. Ⓐ Ⓑ Ⓒ Ⓓ Ⓔ
20. Ⓐ Ⓑ Ⓒ Ⓓ Ⓔ
21. Ⓐ Ⓑ Ⓒ Ⓓ Ⓔ
22. Ⓐ Ⓑ Ⓒ Ⓓ Ⓔ
23. Ⓐ Ⓑ Ⓒ Ⓓ Ⓔ
24. Ⓐ Ⓑ Ⓒ Ⓓ Ⓔ
25. Ⓐ Ⓑ Ⓒ Ⓓ Ⓔ
26. Ⓐ Ⓑ Ⓒ Ⓓ Ⓔ
27. Ⓐ Ⓑ Ⓒ Ⓓ Ⓔ
28. Ⓐ Ⓑ Ⓒ Ⓓ Ⓔ

Part B

76. Ⓐ Ⓑ Ⓒ Ⓓ Ⓔ
77. Ⓐ Ⓑ Ⓒ Ⓓ Ⓔ
78. Ⓐ Ⓑ Ⓒ Ⓓ Ⓔ
79. Ⓐ Ⓑ Ⓒ Ⓓ Ⓔ
80. Ⓐ Ⓑ Ⓒ Ⓓ Ⓔ
81. Ⓐ Ⓑ Ⓒ Ⓓ Ⓔ
82. Ⓐ Ⓑ Ⓒ Ⓓ Ⓔ
83. Ⓐ Ⓑ Ⓒ Ⓓ Ⓔ
84. Ⓐ Ⓑ Ⓒ Ⓓ Ⓔ
85. Ⓐ Ⓑ Ⓒ Ⓓ Ⓔ
86. Ⓐ Ⓑ Ⓒ Ⓓ Ⓔ
87. Ⓐ Ⓑ Ⓒ Ⓓ Ⓔ
88. Ⓐ Ⓑ Ⓒ Ⓓ Ⓔ
89. Ⓐ Ⓑ Ⓒ Ⓓ Ⓔ
90. Ⓐ Ⓑ Ⓒ Ⓓ Ⓔ
91. Ⓐ Ⓑ Ⓒ Ⓓ Ⓔ
92. Ⓐ Ⓑ Ⓒ Ⓓ Ⓔ

Free-Response Answer Sheet

For the free-response section, write your answers on sheets of blank paper.

PRACTICE EXAM 2

AP Calculus BC

Answer Sheet

Part A

1. Ⓐ Ⓑ Ⓒ Ⓓ Ⓔ
2. Ⓐ Ⓑ Ⓒ Ⓓ Ⓔ
3. Ⓐ Ⓑ Ⓒ Ⓓ Ⓔ
4. Ⓐ Ⓑ Ⓒ Ⓓ Ⓔ
5. Ⓐ Ⓑ Ⓒ Ⓓ Ⓔ
6. Ⓐ Ⓑ Ⓒ Ⓓ Ⓔ
7. Ⓐ Ⓑ Ⓒ Ⓓ Ⓔ
8. Ⓐ Ⓑ Ⓒ Ⓓ Ⓔ
9. Ⓐ Ⓑ Ⓒ Ⓓ Ⓔ
10. Ⓐ Ⓑ Ⓒ Ⓓ Ⓔ
11. Ⓐ Ⓑ Ⓒ Ⓓ Ⓔ
12. Ⓐ Ⓑ Ⓒ Ⓓ Ⓔ
13. Ⓐ Ⓑ Ⓒ Ⓓ Ⓔ
14. Ⓐ Ⓑ Ⓒ Ⓓ Ⓔ

15. Ⓐ Ⓑ Ⓒ Ⓓ Ⓔ
16. Ⓐ Ⓑ Ⓒ Ⓓ Ⓔ
17. Ⓐ Ⓑ Ⓒ Ⓓ Ⓔ
18. Ⓐ Ⓑ Ⓒ Ⓓ Ⓔ
19. Ⓐ Ⓑ Ⓒ Ⓓ Ⓔ
20. Ⓐ Ⓑ Ⓒ Ⓓ Ⓔ
21. Ⓐ Ⓑ Ⓒ Ⓓ Ⓔ
22. Ⓐ Ⓑ Ⓒ Ⓓ Ⓔ
23. Ⓐ Ⓑ Ⓒ Ⓓ Ⓔ
24. Ⓐ Ⓑ Ⓒ Ⓓ Ⓔ
25. Ⓐ Ⓑ Ⓒ Ⓓ Ⓔ
26. Ⓐ Ⓑ Ⓒ Ⓓ Ⓔ
27. Ⓐ Ⓑ Ⓒ Ⓓ Ⓔ
28. Ⓐ Ⓑ Ⓒ Ⓓ Ⓔ

Part B

76. Ⓐ Ⓑ Ⓒ Ⓓ Ⓔ
77. Ⓐ Ⓑ Ⓒ Ⓓ Ⓔ
78. Ⓐ Ⓑ Ⓒ Ⓓ Ⓔ
79. Ⓐ Ⓑ Ⓒ Ⓓ Ⓔ
80. Ⓐ Ⓑ Ⓒ Ⓓ Ⓔ
81. Ⓐ Ⓑ Ⓒ Ⓓ Ⓔ
82. Ⓐ Ⓑ Ⓒ Ⓓ Ⓔ
83. Ⓐ Ⓑ Ⓒ Ⓓ Ⓔ
84. Ⓐ Ⓑ Ⓒ Ⓓ Ⓔ
85. Ⓐ Ⓑ Ⓒ Ⓓ Ⓔ
86. Ⓐ Ⓑ Ⓒ Ⓓ Ⓔ
87. Ⓐ Ⓑ Ⓒ Ⓓ Ⓔ
88. Ⓐ Ⓑ Ⓒ Ⓓ Ⓔ
89. Ⓐ Ⓑ Ⓒ Ⓓ Ⓔ
90. Ⓐ Ⓑ Ⓒ Ⓓ Ⓔ
91. Ⓐ Ⓑ Ⓒ Ⓓ Ⓔ
92. Ⓐ Ⓑ Ⓒ Ⓓ Ⓔ

Free-Response Answer Sheet

For the free-response section, write your answers on sheets of blank paper.

PRACTICE EXAM 3

AP Calculus BC

Answer Sheet

Part A

1. Ⓐ Ⓑ Ⓒ Ⓓ Ⓔ
2. Ⓐ Ⓑ Ⓒ Ⓓ Ⓔ
3. Ⓐ Ⓑ Ⓒ Ⓓ Ⓔ
4. Ⓐ Ⓑ Ⓒ Ⓓ Ⓔ
5. Ⓐ Ⓑ Ⓒ Ⓓ Ⓔ
6. Ⓐ Ⓑ Ⓒ Ⓓ Ⓔ
7. Ⓐ Ⓑ Ⓒ Ⓓ Ⓔ
8. Ⓐ Ⓑ Ⓒ Ⓓ Ⓔ
9. Ⓐ Ⓑ Ⓒ Ⓓ Ⓔ
10. Ⓐ Ⓑ Ⓒ Ⓓ Ⓔ
11. Ⓐ Ⓑ Ⓒ Ⓓ Ⓔ
12. Ⓐ Ⓑ Ⓒ Ⓓ Ⓔ
13. Ⓐ Ⓑ Ⓒ Ⓓ Ⓔ
14. Ⓐ Ⓑ Ⓒ Ⓓ Ⓔ

15. Ⓐ Ⓑ Ⓒ Ⓓ Ⓔ
16. Ⓐ Ⓑ Ⓒ Ⓓ Ⓔ
17. Ⓐ Ⓑ Ⓒ Ⓓ Ⓔ
18. Ⓐ Ⓑ Ⓒ Ⓓ Ⓔ
19. Ⓐ Ⓑ Ⓒ Ⓓ Ⓔ
20. Ⓐ Ⓑ Ⓒ Ⓓ Ⓔ
21. Ⓐ Ⓑ Ⓒ Ⓓ Ⓔ
22. Ⓐ Ⓑ Ⓒ Ⓓ Ⓔ
23. Ⓐ Ⓑ Ⓒ Ⓓ Ⓔ
24. Ⓐ Ⓑ Ⓒ Ⓓ Ⓔ
25. Ⓐ Ⓑ Ⓒ Ⓓ Ⓔ
26. Ⓐ Ⓑ Ⓒ Ⓓ Ⓔ
27. Ⓐ Ⓑ Ⓒ Ⓓ Ⓔ
28. Ⓐ Ⓑ Ⓒ Ⓓ Ⓔ

Part B

76. Ⓐ Ⓑ Ⓒ Ⓓ Ⓔ
77. Ⓐ Ⓑ Ⓒ Ⓓ Ⓔ
78. Ⓐ Ⓑ Ⓒ Ⓓ Ⓔ
79. Ⓐ Ⓑ Ⓒ Ⓓ Ⓔ
80. Ⓐ Ⓑ Ⓒ Ⓓ Ⓔ
81. Ⓐ Ⓑ Ⓒ Ⓓ Ⓔ
82. Ⓐ Ⓑ Ⓒ Ⓓ Ⓔ
83. Ⓐ Ⓑ Ⓒ Ⓓ Ⓔ
84. Ⓐ Ⓑ Ⓒ Ⓓ Ⓔ
85. Ⓐ Ⓑ Ⓒ Ⓓ Ⓔ
86. Ⓐ Ⓑ Ⓒ Ⓓ Ⓔ
87. Ⓐ Ⓑ Ⓒ Ⓓ Ⓔ
88. Ⓐ Ⓑ Ⓒ Ⓓ Ⓔ
89. Ⓐ Ⓑ Ⓒ Ⓓ Ⓔ
90. Ⓐ Ⓑ Ⓒ Ⓓ Ⓔ
91. Ⓐ Ⓑ Ⓒ Ⓓ Ⓔ
92. Ⓐ Ⓑ Ⓒ Ⓓ Ⓔ

Free-Response Answer Sheet

For the free-response section, write your answers on sheets of blank paper.